How to List and Sell Real Estate

In the 90s

Danielle Kennedy
Warren Jamison

Prentice Hall Career & Technology
Englewood Cliffs, New Jersey 07632

Library of Congress Cataloging-in Publication Data

Kennedy, Danielle.
   How to list and sell real estate in the 90s.

   Rev. ed. of: How to list and sell real estate. c1983.
   Includes index.
   1. Real estate agents.   2.   Real estate listings.
3. Real estate business.   I. Jamison, Warren.
II. Kennedy, Danielle. How to list and sell real estate.
III. Title.
HD1382.K46 1990   333.33'068'8   89-10193
ISBN 0-13-402249-1

ISBN 0-13-402249-1

90000

9 780134 022499

Editorial/production supervision
  and interior design: **Janet DiBlasi**
Cover design: **Lundgren Graphics, Ltd.**
Manufacturing buyer: **Laura Crossland**

 Published by Prentice Hall Career & Technology
Prentice-Hall, Inc.
A Simon & Schuster Company
Englewood Cliffs, New Jersey 07632

Printed in the United States of America

10

ISBN 0-13-402249-1

Prentice-Hall International (UK) Limited, *London*
Prentice-Hall of Australia Pty. Limited, *Sydney*
Prentice-Hall Canada Inc., *Toronto*
Prentice-Hall Hispanoamericana, S.A., *Mexico*
Prentice-Hall of India Private Limited, *New Delhi*
Prentice-Hall of Japan, Inc., *Tokyo*
Simon & Schuster Asia Pte. Ltd., *Singapore*
Editora Prentice-Hall do Brasil, Ltda., *Rio de Janeiro*

For My Children

CONTENTS

6   SOW THAT FARM AND REAP AND REAP AND REAP   57

9 OPEN HOUSE—BRING YOUR OWN BANANA, AND PROSPER   **124**

12   SERVICING LISTINGS   207

13   PROMOTION   228

14   THE SUBTLE AND LEARNABLE ART OF CAPTURING CUSTOMERS   241

25   DEAD CATS, WEEDS, AND HOLES IN THE WALLS   418

26   GOALS   429

FOREWORD

The book you are holding contains some of the finest proven techniques and strategies for the field of real estate ever written. It is with great pride that today I join the thousands of people who have enjoyed watching Danny Kennedy climb the ladder of success as a salesperson, lecturer, author, mother, and wife. You are about to read a very special book by a very special, special human being.

Tom Hopkins

ACKNOWLEDGMENTS

Special thanks to: Kitty Jamison for her unending emotional support and work to help tie this book together; Larry Asbill, Rick Bosmer, the late Jo Brown, Danny Cox, Herb Lewis and Marlene Lietzel for marvelous ideas and expertise; my client friends; and my Realtor® friends nationwide who keep doing their homework and raising the professional standards of our industry.

Most of all my thanks go to my mother, Rose M. Barrett—a pal for all seasons of life, and my husband Mike and all the kids: Kelly, Beth, Joe, Kevin, Dan, Bob, Mary and our over-40 bonus—Kathleen Rose.

ATTENTION BROKERS AND MANAGERS

This book is a complete, detailed, ready-to-go training program that you can simply hand to new agents. **Call their attention to the Breakaway Schedule in the back.** Every achievement called for there is keyed to, and fully explained in, the preceding text. The Breakaway listing and selling training program will get every new agent who has the determination to succeed out into the field fast. It'll quickly arm those new agents with the ability to list and sell, and do all this without taking up your time.

Nothing helps the new agent more than collecting a fee. No amount of managerial encouragement matches the power of the bankable. *How to List and Sell in the 90s* acts on the theory that nothing succeeds like success. It's organized so that the new agent learns before trying to practice, acquires some expertise in a limited field, operates first in that limited field, and always moves in a confidence-building manner from inexperience to effective action. Although it's a tough course, this book is graduated so that no single step is too formidable.

But be sure to review the book yourself. Make certain that none of its techniques conflict with your local ordinances, board rules, and office policies. If you find an idea or two here that won't work in your situation, make a note of the items your agents are to pass over.

Seasonal agents will benefit too. There are winning scripts in this book for every standard situation your associates will encounter in residential real estate, as well as advanced techniques and insights that will be helpful to experienced agents. Chapters 11 and 16 have role plays for three agents plus yourself. Use all this material to inspire your present sales staff with fast-paced training sessions.

1

BREAKAWAY

Barriers and Fundamentals • If You're New to Real Estate • Take Off Strong from the First Day • Check with Your Broker • Surface Details • If You're Not So New • What Do You Need to Begin Your Breakaway? • What Do You Need to Complete Your Breakaway? • Formula III Schedule

BARRIERS AND FUNDAMENTALS

"What's the most important barrier between me and the success I want from real estate?"

That's a question you should ask yourself continually. The purpose of this book is to give you the skills you need to break away from whatever now prevents you from attacking that most important barrier. Once you've knocked the first one flat, you'll see that there's another behind it. But that second barrier won't be as difficult as the first, because then you'll know that barriers aren't as tough as they look. They can all be knocked down—or walked around. Whether you're new to real estate, not-so-new but in need of a lift, or already a high flyer, you can break away to new heights of income and professional standing. Put the systems, the insights, and the tips in the following pages to work—and soar as high as you wish.

It probably won't be easy for you to recognize your weak points. It'll be even harder to make the necessary changes in your work style to eliminate those weak points. Success doesn't come easy. It only seems easy when someone else does it— or when you look back after you've forgotten the hard work. But, curiously, real estate is the best-paid easy work in the world—after you've learned the fundamentals and paid the price. If you refuse to pay the price, and don't learn the fundamentals, real estate is one of the lowest-paid hard jobs available.

Having that expertise enables you to work confidently with clients, to solve their problems, and to collect fees for doing so. Sure, you're impatient with the basics. Certainly, you want to get right at the action. But it's no good going where the action is if you can't handle it when you get there.

IF YOU'RE NEW TO REAL ESTATE

Is 21 days too long to wait for professional competence? If you're new to the business, read quickly through this book, and then put yourself on the Breakaway Schedule. You'll find it right behind Chapter 28. *The 21-Day Breakaway Schedule is designed to give you a thorough knowledge of your area, its inventory, and of professional real estate skills in just three weeks.* It's a 21-day cram session organized with high-speed learning methods. It's on-the-job training. And it's tough. Deliberately so, because real estate is tough. But don't be discouraged if you can't finish it on time. Few can. Other commitments, and often new clients discovered through Breakaway, eat into the available hours. Simply repeat the course until you've completed all of it.

Many of the most important achievements in the Breakaway Schedule don't require a real estate license. You can do them while you're waiting for, or studying for, your license. Then, when it comes, you'll be enormously better prepared to work with clients. You'll have the realistic self-confidence that can only be won by hard work.

TAKE OFF STRONG FROM THE FIRST DAY

Accept that you're ignorant of many things you'll soon know; accept that you'll frequently reveal your ignorance to others; accept this as part of the legitimate price that must be paid for competence in every new endeavor.

Decide now that you won't be embarrassed by your freshness. Decide now that you'll waste no time, not your own, not that of the more experienced agents around you, by apologizing for your ignorance. And, no matter how it's put, receive as a gem given free any instruction offered by the top producers in your office. Thank them warmly for any hint of advice. Tips and encouragement are priceless, but remember that winning must always be learned by your own efforts, by your own study, practice, and doing. And never forget that from losers you can only learn the skills of excusing losing.

Do what I did right, and don't do the things that most agents—myself included—do wrong when starting. That's what this book is all about: doing the positives, avoiding the negatives. Success is a series of habits and skills—and they're all learnable.

I can still see the way I worked during the first three months: the phone on a 25-foot cord under my ear while I travelled around the kitchen frying hamburgers, waving my arms like an idiot at one of my kids fighting with his brother or sister, trying to burn them with that "when I get off this phone I'm going to give you a good spanking—don't you know this is a very important customer?" type look. Slung under my arm is my brand new baby, Mary, who must have wondered what

God had in mind to bestow such a nut of a mother on her. On the kitchen table is a deposit receipt with spilled milk smudging my buyer's signatures.

As soon as I can find a friend, neighbor, or babysitter to rescue me, I'm going to present that offer, smudged signatures and all. And, walking into that seller's home, I'm going to look as though I don't have a care in the world. How I did that during those early months is a mystery to me now. But I did know how vital it is *not* to come in, boiling over with my own pressures and problems, and dump them on the buyers or sellers. The principals of a transaction are already cooking. They're in the special oven that making a large and unfamiliar decision puts most people in. Buyers and sellers don't need even the smallest piece of my problems; they have plenty of their own just then.

That was back in the days before any trophies for top listing and selling stood on the shelves of the pantry I used as my office; before I put up a little sign that said, "Never forget a humble beginning."

Because my beginning was indeed humble. And staggering. At the time I was six months pregnant with my fifth child, and completely unsure of myself. I looked like a tank. People couldn't believe some idiot would try to start a real estate career in my condition. "Why don't you just drop out and have your baby, darling." Pang, Pow, Ouch. Those early days, weeks, and months hurt. The whole thing was like a soap opera. Girl's feelings hurt daily. Girl unsure of real estate business. Girl weeps, mopes. Girl hopes again.

Somehow I eked out a few good cold calls, banged on about 700 doors that first summer, and patiently courted FSBOs* all over town. After about three months I had clients to work with, and I knew what I was doing. You can reach that same point by following the Breakaway Schedule for just three weeks.

When you start in real estate, you stand at the entrance of a treacherous tunnel leading to success. That tunnel was so dimly lit when I went into it that I paid for every step with bruises. While I struggled there, my survival in real estate still uncertain, I promised myself: "If I make it, I'm going to light up the way for the people who'll travel this tunnel after me." From that early resolve sprang my speaking career and this book.

So come with me and break away. I've strung beacons along your path, though you must still travel it yourself. You'll find that Breakaway concentrates on the specific competencies that will enable you to nail down fees. No useless keep-busy stuff. Heavy work on your professionalism's foundation is included because that foundation must be solid before you can build a tower of high volume above it. Some of the places where this heavy work falls may surprise you. Trust me that it'll be worthwhile. Plunge in. Make this material yours instead of wasting time debating whether to start.

---

*FSBO is pronounced fizz-bo. It means "For Sale By Owner," that is, sellers attempting to market their property without professional real estate assistance.

CHECK WITH YOUR BROKER

Many areas have rules or ordinances against some of the activities suggested in this book. For example, it may be illegal in your town to farm door-to-door as suggested in Chapter 6. Always check with your broker before trying a new real estate activity in your area.

SURFACE DETAILS

I travel worldwide conducting real estate training seminars. I'm always struck by how much the surface details—the procedures, jargon, and local rules—vary from area to area. And I'm also struck by how little the underlying truths of this people business of ours change over time and distance. Buyers and sellers have the same basic fears in Saskatoon as they do in Schenectady, although the documents they sign differ. If you encounter a surface detail in this book that doesn't apply in your area, skip to the next item. Better yet, figure out how to adapt the idea so that you can use it.

IF YOU'RE NOT SO NEW

If you're an experienced agent, skim through the Breakaway Schedule in the back after you've read the book. All of us have our weak points. Skip the achievements that are too basic for you, and use the others to strengthen your expertise in those areas where your present level of performance doesn't satisfy you. Three weeks of systematic, concentrated effort will do wonders for your confidence and income potential.

"Wait a minute," you say. "I've been in real estate a while now—and I've been working hard—but I still don't feel competent. How're you going to change me into a pro in three short weeks?"

A fair question. Right up front, we should get three things straight:

- You're the one who'll do it. I've made my start. Now it's your turn.
- Breakaway is a tough course. I didn't say the days would be short, or easy.
- You can do it if you so choose. You can go all the way to top producer if you're willing to pay the price. The fee is payable only in the hard coin of effort.

Accept that your break into the big scene will be painful. But that pain is easily forgettable in the knowledge of great professional growth and the joys of success that follow close behind.

There's no sit-back-and-watch to Breakaway. It's all DO, with you the DOER; it's all solid meat that you must chew before swallowing. Breakaway requires three weeks' investment of all-out effort in your future.

Can you handle it? Will you? Your answer may well determine your success in the real estate field.

Caution.

Before you skim over the Breakaway schedule and decide, "I'm not doing this part," be aware that you're rejecting what you fear, not what you don't need. You'll be tempted to avoid precisely those things that will help you most. Fear does that to us if we let it.

In order to succeed, we must grow. To grow, we must endure the pain of doing what we fear until, by meeting and conquering that fear, we pass through to success. Control fear or fear controls you. That's a hard rule but a fair one, for it applies equally to us all.

WHAT DO YOU NEED TO BEGIN YOUR BREAKAWAY?

Three things:

- The desire to improve yourself
- Access to a cassette recorder-player
- A supply of cassettes and 3 × 5 inch cards

WHAT DO YOU NEED TO COMPLETE YOUR BREAKAWAY?

- The determination to improve yourself.
- Access to a car and the Multiple Listing Service, if your area has one.
- Your real estate license, and association with an active broker. One more item: Get an appointment book. You'll need it.

Each night of Breakaway, plan your tomorrow. Schedule how you'll accomplish your daily Breakaway commitment within not more than twelve hours. Then get on with it. Avoid distractions. Waste no time nerving yourself for the next step. Plunge ahead, and you'll get through in less than nine hours of thorough, effective work.

Planning tomorrow every night is only one of many important new money-making habits you'll instill in yourself through Breakaway. The program is packed with carry-over ideas. These ideas will help keep you on course for high income after you've completed possibly the most exciting and demanding period of your work life so far. But be prepared. Breakaway will crowd everything off your tomorrow's action list except itself and the money-making opportunities you generate through it.

Another caution.

If you nibble around the edges of Breakaway for long, you'll lose your taste for the whole course. Don't let this opportunity to dramatically change your life slip away from you: Set the earliest date that you can possibly begin Breakaway.

What's wrong with right now?

This minute?

There's no need to put off your Breakaway until a new day dawns; you can instantly blast off by deciding to, and by acting on that decision. Set tomorrow as your Breakaway's Day One. Then pick an achievement from the schedule and start making it yours now. Commit yourself to Breakaway. Stick to it. Your bank account will thank you!

One of Breakaway's greatest values lies in your commitment to an all-out investment of energy in your future. Racing the clock to meet the schedule forces extra effort and concentration from you. That extra output will send your abilities and performance to new heights. Completing the work on time will create an unshakeable confidence in your own competence, and a faith in your own worth that will be of great ongoing value to you.

FORMULA III SCHEDULE

One of the earliest concepts the new Realtor must grasp is my Formula III Schedule.

This illustration is the typical pattern of agents who put all their eggs into one basket. These agents start up very enthusiastically about business developing. This includes FSBOs, open houses, farming, working centers of influence, and other prospecting tips learned in training. As soon as a sufficient number of appointments begins to generate, these agents quit focusing on business development, and begin overpreparing for the appointment. They start putting all their eggs in one basket. This habit soon communicates to the public that the agent is desperate. If an appointment doesn't work out, the Realtor may starve. This pattern also happens to the Superstar who suddenly doesn't think he needs to work FSBOs or to farm anymore. Because referrals can dry up at a minute's notice, never stop developing business, no matter how long you've been in real estate. Constantly picture yourself balancing three balls of equal weight and size: business development, appointments, and service. But remember: Appointments and service follow only after business development has been cultivated.

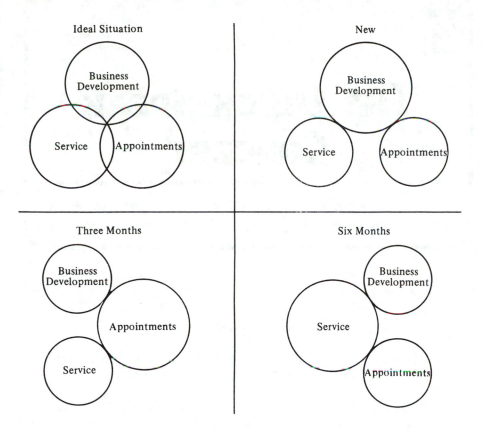

Ideal Situation

New

Three Months

Six Months

2

THE QUICK-SPEAK CONCEPT

The Concept • Buyers' Phobia • The Quick-Speak Inventory • Money-making Games with your QSI • The Jet-powered Selling Tool

THE CONCEPT

A prospect says, "I want a two-story, four-bedroom house with a green carpet and a big kitchen—and a family room right off the eating area. Oh, and I also want a view."

You immediately answer, "I know of a home just like that: It has two fireplaces, a wet bar, and it's air conditioned. That's one you'll want to see. Then I'll show you another that's available for a lot less money, and it has everything you mentioned, except the carpet is orange. But it needs replacing anyway. And we should also look at—"

That's Quick-Speak. The client has the need, you have the house. No delay. No desperate search through the Multiple Listing Book.* They ask—zap, you answer. That's competence. That's problem solving. That's doing the thing you're in business to get paid for doing.

Of course, you'll often have to answer. "We can come close. Here's what's available—" The point is, you *know*. If a house that fits their specifications is available, you know about it; if not, you're certain that no such house can be found.

It's not surprising so many new agents don't understand that to become successful in real estate they must know the inventory. Many experienced (in just getting by) agents don't understand that point either. Knowing the inventory does

---

*If your area doesn't have a Multiple Listing Service, put your office's inventory of listings on Quick-Speak.

not mean knowing how to look houses up in the Multiple Listing Book, nor does it mean spending half a day researching before showing property to every buyer. It means knowing the homes before you start working with a customer.

Of course that's harder. Many agents say, "I can't remember homes unless I'm looking for a customer. Then I remember them really well. And it's a lot easier. The inventory changes so fast."

Of course it's easier—that's why so many agents operate in this self-defeating way. It's also why an agent with a large Quick-Speak Inventory stands out from the crowd. If you've decided not to remember four-bedroom homes with pink wallpaper unless someone wants to look at four-bedroom homes with pink wallpaper, you've decided not to make much money in real estate.

The Quick-Speak Concept applies to everything you need to know. Not only inventory, but all the phrases needed to treat objections, all the facts and figures and formulas, all the Winning Scripts, must be on Quick-Speak if you're to seize the instant when they can be used effectively. This knowledge on the tip of one's tongue is power.

Quick-Speak means knowing all the things you need to know so well that you go far beyond merely repeating them to customer. You state them, each time, with sincerity. You present facts with tight application to your customers' aspirations and abilities. Anyone can learn the phrases, but that's not enough. Learn to sound spontaneous. And never bat them down by snapping off the perfect answer to every objection with mechanical precision. Let it show how much you've practiced and you've practiced in vain. People want to solve their problems with a sympathetic human being, not a calculator with a mouth.

Half-knowing your material reveals that you've memorized it; putting your material on Quick-Speak allows you to play infinite variations without losing the rhythm. Don't stop working when you have all the openers and closers down word for word; just be glad that the hard work is done, that now the fun and the fees begin. Be expressive with your clients; sing their song; dance to their beat—and conduct them right through the closing with bright, warm sincere interest.

BUYERS' PHOBIA

This is the fear of missing the best house that's available. If you allow even a crack of doubt to creep in on this point, your customer will suddenly develop acute Buyers' Phobia. They'll disappear, and seek the cure elsewhere. Those buyers probably won't find a salesperson or house they like better, but they will get tired of looking. An agent who does convince them that he or she knows the entire inventory will find it easy to close them.

The successful real estate salesperson convinces every buyer that he or she will show everything they'll be interested in. Sometimes the salesperson has the inventory knowledge, but doesn't state it convincingly. Never groan about how tough it is to know all the homes. Know them. And tell your people that you do.

Mrs. Buyer: "I like the colors here, but I want a larger dining room."

You: "There's a house like this over on South Street with about these same colors. It has a very large dining room. The yard is so small there that you won't have room for your garden. But would you like to see it anyway?"

There's a specific cure for Buyers' Phobia.

THE QUICK-SPEAK INVENTORY

What's a Quick-Speak Inventory?

It's the total number of houses you can instantly describe without delaying the buyers by hunting around for information. Using accelerated methods, you can add five houses to your Quick-Speak Inventory (QSI) every day. By doing that, you'll soon be ready to show, without prior notice, at least three properties that are of interest to any buyer, and to talk knowledgeably about competitive inventory with any prospective seller.

All these good things begin with a simple form that guides you to a manageable mental inventory of best-buy homes. It tells you what to look for, so your mental inventory isn't concentrated in a narrow price, location, and amenity field, but instead stretches across the entire spectrum of housing available in your chosen specialization area.

I call the form QSI slot sheet because it's short and descriptive. If that's too fanciful for you, name it Guidelines to Best Buys, Inventory Control Sheet, or whatever. The important thing is to quickly zero in on your initial area of specialization and take a fast grip on the inventory there.

With a pencil and a plain piece of paper, make up a form master for your Quick-Speak Inventory Slot Sheet and have a dozen copies run off. Use sample 1 in Chapter 24 as a guide.

Preparing your QSI slot sheet requires that you first select your zone of specialization. Don't agonize over this decision. It's no problem to shift your emphasis later, and you'll profit from the special knowledge you've gained in your first specialization zone as long as you stay in the same Board of Realtors®.

If single-bedroom units or houses with more than five bedrooms are important in your area, make space for them on the form. Choose the special categories that seem most useful to you. Fixer-uppers and especially attractive terms are probably found everywhere; for the other three special categories select the three most important amenities in your area.

UNDER 200K	UNDER 150K		CONDOS	ELM DIST.	CLUB ESTATES
140 W. "E" ST.		v	66 S. NET	5502 W.ACE	
1020 BLUFF		o	2131 4th E.	4901 DANTE	65 PRESS WAY
2 BEDROOMS	2 BEDROOMS	v	2 BEDROOMS	2 BEDROOMS	2 BEDROOMS
		o			
3 BEDROOMS	3 BEDROOMS	v	3 BEDROOMS	3 BEDROOMS	3 BEDROOMS
		o			
		v			49 S. 60th
4 BEDROOMS	4 BEDROOMS		4 BEDROOMS	4 BEDROOMS	4 BEDROOMS
		o			
		v			
5 BEDROOMS	5 BEDROOMS		5 BEDROOMS	5 BEDROOMS	5 BEDROOMS
		o			

QSISS   **QUICK-SPEAK INVENTORY SLOT SHEET**

V Vacant   O Occupied

FIXER-UPPERS	GREAT TERMS	VIEW	POOLS	

If necessary, take one of the vertical columns for additional special categories, but keep the total slots in your initial QSI around 50. Get that many firmly into your mental inventory and then consider adding more slots. Don't limit the total number of houses in your QSI; instead, work at maintaining variety in your mental inventory of salable properties. You'll find yourself carrying 75 to 100 houses in your QSI to fill those 50 slots. The goal is to keep the most houses in your mental inventory with the least effort, because fees are earned working face-to-face and phone-to-phone with clients. The entire point of QSI is to give you the tools to earn fees with the least amount of time taken away from direct-with-customer work.

Building a powerful Quick-Speak Inventory in the shortest time is possible, using the least time per day, demands fast learning. And it also demands keen retention.

But that's easy. Here's how you do it:

1 Keyview houses instead of merely previewing them. The next chapter tells you about the effective keyviewing method.

2 Flashdeck your Quick-Speak Inventory. This simple method of brain-clamping information fast is also detailed in the next chapter.

MONEY-MAKING GAMES WITH YOUR QSI

Once you've built your Quick-Speak Inventory (QSI) above 50 houses, you can increase the mental clamp you have on that information by challenging yourself with questions: "Name the three four-bedroom houses (on your QSI) that have the most square footage." Don't hesitate. Write three down immediately: "The tulip house on Birch. 2020 Country Club Drive. The brick-front on Aspen."

Then see how well you did on that question by checking your QSI Flashdeck, or your QSI slot sheet. As you do that, you'll learn even more about your Quick-Speak Inventory. The questions in this money-making game are limited only by your imagination and the keenness of your eye when keyviewing. Now you're developing your QSI into:

THE JET-POWERED SELLING TOOL

"Quick, name a three-bedroom house with fireplace and blue carpet." With 50 homes that you're constantly drilling yourself on, you have an extremely useful selling tool. Follow the Breakaway Schedule given after Chapter 29 and you'll build a 50-house QSI during the next ten days. Using the speedy learning systems given in the next chapter, you can have 150 houses on Quick-Speak a month from today. No more will you be stopped cold when customers suddenly switch specifications, as they so often do. It happens like this: You research homes with a view for customers, show them one or two, and then they decide to forget about a view and go for more space. If, instead of telling them to come back another day, you can drive right to some houses that meet their new requirements, and knock on those doors for permission to show right then, you can turn a loss into a win. I've made a lot of money doing this.

Suppose, the next time you're sitting at your desk, that someone you know phones and says, "My new boss and his wife are here, and he wants to look at houses right away. Can you come over and pick him up?"

You do. Your friend's boss climbs in your car and gets right at it. "Look, I know all about this qualifying bit. I can go to $50,000 down, and I can quality for a $200,000 loan, but I don't want to put that much into a house. Our kids have just gone out on their own, and we might buy a smaller house than we have now. But maybe not. So show us what you've got."

If you have 50 houses on QSI, you can show him a different house every 15 minutes for *twelve and a half hours*—without stopping for meals. That'll satisfy the most eager curb jumper. But, you're thinking, this is nonsense. Nobody wants to look at houses for twelve hours, and nobody wants to see them all.

Right. But, if you've selected a good cross section of the available houses for your QSI, you can instantly pick out at least three houses that anyone qualified to buy in your area might be interested in. You came on like a champion all the way.

Your customers know they'll never find anyone who is more certain to guide them straight to their best housing buy than you are.

Suppose you work in a board that publishes a weekly Multiple Listing Book of a thousand or more properties that are for sale. There's no way you can keep that large an inventory on ready recall in your mind. Fortunately, performing such a feat isn't necessary. Carrying between 50 and 250 listings in your Quick-Speak Inventory gives you a powerful machine for selling real estate.

Before you decide to amble along with only 50 houses on Quick-Speak, reflect on these two facts: (1) top producers make at least five times as much money as average producers in the same office; (2) top producers have at least five times as many properties on Quick-Speak as average producers. High income and high QSI fly together, just as low income and low Quick-Speak Inventory grumble along together.

Top producers don't have a snobby attitude about previewing or showing listings from competing offices. If you are a true "public servant" you will not show any partiality regarding listed properties. Of course everyone wants to sell their own or their office's listings because they make more money, but personally I think that's secondary to the customer's need. Don't kid yourself, the public knows what we are after. I have heard people from all over discuss real estate agents who won't show certain properties or try to talk the public out of one house because it's not an "in-house" listing. In the long run, when you cooperate with all brokers and their properties your reputation within the industry and with the public will be rated as highly ethical. Take it from me, your pocketbook will also reflect your golden rule philosophy.

3

BUILD MONEY-MAKING SKILLS FAST WITH HYPERLEARN

Hyperlearn's Six Easy Steps • Hyperlearning Techniques • Specific Hyperlearn Applications

Hyperlearn is a method of extending your perceptions and intensifying your concentration so that you can more quickly grasp new knowledge and acquire new skills. It only sounds formidable; in practice it's simple. And Hyperlearn is fun because the good results start at once, and you're creatively involved.

Haphazard study is inefficient and delivers haphazard results. Hyperlearn is organized and delivers the results you want when you want them. It's a flexible system. You adapt it to the knowledge or skill being acquired. The brief time you spend organizing your Hyperlearn course often takes you halfway or more toward mastery of the material or craft.

HYPERLEARN'S SIX EASY STEPS

Here are the six easy Hyperlearn steps that will allow you to learn anything quickly.

1 *Define* precisely what you're setting out to learn. Write down your learning goal. Be concise. Use numbers to make your goal clear and definite. Short

sentences are best. If you need more than a short paragraph, you're trying to include too much material in a single learning course.

Suppose you write your goal as, "I want to know the floor plan of every available house in my sales area; I want to know the amenities each house has; I want to be able to give buyers the prices, number of bedrooms, and—"

You stop because your goal seems too wordy and the task seems too big to cope with. Break this large learning problem down to several manageable courses, and concentrate on becoming an expert in part of the sales area fast, rather than remaining a mumbler about all of it for a long time.

Write your Chief Goal down first: "To master the inventory of the entire Greenpretty Valley." Now pick a subgoal: "To master the inventory in the Elm School neighborhood."

At one stroke, you've changed a formidable goal requiring many months to achieve into one that can be conquered within a few days—without altering your basic thrust.

2 *Gather* the information to be learned into one place. In the case of the single named neighborhood's inventory you've set out to learn, clip the listings for sale there from last week's Multiple Listing Book, and put them in one stack.

3 *Understand*. Give the information to be learned a rapid first reading to familiarize yourself with its depth and scope. Then reread it, this time carefully. Make sure that you understand every detail well enough to explain it to a customer.

4 *Break down* the material you're learning to the smallest study units possible. Express the data as single facts or in short paragraphs.

5 *Reassemble* the material you're learning into a self-created, self-teaching course. Use one or a combination of the following:
  • Flashdecks
  • Blank-interval cassettes and solo role working
  • Outlines to details
  • Mnemonic hooks
  • Feelings remember
  • Variety of skills and senses

These methods are explained in the order given. Note that none of them require expensive equipment or supplies.

6 *Review* the material twice each day, using whatever learning method(s) you've selected. Concentrate as you review the material, work fast, and be thorough. Do that every morning and night and you'll master what you want to learn with astonishing speed.

HYPERLEARNING TECHNIQUES

Create Your Own Flashdecks

All you need is a pack of 3 x 5 inch cards. Cut them in half for easier carrying and lower cost. Write one question or situation on the front of each card; write the answer or response on the back. A dozen cards make an effective flashdeck that's ready for instant study any time you have a few moments.

To use the flashdeck for learning, read the question, answer it, and flip the card to check on the completeness and accuracy of your response. Don't hesitate. Demand fast answers from yourself. If you can't answer within two seconds, read the answer on the back of the card. When you miss a question, study the answer intently. Then put the card where you'll encounter it again on that run through the deck.

The time you spend organizing and writing your flashdeck cards is the most effective learning experience you can have with most types of material. From there to complete mastery of the data through spaced repetition (twice daily drills) is an easy downhill slide.

Shuffle the cards once or twice a week so your responses won't be keyed to a familiar card sequence. If a few questions are especially troublesome—and this is the usual case—create a constant companion deck by making a second copy of the card you're having trouble with. Carry this deck with you during the day and review it whenever you have a few free minutes. Drop cards as soon as you've learned them.

Examples of a flashdeck card:

How many homes in Elm School area?	740

Side 1   Side 2

Blank-interval Cassettes for Solo Role Working

First, let's distinguish between role playing and role working. Chapters 11 and 16 include role plays for office meetings. Volunteers play the parts by reading them from this book.

This is training with live ammunition. The situations that agents face when they work with clients are recreated for the benefit of the players and the rest of the staff who are watching the role play. But you can't make the words yours by hearing them once. That's where role working comes in. You role work, solo, as often as you like. There's no time wasted trying to schedule mutually convenient times for group role playing. Getting ready for solo role working—creating flashdecks and blank-interval cassettes—is a big step toward memorizing the material.

Preparing Your Own Blank-interval Cassettes

You need four things: a clean cassette, a recorder-player, a flashdeck you want to learn, and a quiet place to work for a short time.

With the machine in "record" mode, read the question *out loud* from the first flashdeck card. Then, with the machine still recording, turn the card over and *silently* read the answer. Repeat this process for each card in the deck. That's all there is to it.

Using Your Blank-interval Cassettes

Rewind the tape you just made and play it from the beginning. When your taped voice finishes asking a question, say the answer. (Don't record your answer, of course.) Use the flashdeck to prompt yourself at first. This is a let-it-roll operation. While the blank-interval cassette plays, you're free to walk around and concentrate on what you're saying without having to stand over the recorder punching buttons.

Four tips:

1 From the very beginning *work at speaking with clarity and verve*. But don't overdo it: Naturalness is the key.

2 As you listen to each question, *visualize the situation* that would give rise to that question in real life. Once you know the answers, the only problem left is that of recognizing the situations.

3 *Don't rush* through the silent reading when recording the blank intervals. Be sure you allow yourself a second or two to get set, plus enough time to say the full answer with conviction and unhurried phrasing.

Number each card before recording so the flashdeck will be convenient for prompting yourself and checking the accuracy of your spoken answers.

4 *Perfect your responses*. Occasionally tape your replies for review. Go through the entire blank-interval cassette, then review all your answers. Make notes of your responses that need further rehearsal to give them more zip and zing.

Expect to hear a host of minor mistakes; refuse to be dismayed by them. Practice perfects, and this may be the first time in your adult life that you've set aside time to improve your verbal performance. You're in sales, yet how much time in the past month—or the past year—have you devoted to improving your performance as a speaker? How well you speak bears heavily on how much you get paid as a salesperson.

Outlines to Details

Take your outline of the detailed material to be learned, and tape-record, write in longhand, or type the details out from memory. You can also use the answer side of a flashdeck to cue this self-testing. Check your answers for accuracy or you may thoroughly learn wrong information.

Mnemonic Hooks for Nimble Numbers

Feelings about numbers divide people into two groups. Group one has experienced pleasure at being able to remember numbers well at some time in their lives. Group two is composed of everyone else, of all the people who keep telling themselves, "I'm no good at remembering numbers." It's easy to change all that.

Every successful agent has had many instances where a snatched moment has saved a transaction that would otherwise have been lost. When a customer goes to the john or trots out to the car for something, I've often snapped off the phone call that held another situation for me until I could finish with the first customer, and meet the second again. I've made these calls (local, of course, or charged to my office phone) while showing houses to buyers. Address books are great. Use them. Write down those phone numbers. But, if you know the number, you can be talking to the person you need to reach before you can pull an address book out and find anything in it. Your brain is eager to give you that phone number in 1/100 second. All you have to do is program it right and it'll do it for you every time. No charge.

Phone numbers are only the tip of the numeric iceberg. Interest-rate factors, square footages, prices, all the numbers you need, if they're on ready recall, will help you solidify your foundation of competence. Nimbleness with numbers contributes mightily to the relaxed, alert, I'm-on-top-of-everything attitude that does so much to reassure people when they need all the reassurance they can get to make a major decision. When you've got it, that positive attitude radiates from you in countless subtle ways, winning respect and building confidence. When you don't have it, when you're crackling with tension, you radiate stress that your prospects pick up as fear and uncertainty. Calm Confidence closes better than Hectic Hassle ever will.

There is no such thing as a hard-to-learn number that you need to know in real estate. Concentrate on any number for an instant and you'll see patterns. The concentration is the first step to your goal, the ability to project that number in 10-foot high figures on the screen of your mind. Let's try instant concentration on a phone number, and suppose that 547-8332 is the home phone of your client, James Fagan.

547-8332   The five is alive; 47 is Fat Fagan's Waistline—8 less two 3's is 2. Visualize a very alive Fat Fagan jiggling his 47 inch waistline while yelling, ''Eight minus 3 twice is 2.''

Write this number a couple of times. See the figures standing high as you write them. That one sample may suffice to show the method. The point is to learn the method, not this jibberish number. Practice learning the method on the numbers in your own address book. Make the dull numbers throb. If this trick eludes you right now, take a memory course at your local college, or buy a book on memory building—you'll find both are loaded with recall hooks that make memorizing numbers a snap.

Feelings Remember

Can you remember a painful childhood accident? Most people can vividly recall such incidents that happened many years ago, although the hour that just passed may be a blank. The emotion and pain of such incidents have imprinted a number of details on their minds that would otherwise have vanished long ago. But you don't have to give yourself a crack on the head every time you see a house you want to remember: Pleasant emotions are effective memory clamps too.

Be alert for emotional associations you can form between events in your life and information you now wish to remember. This idea is particularly helpful in keyviewing houses. All of us can find parallels between the houses we're selling and the houses we grew up in, or have lived in since. This can apply to furnishings as well as floorplans. A solid memory hook to hang a house on could be a grandfather clock standing in its hall that's just like the one your aunt used to have. Another solid hook is a house where you've worked many open houses. Make a conscious effort to find these associations for a month and you'll find they'll flow to you after that, making your observation sharper and your recall keener. Make a note in each house you keyview of the specifics remembered. ''242 Elm, 3-bedroom, reminds me of Aunt Lou's house in Chicago.''

Use a Variety of Skills and Senses

Use every different sense and skill you can reasonably employ to perceive, express, and impress the material on your mind. Read it silently and then aloud. Copy each of the study units you've laid out for yourself word for word in longhand. Outline the basic ideas. Then, using only your outline, write the material you're learning in detail. Prepare a flashdeck and drill yourself on the facts you're acquiring. Record one of your readings of the material and then listen to your tapes. Discuss the details with someone who shares your interest.

When you're learning about houses, walk through and around them. When you're learning about an area, drive it, walk it—and fly over it if you can.

The two essential elements of the Hyperlearn process are:

- Break down the material to be learned into small, easily understood parts.
- Reassemble those parts in your brain by drawing them in through as many different channels as possible. To shorten your learning time and make your recall keener and quicker, experience what you want to learn in all the different ways and with all the different senses, skills, and emotions that you can.

Remember that only full mastery of your material permits you to concentrate all your attention on the prospect.

"And while I at length debate, and beat the bush, there shall step in other men and catch the birds".

—John Heywood, 1549

Run through your Hyperlearn exercises rapidly and intensely. Avoid distraction's slowness. Two short drills spaced several hours apart teach more effectively than one long session. Schedule twice-daily study times.

SPECIFIC HYPERLEARN APPLICATIONS

Learning the Named Neighborhoods Fast

Can you drive to any property in your area, from wherever you happen to be, without wrong turns and without consulting maps? You're paid in proportion to the knowledge and skill you employ helping customers do what they want to do. House hunters need guidance through the unknown to the property they can afford in a neighborhood they'll like. They too can study the map, research the area, and knock on strange doors, but they prefer tapping your reservoirs of knowledge. Those reservoirs had better be full or they will go elsewhere.

There's no quicker way to lose people forever than by getting lost driving them around your own area of expertise. It's basic, but don't make the mistake of thinking it's too boring to bother with. If you have no knowledge of the territory, you'll make no money in it; if you have good knowledge, you can make good money; if you have top knowledge of the territory, you can make top money there. Learning your area's streets so well that you zip around them with blithe confidence, and make your folks glad they're working with you, takes work. It'll take a lot less work if you apply system to your street-learning process.

The first step is to take out a piece of paper.

Draw a map of your sales area.   Include only the main thoroughfares serving your area of primary interest. Do it fast and then compare what you've drawn to the printed map. If you're not satisfied with your accuracy or completeness, draw another from the printed map. Don't trace. Draw it. Until you can quickly sketch an accurate, main thoroughfare map of your area, as you might need to do while sitting with a customer in a coffee shop, repeat this exercise daily.

That's your personal and customer orientation map. Get it straight in your head now, so you can start operating with a happy can't-get-lost feeling right away.

Many an agent doesn't see the point of putting out further effort to learn the territory in detail. Yet, if his own house were going up in flames, that same agent would be enraged if the fire department wasted time figuring out how to get there. Hot buyers are aflame with impatience. Fiddle around looking for houses while they burn, and you'll send them to a better-prepared agent. You can take that lesson from this page, or wait and learn it when you've sent several thousand dollars to the professionally prepared agents who know exactly where the salable inventory is.

You can lose some buyers simply by not knowing whether there's a church of their denomination in your area, and exactly where it is. Again, you can lift a fee-saving idea off this page. Or you can wait and learn this small amount of information when you lose a sale. It's often said that experience is the best teacher, but few people find that experience's lessons come cheap.

As soon as you're familiar with the area's major streets and points of interest, you're ready for the second step: mastering the residential streets in detail. Here's how to do that efficiently.

Define 30 neighborhoods of about 20 streets each on a printed map of your sales area. Use a pencil to draw lines around them.   These 30 neighborhoods will cover much more than your area of primary interest. The purpose is to ready you for working with buyers on short notice. You'll often find yourself working with buyers on short notice. Agents who aren't prepared to work on short notice lose lots of buyers. Don't let that happen to you. Prepare. Now.

Use main thoroughfares or natural barriers for the neighborhood boundaries; where none are available, pick a key street to draw your line down.

After you've defined these 30 neighborhoods, take a moment to put a hook on them so that each one will stand out in your memory.

Name each of these neighborhoods.   If a church, school, or landmark is located in one, use that name. An intersection in the neighborhood, a park, street, or any other feature can furnish a distinctive name.

When the neighborhoods are all defined and named, you're ready to schedule a rapid-learning sequence. You'll probably find that learning two Named Neighborhoods a day is about right. Here's how you go about it.

- Study the streets and how they connect on the map.
- Set the map aside and sketch the streets of that neighborhood from memory.
- Compare your sketch to the map and make corrections.
- Repeat the above until you can draw a complete and accurate sketch showing how the streets connect in that neighborhood.
- Make a list of the streets in that neighborhood by copying the names from the map.
- Make up a Named Neighborhood Flashdeck (next topic) and run through the cards.
- Repeat this process morning and night until you've overlearned each neighborhood. Be sure to drive the streets twice daily. As you do so, keep in mind which Named Neighborhood you're in.

One of the repeating achievements of Breakaway is to thoroughly learn 2 of these 30 neighborhoods each day. Do this and you'll always know exactly where you are on 600 streets. You'll have an inexhaustible bag of tricks to save time, impress clients, and win fees. Streets don't change. Learn them, and you'll make big money from that knowledge as long as you work the area.

Named-Neighborhoods Flashdeck

Use a 3 × 5 card for each street. On the question side, write only the street name. On the answer side, write the main cross streets, how you get there, and where the subject street begins and ends. The quickest and most effective memory tool is a sketch of that street.

Be sure to note the neighborhood on the answer side of the card. This will permit you to mix learned cards into one Named-Neighborhoods Flashdeck for occasional review.

Keyviewing

Here's how to look at houses and organize your thoughts on 3 × 5 cards so you can build up a large Quick-Speak Inventory of properties fast.

Spot a single distinguishing feature about every home you're putting in your Quick-Speak Inventory. This could be a fountain, a spectacular view, a weird decoration—anything you notice will do. Then key your memory to that feature.

On the front of each 3 × 5 card write your memory key: "Purple hairy wallhanging in living room."

On the back of the same card, jot down the following information:

> "4567 Arrowhead Drive
> CBS M/M Strangeideas 987-5432
> 3 beds 1¾ ba
> shake rf, rm 4 pool, no vu, gold cpt, clean, AM."

Spelling out the abbreviations, we have: "Call before showing, Mr. and Mrs. Strangeideas, 3 bedrooms, 1¾ baths, shake roof, room for a swimming pool in the back yard, no view. Gold carpet. The house is clean (but not immaculate). Priced at the market. This last comment (AM) is your feeling, not what the listing agent said on his flyer. For your QSI Flashdeck and similar purposes, it's handy to have a simple, three-term price indicator:

UM   Priced under the current market: a bargain that's likely to sell fast.
AM   Priced at the market. The comparables will validate this price.
OM   Priced over the market. This one will be around for a while.

Have a reason for putting every house on your QSI. Price. An emotional feature or features. View. A real fixer-upper rat—but cheap. A creampuff. A dull dog with lots of space. Highlight what's special by circling that item or items. If it's price that causes you to put it on your QSI, draw a circle around the price.

The most convenient way to work your QSI Flashdeck, usually, is to file the cards by price. Be sure to date each *price*. Leave room on the card for later price changes.

Standing around an open house, waiting in the office for an important call, or when you're early for a meeting, pull out your QSI Flashdeck and refresh your inventory knowledge. When you see "Hairy purple wallhanging" on a card, that whole house should flash on in your head. With just a little practice, you'll find that you can mentally walk around in that house and see the family room, the fireplace there, the shelves in the library. You'll be able to remember all the other pertinent details that you related to the purple hairy wallhanging. Keen memory is merely intense concentration hung on a hook. Everyone has a keen a memory as they're willing to concentrate on having. By pulling on that hook—the key element you tied your details to—you'll be able to pull out your memory of the entire house. It's really fun to recall minor details about a house you've keyviewed several weeks before, and it can be very profitable.

Drill yourself with your stack of QSI cards morning and night. Polish that knowledge and it'll fly you to Tahiti.

Visual Flashdecks

Photograph whatever you want to be able to identify by sight with an instant-print camera, and then write whatever you want to memorize on the back of the print. Voila: a Visual Flashdeck.

Use this technique to create a beautiful sales tool in no time at all for working with both buyers and sellers. Compile a Visual Flashdeck of

- Distant properties, or those that require long advance notice to show;
- Common types of houses in your sales area for establishing price ranges;
- Tract model exteriors, to speed your memorization of them, and then to show resale buyers what's available;
- Best buys; or
- Your entire Quick-Speak Inventory.

Make this part of your keyviewing routine. An instant print of the exterior will allow you to concentrate your keyviewing effort on the interior.

Learning Floorplans Fast

You'll be pleasantly surprised at how firm a grip you'll get on floorplans by using this routine when keyviewing:

- After walking through the house, sit down there and make a quick sketch of the floorplan. Don't look around as you do this, sketch entirely from memory.
- Then jump up and check the accuracy of your sketch.
- Repeat the process until you can sketch the basic floorplan from memory.

Conquering the Agreements

There are two ways you can become thoroughly familiar with the listing form and the purchase agreement: Work with them for a few years—or Hyperlearn them in a few hours. Command of this verbiage will boost your self-confidence and imbue your clients with faith in you. It will help mightily to create in your customer the willingness to be closed. All too many new agents delay giving these two vital forms intense study until they're sitting with buyers or sellers and trying to close. Hesitation or incompetence revealed at that time can chill the clients and kill the transaction.

Don't risk it.

Here's how to acquire absolute command of the clauses in these forms easily:

- Read aloud the agreements your office uses to take listings and make offers. Make sure you understand every paragraph, sentence, phrase, and word well enough to explain them. Get answers to every question you have.

- Visit an escrow officer, attorney, title person—whoever is involved in closing in your state. Spend time with them and just watch.
- Then create a flashdeck for the paragraphs of that form: on one side the number, on the other the exact, complete text of that paragraph.
- Drill yourself with that flashdeck until you know exactly what's in that agreement form, and precisely where everything in it is.

This won't seem like wasted effort after you've had a distraught seller say, "I can't find where it tells what happens to the earnest money if the buyers back out."

You can scurry over and frantically scan the form to answer his question while he thinks, or says, "Don't you even know your own form? Am I dealing with an amateur?"

How much better if, without glancing at the form, you immediately say from where you're sitting, "Paragraph 12* covers that point, Mr. Nagle." That action quietly shouts, "I am a competent agent. Your interests are safe in my hands." Large fees are won on a series of just such small wins!

Writing Offers with Hyperlearned Phrases

Being able to write clear offers is a vital skill. Loosely phrased offers frighten sellers. How would you phrase an offer if your buyers want

- To sell their house first?
- To assume the existing low-interest loan?
- To be assured that the landscaping will be properly cared for until they take possession?
- To do, or be protected against, any of the other things that come up, time after time, during purchase negotiations in your area?
- To lock in a maximum interest rate in a buyer's agreement?
- To close concurrent with the closing of the buyer's present home that is sold but not recorded?
- To rent back prior to the closing (not a very smart thing to do but sometimes necessary)?
- An all-cash offer?
- A geological report within a certain time frame (or any other valid inspection that could affect the ultimate value of home)?

---

*The form used in your state today probably covers this information under a different paragraph number.

Here's how to take a quick fix on these phrases.

- Examine your office's files of closed transactions, note the most common situations that arise on offers, and study the wording used to cope with those situations. Pass over complex, unusual circumstances. Concentrate on learning the solutions to the most frequently encountered questions first.

- From this study, create your own list of effective offer-to-purchase phrases in flashdeck form. On one side of a 3 × 5 card, write the deposit receipt problem. On the reverse of that card, copy the most effective phrase you've found dealing with that particular circumstance. Avoid rambling sentences. Choose those that are short and precise.

- Practice working fast and accurately under pressure by writing up offers with intense concentration for 30 minutes a day until you are supremely confident in this area of real estate expertise.

4

CONFRONT OLD PRO—AND WIN!

How to Win FSBO Listings from Old Pro • Eight Tips on Winning Any Listing from More-experienced Agents • When Old Pro Has an Offer on Your Listing • What Old Pros Hate • When You Have an Offer on Old Pro's Listing • Both You and Old Pro Have Offers on a Third Agent's Listing • Hearing Simultaneous Offers on Your Listing

When they find themselves competing against an oldtimer of considerable reputation, many new agents assume they're beaten, merely go through the motions of trying, and let Old Pro collect the fee by their own default. By making such feeble efforts, or by telling the client or customer (with words or manner) that Old Pro is the big operator they should be working with, these new agents set Old Pro up for an easy fee.

New agents should seek and welcome encounters with established agents who have an impressive track record. Win, lose, or draw, such encounters are instructive. Dwell on the positive benefits such a learning experience will bring you, and refuse to worry about whether your inexperience will show. Seize each of these exciting learning opportunities, wring all the knowledge you can from them, and you won't be inexperienced for long. Let's consider the basic situations where you'll find these priceless learning opportunities.

HOW TO WIN FSBO LISTINGS FROM OLD PRO

Since the new agent has more time, he or she holds an important advantage over Old Pro in working this aspect of real estate practice. Fizzbos are heavy time eaters. Old Pro will swoop in and gobble up a FSBO now and then where he or she is referred, has a buyer for the property, or may just feel like it. But the top producers (with rare exceptions) can't work constantly in the For Sale By Owner field. If they try, they'll have to neglect the referral business that brings in most of their top production.

If you're a new agent battling for a fizzbo over a period of time with Old Pro, take heart. Time is with you. The longer the fizzbo holds off making a decision, the better your chances are of eventually winning. You have the staying power and the determination; you are rapidly plugging the gaps in your knowledge and skills; you are closing fast on Old Pro's lead in expertise. It'll take time for you to match Old Pro's inventory knowledge of the entire sales area. You can't match his whole bag of skills overnight. But you can, within days, learn enough about the sellers' neighborhood to convince them that *you* are the upcoming expert on their location. Do this by concentrating on their block and neighborhood. Old Pro can't concentrate to that extent; he or she must cover a wider area. And, when people think about who's keeping current on their turf, your knowledge of what happened there last *week* will be much more important to them than Old Pro's knowledge of what happened there last *year*. Knock on doors. Talk to the people. Find out who's thinking of selling, who's getting promoted and what people think of the neighborhood today. You're in a far better position than Old Pro is to discover what's happening *now* on that block because you have the time to do it.

EIGHT TIPS ON WINNING ANY LISTING FROM MORE-EXPERIENCED AGENTS

- Concentrate on the one situation. Overprepare for it.
- Keep your cool, your humor, and your integrity.
- Be professional, and be courteously assertive.
- Emphasize your strong point: that you have more time for thorough promotion (especially open houses) and for servicing the listing.
- Defuse Old Pro's advantages by quickly conceding his or her fine reputation. Then point out that your office's enormous fund of knowledge and skill is available, if needed.
- Don't fight on unfavorable ground. If you're competing for a listing in the farm Old Pro is actively working, don't try to prove you know more about that neighborhood than Old Pro does (though you might be able to show more knowledge about that *house*). In this situation, you're in the running only if the sellers are disenchanted with Old Pro for personal or business reasons, and they very well may be.
- Believe in and act on this maxim: "I win by demonstrating my own competence; I lose by casting doubt on my competitor's competence." You can't have clean hands if you throw mud.

- Try to have the appointment after Old Pro. If that's not possible, say to the seller, "Could I have just one more chance to talk to you before you make your final decision? I know Old Pro is an excellent agent, but please don't list with someone based on pricing. Any of us can agree to a price."

It's critical, when you're up against Old Pro, to use a listing presentation manual to make sure that you fire all your ammunition.

Role play your presentation to your spouse, or another beginner in your office. Rehearse presenting the seller's net sheet and the guidelines to market value. Find out if you and the prospective seller have a mutual friend. If you do, call the friend to enlist help. Say to your friend: "In real estate, I get by with a little help from my friends, so could I ask you a favor?" (Don't pause). "Mary and Bud Johnson have asked both me and a competitor to give them a market evaluation on their home. Sometimes if an outside third party, a mutual friend not in real estate, puts a good word in, I have a better chance of getting the opportunity to serve them. Would you call Mary and Bud and possibly put that good word in for me?"

WHEN OLD PRO HAS AN OFFER ON YOUR LISTING

(Practices vary from state to state. Check with your broker on how this is handled in your area.)

You set up the appointment to meet Old Pro at your seller's home. Naturally, you don't want to look inept. Here's how you avoid that. First of all, as a new agent, you have had time to thoroughly research your listing long before the offer came in. You have a complete Guidelines to Market Value already prepared. Visit all the houses on that list so you know how comparable those houses are. Know them well and be able to talk knowledgeably about them.

Never forget that Old Pro is human too. He or she is not a machine, or some supertoughskin. Every Old Pro has been humbled, frustrated, and defeated many times in this business. He may be supremely confident—or suspicious, alert, and unconfident. He may be desperately pressed for time and wholly unprepared, although it's more likely that Old Pro will come to the meeting very well prepared because of the long-time accumulation of knowledge and the constant updating of it.

As a new salesperson, you'll constantly be confronting the Old Pro in the business. When I was new, I had this attitude: I looked up to the big producers in the board because they were where I wanted to be. I realized how much more they knew than I did, and I never tried to be something I hadn't earned the right to be yet. But I wanted Old Pro to respect and like me, and to think I was taking my job seriously.

That first summer was strange. Back in those days, there were only 100 members in our board. We all used to meet for coffee and rolls every Thursday morning at a savings and loan office. Then we'd follow each other's cars and preview all the new property that had come on the market that week. The first few times I walked into the coffee room of the savings and loan building, where groups from each office were banded together in tight little groups, I was alone—and pregnant. Everyone seemed to stare at me. I'd try to hide in a corner but my tummy stuck out like Mammoth Mountain. Sometimes they'd look at me and giggle, or whisper. I felt angry and isolated—but I had conviction. "These people think I'm pregnant, fat and dumb. I'll show them that I'm pregnant, rich, and smart." First a listing of mine came out on caravan. It was a mile too high but there I was, parading around my own listing with all these other brokers. They said, "It's beautifully done but overpriced," as they stepped through, and "Whose listing is this?"

"Mine, thank you."

"It's too much money."

"The seller and I are reasonable people," I'd say quietly. "Bring us a prospect and we'll work with you."

Bong, they'd go, "Who's this little pipsqueak?"

Then another listing. And then an offer. My first offer involved a high-flying lister and farmer from another office. I practiced, drilled, and rehearsed before I presented. Old Pro was happy. I was happy. I told him after the offer was accepted, "It's such a privilege to sell your listing. You are a legend in your own time." Always stroke Old Pro's ego. He loves it. I sure did later. Then I sent him a thank-you note, "Thanks for the opportunity to work with you. I appreciate your patience. I'm sure you remember what it was like to be the 'new kid in town,' when you first moved into real estate. Keep me posted on our transaction and I'll do the same. Danny."

Then he told the people in his office that I was a hard-working lady. If Old Pro is impressed, he'll tell his buddies about you. Then you've got one office on your side and you go for the others little by little. How do you think so many of my listings sold during the first year? Lots of Old Pros worked with me because I dug in and did my part.

WHAT OLD PROS HATE

The New Agent Who Knows It All. Here are three examples that occur when New Agent has an offer on Old Pro's listing.

1 New Agent remarks to Old Pro and her seller that the photo in the Multiple Listing Book isn't very attractive, and that if he were Old Pro, he'd have it retaken for the seller. Old Pro thinks, "Another smart aleck."

2 Old Pro, during the presentation offer, explains to his seller what this offer means to him in dollars and cents by breaking down the seller's net sheet. New Agent interrupts Old Pro when he gets to miscellaneous charges and says, "You've only plugged $100 in there. I always use $200, because I want

to cushion 'my people' extra high, and avoid any last minute shocks. I really think we ought to use $200 here." Old Pro knows New Agent heard another agent say that, and sees through the big dealer act.

3 New Agent tries to become "fast friends" with Old Pro's sellers. Always address Old Pro (who's acting as listing agent) in this manner: "For you and your sellers we are offering, hoping or presenting . . ."

In all of these examples, the New Agents made an enemy of Old Pro, gained nothing now, and set themselves up to lose much in the future. This is a people business, and Old Pros are people too.

WHEN YOU HAVE AN OFFER ON OLD PRO'S LISTING*

Use this dialogue to secure Old Pro's cooperation now, and start building the solid rapport that will bring you many benefits in the future:

"Hi, John. I'm Danny Kennedy of Sell Fast Realty. I haven't had the opportunity to work with you yet, but I hear you're one of the pros. Anyway, I have an offer on your listing and I'm excited and eager to present it as soon as possible." Be sure to say that. Sometimes Old Pro gets lazy, would rather keep his previous dinner plans, and present your offer the next day. "Please call me back immediately. I'm anxious to meet you and present this offer. I've spent a lot of time making sure it would meet your requirements."

The key is friendly persuasion—humility with firm confidence. You may be new, but you're definitely one of the up-and-coming pro agents. Your attitude displays that to Old Pro.

Old Pro says, "Tell me your offer before we go over there."

Caution. Protect yourself. Don't tell *anyone* what the offer is until you're with the seller. "Old Pro, I'd rather wait and discuss it when we're both in the presence of your seller. That way your seller won't think that you and I and my customer are in cahoots."

When you present the offer, tell Old Pro in the sellers' hearing. "John, I know how much these folks respect you." Expand on this a bit, and then say, "First, I'd like to give all of you a little background on my buyers. Then I'd appreciate it if you'd present the terms and price, John—unless you'd prefer to listen along with Mr. and Mrs. Sellers, and shoot questions at me after the presentation. Which would you prefer?" Tie downs work with Old Pro, too.

Give him the opportunity to make the choice. If Old Pro is the buyer's agent, and you are the lister, then reverse the words: "Old Pro, would you prefer that I sit back and listen with the sellers while you present the entire offer—and then shoot any questions that we have at you afterwards?"

---

*Check with your broker and make sure that these suggestions conform to the customs of your area.

BOTH YOU AND OLD PRO HAVE OFFERS ON A THIRD AGENT'S LISTING

Introduce yourself to Old Pro. "I certainly wish we were meeting under better circumstances, but I guess our customers have the same taste. We must both be doing something right."

Insist on presenting your offer alone with the seller and his agent, and not in the presence of the competing agent. If you're alone with Old Pro before the offers are presented, keep it light. Chit chat, trade tips on other properties, but don't discuss your offer or your clients. Not a word.

HEARING SIMULTANEOUS OFFERS ON YOUR LISTING

As a first-year salesperson climbing rapidly to the top, I caught my share of icy stares from the Old Pros. Some of them want to see you get good, especially if they've given you a few tips, but they aren't comfortable if you get too good too fast. So don't push them unless you have a reason to.

I was the listing agent on a property that drew six offers one evening. At least three of them involved strong-willed Old Pros. When the "Woman in the Shoe" (my nickname around town because of all my kids) lined up those six agents at the property and said, "My sellers and I are honored to have six offers. I wish we could accept all of them, but, of course, that's impossible. So here's the procedure: We'll listen to all six in the order that you came in. Then we'll do one of two things: accept the best offer, or make a counteroffer.

Of course I wanted my sellers to get some reassurance regarding the financial strength of the individual buyers as well. How frustrating to walk away from strong prospects only to find out the offer they accepted (though it looked appealing on the surface) was from a risky buyer. It's always great to get some loan interviews set up prior to the offer. Then the seller can get some input from a loan representative or lending institution during the time of the offer, for further reassurance. Be sure that you keep the hotline phone number of your state association's on-call attorney handy to be sure that, in case of multiple offers, you are giving correct advice. There have been so many debates regarding counteroffers. Never put your sellers in jeopardy. You can do this by giving incorrect advice that may cause them to have to pay more than one real estate fee if two parties perform as agreed.

Everyone had a better way to handle the situation of six offers at the same time, of course. Some Old Pros had their buyers outside in cars waiting to consider counteroffers. It was a touchy situation.

I had called the Board of Realtors® that afternoon for advice on the proper procedure. I told my sellers I'd done that, and asked for their confidence.

I kept my cool, although when you have to deal with a couple of cocky buyers' agents at a time like that, it can make you seethe under your smile. It was, of course, a difficult time for those six agents too, and afterwards I sent them all a thank-you note. At the time, I knew I had to extend myself to avoid making anyone mad.

Sooner or later you will run into the simultaneous-offer situation on one of your listings. When you do, plan ahead to avoid upsetting anyone and to keep control. Maintain good eye contact with each agent as you take them into a separate room with the sellers. Say to them, "We certainly appreciate having more than one offer. Please understand I have a fiduciary relationship with my sellers. I must guide them to the best decision for them, without bias."

Keep in mind that someday you will be a seasoned campaigner. The secret is to ask Old Pro to remember when he or she was the new kid on the block. "Frustrating and confusing, wasn't it?"

New agents: Keep in mind that you haven't quite earned the right to throw your weight around. Have a little respect for your elders; you are not yet one of the "walking wounded." The word here is *compassion*.

Why should feisty youngsters have respect for entrenched oldtimers? Because the Old Pros are the people who know where it's at and how to get it. They're the ones who did most of the business in the past, and they'll keep on doing most of the business in the future. They aren't afraid of the capable, hardworking newcomer— it's the incompetent, careless clowns who worry them.

The Old Pros will be around tomorrow, and ten years from now, still doing good business. They'll sell a few of your listings whether they like you or not, but if they like you, and respect your professional ability, they'll sell lots more of your listings.

Sure, confront Old Pro when that's the ball game. Play hard, but fair. Win their respect and the fee if you can. If you can't, it's a big win to gain Old Pro's acquaintance, confidence, and respect.

5

How to Flip Those Fizzbos Right into Your Fold

The One Winning Move that Brings in 100 Listings • The Four Tactics that Make Money • The Full Treatment • Putting Your Winning Move to Work • The Four-Kinds-of-Buyers Listing Close • Avoiding Recalls: the FSBO X-File • Call Fizzbos from Open House • Potpourri

Fizzbos are the people who put out signs that read "For Sale by Owner." Fizzbos are wonderful—I've always been very happy that there are plenty of them around. Why do I say that? Because whenever I've needed to rejuvenate my business fast, I've done it by hitting the fizzbos.

Experienced agents often need to rejuvenate their activity when, for one reason or another, their production has fallen off and they want to get back on the track. They can do it quickest with the for-sale-by-owner people. The same thing applies to the new agents—fizzbos are a quick way to get on the fast track to higher earnings for the first time, too. What a great place to start a real estate career.

The need for your services as a real estate professional will continue to grow because financing and other aspects of real estate knowledge will continue to become ever more complex. This means that owners attempting to sell by themselves will encounter greater difficulties every year. To solve the difficulties, owners will turn ever more often to highly trained fulltime real estate professionals.

As we draw close to the twenty-first century, keep in mind that it's a trickier business for a for-sale-by-owner to sell his or her home today than it was 20 years ago. With adjustable interest rates, indexes, 2.5% spreads over the life of the loan, and a million other facts people want to know about before they buy a home, the public mistrusts the average seller trying to sell his or her own house. Also, for-sale-by-owners are part-time, unlicensed people trying to market their most valuable asset—their home. Not only are they unqualified, but their chances of holding the sale together for 30, 60 or 90 days is questionable.

When do most Realtors do most of their work? After the sold sign is nailed on the front lawn sign. Buyer's remorse, changes in loan amounts and rates, possession problems, geology reports, plumbing, and so on, all crop up before the close. The average homeowner is ill-suited to represent himself on such touchy topics. That's why I remind agents never to give up on a FSBO they have good rapport with. Even after the fact (the homeowner tells you the property is sold), changes take place. FSBOs have high cancellation rates. You should be waiting in the wings to help or list the home immediately. After a false sale erupts, the homeowner probably has had it up to his ears playing real estate agent.

You need one effective tactic, one winning move, one system that produces. Once you have your single FSBO system perfected and are consistently bringing in salable listings with it, your success in real estate is assured. The fizzbo situation lends itself to the use of a single system because you have complete control over who you approach, when and how you approach them, and whether or not you'll call back. So throw yourself into perfecting.

THE ONE WINNING MOVE THAT BRINGS IN 100 LISTINGS

Most agents devote little or no quality time and effort to developing their methods to a high level: They always *act* in terms of getting the one listing or sale that's in their minds at the moment. They may believe they're taking a longer view, but when it comes to action, they do little beyond improvise their next phone call, door-knock, or face-to-face meeting. They function entirely outside the concept of perfecting systems for gaining listings and closing sales. They operate on the play-it-by-ear plan. Unless they have an extraordinarily keen ear, they continue on this catch-as-catch-can basis throughout their real estate careers, however long or short those careers may be. Leaning now this way, now that, they never put together an act good enough to make the money that will raise them safely above the get-by stage.

Don't drift in that aimless manner. Set your sights on acquiring a system that will permit you to manufacture salable listings from the fizzbo raw material at a steady rate. To do that, you must make—and carry out—decisions to put forth considerable effort. Think in terms of developing a system that will enable you to win 100 listings at prices realistic enough to allow 80 of those listings to sell. Stop reading how and calculate how much money that will put into your hands: 80 listings sold at your area's average price times your listing brokerage split.

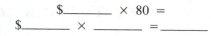

$$\$\underline{\qquad} \times 80 =$$
$$\$\underline{\qquad} \times \underline{\qquad} = \underline{\qquad}$$

The sum you're going to earn by learning how to de-fizz fizzbos adds up to important money, doesn't it? Thinking positively about adding that substantial amount to your assets will give you a different viewpoint. It's an effectiveness-expanding exercise—do it often.

To earn that sum, you'll need discipline, determination, and desire. Earning it will involve study and practice. It will involve working to a schedule and managing your time well. It will involve going in rejection's way. But now your corrected viewpoint will put rejection into its proper perspective. The rejection you'll brush aside earning that interesting sum of money will leave no more impression on your mind than the contrails of yesterday's jet flight overhead.

You'll be working with people in all their human caprices, confusions, and contrary convictions. To do that successfully, you must be flexible. Every phizbow is different. Some fizbeaux are impatient, get-it-on types; other fizzboughs are slow and suspicious and poor listeners. Know your system so well that you concentrate on them, not on what you're supposed to say next. You'll often need to compress your plan into fewer words, or omit entire parts of it—or repeat some of the parts over and over in different words. You'll need to psych up for the crucial periods, and tune all your antennas for signal catching: You'll need to know when to move right into the close, and when to make an emergency landing to wait out a storm.

The single system that will enable you to consistently produce salable listings from for-sale-by-owners will be the one you create yourself to exploit your strong points, and to meet the needs and conditions in your area. The two most important steps you can take toward developing that well-paid FSBO business are:

- Design a clear-cut system and work that system hard. Replace any parts that don't work for you with other ideas that do. Think constantly in terms of system, of perfecting your performance of the repetitive phrases that will lead you with constantly accelerating speed to a steady flow of salable listings from fizzbo contact.
- Select and adhere to a schedule for working with FSBOs at the most effective times to do so where you operate.

First, select the basic tactic you'll use to win victories on the FSBO battlefield. Four choices are given under Decision A. Select one, perfect it, and start the fees rolling your way before you consider spending time on a second FSBO tactic. You'll probably never need the second FSBO tactic, and concentrating on one will leave you more time for other aspects of successful real estate practice.

Details for each of the four tactics follow Decision D.

THE FOUR TACTICS THAT MAKE MONEY

Decision A: Select a FSBO Tactic that Makes Money

1 *Letter-a-day*. Preprinted letters combined with phone calls pave the way for a successful listing meeting. The figure is escalating daily, but well over 60 percent of American households are two-career families. That means both folks are at work when you try to call on their FSBO ad. It sounds dumb, but they advertise and then disappear. A lot of two-career FSBO couples are what I call "forced fizzbos." They had their house on the market with a broker. Communication was at a low level (Every time I call those owners, they aren't home."). No offers ever came in. The listing expired. The sign was never picked up for 6 weeks. The owner actually threw it in the side yard. The owner's opinion of Realtors is bleak. They decide to sell it themselves, out of desperation and frustration. If a sharp Realtor can get his or her foot in the door, I know this two-career couple would love to get the business of selling their own home off their hands.

2 *Free service package*. Once you've done the preparatory work, you can use this phone tactic on every fizzbo that pops up in your sales area, and put off researching individual houses until their owners send you clear come-list-me signals.

3 *Knock on their door*, after researching market values in the area.

4 *Phone for an appointment*.

Decision B: Decide How You'll Find the Fizzbos

1. Drive the streets.   Of course, you must be careful to drive below the speed limit for residential areas. With practice, and by routing yourself on a map, you can cover a large area in one early morning hour when there's little traffic. Late in the evening is also a good time. (Ladies lock your car doors.) My first sale was a FSBO I found in the middle of the night. They gave me a one-party show (a written agreement to pay brokerage if I sold the property to my customers, who were named in the document). I had already shown my buyers everything in the area and I thought they'd buy from me if I could find a house they'd get excited about. I knew what they wanted, and where they wanted it, but there simply wasn't such a house available at 6 P.M. when we stopped looking. Worry that I'd lose my buyers to another area kept me from sleeping, so I got up and drove their favorite neighborhood once more. On a street I'd covered a few hours before, I found a brand new FSBO sign. The sellers had decided to move that evening, and after dinner the man tacked his sign up. Before they sat down to dinner the next night, they had accepted my customers' offer. When you have the buyer, cruise those streets no matter what the hour.

2. Read the newspaper ads like all the other agents do.

Many agents have never seriously considered automobile search for FSBOs as a regular part of their routine. They may occasionally list a FSBO they stumble onto, and do it rather easily, but they continue to rely on serendipity and newsprint for their supply of FSBO prospects. It does not occur to them that there may be a fundamental difference between the group of FSBOs who advertise and the group who puts up signs on their property.

"But," you may say, "they are the same people."

Many are, of course. But many aren't and therein lies the opportunity. Some sellers think that the easiest way to find a strong agent is to stick a For Sale sign in front of their house. Some fizzbos are too broke to advertise. Some are too stingy. A few can't make the necessary decisions. Some never placed an ad in their lives and have no idea how to go about it. Others know how to advertise but just can't get around to it. And some know that more agents than buyers read and call on FSBO ads. There are hundreds of reasons why FSBOs fail to advertise beyond tacking up a sign on their property.

And, to be sure, some fizzbos will place ads but won't put a sign on their property. Searching by car isn't necessarily the best method of finding for-sale-by-owners. But it does have these advantages:

- You'll find many fizzbos before the pack does.
- You'll find many fizzbos before they spend money advertising, an act that heavily commits some people to the sell-yourself idea.
- You see the property before you speak to the owners, so you can talk knowledgeably about their property, their neighborhood, and how to solve their problems.
- Some of the fizzbos you find by search will be the wow-do-we-need-help types that are easy to list.
- And others, as I mentioned earlier, are couples who both work. No one's there to show the house or answer the phone, so how do they expect to sell it themselves? Most of the both-work FSBO couples haven't figured out that, by effectively keeping their house off the market throughout the week, they cut themselves off from the main buying stream. Most buyers need a home so badly it's their number one priority; they're househunting all week long. But on the weekend, when the both-work FSBO couple can be home, it's the lookie-lews and the bargain-dreamers who are out in full force. Often, the agent who lists the both-work FSBO couple is the first one with the persistence to track them down.

If you work the ads, pay special attention to the offbeat or throw-away publications that have small circulations and the lowest rates. Advertisers in such papers are the least determined to see the FSBO thing through to the end. Car-search is not necessarily the best of the two methods; working the ads is not necessarily the least time consuming. Try both. Let results, not Mr. Sloth, decide which is best for you.

Decision C: Selecting the FSBO Opportunities You'll Work

Whether you work the ads or hunt in the field, you've limited the area in which you seek FSBO opportunities. Now consider what system you'll use to select the fizzbos you'll work on within that area.

1 Work them as you find them.

2 Select the houses that appeal to you.

3 Select the price range or type of housing you believe is most in demand.

4 Select the best buys.

1 and 2: Working fizzbos as you find them means you work with lots of poor prospects. Selecting only houses that appeal to you, without regard to demand or value, will load you up with unsalable listings that devour your time, energy, and enthusiasm.

3 and 4: Your selection process is simply time management. You choose to manage your time well, or poorly, by your actions—or lack of them. Good fizzbo time management means that, each day, you do everything you can to list those properties that are in demand and are priced to sell before you give any time to the poorer prospects for successful transactions. As with every system, there is a hazard in this one: You can immobilize yourself worrying about what opportunities are the best. The point is not to spend time debating which of two good prospects to work on, the point is to be continually on the lookout for salable opportunities, and to work on them first.

Decision D: Select an Effective Schedule

Timing is vital. Late Sunday afternoon is a great time for closing FSBOs who are discouraged by a poor turnout that weekend. But you can't do it all during four Sunday hours. And other aspects of real estate compete for your time. You'll need to block out times during the week when you'll follow up with all the fizzbos you're working with now, and when you'll initiate your program with new fizzbos. You'll need to set goals for how many new fizzbos you'll take on each week, for how many old fizzbos you'll continue to work with week after week, and for how many fizzbo listings you want to take.

Here are the details and the phrases that pump success into each of the four basic FSBO tactics that make money:

1. Letter-a-day.   You can run this system wholesale on all fizzbos that come up in your sales area, without any research beyond learning each fizzbo's name, address, and phone number. Enclose one of your business cards with every mailing.

- *First day*: In a large brown envelope, send a blank copy of your purchase agreement. Hand write on one of your imprinted scratch pad sheets (so your photo and phone number will be there) these words:

  "Sorry you're leaving us! Here's a copy of the form you'll need to sell your house. If you'd like an explanation of any of its terms, please give me a call. No obligation. Sincerely, _____" Sign your first name, and enclose your card.

  You can write that once, and then have a printer run off a handful of copies.

- *Second day*: In a regular #10 correspondence envelope, send them a blank sellers' net sheet and this note, also handwritten on your imprinted scratch pad:

  "Here's the form we use to figure your net walkaway dollars. Please feel free to give me a call if you don't have the formulas to figure any of these items. Again, no obligation, Sincerely, _____" Be sure you don't say "if you don't know how to figure any of these items," which implies that they're stupid if they can't.

- *Third day*: In a Christmas-card-sized envelope, send a blank Guidelines to Market Value form and this handwritten message:

  "Here's a form we use to summarize the facts that set market price. If you'd like me to develop this data for your home, please give me a call. No obligations, of course. We're here to serve you. Sincerely, _____."

- *Fourth day*: Wait until they've received the day's mail. Then knock on the door, or phone, and say: "Hi, I'm Al Vaughn with Belmont Realty. Are you getting the forms I've been mailing to you to help you market your home?" You've already given them service, and demonstrated a nonabrasive persistence. They'll usually feel obligated to give you some information about the house. From their response to this contact, decide whether to (a) try for an immediate listing appointment; (b) put them on the Full Treatment spelled out later in the chapter; (c) put them on Letter-Every-Saturday; or (d) drop them as an unpromising situation.

- *Letter-every-Saturday* calls for you to send them something about selling their home once a week. Mail it on Saturday so they'll have it on Monday, right after their house didn't sell over another weekend. Each week, send them a handwritten update on the market plus one of your newsletters, a reprint that spells out why it's so tough to sell your own home, a flyer telling them something about selling their house (such as setting the stage), or some similar item. Mail on Saturday, and then call them every Wednesday or Thursday evening. Each time you call, consider whether you should intensify your campaign to list them.

2. Free service package.   Work up written material that will help the fizzbos market their house, and then offer this package to them free during an evening phone call. The package should provide information they can use, and it should also introduce them to the complexity of real estate transactions.

Once your free service package is ready, you need only compile the list of fizzbos you want to call, and you're all set for your evening phoning session. Because no time is spent in research, this system does not require a high success ratio. You can call large numbers of fizzbos, and deliver the package to only those who give you encouragement. That gives you select group to concentrate your follow-up efforts on.

Don't call during the day with this tactic; call in the evening when both husband and wife are home. And avoid pressing to deliver the package the same night you call because that's too sudden for most people and frightening to some. Making an appointment for a later night has a reassuring, professional ring to it.

The package consists of flyers and blank forms. The flyers should be neatly typed on the company letterheads and have your photo and name imprinted on them. If you don't have such a letterhead, type your flyer on a regular company letterhead, rubber-cement your photo to it, and have a quick-printer run off some copies.

Supply one copy of each form. Be sure all these papers are fresh and clean, not creased and dog-eared. As you make up a batch of these packages, protect them in large envelopes.

Here's the list of items for your Free Service Package:

Forms

- *Real Estate Purchase Contract and Receipt for Deposit* (or whatever agreement form is used in your state for making offers).
- *Buyer's Net Sheet.*
- *Seller's Net Sheet.*
- *Power of Attorney* (in case only one of two buyers will be able to be present when the contract is finalized).
- *Guidelines to Market Value.*

Flyers

- *Advertising Rates and Numbers to Call to Place Ads in Our Local Newspapers.*

- *How to Get Your Home Ready for Sale.*
- *How to Set the Stage for Your Open House.*
- *Government Financing Plans that May Be Available to Finance the Purchase of Your Home.* (This will necessarily be complex.)
- *A Brief Discussion of Conventional Home Financing.*
- *Fixed-rate Mortgages.*
- *Adjustable-rate Mortgages.*
- *Your latest (or best) newsletter.*
- *Items You'll Need to Complete Your Sale.* (List such things as termite inspections, roof inspections, appraisals, assessor's parcel numbers, legal descriptions, building permits for any improvements, title insurance, etc.

Other

- *"Want to Sell Your House in a Hurry?"* This compact article has good house-selling information for homeowners, and it makes a powerful case for using an agent. Write to Reprint Editor, Reader's Digest, Pleasantville, NY 10570.
- *Title Insurance Rate Card.*
- *Reprint* of the most complicated magazine or newspaper article you've come across recently that discusses housing prices, interest rates, and the availability of mortgage funds.
- *Guest Log Sheets.* Make these up on blank paper. Type across the top on the long way of 8½ × 11 paper:

GUEST LOG

Name	Address	Phone	Remarks

Run the horizontal and vertical lines to the bottom of the sheet. Don't put anything like "Courtesy of Harry Hotseller, Go-Get-Um Reality," on these guest log sheets, or the lookers coming to the fizzbo's open house won't sign them. Give every fizzbo three or four copies. Win a fizzbo's confidence and you'll get a chance to work with the list of house hunters they gather on these log sheets.

- *Preliminary Title Report.* (Select an intricate report from your office's files of completed home resale transactions so the fizzbo will gain some insight into the complications that arise here. Your copies should have identifying names and numbers blocked out.)
- *Sample Escrow Instructions*, if this is applicable in your state.

That's the package. Winning scripts in this chapter give you the phone and face-to-face conversation, and the cut-off points, that make this system a time-effective producer.

3. Knock on their door.   Here are two winning scripts you can use when driving your area to get something going. Many successful agents simply can't drive past a FSBO sign in their area of interest without stopping to knock on that door because they've already made so much money doing that. Set aside at least half a day a week to go out looking for FSBOs with the intention of charging right up and talking with every one you find. Between 3 and 6 P.M. on Friday is an excellent time in most areas because more people are home and they seem to be in a better mood—perhaps because for many people it's payday and the start of two days off.

First knock-on-the-door winning script:

"Hi. I'm Danny Kennedy of Sell Fast Realty, and I noticed your sign out front. [Don't pause here.] As you know, the real estate market changes constantly and for this reason you should have a knowledgeable local professional to call to answer a quick question—even if you are marketing your own home. So here's my card, and if you need a fast answer about how your home stacks up against the competition or are wondering about some other aspect of marketing your home, give me a call and I'll be happy to discuss the situation with you."

After their response, you may want to give them some pertinent information: "Did you know that the interest rate on treasury bills dropped half a point this morning? That can affect the sale of your house because mortgage interest rates tend to follow the direction that treasury bill rates take."

Second knock-on-the-door winning script:

"Hi, I'm Danny Kennedy with Sell Fast Realty, and I was wondering if you're cooperating with Realtors® in the marketing of your property on a one-party basis."

They'll usually respond by asking what you mean.

"Well, for instance," you say, "in today's market the buyers being transferred in (moving in) are even more conservative than before. These are the people who have cash and can buy in this market. However, most of them want to be represented by a Realtor® because of the time and distance involved in their move.

"So, when a buyer of mine especially loves an area, I often ask a for-sale-by-owner if I could show his property on a one-party agreement. This agreement applies to just the one person or couple that I represent, and makes it possible for me to expose your property to that one buyer. If I am able to sell them on your property, the next step would be that I'd bring you a written offer to buy.

"That offer would be backed up by a substantial good-faith cash deposit. If you decide to accept my buyer's offer and sell your home to him, I would then be entitled to receive a fee when the sale is completed. The agreement is made in writing, of course, because it's a common business arrangement.

"The advantages of the one-party agreement are that you can continue to market your home to everyone else in the world, and still have the opportunity to sell to my buyer if you choose to do so. So it's a winning situation for you both ways.''

Always use the low-key approach with the for-sale-by-owner. Never get pushy; never act as though you must have the listing. Learn to think and act decisively without putting must-haves in your life, must-haves always create more barriers between you and your goals.

Many FSBOs are suspicious. This means that the harder you push, the more you'll convince them of what they want to believe: that your buyer will cruise the area and find them anyway. You can get away from this by approaching every FSBO in your area of interest as soon as possible with the one-party agreement idea, and then returning every week to remind them of the opportunities to sell that they may have missed by not agreeing to cooperate with you.

Act with purity of intention with everyone—and especially with the for-sale-by-owner. This means that you truly want the same good things for everyone that, in the same situation, you'd want for yourself.

And be patient. Don't give up. We have to work some FSBOs a little bit at a time for months before they list. I've heard many agents say, ''Those people will never go with a Realtor®.'' I always cringe at that comment because I've seen the same thing happen over and over: A few days or weeks later, there on the list of new listings is that ex-FSBO, listed with persistent Paul(ine) who hung in there.

Here's another winning way to get started with a fizzbo:

''Hi, I'm Danny Kennedy with Sell Fast Realty—I know that you're marketing your own property and don't want to be bothered with agents, but you should have my free service package.''

Pause here to get their response. They may agree to getting anything that's free, ask what your service package is, or tell you they don't need it. Practice phrases for each of those responses that'll allow you to bridge into your main speech:

''If it's free, okay.'' Your response: ''There's no obligation at all. My free—''

''What's that?'' Your response: ''I'll be happy to tell you about it. My free—''

''I don't need it.'' Your response: ''It'll only take a moment for me to tell you about it—why not listen and then decide? [Don't pause here.] My free—''

Here's the main speech: ''My free service package is prepared especially for you. It gives you the information you need to market your home and there's no obligation. In fact, you'll find that it'll save you time because you can use it to speed things up when other agents call. I promise that I'll just drop it by and not bug you to death. But in these days of ever-increasing competition in the marketplace, you should have someone you can call on locally during the marketing of your home who won't be just out for the listing.''

Give the owner time to respond at this point. Of course, whenever they agree to let you drop the package off, you switch into making an appointment to do that. But many times the owner will say something like, ''What's in it for you?''

Your response: "Maybe nothing but good rumors—after you see my package, and perhaps get a few answers from me, either now or at some time in the coming weeks. You may at least be able to tell some of your friends that you know a Realtor® who is really interested in giving service. Many people don't want to market their own homes for a variety of reasons; perhaps someone you know will want professional help with selling their home in the future. Perhaps you'd be willing to pass my name along for them to consider if you're impressed with my service. Word-of-mouth advertising is the best kind there is, and that's what I'm always trying to deserve. So, can I drop my free service package off at six this evening, or would around eight be a better time?"

4. Phone for an appointment. For both these systems, knocking and phoning, it's vital that you check their street, and the streets on either side of them, for recent sales. Before you knock on the door, or phone them, you should have the sales information from your comparable file memorized for those streets, or on a Guidelines to Market Value form in front of you. If they know more about their home's value than you do, how are you going to convince them that they need your expertise?

Your first contact, whether by dial or knock, is merely the takeoff. Now you have the flight ahead of you. Success with fizzbos demands persistence—but it also requires that you develop the ability to recognize unpromising situations. Decide on how many fizzbos you can work with week in and week out, giving them the Full Treatment outlined next. Contact new fizzbos, but do it less frequently now, and be more choosy about which of them you take on for your persistent follow-through. Whenever you draft a new fizzbo for the squadron you're giving the Full Treatment to, drop the one you're already working on who shows the least promise of giving you a salable listing. In this way, you'll constantly upgrade the quality of the fizzbos you're working with. *Quality* here means the likelihood that you'll obtain a lucrative listing.

If you're using Tactic 4, and you've driven past their house, be sure to flash your knowledge fast when you call. Even if the newspaper with their ad just hit the streets, the chances are good that several agents have already called them. If so, you can be sure that fizzbo is tired of talking to agents who know nothing about their house except what's in the ad. They put their castle on the market and the world yawned. As far as they know, no one has even bothered to look at it—until you called. Here's how you open the conversation—say it all in one breath:

"Hello, I'm Danny Kennedy with Sell Fast Realty. You're the party with the lovely two-story home on Elm Street with the white picket fence?"

THE FULL TREATMENT

Give them forms.

Lend them flags, arrows, signs.

Go see them late every Sunday afternoon, and call, or drop in, once during the week. Be quick. Get in and out fast. Always tell them something they don't know about new sales or listings, or other developments that influence the salability of their property. Never tell all you know. Leave the impression that you're busy, but interested, that you have more vital information than you have time to pass on to nonclients.

As soon as they're talking pleasantly to you, say, "If things change and you decide to list, do you have an agent in mind?"

What you're looking for is a *no* to that question (unless they say, "Yes, you.") and a *yes* to the next: "In that case, if you do decide to take advantage of professional real estate service, will you consider appointing me your full-time representative?"

As soon as you have established some rapport with the fizzbo (but not before, or you'll shoot yourself in the foot every time) you must ask that question.

If they answer, "Well, I guess so. But my husband's cousin Bob just got his license and Jim wants to let him try. But I don't want to. Let him learn the job first."

Note the winning list scripts on page 196 . The excuse: "If I list, I'll list with my friend" is an excellent pre-script-tion suggestion for people with relatives or friends in the business.

If this option doesn't work the first time, wait until Cousin Bob drops the ball, until his listing expires. When they're mad at him, anxious to sell, and ready to think realistically about price, they may recall your earlier conversation.

PUTTING YOUR WINNING MOVE TO WORK

Outline your fizzbo plan and your fizzbo goals in writing. Do this fast because you'll make changes and improvements as you work your plan and achieve your initial goals. Constantly think in terms of developing a *system* instead of bouncing around doing whatever seems like a good idea at the moment.

Never let it show that you're working systematically. People resent being processed. Cultivate the habit of personalizing your scripts with references to the interests and situation of the individuals you're talking to.

And be alert for opportunities to skip any steps of your system—of your winning fizzbo move—that aren't required with a particular prospect. Know when to close. If you fail to recognize when you've talked yourself into the listing, if you relentlessly plow through your entire routine after the fizzbo's folded, you'll talk yourself right back out of that listing.

You must also be alert for steps of your presentation that must be repeated. Don't keep on talking about point Q to someone whose eyes are still glazed in concentration over your point L. Keep checking with the prospect in a friendly way. Be very careful here. On the one hand, you must make sure you're getting through. On the other, you can't give any hint that you suspect they may be slow-thinkers. Many people are quick to take offense at any such hint.

Goals help most when they're realistic and challenging. Set them where they'll give you a pull without knocking you over. Set goals where they'll give you wins to cheer you on, rather than defeats to discourage you.

Your schedule must be flexible enough to allow you to work with hot buyers until they buy, yet rigid enough to keep you in contact with many old prospects, and bring you into contact with many new prospects each week.

Ask your fizzbos to consider who their potential buyers are. Why are those buyers going to all the trouble of scouting around by themselves, if not to save the fee themselves? Now let's consider:

THE FOUR-KINDS-OF-BUYERS LISTING CLOSE

This is a great winning script if you use it right. Don't waste its impact by hitting fizzbos with it when they're fresh on the market and bursting with false confidence—wait until you've built some credibility and rapport with them through several visits, during which time the realities of the marketplace have introduced a glimmer of reality into their thinking. How soon can that happen? It depends on their personalities and problems. I've seen it happen within a week. More often, their process of facing reality takes several weeks, and it can stretch out over six months or longer. When you feel the time is ripe, stop by on a Sunday afternoon and say something like this:

"Hello, Mr. Botkins. I thought I'd just stop by on my way home from the open house I held on Elm and compare notes. Did you have pretty good traffic today?"

"Well, I always get a lot of traffic every time I put out my open house sign, much more than when I had it listed with a Realtor® last year, but for some reason I don't have a check in my hand yet."

You: "I can understand how frustrated that must make you feel, Mr. Botkins." Since it's true, I add the following statement because it helps people see me beyond the Realtor® role. "Before I got into real estate professionally, I was a for-sale-by-owner myself, so I know what you're going through."

Go on with, "Can I give you some information about the buying public that I learned once I got into real estate professionally? This information could help you market your home, and it won't take long."

Notice that I tell them I acquired this knowledge after entering the business, which piques their interest and causes them to think that I'm going to give them the answer they need. If possible, proceed to their kitchen table with both Mr. and Mrs. Fizzbo and begin the following winning script:

"You see, Mr. and Mrs. Botkins, there are **four distinct kinds of buyers** out there. The first kind are the people making their **first purchase of a home**. Most **first-time buyers** are afraid of people selling their own homes because they feel those sellers are far more experienced than they are. To the first-timer, purchasing a home is a frightening experience. Aunt Mabeline tells them that property isn't what it used to be, and that the bottom is falling out of real estate prices. Uncle Ned tells them to keep their money in the bank in case times get tough.

"Without the help of a third party to guide them through all the unfamiliar decisions involved in buying a property, they simply won't make the purchase. They're afraid of a seller because they know that an owner has only one property to sell them. First-time buyers don't buy until they find a real estate expert they trust and enjoy working with.

"The second kind of buyers is the local **house changer**. These are local people who can take their time looking for a home, and they're only interested in the bargain of the century. They also resent the fact that the seller isn't paying a brokerage fee, so they automatically deduct the fee off the top when they think about the price of the house. Their purpose is to find a seller who's in trouble or an underpriced house. They work the for-sale-by-owners hard, and there's no way they'll let the seller save a thing. If they didn't intend to save the brokerage fee themselves, these buyers would work through an agent.

"The third type of buyer is the **investor**. If you think the house changer is tough on price, you haven't met an investor yet. Investors are especially difficult to work with if the owners have any type of financial problem that makes them more vulnerable. Investors want bargains, but they also need counseling—most of them don't understand all the ramifications of the tax laws or have the thorough knowledge of an area's values that a real estate professional does. So most investors work through agents to save time and assure themselves of access to more properties.

"The fourth kind is the **out-of-the-area buyer**. Most of them need a house right now. Whether they're being transferred in or are moving here on their own, their time to house hunt is limited. And they're suffering from the cultural shock of moving to a new area. They don't know the values here; they don't know the communities they can choose among; they're almost always very unfamiliar with our entire region.

"Usually, they fly in. Often, instead of renting a car, they'll depend on the real estate agent they've been referred to for transportation. These people are under heavy pressure to make a fast decision, and they need all kinds of questions answered fast—about schools, business, travel conditions, and many other things.

"They want to have their own local representative, someone they can trust to look after their interests. When they go back to wind up their affairs wherever they're coming from, they want to know that they have a reliable representative here who'll keep them informed and carry out their decisions by phone.

"Many times when I worked with out-of-area buyers, they saw a for-sale-by-owner sign and said, 'I'd never walk in cold turkey and try to deal directly with an owner. I'm a babe in the woods around here.'

"What's the bottom line in all this? It's this: The only buyers you have much chance of getting an offer from are the local house changers and the investors—the toughest kinds of buyers there are. These people won't pay top dollar—they won't even pay market price—they'll only go for a giveaway.

"I can get you what is the fair market price for your home at this time. How can I do that when you can't? Because I am a full-time real estate professional. Listing your property with me means that I will expose it to the people who can and will pay fair market price: first-time buyers and out-of-area buyers. Would you consider listing your home with a part-time agent?" (They'll probably reply with, "Absolutely not!")

"After 'testing' your property for the past [add length of time], I'm sure you'll agree it requires a full-time commitment. In short, you are a part-time, unlicensed individual trying to market your most important asset—your home.

"If you decide to take the commitment to *sell*, not *test*, seriously, please consider me—a full-time, committed, licensed real estate expert."

This is the time to show the Listing Presentation Manual that includes testimonial letters, and so forth, as discussed in Chapter 11.

The previous script has kept me in for-sale-by-owner conversations for years. It works because it's solidly based on truth. Modify my words to fit your style and reflect your situation honestly, and this script will work as well for you as it has for me. Its purpose is to make the owners face facts and think:

"We're not getting the proper kind of exposure trying to sell it ourselves. Dealing with local bargain hunters is tough—I can't do better than I could by going through a professional. It's hard to be patient with most of the people who come and waste my time, and the ones I think would buy don't trust me. And I don't know enough about real estate. There are lots of things about financing that I just don't understand."

After you deliver that script, pull out a Sellers' Net Sheet and work things out for them. Figure the brokerage fee and go over each item with them. When you get to the brokerage fee, point out that they really don't have that to play with—bargain hunters would deduct it anyway.

AVOIDING RECALLS: THE FSBO X-FILE

You need a fast-working file that'll tell you whether you called each fizzbo before. Calling them repeatedly is great—if you know that's what you're doing. Not knowing means you blunder; knowing means you can build rapport by taking a different line on subsequent calls than you did on the first one. Just as important, you also save the time, and avoid the frustration, of talking to hostile fizzbos a second time. Here's how to set up your file so it saves time instead of taking it.

Tape each ad to a 3 × 5 card and write the phone number in large figures in the upper right hand corner. Abbreviate the name of the publication and show the date of the ad. File the cards by phone number, lowest number first. Then, the next

MB	DC			

WHERE/WHEN ADS WERE RUN BY THIS FSBO — MB 9/7 DC 9/14

PHONE NUMBER — 123-9876

LAST NAME — Stone

Man's — Jerry — **M**

Woman's — Rita — **W**

FIRST NAMES

ADDRESS — 4126 Barmie Dr   Westport

| | ▼ DATE | ▼ TIME | ▼ PERSON REACHED | CALL RECORD |

9/7 (11 AM) PM (M) W	9/14 AM (8 PM) M (W)	9/16 (9 AM) PM M (W)	AM PM M W

| Call 9/14 | Call 9/16 | Appt for 9/17! | |

FSBO X-FILE   Form KJ-2 PRINTED IN USA

time you work a batch of fizzbo ads, it's the work of a moment to check the phone number in the new ads against your existing cards.

On the card shown here, "MB9/7" means you saw this fizzbo's ad in the September 7 issue of the *Morning Bugle*, a local newspaper. Ads are taped to the back of these cards to keep all the details handy. The notations and circles in the first call box show that you reached a man at that number at 11 A.M. on September 7. That September 7 was a Friday is worth recording because it alerts you to the possibility that the man works nights or at home, or is unemployed.

Another local publication you check regularly for fizzbo news is the *Dollarclutcher*, a bargain-ad magazine. The next week, checking the *Dollarclutcher's* ad against your FSBO cross file, you pull this card. After entering "DC9/14" in the second ad box, you dial the number again. The man answers.

"Hello. This is Alex Campbell with Fastrunner Realty. I talked to you last week. Are you getting as many calls from your ad in the *Dollarclutcher* as you did off your *Morning Bugle* ad?"

FSBO X-File Cards save time and organize the information, but ordinary 3 × 5 cards will work. Chapter 24 has more details about FSBO X-Files, and tells you where to get them.

CALL FIZZBOS FROM OPEN HOUSE

Should you admit you're on an open house, calling other *sellers*?

Certainly. That's one reason why you call FSBOs late in the afternoon; so you can tell them, "I've called all my buyers—all the ones I haven't already shown this house to—and I've called all the neighbors around here, and a lot of them came over.''

Suggest to the FSBO that they call their own neighbors, and have them come to their open house. Why give them ideas like that? Because they won't want to do it. If they start to, they'll soon get discouraged. The first grumbler they hit will stop them cold, and the experience is certain to inject new respect for the real estate professional into their blood.

Will the first grumbler stop *you* cold? He shouldn't. You're the professional, the trained telephoner, the get-it-done type. And you're fully aware that every hard *no* you hear gets you much closer to the soft *yes* that's out there too, ready to put money in your pocket.

And, without a reverse directory, the fizzbo will be limited to calling the neighbors whose names he knows—people who already know about his open house anyway.

Chapter 9 has additional tips on working fizzbos from open house.

POTPOURRI

Talk to the stay-at-home fizzbo ladies in the morning. Try to make an afternoon appointment. If you can look at the property before an evening appointment, you'll be able to prepare a better Guidelines to Market Value form. Have the cold, hard facts for the evening appointment because they are often essential to closing fizzbos on listing with you.

All agents need to immediately identify themselves and not allow the lady to think for an instant that she may be talking with a possible buyer of her property. This is a real must. You can't build trust on a foundation of deceit.

Identifying yourself will get you an immediate shutoff now and then. Accept that. Expect it—but don't let it tarnish your honor. One of the pillars of your integrity and professionalism is your unfailing respect for the rights of others. And, by choosing to respect the rights of others, your rights get respected. In this case, you are informed immediately that you're not going to make any headway with that person *that morning*. You can try again at a later time. Congratulate yourself that you've wasted no time. Thank them for being frank with you. If they've been instantly nasty, your courteous response will make an impression that could be valuable on a future contact.

Always be alert for fizzbos who are ready to stop fooling around and get their house listed and sold. With some people, the mood strikes suddenly—and doesn't last long. Always be ready to cut the preliminaries and write up the listing; always be equally ready to back off when you're pressing too hard.

Top producers don't work for-sale-by-owners because fizzbos take up too much of their time. So, to be a top producer, you should avoid fizzbos, right?

Wrong. They have less time for each fizzbo than you do, of course. With the kind of fizzbos who have to be nurtured toward listing through a series of visits (preferably spaced close together) the top producer is at a disadvantage—you can give prospects six hits to top producer's one.

Fizzbos Are Where You Start

They're where I started. The new agent is the only one who has the time to work the fizzbo field widely, heavily, and with the consistency and persistence it takes to close them.

Many fizzbos compile a list of people who come through to look at their house. These people are often bona-fide prospective buyers, although some will be bird dogs for other agents, lookielews, and people interested only in a distress situation. Volunteer to help the fizzbos and they'll usually give you that list.

If one of your clients (or friends) goes fizzbo, don't snarl at him. Smile warmly and sincerely—be careful not to let that friendly smile turn into a you'll-see-what-a-dummy-you-are smirk—and say, "If you can sell it on your own, I'll be happy to answer any questions or guide all parties in good directions."

"Well, uh, thanks. But I don't want to take up your time if you're not getting anything for it. I think we can manage okay."

"Fine. But if that's your only reservation, there's a way you could pay me back for helping you that won't cost you a dime. Are you keeping a list of the people who come through your open houses, or of those who call?"

"Well, we haven't bothered. Actually, I kind of hate to ask."

"Let me tell you how that'll help you and the buyer. Supposing you go along for a while, it doesn't sell, and you decide to drop the price. Calling everybody who expressed interest could find a buyer in a hurry at your new low price."

"I don't want to tell them I might drop my price later. That's like saying it's too high."

"I agree. Don't put it that way. Say: 'Look, if it doesn't sell by June 1, I'm going to list with Danny Kennedy of Sell Fast Realty, but I'll reserve the right to sell to you without brokerage if you'll give me your name and address.' Then hand them the Guest Log Sheet."

"That's a good idea."

"If I help you with the processing, perhaps you'll consider giving me that list. I'll call them and see if I can help them find another house."

"Naw, that sounds kind of sneaky to me."

If they say that, you pushed too soon, before you built confidence in your integrity in their minds.

Work the Buddy System

Work the buddy system in your office, not the stab-in-the-back system. What you send up is what comes down on your own head. Let me tell you a true story about a good listing I got from an office that practiced backstabbing. Only the names have been changed to protect the guilty.

Mr. Bell was trying to sell his own property and, of course, he wasn't having any luck. I was working on him, but he indicated that if it didn't sell by July 15, he was going to list with Jack Toeline of Selzip Realty, the agent who'd sold him the property when Mr. Bell was transferred into our town.

Mr. Bell liked Jack, and Jack was keeping in touch with him. I was, too—I hadn't given up. One afternoon Milton Cutter, another agent from Selzip Realty, saw the FSBO sign in front of Mr. Bell's house and stopped in to see him. As it happened, Jack Toeline had been in to see Mr. Bell that very morning.

When Mr. Bell told Milton Cutter that, here's what Milton said: "You mean Jack was here this morning? That amazes me—Jack is so busy he barely has time to return his messages. He's already got about all the business he can handle."

Did that allow Milton Cutter to steal the business away from his co-worker, Jack Toeline? Not at all. Mr. Bell was turned off on the whole Selzip organization. Even though he liked Jack , he wasn't about to list with a company whose agents were fighting among themselves. He wanted to list with a company whose agents got along together, helped each other, and all tried to sell each other's listings. So, since I was Mr. Bell's number two choice, I moved up to number one and wrote up the listing.

When it sold and I collected my fee, I started thinking beyond just not knocking the guy who works at the desk next to you. Why be neutral? Why not help each other instead of simply not knocking each other? Why not use the buddy system? Here's how it works:

Two agents, let's call them Wendy and Eloise, decide to buddy their fizzbo calls. They talk about how they'll divide up the fizzbo opportunities in their service area, and decide that Wendy will take the west side of town and Eloise will work the east side of town. In other words, they come up with a simple way to avoid conflict. Then they put the plan in operation. The first day Wendy works the west side and Eloise works the east side, calling all the fizzbos.

The second day they trade lists of fizzbos phoned or called on, and Wendy calls the people on the *east* side of town that Eloise talked to the day before. Meanwhile, Eloise is calling on the people that Wendy talked to the day before.

Let's run through one of those calls. Eloise calls up a fizzbo she knows Wendy talked to yesterday and identifies herself and her company.

"Somebody called me from your company yesterday."

"Oh, was that Wendy Fullbright? She's very active in your area."

"Yeah, that's who it was."

Eloise says with much enthusiasm, "Well, I'm not going to try to compete with Wendy Fullbright—she's one of the best agents in town—she sells a lot of property."

The buddy system works best when both agents knock on the doors and meet all the people in person:

"Somebody from your office has already been here."

"Oh, really? Who?"

"Well, I think she said her name was Wendy, or something like that. I've got the card right here. Yeah, Wendy Fullbright."

"You're lucky to have Wendy Fullbright interested in your property—she sells a lot of houses around here. Well, I better be going—no need for me to stay here and take up your time since you've already talked to the best in our company."

The owners love it because people like to work with organizations that pull together.

Bring the Whole Gang Over to Meet Mr. Fizz

You've been stopping in on Sundays, you've given them the four-kinds-of-buyers script, you've worked the buddy system, but they aren't quite ready to approve the agreement. Try this:

"Mr. Fizz, Tuesday is our sales meeting at Sell Fast Realty. I'd love to bring my team of experts out to see your property then. They're all working with customers right now, and you never know—one of them may know a buyer who'd fall in love with your place. In that case, we could work a one-party agreement on a showing. And I really want you to meet all these people—they're the best in the business."

Say it enthusiastically. Sellers can't resist enthusiasm when it comes to marketing their homes.

How to Scare People and Lose Friends

A fizzbo opens his front door one Sunday afternoon and there sits a beautiful potted plant with an envelope on top. "How thoughtful," he says, and opens the envelope. Inside is a newspaper clipping about another for-sale-by-owner in town who was abducted and robbed at gunpoint by someone who'd posed as a possible buyer. There's also a note from an agent saying, "Be sure this doesn't happen to you."

This is a true story. It's not a problem anymore because the agent who was doing it didn't last. He had to get out of the business because trying to intimidate people didn't work, and he wasn't the type to give service and deserve people's trust.

Build Future Business with Today's FSBO

My first fizzbo experience wasn't too thrilling because, in a strong seller's market, the Millers were able to sell it themselves. But I had promised to help, so I shopped the loan for their buyer, did some footwork for everyone, and the Millers were able to move to their new home a couple of miles away. Eighteen months later I got a come-list-me card from someone I'd never heard of. When I went there and wrote the listing, I stopped next door to thank the Millers—they'd told their neighbors about me.

Don't look only for the quick dollar—you're in this business for the long pull. Working the fizzbos is like any other form of prospecting—it's a great way to get the word out about who and where you are.

Work those fizzbos until it hurts.

6

Sow That Farm and Reap and Reap and Reap*

Learning My First Farming Secret • The Different Farms • Four Sizzling Starter Letters • Selecting Your Farm • Annual Turnover Rate • Organizing Your Farm • Working Your Farm File • Coping with E-Agent • The Evergreen Listing Farm • More Farming Secrets • Farm Decision Day • Professionalism • Your Attitude on the Farm • Careless Slips • Every Door Is Different • Speed Counts • Humility Helps • Success Breeds Success • The Best-Looking Homes • Exceptional Properties • Winning Scripts

LEARNING MY FIRST FARMING SECRET

"Kennedy, I know it's tough not getting in on the great floor time here," my manager told me a few weeks after I started real estate, "but you can turn that to your advantage." Nell Shukes was trying to cheer me up. With nothing to show for many hard hours except a couple of unpromising FSBO situations, I needed cheer.

"Tell me how, Nell."

"Do what that kid out in Simi Valley is doing."

"What kid?"

"Tommy Hopkins."

That was the first time I'd ever heard the name.

"So what's he doing?"

---

*Don't, and you'll weep, and weep, and weep.

"Breaking records," Nell said. "I've been trying to break *his* record all year. I came close, but—" Nell leafed through her messages and then looked at me. "For Halloween, he rents a truck and loads it up with pumpkins. Then he gets into a ghost costume and drives around his neighborhood giving away pumpkins. For Christmas, he throws parties for all the neighborhood kids."

"But how can that pay off? All that expense—"

"There are four or five hundred houses in his neighborhood, Danny. It's active—about 20 percent turnover— and he's getting it all."

"Then he's averaging two listings a week!"

"That's right, Danny. And he's selling most of them himself."

"Four transactions a week!"

She nodded. "Plus the referral business he's doing outside his farm. It does add up."

"His *farm*?" If I'd heard the term before it hadn't sunk in. Pumpkins, Christmas parties, farms. This is the real estate business? My mind was reeling. "Nell, I can't afford a truckload of pumpkins. So far, it's all been outgo: babysitters, gas—"

"You don't need to spend a dime now. The storeroom is jammed with rain hats and other giveaways. You can reimburse the company later out of your earnings."

When you're seven months pregnant, tramping up to several hundred houses handing out plastic coasters is an idea that lacks instant appeal. "I can see how the pumpkin truck and the parties would make an impact, but these little giveaways— who cares? If I could start big, like this Tommy did—"

"Danny, let me tell you how big Tommy Hopkins was when he started. He couldn't afford a suit, so he wore his high school band uniform to the office *and* out farming."

"You're kidding me!"

"Danny, he did the best he could instead of stalling. He knocked on the doors, handed out the scratch pads, and told the people about himself and his company. It worked. He started getting listings, and when he collected a fee, he put a chunk of it back into better farming tools—"

I'm not sure I heard the rest of what Nell Shukes told me about Tommy Hopkins that day because I was thinking, "If that nut can knock on doors in a band uniform, I can knock on doors in a maternity dress." The idea of actually doing it took hold, and I left Nell's office with fire in my eye and hope in my heart.

I've never forgotten that conversation. Four years and eons of experience later, listing and selling awards put me on the same speaking platform with Tommy Hopkins one day in Palo Alto. Once again he was to inspire me, this time to become a national real estate trainer. Now let's talk about how *you* can set a sizzling pace on *your* farm.

THE DIFFERENT FARMS

The Best Farms

Some of the best farms can't be delineated on a map. One of the most effective real estate farmers I know, David Garris in Laguna Beach, CA, played tennis at 7:00 A.M. every morning for years, with doctors and executives at the country club he belonged to. That's reaping the harvest with a sharp scythe!

He didn't hang around the tennis courts all day. He was too busy with his real estate business. But he always found time to line up some early-morning tennis partners. He made a point of inviting new members to join him for tennis. Invariably they were pleased to be noticed and, whether they played tennis with him or not, he was on his way to becoming acquainted with them.

It took him time to build that farm. There were thin periods in the beginning, times of doubt, but he persevered. Now he gets come-list-me calls from friends of club members who are golfers, not tennis players. The good word gets around, especially when you keep spreading it yourself in a way that's right for you and right for the working environment you've chosen.

Ask yourself: What's my comfort zone? How many homes can I farm? Would I be better off working a club, civic organization, or sports group than an ordinary farm?

Three to four hundred homes make a good farm. Over that number, you lose control. Don't take on more than you can handle. You should visit with everyone in your farm at least three times a year—preferably four times. You should have something useful with your name on it in their house all the time. You should send them a note or a newsletter or leave a giveaway on their doorknob every month. As soon as you can afford it, you should stage at least three super promotions a year. The next chapter gives you details and promotions for every month.

People Farms and House Farms

The tennis player's farm is a specific group of people: the members of the country club. Their real estate holdings are scattered over a large area and the tennis player reaches those properties only when personal contact at the club has set the stage for a further step. This is a people farm.

The house farm is a specific group of dwellings outlined on a map and concentrated in one or a few areas. The agent reaches the owners through their properties.

In a house farm, people come and go; the houses remain. The reverse is true in a people farm; members of a club often change homes, or invest in rental property, without leaving the club.

Whether you have a house farm or not, you do have a people farm. Call it the Everybody-I-Know Farm, and include everyone who isn't loyal to another real estate agent. Don't leave people out just because they live far away. They or one of their friends may decide to move nearby at any moment.

Think about your everybody-I-know farm. It exists. Out there somewhere are more people who know you than live in your house farm. Are you cultivating them? Do they know you're in real estate?

An everybody-I-know farm, properly worked, returns invaluable referral business from small efforts. The next section tells you how it's done. Before you turn to it, consider whether one of your interests or hobbies is served by a club that will give you valuable new contacts while you enjoy some much needed recreation. If so, get active in that club or group. Have fun. But avoid obligating yourself to a heavy schedule of club duties. Explain that your real estate business requires you to work unpredictable hours, especially in the evening and on the weekend. Then take part in your group's fund raisers, tournaments, and social activities with gusto whenever you can squeeze them in.

Let all the club members know you're in real estate as you get the chance. Don't push it. Let the subject come up naturally. It will—frequently. You'll soon find that you'll get a good shot at many fellow members' real estate business merely by demonstrating courtesy, friendliness, and a willingness to participate energetically in your group's social activities.

Your Everybody-I-Know Farm

It all begins with the list, and your first resource for names is yourself. While I was studying for my license, I used spare moments to organize my mailing list. In a green cardboard box, filed A to Z, I put a card for everyone I could remember from when I was ten years old. As soon as my license was hanging on a wall, I had my letter of introduction printed. It went to everyone who wasn't so close that a handwritten note, also shown in the next section, was required.

Make up the list first. If you're already busy in real estate and looking for more business, you won't be able to spend much time pulling this vital list together. Try this: Add three names to your list every morning, starting today. Do that and, one year from today, you'll have 1095 names on your list—the equivalent of three regular house farms! How long can it take each morning to put three names and addresses on cards?

I use 4 × 6 inch cards because they have room for lots of information, and for several changes of address. Start by copying current addresses out of your Christmas card list and whatever little address books you have squirreled away. (Old girl friends are taboo.) At the same time, address an envelope. In the envelope place your latest newsletter, a copy of your Profile of a Champion, your printed letter announcing your entry into real estate, or a form letter especially written to tell friends you're well qualified to handle referral business.

Don't do a junk mailing. Send only one of these items at a time. On the front write, "Hi, Jeannie. See over." Then on the back jot some friendlies and ask, "Whatever happened to Deanna Droptfrumsyte? Got any idea what her current address is?" In this way, work through all your old rosters from church, school, service, previous employment, and clubs.

Add the people you're buying from now, and those you've bought from in the past. List former neighbors and distant relatives. What about customers in your former occupation, and suppliers to that company? As you work with these old rosters and memories, names long forgotten will pop up. Jot them down, one to a card. You'll remember some faces but the names will elude you. Can you think of someone who'd know their address if you could remember their name? If so, jot down in the middle of the card whatever you can remember: "Tall, skinny kid in the mailroom. Was studying advertising in night school. Liked to do imitations."

You can't force your memory, but you can encourage it. Go over the cards once in a while just before going to sleep. Visualize the person you're trying to remember and the scene you knew them in. Sooner or later, the name will jump out at you.

The larger public libraries have collections of phone books from all over the nation. Spend an hour once a month checking your "names only" cards against directories of the cities you think your old friends might be living in. Some of the people you find listed will give you the addresses of other old friends. You'll be surprised at how rapidly your list will grow with only brief but systematic effort.

Mail to your everybody-I-know farm at least twice a year, but not oftener than four times a year. Send one of your newsletters, or a specially written form letter. Each time, ask them to tell anyone they hear is moving in your direction about you. Don't forget to say you are a capable, hard-working real estate expert who takes great care of clients and customers. It works. People feel important saying, "I know a sharp real estate agent out there." And your friend's friend would rather work with someone recommended by a friend than with a stranger in a strange place.

Don't neglect the contacts you've spent a lifetime gaining. Tell them where you are, what you're doing, and that you're good at it.

When you address these letters, don't write, "Mr. and Mrs. Prospect." Write, "The Prospect Family." You don't know what's happened in that house during the last few days or weeks.

Sensitivity in writing and in one-to-one negotiations with people is so important. The divorce rate is high. People pass away. If you mail a letter addressed to "Mr. and Mrs. Prospect" and that family has suffered a shock the week before, it's going to hurt.

For your introductory letters, break your everyone-I-know list into two parts: close friends and relatives go in the first part; everyone else goes in the second. Your close friends should be informed first by a handwritten note. For this purpose, your personal stationery or blank paper is superior to your company's letterhead (with or without your imprinted name and photo). You are sending a handwritten note to reaffirm that you have a personal relationship that does not preclude your also having a business relationship with the person written to. Using your company's letterhead will say to some people: "We used to be friends, but now I'm changing our friendship to a business relationship." Writing on plain or personal stationery says, "We're friends and I'm in business now." Take the time to tailor your handwritten message to fit each of your close friends and relatives. You'll find it's time well spent.

Although it's important to inform your friends first that you've gone into real estate, these people are the last ones who will come throu_h for you. Their support will come—when you've earned the right to service their real estate needs. Don't be hurt. Because they know you so well, or think they do, they'll discount your abilities until you've won your wings working with other people.

The other day a note came from a friend telling me she'd just entered the business. I was pleased to get that information direct from her. Some people might think it's pointless to write someone who's in real estate that they've gone into it too, but I took it as a compliment that she had joined my industry—and thought enough of me to tell me so. Send a letter to real estate people? Certainly. Send it to everybody. We all need each other's help. If you have friends in real estate, be sure to tell them you're coming in because they'll need your help later and you'll need theirs.

FOUR SIZZLING STARTER LETTERS

1. Here's an example of the kind of introductory letter you should write by hand and send to the people you know well.

   Good Morning—
   Guess who's gone into real estate? That's right—I'm proud to say, "I have." For a long time I've had a deep concern and interest in our community. I've lived here for _____ years, and during that time I've [describe your community service, clubs joined, and so on].
   I know the properties here and have a deep pride of *ownership* in our home. Now I want to take these qualities into the active market. I want to ask you for your trust and confidence in important real estate matters.
   Do you feel I'm worth the risk?
   I hope so, because I've dedicated myself to marketing our wonderful community to people like yourself who have my love and respect.

   Sincerely,

2. The next introductory letter is intended to be professionally printed. Mail it first class (hand addressing is best) to everyone you haven't sent a handwritten note announcing your entry into real estate.

Hi Friend—

Yes, I want to call you friend, and I hope you'll consider me one. Everyone needs a friend in real estate—someone you can trust with such important matters as your security and your investments.

Would you place this kind of trust and confidence in me?

You may ask, "Why should I?"

Here are a few reasons:

(1) I am honest. I don't shade the truth. My word is good.

(2) I am reliable. If I tell a client I'll do something, wild horses won't stop me from doing it.

(3) I have time for you. Most people today are "too busy." I'm never too busy for you!

(4) I'm a licensed real estate agent. This means I passed a state licensing examination that required much dedicated study.

(5) I am constantly taking courses on all facets of real estate: appraisal, negotiation, financing, and so on. I'm taking these courses *for you*—to be a better me for you.

(6) I live here and have pride in and concern for our community.

(7) I have dedicated myself to serving our community by active participation in [name the service organizations you belong to and are active in].

(8) I am proud to be associated with Sell Fast Realty, which many people, myself included, believe is the finest real estate organization in Greenpretty Valley.

(9) If you give me the chance, I promise that I'll prove that I care, and that I'm highly capable of serving your best interests.

Thank you for taking the time to read this.

Sincerely,

Tillie Newcomer

Bear in mind, when sending out several hundred letters saying "I'm reliable," shows you're making quite a statement about yourself. Think that through. Get yourself organized fast, because you'll have response from that large mailing—you'll have things to do and people to see. Maybe at first some of these people will only be testing you. If you've been disorganized, keeping irregular work hours, and doing only what you have to do, set up a realistic work schedule. Keep to it. Prove to yourself that you're reliable—if there's any doubt in your mind—as you put together this mailing list and letter mailing. Get your attaché case, desk, auto, and—most important of all—your mind organized to handle real estate business. Go over every item on your office's checklists for processing new listings, reporting sales, opening and following through on transactions, working up-time, writing ads, holding open houses. Make sure you understand everything. The Breakaway Schedule at the back of this book has a program that'll make you an expert fast.

There's a lot to do. At the beginning, before the business makes you busy, get as much of this initial organizing out of the way as you can.

3. Introductory letter to your farm.

Consider me a new friend!
How do you do?
I'm Danny Kennedy. My home is just around the bend from you on Gridiron Drive, and I'm also a real estate counselor. Since your neighborhood and mine is my favorite, I'm delighted to be its specialist for Sell Fast Realty.

This means that I know all the developments on real estate listings, sales, and new neighbors here. I'm well posted on our entire area's cultural activities, tax proposals, and school bond issues. I also keep current on specialty shopping that's open now or due to open soon, and on other community services and events—from attorneys through handymen and physicians to zoo admission hours. Please call me if you have a question you want answered.

You might even get a good recipe or two from me now and then. I'll be distributing scratch pads soon for your convenience. Please consider me a friend and a community professional who is deeply committed to keeping our neighborhood one to be proud of.

Sincerely,

4. Introductory letter, or follow-up letter to be sent 60 days after letter 3 goes to your farm.

Hi Neighbor—
Can we be friends?
A good Realtor® who believes in the town he or she lives in and serves should be considered a friend. So please think of me that way.

I am your home-town representative for the area served by the Birch Street Elementary School, and I keep totally current on all properties marketed in the entire Greenpretty Valley. I know the streets, schools, shops, and churches. If you need home-town advice, you may lose out if you don't talk to me. Keeping current with our local scene is my work and what I love. Just ask my broker. I spend many hours studying and working to be a better me—for you.

Cordially,

P.S. Watch for my handy notepads!

Here is a year-end letter to be mailed the last week of December to the old and prospective clients in your updated everybody-I-know list.

(This letter must always reflect confidence and optimism. If you don't have both, don't send it.)

Hi!

Am I lucky. Because this year I had the opportunity to serve _____ clients in our home town. 19_____ was a good year for owners of real estate. The average days on the market for property in our area was just _____ days. The financing picture was flexible. Interest rates were a bit high at _____ as the year ended, but that figure must be compared to the rapid appreciation rate of _____ percent. As so many astute buyers demonstrated during the year, a person would be silly to let the interest rate stand in the way of a sound purchase of real estate.

The general economic trend was stable according to an article in *The Wall Street Journal* dated _____.

Here are some predictions for the coming year:

[Quote from Kiplinger, Board Room Talk, *Wall Street Journal*, *Forbes*, *New York Times*, or any large out-of-state newspaper—distant prophets carry more weight.]

"Building starts will be slow during the first half of the year" according to _____. A slowdown of new construction, of course, throws additional buyers into the resale market.

"Car sales will hit _____," states the _____. "Retail sales are expected to reach _____, and personal incomes will set new highs at $ _____," says the _____.

The outlook is that people will be spending money, and that means that real estate will continue to be a first priority in millions of households.

All in all, things look bright. I hope to see you during the coming year. Please consider me a friend. Realtors® are the best kind—we care about your security!

Cordially,

Your wrist should hurt the first year. Grab any reason for writing a note. If you see someone in the grocery store who says, "I heard you're in real estate," go home and write that person a note: "Thanks for mentioning that you know I'm in real estate because I need people to know that. I've got to spread the word now about myself being in the business." People will do it for you if you ask them to, not every chance they get, not as often as you'd like them to, and some won't, but many will—frequently.

Be alert for the people who'll be your heralds, and make sure you keep feeding them stuff to talk about: your first listing, your tenth, your sales, copies of ads.

Sustain the momentum your mail campaign will start, but don't sit back and wait to be overwhelmed by its results. Prospect. Work with fizzbos. Call on expired listings. Hold houses open. And farm, farm, farm—get out there and knock on those doors. Behind them is where the money is.

SELECTING YOUR FARM

Define the various areas you can choose from on a map, and take a quick count of the houses involved. You should be looking for about a 300-house (or housing unit) farm. As soon as you're familiar with what's available, start to rate your choices on these three factors: diversity, affinity, promise.

Diversity. A variety of floor plans, exteriors, amenities, and values is desirable in a farm for an important reason beyond the obvious one of attracting a variety of buyers to the area. The market often moves in parts rather than as a whole. Three-bedroom moderns may be hot sellers when four-bedroom rustics are cold; demand may be brisk in the top price ranges when it's dormant in the low ranges; and a few weeks later all these conditions may reverse themselves. Avoid trapping yourself in narrow price, style, and amenity ranges that can make your ride to success a rough and jolting one.

To get the kind of location and price spread that makes for steadier income, consider the advantages of farming 100 houses in each of three different areas. Such noncontiguous farms aren't harder to work. You can diversify in this way without paying any significant time penalty.

Affinity. You'll feel more at home in some areas than others. This feeling may strike you with great force just driving through, or you may have to spend hours there with your senses open. Walk the streets. Talk to the residents. Take time to develop your feelings before you commit yourself to a farm. It's vital that you feel enthusiastic about the area and feel in tune with the people there. Get into all the neighborhoods you're considering in the evenings and during the weekends, and talk to everyone you can. Open yourself up. Be receptive. Taste the flavors and sniff the breezes until you're certain which area you want to throw your efforts into.

Promise. Use the past turnover rate as a guide in making your decision, but keep firmly in mind that this too changes. An area with a high turnover rate may be turning into an era of long-term residences; an area with a low turnover rate may be about to bust loose. Don't go on blind faith that it will—discover a reason why it should bust loose or you'll probably be stuck with a low turnover rate.

Why would a stable neighborhood suddenly start to break up? The reasons may be complex and unknowable, or simple and obvious to the attentive eye. Sometimes an area around an elementary school consists mostly of first-time homeowners who, as newly married couples in their twenties, moved in at about the same time. Real estate turns over slowly while their incomes gain on the mortgages and the babies. Then suddenly the comfortable coffee klatches aren't so comfortable any more. ''Now the fit feels different,'' the women say and the 30 couples glimpse new vistas. Larger families and growing incomes shrink the satisfactions of yesterday's dream cottages. Promotions open new horizons. New opportunities become compelling urges to seek new solutions. Then an influential couple breaks out of the mold and moves up—and in the following months their entire group scatters. Now the neighborhood's property will turn over rapidly for quite some time because change is in the air. You can conduct that entire movement if you know the score—and get to the performance on time.

ANNUAL TURNOVER RATE

The annual turnover rate for a given farm is easily determined. Your Multiple Listing Service will have the records of sales by street. Count the number of sales made last year on all streets that interest you, and then count the houses on those streets. Divide the total number of sales by the total number of houses: The result is last year's turnover rate for that farm.

If, in the 309-house farm that you're considering, 63 houses were sold last year, that farm had a turnover rate a bit better than 20 percent, which is very good. The calculation is: 63 ÷ 390 = .20388 or, roughly, 20 percent.

You may love an area, but does the property there turn over? The time to think these things through is before you choose your farm. Once that choice is made, charge ahead for total control. The first step is to organize your farm.

ORGANIZING YOUR FARM

Organizing your farm means ''organizing to become the world's outstanding expert on your farm.'' Here are four time-effective methods of quickly grasping the in-depth knowledge of your farm that readily translates into solid control. From that solid control of your farm will come a burgeoning real estate practice and a rapidly rising income.

1 *Farm file.* Information about the homeowners.

2 *Deed details folder*. Holds the dry, rarely changing stuff of record: legal descriptions, assessor's parcel numbers, exact lot sizes.

3 *Farm flashdeck*. A simple technique for speedily learning the names of everyone on your farm.

4 *Property catalog*. Information about the houses, the improvements and amenities, and the grounds they stand on.

Part of your farm file is obsolete every time a family moves out. If you have collected information there about the house, you must recopy it, or crowd in data about the new owners. Confusion results. Avoid these problems by keeping your property catalog separate. Once compiled, your deed details folder will never need updating. The farm flashdeck reduces what most agents believe is an impossible task—learning everyone's name in the farm—to a readily accomplished goal you'll quickly achieve.

The methods are detailed in the following four sections.

Setting Up the Farm File

The farm file must be a convenient system for recording new details about the people in your farm; the system must be equally convenient for reviewing those details quickly in the field.

Some agents like to use loose cards for their farm file. I preferred a three-ring binder with a divider for each street. On the back of each divider I stapled a list, typed in easily-read capitals, of the people on that street. At first, to refresh my memory, I always pulled over to the curb and ran my eye down a street's occupant list before turning the corner.

MARK & LINDA BROWN (Billy, Wanda)
RICKY & LILA HARTFORD (No Kids)
JUNE & HARRY LARSON
(Chad, Baby Nancy)

Behind each divider was a special page for each family. On this sheet I gathered the friendly things I learned talking to people, all good stuff for starting the next conversation with them. The address, names of the owners, and their phone number headed the paper. Below that I entered facts about their children and pets. I used the top quarter-page for this information, and gave a brief description of the property as seen from the street, leaving space for adding more details later.

The next quarter-page I reserved for what they told me about their leisure time interests, associations, and hobbies. On the bottom quarter-page I recorded what they volunteered about their jobs and career interests.

By always entering certain kinds of information in about the same place, I could more quickly review my farm file, more readily see what I didn't know about each family, and more surely avoid showing ignorance of something they'd already told me.

Write a small, legible, permanent record as you go, not a huge scrawl that'll soon fill the page. Transfer a street's pages to a clipboard if more convenient. Discipline yourself to write concisely and readably as soon as you're alone.

At the top of each page's back, note the dates you visit each family and their reaction to you. Gather this information as you go or you'll get confused: twice around your farm probably is six hundred visits.

When I was farming, I didn't have anything better than ordinary ruled notebook paper. It's handier, to keep the items used on every contact on the front side of the page. Farm File, in Chapter 24, Money-making Forms, allows you to do just that.

A glance at your notations of visit dates, homeowner reactions, and at the other facts about each family you've recorded, enables you to begin each new visit where you left off your previous one. You'll find people paying friendly attention to you because you're paying friendly attention to them by remembering details about their lives and interests.

Know who's on your team, and who their friends are, but remain the professional at all times. Nothing will turn your farm's crops to weeds quicker than becoming known as the neighborhood gossip and tale-carrier.

Where do you get the homeowners names, addresses, and phone numbers to begin with?

A fast and convenient source, if one is available in your area, is the reverse (crisscross) directory that lists telephone subscribers by street and number. Use this valuable tool for all its worth, but recognize that it has limitations: people were moving while it was being printed and distributed, it won't tell you who owns rental property, and people with no phones, unlisted phones, or new phones won't appear in it.

It's vital that you start the clock running on the rapport-building stage of farming. The sooner you're through that period, the sooner you will be closing fast on effective control of your farm. So get out there today and make your first visits. Keep them brief. Keep moving. As you go, gather and record information. All you need to start is determination and a few sheets of school notebook paper.

Divide your farm into 30 groups of about 10 houses each that you can conveniently visit by parking your car once. You shouldn't always work your farm the same way, but for the first three to six visits, the 10-house group will work fine.

Visit one group of 10 houses each day, and make prospecting calls to verify the names and addresses given in your reverse directory for two groups of 10 houses. You'll soon be calling at houses where you feel confident in calling the people by name.

As you walk the areas, record the addresses not given in the reverse directory. Bypass those houses unless someone's out front and you get into an easy conversation with them. After exchanging pleasantries, they'll usually introduce themselves.

Information on properties not appearing in the reverse directory will be in your deed details folder. The next section tells how to create one.

Creating Your Deed Details Folder

In some areas, title companies will furnish you with owners' names, legal descriptions, and similar data on a courtesy, no-change basis. Call your title company representative and ask for a farm package. In regions where this isn't done, your best source may be the assessor's office, which is often found in the county courthouse.

Legal descriptions, assessor's parcel numbers, and lot sizes usually stay the same for many years. Since you rarely need this information except when writing up a listing, there's no need to carry it when door knocking.

Avoid handcopying deed details except onto a listing form that you'll double-check for accuracy. Errors in this information that creep into transactions are time consuming, embarrassing, and troublesome at best; at worst they'll cost you a lot of money. Defend against them by working from photocopies of official or title company records.

Once you have your own photocopies, a few minutes with a pair of scissors and your office copy machine will give you the data in the format you prefer: legal or letter size. Make two sets, one for your office and the other for the farming kit you carry in your car. This assures you of having these vital details handy and accurate whenever they're needed. Once it's made, your deed details folder probably will never need updating as long as you work that farm.

Flashdeck Your People

The idea is to clamp the names of everyone in your farm into your memory as quickly as possible, and with the same effort associate those persons with a house you can visualize: their home. Only facts you will memorize should appear on the farm flashdeck cards.

On side A, write the family surname only, On side B of each card, enter the first names you find in the reverse directory. Add the names of spouses and children as you discover them.

As you work your farm, compose a brief description of each house in it. Add details about the interiors later. Start with what you can see from the outside and describe what distinguishes each house from neighboring structures in the most emotional *favorable* phrases you can think of that apply. Use this opportunity to develop your sensitivity to the sales features of your farm's properties. Emphasize the positive elements of the real estate you've appointed yourself the world's expert on. That last sentence was not intended as a joke. One of your highest-priority goals must be to become the world's foremost expert on your farm in the shortest possible time.

```
┌──────────────────────────────────────────┐
│                                            │
│                                            │
│                                            │
│                  KERSHAW                   │
│                                            │
│                                            │
│                                            │
│                                            │
└──────────────────────────────────────────┘
```

			Lulu 5
HUSBAND	Joe Kershaw	CHILDREN	Steve (about 8)
WIFE	Mary		

HOUSE This is the ''Tiptoe through the tulips'' house Outside
reminds me of a cozy cottage by the sea — window boxes
w tulips, freshly painted white picket fence

Farm Flashdeck

Review your farm flashdeck twice daily until you've overlearned the facts in it. (The flashdeck learning system is described in Chapter 3.)

The Property Catalog—What It Is and How It'll Make Money for You

The people go, the houses stay. Farm expertise is knowing about both. Pay keen and systematic attention to the houses as you learn about the people and you'll acquire this complete, double-barreled farm knowledge faster, and retain it longer

Compiling a property catalog for your farm spurs your observation. Writing down the facts you observe is a learning process; reviewing the facts you've entered in the catalog cuts your memory grooves deeper. If you're someone who's been telling yourself for years that you have a poor memory, you'll be delighted at how easy it is to install 300 instant-recall images in your brain, one for each house in your farm, when you do it systematically. Piggybacked on each of those images will be others: the owner's faces, names, and various details about their interests, children, and prospects. When you've acquired only a part of this knowledge, you'll find that it's building on itself. It happens like this:

Let's watch Al Pike, a new agent who is working smarter, not harder at a social gathering. Finding himself talking to a man he's never met before, Al introduces himself, but doesn't mention his business yet because he feels that would be too pushy too soon.

"I'm Dick Taylor," the other man responds.

"There's someone by that name living on Maple Street. Is that you?"

"Sure is. Have we met, Al?"

"We haven't, but its a pleasure to greet you now, Dick. You live in that beautiful white Colonial with the huge oak tree in front, don't you?"

"You're right." Dick gives Al a quizzical look. "How do you know all this?"

"I'm with Shakey Shacks Realty, and I specialize in the area you live in, Dick."

"I guess you do. Very impressive how you tied my name up with my house. I'm surprised I haven't heard of your before this."

"I decided to specialize in your area just three weeks ago, so I've still got a lot to learn about it."

"Well, you're moving fast, I can see that. Say, you should talk to Lindsay Long. Do you know him?"

"Only that he lives on Maple Street, too."

"Right. Well, he's been offered a job on the coast. I think he's going to take it. You ought to talk to Lindsay right away."

"Thanks for the tip, Dick. Would it be asking too much for you to give him a jingle and put in an icebreaking word for me?"

"Glad to, Al. Anyone working as hard as you are deserves a break."

And many a sale has been made by a sharp agent who knocked on a house and said, "I have a buyer who wants a home exactly like yours. Are you thinking of selling in the near future?" The answer quite often comes back as, "We *are* thinking of selling. Do you really have a buyer, or is this just a gimmick?" The industry's image and this great ploy should never be tarnished by using it as a foot-in-the-door scheme. Used with integrity, it can readily result in a double-fee transaction, or a listing. These opportunities flow from knowing every property in your farm, not just those currently for sale.

A small loose-leaf notebook that you write in as you go makes an ideal property catalog. Record in it all the amenities you find on each property that people want and will pay extra money for. Make note of the colors, number of bedrooms, and unusual features. Compiling this catalog gives you a thousand conversation openers with the residents of your farm. Make the most of this opportunity to learn about the houses and their owners—but don't be nosey. Judicious questions don't arouse hostility. Avoid asking a homeowner for information you can gather by looking at the house or at the public records.

And don't ask any questions unless you're certain the homeowner can answer it. People usually know how many bedrooms they have, but not the total square footage in the house. Remember what the rancher told his son: "Never ask a man where he's from because he might not be from Texas, and then he'll be mad at you for making him own up to it."

Here's a great opener: "What do you like best about this house?" That's not nosing around for information the homeowner may think is none of your business, that's asking for his opinion. People like to be consulted. If that one goes well, follow it up with "Would you be offended if I asked you what you like least about this house?"

Before asking any questions at all, of course, you identify yourself and state your purpose. "Good morning. I'm Tillie Newcomer with Sell Fast Realty—and I'm the specialist in this area. I'm just going to take half a minute to say hello and leave a scratch pad, and ask just one question for the property catalog I'm compiling on this neighborhood. This is a three-bedroom house, isn't it?" (Of course, you'd ask this question only in a custom home area, where the answer isn't obvious, as it would be in a mass-built tract.)

"No, we have four bedrooms."

Noted when walking by _____	12345 Maple 3 bedroom, 2 ba.
	2 story Colonial — white eagle over front door. Huge oak tree in front yard. Sweeping brick wall. Tucked against hill. No view, but quiet.
	RV acc. poss. (There's room for recreation vehicle access and storage.)
Learned when Dick invited you in _____	Elegant dining room with smoked mirrors
	Gold carpet Yellow check lino in B & K.
	Owners Dick/Rachel Taylor
Space for changes _____	

If they're closing the door on you, give them a bright "Thank you," and head for the next house. But if they seem willing to talk for a moment, use the what-do-you-like-best opener.

Notice how Tillie handled the how-many-bedrooms question. She was fairly sure it was a four-bedroom house, but she said: "It's three, isn't it?" and handed the homeowner a win. Suppose Tillie had said, "You have four bedrooms here, don't you?" to the owner of a three-bedroom house. The homeowner than has to say, "No, we only have three." That's not a win, and she's standing there thinking, "Why am I talking to this klutz who's taking up my time and making me feel bad for no reason?"

Suppose you guess that a house has four bedrooms, say three to be safe, and the homeowner answers, "We only have two bedrooms."

You can save the win by quickly saying, "I'm amazed. It's such a big house—you must have some very impressive-sized rooms here."

Here's a real cruncher: "And, of course you have a swimming pool like everyone else on the block does," Agent Footmouth says to a pool-less lady.

"We're the only underprivileged family on the block," she snaps, and slam goes the door in Footmouth's face.

Note the sample of what a property catalog sheet looks like.

WORKING YOUR FARM FILE

One day you sell a house in your farm on West Street. It's the work of a moment to compare the ages of your buyers' children to those on West Street they'll be living near. On your next sweep through your farm, you knock on a door and say, "Hi, Mrs. Hall. I just sold the house across the street. And guess what? They have a daughter Kelly's age." Or the newcomers both like to bowl, and you know the Halls do, too. People want to know who's coming into the neighborhood. You're not disclosing anything personal.

COPING WITH E-AGENT

Did you select a farm where an agent from another office is powerful—powerful, but not in total control? It's pointless to challenge an agent who has total control of a farm. You can take total control of some other farm with less effort than it'll require to make a bare living fighting someone else's total control. Talk to the people. If half of them tell you that Millie or Jack has the whole neighborhood in a sack, go elsewhere. But, in any desirable farm, you're likely to find out that one strong agent is already operating there. That agent has been taking a steady flow of listings out of that farm for some time, but hasn't extended himself to take total control. Let's call that entrenched person the *E-agent*.

Here's how to cope with E-agent. If you're of the same sex as E-agent, take heart: he or she has no advantage there. If you're of the opposite sex, take heart: some people prefer to work with a man, and others prefer to work with a woman.

Never have anything but praise for the entrenched agent, or else keep silent. You never know when you're talking to one of E-agent's bird dogs, or someone who'd like to make mischief between the two of you. Be sure the grapevine is passing good things back to E-agent; there's no sense at all in goading him or her into strenuous competition to get even for some careless remark you've made.

E-agent has strong points and weak points. He or she has been tough about taking listings at market price, or has taken overpriced listings that didn't sell. Maybe E-agent doorknocks but doesn't hand out giveaways; maybe he doesn't put out a newsletter. Even if he does use a newsletter, he has to take a certain slant with it. You take a different slant, Chapter 7 tells you about giveaways and super-promotions; Chapter 13 about newsletters.

Notice what times and days E-agent farms. Then go farming at a different time. Find out—by casual conversation with someone who seems friendly on the farm—if E-agent specializes in sending out written material. Hopefully, he's become so busy that he's relying on the mails—so you rely on face-to-face contact. That's always the most effective method.

E-agent has loyal fans. Stay away from them.

Get your own.

Hang in there. E-agent most likely won't. He's been getting a nice business from your mutual farm for a long time—with less and less effort expended. Persevere, because perseverance is the hardest game in real estate, and it's the one that pays off the best.

Compete hard, but don't let it show—don't make E-agent come out and fight. You can't bank brag. Do him little favors. Talk a sweet story. The only thing that counts is listings sold; do your best to sell his, because then the new owners are *your* clients.

Never forget that achieving your personal goals, not beating E-agent's record, is your purpose. Paddle your own canoe and let E-agent paddle his; the river is wide enough for both of you.

THE EVERGREEN LISTING FARM

There are three common methods of farming. Let's discuss them in order of popularity.

"I hate it, but I hit it when I have to." This is a labor-saving system of farming: Not much needs to be done because not much is expected. Devotees of this method tolerate other office's signs in their farm quite well; what really upsets them is another agent from their office working expireds or fizzbos in their farm.

"I really worked it—once." Nothing happened, so why continue? Door-knock on a dull afternoon, send a kid around hanging newsletters—and the ungrateful public refuses to respond. That's all—forget it—farming is a waste of time.

The evergreen attitude. "My goal is effective control of my farm. I know that steady output requires steady input. To reap regularly, I must fertilize frequently."

Effective control of a farm begins when you're taking one-third of the listings produced there—and getting them sold. Except in special circumstances, such as when your office has a commanding location, writing two-thirds of the listings from a given farm is about the best you can reasonably expect to achieve over an extended time span. Sellers loyal to the agent they originally bought from, and those with friends or relatives in the real estate business, will impose that limit. There'll also be an occasional maverick you somehow can't click with.

A very active farm has an annual turnover of 25%, but let's use 20%. In a farm of controllable size (about 300 houses) that means 60 listings per year. Writing 40 of those listings, selling 10 of them yourself, and promoting other brokers to sell the other 30 earns one fee per week. That's effective control—of your farm and of your bank account.

So set your goal at one transaction per week from your farm. That's achievable if you're willing to make the effort. Keep that goal constantly in mind whenever excuses for not pounding the pavement or flailing the phone tempt you. Give farming high priority. Schedule heavy time and effort for it—and then do it. And, as you get busier and busier, get more and more efficient so you can maintain the powerful thrust in your farm that made you busy.

Too many agents think of farming as a distasteful chore—and it shows. You've got to feel good about the homeowners before you can expect them to feel good about you. Psych yourself up until you *know* you're the best agent who'll offer real estate services to them. You're not necessarily the most experienced agent, but you can be the most determined to deliver thorough service in that area. Even the newest agent can make that commitment.

The Three Stages

There are three stages to gaining effective control of an evergreen farm.

- Getting to know me.
- Getting to like me.
- Getting to love me.

Each stage takes about six months. If you've selected a good, active farm and work it properly, you'll get *at least* two listings during the first stage, four during the second stage, and eight during the third stage. After 18 months you'll approach effective control—the condition where your presence is so strong that it discourages competition. At this crucial point many salespeople become too busy and slack off in their farms. When the confusion clears, they often find that an aggressive competitor is gaining rapidly on them. Remember that your farm needs frequent attention. That attention can't be constant, needn't be regular, but must be frequent.

Let's consider those three stages to effective control of an evergreen farm in detail:

1. The getting-to-know-me stage.   Before you start, realize that you've got to have patience. Most of the people who quit farming didn't have the necessary patience. They did a tenth, or perhaps nine-tenths, of the work necessary to make it pay. Then they got discouraged—and allowed all that effort to evaporate. Remember during this first stage that giveaways are essential to get you in the door. Scratch pads with your picture on them are great. Rain hats, litter bags, the list is endless. Make your choices, and then get out there and give those giveaways away. During this phase they're essential.

One excellent tip: Have a note printed, or inserted with a spot of glue (your pad printer can do this) near the end of the pad: "Time to call Danny Kennedy for another scratch pad." You'll get calls and sometimes a lead to a listing in the neighborhood at the same time.

The words we use at this stage are very important: "Hi, I'm Danny Kennedy with Sell Fast Realty. I hope I haven't interrupted. I'm a real estate expert who specializes in your home town. I'll only keep you for a minute, but I want you to know I keep tabs on what's going on in this community." (Mention whatever is topical: tax relief, a new fire station or public pool, school bonds.) "And I also keep current on homes sales and listings in your neighborhood."

Don't be afraid to use the word "expert." Webster defines expert as, "One who has acquired special skill or knowledge in a particular subject." Based on that definition, you are a real estate expert, aren't you?

Keep it simple and basic. At the end of this sales dialogue use these dynamite words: "Thanks for talking to me." Many of the people behind the doors on your farm are afraid of the stranger. They are afraid of a small woman too—this fearful attitude isn't only a problem men have. The fear isn't necessarily of physical danger—it's the instinctive fear of the unknown. So a large part of our work is to alleviate that fear of the unknown by making ourselves known in a pleasant way.

2. The getting-to-like-me stage.   Think for a minute about the representatives of mortgage and title companies who drop into real estate offices soliciting business. One day you see Martin Smith's card and scratch pad on your desk. You've never heard of Martin Smith, and don't think you need him, so you throw his card away. A couple of more times you see his card on your desk, and you keep on throwing it away. Then one day you're in the office when Martin Smith comes in. He introduces himself and you small talk for a moment. A week later you're calling a client whose number you've jotted on a scratch pad—and you notice

Martin Smith's photo and name printed on that pad. But it still wouldn't occur to you to call Martin Smith, a title company representative, when you need title insurance. Then one day a problem comes up.

You're preparing a listing appointment packet for presentation tonight. You have no time to spare. Then a call comes in. A document that was missed when the client came in for settlement must be signed immediately by your buyer in order for the transaction to close the following morning. Martin Smith, who until now has been a face only vaguely connected with a name, happens to be here. He says, "I'll be glad to help you out. I'll drive the 60 miles for you to get it signed." Aha—the moment of truth arrived. You not only know him—you like him! He can be useful as well as informative. Martin Smith is now in position to obtain—not only some of your title business—but also some from the other agents in your office. Because you're going to tell them about how good old Marty saved you from a tight time squeeze. Of course, his title work has to be competitive in price and quality, but now he's part of the team; he's no longer one of the problem people one smiles at and gets rid of as quickly as possible.

The same forces work in the farm. When you finally arrive at the right place at the right time—you enter the getting-to-like-me stage, not only at that one house, but at all the neighbors who talk to those people. For example: It's mid-May and you're out farming. As you walk up to Alice and Phil Cooke's door, he's sitting at the dining room table filling out an application for a home improvement loan. Alice and Phil have the itch for a swimming pool. When he comes to the application's question about the present value of their home, Phil yells, "Hey, Alice, what do think this place is worth?"

"How should I know?" Alice calls from the back yard. "Is that our doorbell?"

Phil opens the door and stares as you say, "Hi, Mr. Cooke—I'm Danny Kennedy, the real estate expert from Sell Fast Realty. Is there any information you need about real estate these days? I'm right on top of things."

"Hey, you are just the gal I need—the face on the scratch pad, right? Listen I'm filling out a loan application, and they want to know the value of my house."

"No problem, Mr. Cooke. Let me make a quick run to my car and bring in my current listings and comparable records. I'll give you an up-to-date market evaluation in five minutes." The getting-to-like-me stage is accomplished. You are useful and informative and not after anything but his confidence. Obviously, he's not moving. But you helped. He tells the neighbors to the left, right, and down the street, "The Kennedy kid is okay. She's not just after the buck. She'll give you service whether you're moving or not."

In this stage be careful not to become a pest—don't let them say, "Who is this clown hanging around the neighborhood all the time?" Act busy in your farm. Move. You're being watched. If you're in the neighborhood too much, they'll say to themselves, "When does he sell houses?"

So watch your timing, and step out briskly in your farm. Drive through, wave, and act busy. Even though you don't visit someone, even though they don't have that person-to-person contact with you every time, once you're in this getting-to-like-me stage, the fact that you're driving around the neighborhood, that you're busy there, keeps you in their minds.

Recommend nice homes for a home tour, or something special like ''The Most Beautiful Homes on the Block'' award that Tom Hopkins talks about. If your local newspaper occasionally does a photo story on some of the area's outstanding houses, find out how they're selected and try to get homes in your farm included.

Perhaps a charitable group in your area conducts an outstanding home tour as a fund-raising event. If so, be on the lookout for homes in your farm that you can recommend for the tour.

If your area has no such tour, develop a plan for one and call the program chairpersons of the various charitable organizations. Ask to appear on their program to propose a fund-raising tour for their organization's benefit. This is a powerful way to make yourself known in the community, and talking with homeowners about whether they'd like their home singled out as a showplace is a powerful way of creating a significant presence in your farm.

Make spot checks on your ''buddies.'' From day one, cultivate the group of homeowners in your farm who are naturally friendly and helpful. Some people are more open and loving. You'll know when you see them. They open the door and say ''Good morning. Beautiful day, isn't it?'' Lean on your newly acquired buddies in the get-to-know-me stage. On each block, visit two or three good guys and say: ''I'm on my way to the office to show property, but I just wanted to see if there was anything I can do for you in the area of real estate—How's the scratch pad supply?—Talk to you later—Bye now.'' Boom, on to the next spot check. Soon you'll pop onto a juicy tidbit on one of your spot checks—''Hi, Dan—say, the Walter kids are telling my kids that their new home will be near Disneyworld in Florida. Something's up—check it out.'' Cheers for spot checks in the getting-to-like-me stage!

3. The getting-to-love-me stage.   When they're putting the bread on your table, you've reached this happy state. You should use a more personal approach now. Send birth announcements when a baby is born in your farm. Drop the parents a note saying, ''Congratulations on the new addition. I hope father's nerves are calming down, and mother is getting some rest. If you think you'll need more space later, remember me.''

Now it's your sign that's all over the place. People are watching to see if you make any mistakes. They'll call up a neighbor and say, ''Is your agent doing a good job for you? Is she keeping the promises she made? Is she keeping you informed?''

''No, she isn't. She's gotten too big for her britches.''

The people asking these questions are thinking of moving, or have a friend who is. How much better if your client says, "Yes she's done a marvelous job. She's really a fine agent."

During this getting-to-love-me stage, remember that bad rumors spread rapidly. You can lose that farm just as quickly as you built it up. "She returned messages fast when we wanted to list. She followed up during the time it was on the market real good. But, now that the property is sold, we can't even find out whether the buyer is getting a loan okayed or not. Am I burned up. But what can I do?"

That irate lady can do plenty. She can ride over your farm like Attila the Hun with phone calls telling everyone who'll listen what a rotter you are. No real estate farm will ever be so lush that its crops won't fall if they're untended. Allow yourself to become too busy with other things, too disorganized, or too tired, and the labor and money you expended building your farm up will be wasted.

MORE FARMING SECRETS

Numbers Game

By striking out 1,306 times, Babe Ruth set one of the longest held records in baseball—but we remember his 714 home runs. Even that legendary figure had to take two slaps for every kiss. Thomas Edison's ratio was far lower: hundreds, or even thousands, of fruitless experiments patiently carried out to achieve each successful invention.

Count the harvests you reap, not the seeds you plant that don't sprout. Sow widely, and sow often. Talk to as many people as you can; follow up every opportunity you sniff; never look back and grumble. Look forward through your victories to more successes. Real estate is a numbers game.

When Is the Best Time to Farm?

Find out when you first begin farming. Hit two or three houses at different times of each day for two weeks and discover when most people are home. Friday afternoons, between 3 and 6, and Saturday mornings between 10 and 12, were my most effective times. After I covered my farm twice, those were the only times I went farming because by then I was too busy to doorknock during the less-effective times of the week.

Always Have a Reason

Always have a reason for follow-up notes and phone calls. Let me give you an example: You're out in your farm talking to a lady. She really doesn't want to talk about real estate, but has a question about the school bond issue, or she's heard something about the school system she wants verified. As you're chit-chatting, she says, "I'd really like to know what the scoop is on that." She doesn't specifically say to you, "Find out."

Don't tell her you will. That becomes a promise you might not be able to keep. Instead of promising, do it. Go back to the office after farming and find out what she wants to know. Then drop her a note, or call her up and say, "Remember when we were talking about the school bonds? Well, this is the story—"

Have a good reason. That was always an effective thing for me to keep in mind. When you have a reason for contacting them, it's not, "That agent's bugging me again." You're giving out information; you're a professional doing the job right.

Beat Square? Try Wacky

When I was a practitioner another gal and I were talking about the people on our farms we hadn't clicked with, and how we might get some of those people on our team. We decided to go out right then and see what we could learn from each other by knocking on problem doors together. The plan was for her to take the lead in my farm, and for me to take the lead in hers. I won the coin toss and we went out to hit three houses on my farm first.

We knocked on two doors, found no one home, and were walking past another house when my friend pointed at it and said, "You're doing good here?"

I shook my head. "There's a 'No solicitors' sign, a big one, right on the door. No way you can say you didn't see it."

"Danny, let's see what'll happen if we blow her a kiss." My friend headed for the door. I followed, reluctantly, and kept well back when she knocked.

A grim-faced woman opened the door, gave my friend a wilting stare, and said, "Don't tell me you didn't see my sign."

My friend fluttered her hands, shook her head, and protested in a bewildered tone, "But I don't smoke!"

The lady opened her mouth, couldn't find words, and finally chuckled. Then she said, "Oh, all right—come on in." We had a nice chat, and the lady invited us back any time we were in the neighborhood. After a few months, a relative she referred bought a house from me, and two years later I listed her house when she moved away.

It was a shot in the dark and we were in a wacky enough mood to try it that day. Our lighthearted approach ultimately made our pockets heavier.

Why not? Why be grim when you can be cheerful? People pay to see comedians, but the only pay cold stone faces get is from pigeons.

Keep a Record

Keep a record of all sales and listings in your farm. Listing this information in the order it happens makes it easy to summarize and helps you spot important new trends. Within 60 days of starting to work a farm, on the information you've gathered and analyzed from the Multiple Listing Service, you should be able to tell prospective sellers and buyers something like this:

"Three years ago 49 houses sold in this immediate neighborhood at an average price of $150,000. Two years ago 57 went for $158,000, and last year 66 homes bought an average price of $160,000. So far this year the lowest any house has sold for is $151,000, and the highest price paid is $185,000. At the rate it's going I expect 75 houses to sell this year at an average price of $167,500."

Your listeners will be impressed.

People will ask you to repeat the information, so be sure you've got it right, and that you can back it up with records. It takes effort to pull together the information necessary to make that short speech, but it pays big dividends of reassurance. Your buyers know they've got a knowledgeable agent on their team, and that they're buying a good investment. Your prospective sellers are reassured to learn that you know the area better than they do, and they'll be more inclined to accept your pricing advice. Check out every reported sale as you work your farm and find out what each sold property is comparable to. If 1234 Elm Street sold for $200,000 a month ago and you know nothing else about that house, that information won't help you a bit to advise a buyer or seller about a property at 4321 West Avenue. But if you know they are both two-story, four-bedroom homes of about 3,000 square feet, and have similar amenities, Elm Street's sale makes a significant statement about West Avenue's market value. That statement will carry weight with mortgage company appraisers and loan committee members; it should give guidance to the seller, and it will be considered by an intelligent buyer.

Publish a Monthly Newsletter

Sounds overwhelming? It isn't when you set it up right. Create a simple format, set a schedule, gather your market information, type it, have a quick-print shop run off copies, and get them out. Detailed tips for doing all this quickly, reliably, and cheaply are given in Chapter 13, Promotion.

But why bother? Because the monthly newsletter gives you a constant presence in your farm. People will notice if you consistently deliver professional market facts about their neighborhood. If they suddenly find themselves sellers, they'll want the agent who can do them the most good. Telling them twelve times a year that you are their best choice is a powerful convincer.

Get Out There!

The hardest part of farming is leaving the office. Details by the dozen conspire to delay us. Excuses multiply. "I'll just do these two things, make that one more call, and then I'll go farming. Oh, but I've got to—"

This can—and usually does—go on all day. Schedule your farm time like an appointment with a buyer. When that time comes, go do it. That's all—just go do it when the time comes. At the end of the year you'll be thousands of dollars richer for following that simple resolve.

FARM DECISION DAY

Pick one day of each month on which you'll make your decisions about farming tools. Mark that date in your appointment book for the rest of the year or, if you use the Tickler 1/31 system discussed in Chapter 22, staple a reminder in that day's folder. The tenth of each month is a good date to make your final decision on the item you'll hand out during the fourth following month. This allows your supplier 110 days to imprint your message on the items and get them to you well in advance of need. If you order early, you won't be tracing shipments when you should be handing out the giveaways in your farm. Ordering early also allows you to shop for price, and to refuse or return poor quality merchandise.

PROFESSIONALISM

In its finest and most complete sense, professionalism furnishes the real estate agent with both armor and weapons. The armor is one's attitude of concern to help qualified buyers while safeguarding sellers' legitimate interests.

Be friendly, relaxed, and natural, yet make clear by action and speech that your professional responsibilities come ahead of your personal whims. Never indulge in idle chatter about your pet peeves, problems, and pleasures. Stick to business—talk about your clients' interests, concerns, and opportunities instead of your own. Maintain under your friendly and relaxed manner a reserved position of dignity.

Professionalism's weapons are knowledge well learned and skills carefully practiced. Know your job. Let people become aware, by deeds instead of words that your time is valuable. Treat your time with respect and you'll find that others will respect it too.

One of the burdens of success at farming is the chatty types who have given you a lot of referrals and tend to get a bit possessive of you. They're inclined to call up at any time and want you to run right over. Although you are grateful to them, you can't let them control your time. Let's take a professional approach to handling that possessive person's phone call:

"Danny, can you come here right now? My girlfriend from Oak Park and her husband just dropped in and they really think Hilton Head is neat, and they're interested in taking a quick peek at a few houses. Who knows? Maybe she'll be able to get him down here. I sure hope so, because we're such great friends, and—"

When two women, or two couples, get together on a visit, they often catch "houselooking fever." The hosts are proud of their home town or second vacation home; the visitors are more interested in looking at homes than at the high school gym. Sometimes they just want to be entertained at your expense. Even if you don't pick up the lunch check, your time, especially your weekend time, is a heavy expense.

Ask to talk to the visitor. When he or she comes to the phone, say, "I'm so happy you love our area. But are you really serious about investing in our area?

Visitor: "I don't know. It depends on what you have in my price range."

Agent: "How long will you be here today?"

Visitor: "Just this afternoon."

Agent: "I have a problem. My schedule is pretty full this afternoon, but I have lots of information on this area. I can put together a presentation of some representative properties that are available right now in your price range." [The flyer packet discussed in Chapter 9 is ideal for this.] "I can drop it off in about 20 minutes on my way to one of my appointments. How about that?"

YOUR ATTITUDE ON THE FARM

Treat people with the alert cordiality that is the essence of good manners so they'll feel a pleasant compulsion to reciprocate your friendly attitude. Be sensitive. Never press when they're troubled or busy.

Above all, avoid even the suspicion of trickery or underhanded tactics. You farm to build confidence and trust, not to breed fear and suspicion.

CARELESS SLIPS

Careless slips of the tongue can get back to people in your farm. You're there to list and sell real estate professionally, not to pass judgment on people. Be careful what you say, and be careful what you write in your farm file. Someone can look over your shoulder, or the book can get mislaid.

EVERY DOOR IS DIFFERENT

Have a planned presentation, have a dozen openers practiced, but remember that you're dealing with human beings.

Look at the person who opens the door. You've got a scratch pad in your hand and a split second to react and adapt your planned presentation to the circumstances. If they only open the door a crack and a wolfhound is barking through at you, don't stand there saying, "I'm Danny Kennedy of Sell Fast Realty, and let me tell you, the real estate market is fantastic—" Sneak your scratch pad through the doorway crack and say, "I'm sorry for the interruption. I'll come back another time." Then beat it out of there.

Every door is different. Now you're knocking on another one. Mrs. Verbose, a little old lady who hasn't seen anyone breathe for weeks, answers. "Oh, Danny, you're the kid with the scratch pads. Come on in." And she pours you tea, and she gives you cookies, and she tells you about her long-lost relatives. You could be there all day. There's a time when you'll have to say, "Goodbye, Mrs. Verbose. I've got to go. But I'll be back and talk to you."

This is a people business first, and a property business second. Gear your outwardly visible emotional level to where they're at.

Before you start doing anything that isn't already common real estate practice in your area, check with your broker. Local ordinances, or your professional association's rules, may prohibit what you're thinking of doing. For example, some areas have laws against cold calling for listings. Other places won't permit agents to go door-to-door. Before you order giveaways, make sure you'll be allowed to hand them out. Before using any new method, make sure it's acceptable. Before you dive in, make sure there's water in the pool.

SPEED COUNTS

When you have the chance to put out *Just Listed* or *Just Sold* door-hangers, speed counts. If these transactions are of special interest to the fizzbos or other prospective sellers you're working with, phone or visit them with the news. These are professional, nonbugging reasons for you to contact them, and nothing enhances your image more than listing or selling a property comparable to theirs.

But you can't know everyone who might be thinking of selling in your farm. Some people are secretive, others are struck by sudden changes. Get those new door-hangers out fast (with the sellers' permission, of course), while they're still news and before another agent does.

HUMILITY HELPS

Humility helps you pass around many a pitfall that pride digs. Real estate agents walk a narrow line between enthusiastic confidence on the one hand, and unfeeling pride on the other. Some of us stray from that narrow line and offend people to our serious financial cost.

After you really have control of your farm, drop notes to people, or go see them and use words like this:

"I never could've won that sales award without your confidence."

"I really appreciate your support—I couldn't have done it without you."

Memorize those phrases. Use them often. And, on a day you think you're Mr. King Pin, put a sign on your desk that says, "Never forget a humble beginning."

SUCCESS BREEDS SUCCESS

Work your farm hard, get some priced-right listings, put the *For Sale* signs up, slap the *Sold* riders on promptly, and you'll start getting neat calls like these.

From a young woman you don't remember (a quick look in your farm file shows you caught her home only once, and she didn't seem too impressed then), "Jerry just called. He got the promotion and transfer we've been hoping for. I told him you're the hot agent around here, and he wants you to come out tonight and put our house on the market."

From someone on your farm you've spoken to several times: "Hey, call up Nancy Dowd. I've been telling her about you. . . . Yeah, and her listing expired at midnight last night . . . that other office didn't take care of her right. . . . Yeah, call her up and I think you've got the listing."

Now your name riders are all over the farm. You have a good month, another, and stretch it to three. Lots of people are calling in, lots of good things are happening, and your name goes in the paper: top lister, first in sales, whatever. Tape a newspaper clipping of that ad or article and send it with a thank-you note to the people who've been giving you leads. Tell them "I really appreciate your help. I couldn't have done it without you."

Encourage people to feel they have an emotional stake in your success with notes and attention. Don't be stingy with praise and thanks for help received. People like to play a part in a winner's success. Your recognition of your team players does more than anything else to build the local referral team you must have before you can list and sell in high volume.

THE BEST-LOOKING HOMES

Usually have the best-informed owners. The pride and commitment they've lavished on their home often extends to concern for their entire neighborhood. They can say to you, "Those people down the street who haven't cut their lawn in six months, there's big trouble behind that door." Don't carry gossip, but do keep your ears open for clues to the future and to how you should deal with people. Knowing that an unfriendly woman has marital and financial problems makes it easier to cope with and overlook her initial surliness. Persevere. A series of short, friendly contacts can gain her trust. You'll then be in position to help and advise if the difficulties require the sale of her house.

Be especially attentive to the people who keep the best homes in the neighborhood, even though they seem to be the least likely to move. You have a common interest: the well-being of their neighborhood. Be kind to your best-kept homeowners: thank them for their help, and reward them with appropriate invitations and small gifts.

EXCEPTIONAL PROPERTIES

Pay special attention to all real estate parcels that don't conform to the pattern of your farm. If it's comprised mostly of well-kept single-family residences, investigate any home you notice that isn't well kept. If the tax bills are being sent elsewhere (the assessor's office can tell you), an absentee owner probably has rented the house. The renter may feel that, because the owner is some distance away, he can let the property run down.

Take an instant photo that shows the property's condition, and send it with a nice letter to the owner. Say nothing about the property's condition; simply tell him you specialize in the area and are available and well qualified to help with real estate matters. Don't write, "I can solve your *problem*," and perhaps stir one up for yourself: the occupants might be pet relatives to one owner and no-good in-laws to the other.

If the property qualifies for this treatment, you'll be able to make some photos from the sidewalk that'll make your point, effectively but subtly. This can bring you a client and get a neighborhood blight cleaned up.

If there are vacant lots in your farm, become an expert on their offering price, terms, and the requirements for building a house there.

Any vacant lot not offered for sale in a built-up area might have formidable title problems, or it might just be lying there waiting for an aggressive agent to work at getting it listed and sold. It's to your advantage to breathe new life into the neighborhood by getting those lots built on. And, to qualify as an expert on your farm, you must know the current status of every property on it.

If there are a few retail business properties within your farm, or on the fringes of it, get to know the managers. If you use their services, consider trading with them. Hairstylists and barbers make great bird dogs.

WINNING SCRIPTS

- "May I ask your permission to give you a complementary scratch pad?"
- Former client: "Are you busy right now?"
  Active agent: "Things are hopping, Jeannie, but I'm certainly never too busy to talk with you. What's up?"

- Spreading the word in your farm about your new listing: "Your neighbors chose me to sell their home. Wouldn't you like to choose your *new* neighbors? Do you know of anyone who's looking in this area for a home?"

- Never linger when farming. "I'd love to stay, but I have another appointment."

- "I know that I could market your home for you. Is there a chance you'd consider me?"

Getting-to-know-me stage, long form.   (Use this approach when they seem friendly. Have a giveaway in your hand.)

"Good morning, I'm Danny Kennedy with Sell Fast Realty, and I'd like to take this opportunity to tell you that I know your street, your neighborhood, and your town on a professional real estate level. That is, I'm an expert on the property here. I'm not bragging, but I have earned the right to say that by hard work. So I hope you'll call on me for all your real estate and community information wants and needs. May I have your permission to leave this scratch pad with you?

"Thanks so much for talking with me."

During this crucial *getting-to-know-me* stage, it's important to take a matter-of-fact attitude about your right to be at their door. After all, you are the specialist in that area, so you *must* keep up with the happenings and trends there.

One way is to take a survey on your second or later visit. Make out a form listing your survey questions and have enough copies run off so that you can use one for each property in your entire farm. Your questions could cover such things as

- How many bedrooms do you have?
- How many members are there in your family?
- How long have you lived here?
- Is this the original building, or have you added some rooms?

If you ask these questions after you've developed rapport, and after you've explained that you're updating your records for the area you specialize in, you'll find that most people will be happy to talk to you.

More know-me scripts.   "Hi, I'm Danny Kennedy with Sell Fast Realty. The lady down the street said someone in the area might be relocating. Do you happen to know who that is?"

Isn't there always a lady down the street who's telling you something?

If they say they don't know, smile and ask, "Would you folks be thinking of relocating in the next three months?"

You're looking for the few who'll say *yes* or *maybe* to that question, of course, so be prepared for that answer. Inquire pleasantly for more details about their plans. Work gradually into the real estate decisions they'll need to make.

Volunteer to get them some specific bit of information that your discussion reveals they don't have about their possible move. And schedule yourself to keep in close touch with them.

If they say no to your question about moving in the next 90 days, tell them, "As you know, real estate needs can come up unexpectedly. Here's my card. If you have any questions in the future, please give me a call."

Let them say something and, if it goes well, add this: "I'll be stopping by from time to time to see how you're doing and give you up-to-the-minute market information. Would that be all right?"

Break off courteously with the few people who answer that question negatively, and make a note of them. You're not done that day until you send a handwritten note to all the people who said they didn't want market updates. Your note should run along these lines.

> I hope I didn't offend you by stopping in today. I am a full-time real estate professional who specializes in your area, so many of your neighbors like me to keep them updated monthly on real estate developments that affect your neighborhood. From now on I'll be contacting you by mail only, but feel free to call me at anytime—no obligation, of course. Thanks for talking to me.
>
> Cordially,

Another opener to use when you're out door-knocking:

"Hi. I'm Danny Kennedy of Sell Fast Realty. Here's my newsletter with up-to-the-minute information that affects property owners in this area—which is my area of specialization."

Know-me stage, short form.   "I hope I haven't interrupted you. I'm the real estate representative from Sell Fast Realty for this area, Danny Kennedy. Please accept this scratch pad with no obligation. And please remember that I'm an expert on the property here. Call on me if you have any questions about this area. Thanks for listening."

Getting-to-like-me stage, long form.   "Hello. It's nice to see you again. How's the scratch pad supply? My shipment of litter bags just came in, so I thought I'd drop one off for you. Have you heard about _____ Industries? They're moving into town, so lots of their people will need homes here. We're really excited about this at Sell Fast Realty because this development is going to have a beautiful impact on your property's value. I'm looking for homeowners who may want to sell soon. I hope you'll keep your ears open for me, and pass on anything you might hear about people who are leaving this area. Have a good weekend, and thanks for talking to me."

Note that you didn't ask for the listing directly, so they don't feel threatened.

But you did drop the hint. It depends on the tempo of the person behind the door whether you use the long or short form. Use the short form if they fidget.

Like-me stage, short form.   "Hi, Mr. Oasis, I'll just take a minute. At my office we're excited about the new company that's moving into town. If you hear about anyone who might be moving out, please let me know because we've got buyers who want to move in. I hope you'll remember me, I'm _____ with _____, and let me leave this scratch pad with you."

Getting-to-love-me stage, long form.   "Hi, Jack. Things are really popping. Did you notice my sold sign across the street? Well, we marketed that home in just 48 days. And guess what? The buyers are collectors too. I think you'll enjoy them. . . . Say, Jack, I'm really running out of homes. This is such a darn nice area that I can never find enough houses around here for sale. I need help. Do you know of anyone who might get transferred or want to sell soon? . . . Thanks for everything."

Love-me stage, short form.   "Hi, Sue. I don't know if you've noticed, but I've been busy around here listing and selling property. Do you happen to know anyone who may want to relocate? . . . Can I tell them that you mentioned their name to me? . . . Thanks for everything."

WINNING SCRIPTS FOR EVERY MONTH

Winning scripts for every month of the year are given in the next chapter.

7

DANNY KENNEDY'S FULL-YEAR FARMING ALMANAC

Blitz Your Farm • Farm by Plan • I've Seen You Around • Operating in a Vacuum • Plan and Review • Two Points • Rating Scale • January Through December: Giveaways, Scratch Pad Messages, Newsletter Lead Stories, Bottom Lines, Farming Technique and Super-Promotions, Winning Scripts for Every Month

BLITZ YOUR FARM

Start with inexpensive giveaways and a consistent newsletter. Then, as the fees come in, invest part of them in your drive for control of your farm. The ideas are here; you can move as fast as you wish. What income would you have earned if you had listed half the houses that sold in your farm last year? Figure that out, and then decide if you can afford *not* to dominate your farm by investing 15 percent of your farm income in promotion there.

FARM BY PLAN

Set up a 12-month almanac for your farm. Have a giveaway planned for every month. Do it on your own; you don't need your company to do it for you. If they're providing farming tools, fine. Use their materials. If not, take the initiative and do these necessary things for yourself. It's your farm, your career. Take charge of them.

People who don't remember you won't call you. They don't even know you're there. A long step in the right direction is to have your scratch pads sitting beside their phones, with your photo, name, and phone number staring up at them. But not much will happen until they connect a warm body with that cold printed photo. When an occasional glance at the scratch pad recalls a person they've talked face-to-face with, the feeling of familiarity that's essential to success in farming begins to develop.

I'VE SEEN YOU AROUND

Put the common reactions to work for you. We all tend to trust the familiar and distrust the unfamiliar. People often say, "I've seen you around," as though having seen someone before automatically makes that person more honest, capable, and likable. The strange part is that having seen someone around before actually does make that person seem more honest, capable, and likable—assuming nothing untoward happened on the previous sightings. "I've seen you around, so you must live and work near here. We probably know some of the same people. You're not a fly-by-night. We have to cope with the same weather, traffic, and school problems. Maybe our kids know each other. You're going to be around tomorrow. We've at least got this much in common: we've both chosen the same part of the earth to live on. I know where I can get back to you." No one consciously goes through all this each time they recognize someone at their door.

But the feeling of familiarity goes through them. "You're part of the community. To some degree I can trust you. I'll have to treat you with a touch more courtesy and respect than I would a total stranger."

That's the first step: to get them to recognize that they've seen you before. On that foundation you can build trust and confidence.

Isn't this the essence of farming?—to impress your image on their minds so that when they think of selling, they'll also think of you? People who don't remember you won't call you.

It goes beyond that: People who don't remember that you are the real estate expert in *their* area won't call you when they decide on a move. This is why the verbal techniques on the following pages call for you to constantly repeat "I am the local real estate expert who is ready to help with any real estate question at any time."

OPERATING IN A VACUUM

Giveaways you personally hand to homeowners have enormously greater impact than those hung on doorknobs. One day I noticed an unprofessional-looking man distributing frisbees for a competitor on my farm. They were beautiful frisbees. Imprinted on them was my competitor's picture, her name, phone number, office, slogan—the works. In two colors yet! And Mr. Unprofessional was doing a good, fast job of setting them on doorsteps. He had been properly instructed to bypass the houses that had other agents' for sale signs on them—no problem there. While I stood at a front door, waiting for someone to answer my knock, I watched the man hustle back and forth across the street, hitting house after house for my competitor. Her system was so easy: All she had to do was pick an item out of a catalog, place an order for shipment to a delivery service, and write a couple of checks. No pounding the hot pavement, no risking rejection, no getting all rumpled and tired. Just order the work done; let the phone ring; pick it up; and make those listing appointments.

Trudging to the next house, I debated whether to quit for the day rather than confuse people by being at their door when they spotted their frisbee. Then two things happened. Mr. Unprofessional hurried around a corner, and a pack of grade-school-age boys appeared. The boys were racing each other to see who could gather the biggest stack. I kept on farming and never saw another of those frisbees; the boys had swept my farm clean of them.

Don't try to operate in a vacuum. The real world you have to function in is quirky, full of surprises, and it hands out very few free lunches.

Let's call the gal who put her faith in frisbees Edna Goeasy. Edna never figured out the real reason why her frisbee promotion vanished without a trace because she was on vacation the week they were distributed. To this day, Edna is convinced the delivery service dumped her expensive giveaways in the trash instead of handing them out as instructed. But she wasn't there to make sure. The supervisor swore he had spot-checked the distribution, and Edna had to pay his bill. She paid for a lesson but didn't learn it.

An effective farm program builds your image as the area expert who is *the* person to deal with, should a real estate need arise. It also keeps you in close touch with the people so you'll often know who's thinking about moving early enough to zero in on them before they make a decision. If your farming program bumps along, and gets done only when you're in the mood, the chances are you're not building toward control of your farm.

PLAN AND REVIEW

Plan your farm program a year in advance. It's not necessary to order everything, or to develop every detail right now, but the general outline should be tentatively set now. Find out now what lead time is required for the giveaways you'll need later. Schedule the dates now when you must place your orders to be sure of timely delivery. Working well ahead of need is simply a habit; playing constant catch-up is also a habit, an expensive and time consuming one.

Planning a year's farming activity is easy. If you have an important annual event in your *community*, or an important annual promotion in your *company*, start with that month. Then work forward to the current month, and back through the full year. Label a folder, "Farming—Next 12 Months," and collect there all your ideas, schedules, and brochures on giveaways and promotions.

In your appointment book, write in a reminder for the same day of each month to review your next 12 months' farming plans, to order anything that needs ordering, and to evaluate how well your current month's promotion is going. Should it be repeated next year? Now is the time to decide that (tentatively, of course).

The practice of considering the entire year's farm program only once a year is a bad one: It's influenced too much by the state of the market at that moment, and how well or poorly the last promotion went. Planning your farm operation is far too important to give it only an annual review.

Your first tentative plan should be simple. List the next 12 months on the left side of a sheet of paper. Then jot down next to them possible farming activities for each of those months. The list that follows in this chapter will give you many ideas. If your company runs a cooperative promotion during one or more of those months, jot that down, and then consider what the most appropriate tie-in with that promotion is for the month before. Should you remind your people of the coming event by means of a lead story in your monthly newsletter?

This plan-a-full-year-and-review-it-monthly approach will bring many things into sharp focus, including some unrealistic expectations and misleading ideas. Remember that it takes repetition to achieve results. Don't expect too much too soon: Farming requires preparation, planting, and nurturing before a big harvest can be reaped.

Dare to be different, people say. That's easy. Just follow a sound plan long enough for it to work for you. That's being different; almost everyone else will quit after one or two quick passes through their farm.

TWO POINTS

When selecting items and activities, keep these two considerations firmly in mind.

   1 Farming activity must reflect **favorably** on you.
   2 Farming activity must reflect favorably on **you**.

Let's take these two different ideas up separately.

   1 Farming activity must reflect **favorably** on you. There's nothing worse than getting a hate letter written in crayon. I guarantee it'll ruin your whole day. If you sponsor a free show or have a drawing for the kids, be very careful to think everything through. Talk to people about your ideas. Imagine the scene you'll stage so you can organize to keep everything going smoothly. Talk to a few of the kids. Get their ideas. Make sure you don't carelessly leave some children out.

If the kids in the farm don't like you, you've had it with the parents. You want the kids to scream and the dogs to bark (with joy) when you come around. "Oh, she's here again; I like her. When Dad gets transferred and we have to sell our house, Mom, she's going to sell it for us, isn't she?"

The whole family should like you. Pay attention to all of them, and work carefully to avoid getting any of them mad at you. Hollywood says there's no such thing as bad publicity but, true as that may be at the box office, it's not true where the listings are signed. Here's something worse than getting a hate letter written in crayon: realizing that you spent money making the kid write it. You can be just as upset—and financially hurt—if you spend money giving out a gimmick you think is funny or different if part of your homeowners consider that item offensive. A wide spectrum of imaginative ideas stand between the dull and the dangerous. You can build your reputation as a strong real estate agent without risking backlash. Make your selections thoughtfully.

2 Farming activity must reflect favorably on **you**. It's absolutely no good at all to put on a whizbang promotion that people don't identify you with. The husband comes home and says, "That's neat, honey. Where'd we get it?" The wife answers, "Oh, somebody hung it on the door. You know, it's one of those giveaway things." Cost, considerable; results, zilch.

Once you have control of your farm, you'll be so strong that your name may come up whether you give the item out or not. Reaching that pinnacle requires frequent contact, and some noticeable promotions spread through the year that have strong identification with you. When you have control, you stand in the back of a truck handing out pumpkins to kids you're calling by name. The first year, you'd better figure out a way to hang your name, photo, and phone number on the pumpkin, and you'd better hike up to the door and hand it to each homeowner. But it's all lost if you only come through your farm three or four times between each October's pumpkin hand-out time.

RATING SCALE

A rating scale is helpful in choosing among the various possibilities. Never buy any giveaway that doesn't score at least 50 points out of a possible 100. Here are the value weightings.

Cost	25 points
Uniqueness	20 points
Identification	55 points

Allow identification points for each of the following that you can have imprinted on the giveaway itself (if the imprinting of your identification goes on packaging that will be discarded, allow only half value).

Your photo	20 points
Your name and phone	20 points
Your company's name and location	10 points
Your slogan	5 points

This scoring system is heavily weighted against mass giveaway items that can't be imprinted with your advertising message. It favors imprinted scratch pads and newsletters, the two most cost-effective promotions I know of. I made a lot of money because I established and maintained identity. Nothing I know of does that as cheaply and reliably as imprinted scratch pads and newsletters backing up an active door-knocking program. However, I believe that it would be a mistake in most farms to limit giveaways to those two items. Think of them as the foundation of your farm program.

Now let's look at a wider variety of ideas to fill out your 12-month farming program. Additional tips on these promotions are given in Chapter 13.

JANUARY

- *Giveaways.*   A calendar of local and regional sports and cultural events that you've compiled
  Imprinted scratch pads
  Cookie cutter: house, snowman, dog

- *Winning scripts.*   "Hi, Mrs. _____. I'm Liz Fuller with Shannon & Luchs Realty. Here's a little something to start the new year off. I hope you'll—" (tell about the unique set of cookie cutters you're going to give them through the year, if that's your plan) "—enjoy it. And I hope you'll remember me if you have any questions or needs in real estate."

- *Scratch pad message.*   "Every month (every other month, every third month) this year I'm planning to run by with a different cookie cutter. Just my way of saying thanks for thinking of me when you think of real estate—Liz."

- *Newsletter lead story.*   "Exclusive Information: All Last Year's Sales Prices in This Neighborhood."

Give the average prices broken down for

2-bedroom homes	$_____	average
3-bedroom homes	$_____	average

and so on. Give the range from high to low also.

- *Newsletter bottom lines.*
  "Knowledge is of two kinds. We know a subject ourselves, or we know where we can find information upon it."

  —Samuel Johnson

  "If real estate is the subject, you know where to find information: Call me."

- *SUPER-promotion.* Stage an Ice-Skating Night. Provide the firewood and hot refreshments if outdoors, the admission if indoors.

- *Farming technique.* A common mistake is to regard newsletters as being freely interchangeable with giveaways. "This month I'll just hand them a newsletter," is a thought that's stalled many a promising farming program. Newsletters are powerful when used in support of a strong face-to-face door-knocking and giveaway program; used alone they will fall flat. Chapter 13 tells how to get out a newsletter every month that'll contribute mightily to your rapid takeover of your farm, and shows how you do it with little trouble and at low cost. Just don't expect the printed page to door-knock for you, open the doors, and make the impressions that giveaways will. But the newsletter is a broad canvas; paint the picture of your professionalism on it. Giveaways are the free program and newsletters are the commercials; so don't leave the commercials out of the program.

FEBRUARY

- *Giveaways.* Tax preparation booklet
  Heart potholder
  Cookie cutter: heart, diamond or square, half-moon

- *Winning scripts.* "Hello there, I'm Betty Jones with Coldwell Banker Realty. Happy Valentine's Day. Here's a little remembrance; I keep current with our local resale housing market, so call me if you have any questions."

- *Scratch pad message.*   "Hope your Valentine's Day will be a sweet one in every way—your local real estate expert—Betty."

- *Newsletter lead story.* "Here's what we can expect the local resale housing market to do this year."

- *Newsletter bottom lines.*
  "A house is made of walls and beams; a home is built with love and dreams."

  —William Arthur Ward

  "What is more agreeable than one's home?"

  —Cicero

- *SUPER-promotion.* Throw a dance party for your farm. Take over a local disco or rent a hall.

- *Farming technique.* Only a few hours each week are really effective times for farming. You'll want to make the most of those vital hours: You'll want to concentrate on people, not fumble with farming materials. Several days before you're planning to farm, take a moment to practice how you'll handle your handouts from door to door. Remember that you'll want to make notes about the people you talk to as you go. If your materials will be awkward to handle loose, drop them in light plastic bags. Fold the end of the bags around rubber bands, and staple them closed. Then all you have to do is carry a few of the filled plastic bags and hand one to each homeowner as you plant your verbal seeds with that person. No fuss. You're free to talk, listen, learn, and make notes.

The rubber band allows you to hang the bag on the doorknobs of no-answers. That's who the scratch pad messages are for, the no-answers.

- *Good idea.*   Handcopy the current scratch pad message on 50 or more pads ahead of time, and use them only on no-answers.

- *Better idea.*   Write the message on two sheets of your pad, paste them down side by side, and run off 150 copies on regular sized copy paper. When you cut these sheets in half, you'll have 300 messages—enough for your whole farm. (I recommend scratch pads that are half the size of a regular typewriter sheet.) Chuck one of these messages in every one of your plastic bags, along with your giveaway, imprinted scratch pad, and newsletter. Then you give the same thing to homeowners who answer as you hang on the knobs of no-answers. Keep it simple.

MARCH

- *Giveaways.*   Kites for the kids
  Fuzzy green shamrock for lapel (Below your imprint on the
      package, put this slogan: "Wear a little green on us.")
  Imprinted shoe horn
  Cookie cutter: shamrock, egg, cat

- *Winning scripts.*   "I'm Sue Chalmers of ERA Real Estate, your local real estate expert. I hope the kiddies, and even Mom and Dad, enjoy flying our special family kite. Have a good month and thanks for talking to me."

- *Scratch pad message.*   "Hope you have the luck of the Irish this month. Please keep this pad handy for writing reminders, and please remember your local real estate expert—Sue."

- *Newsletter lead story.*   "What every homeowner should know before selling his home."
  Give tips on setting the stage.

- *Newsletter bottom lines.*
"A verbal contract isn't worth the paper it's written on."

—Sam Goldwyn

"What the world needs most today is happy homes. Not rich homes. Not frustrated homes. Not empty homes."

—Elsie Landon Buck

- *SUPER-promotion.*   Take over a local bowling alley for a few hours and invite the farm to a night of bowling on you. Give out trophies for high score, low score, most balls in the alley.

- *Farming technique.*   The purpose of super-promotions is to make a heavy *personal* impact on your farm, so the more personal you make the super-promotions, the greater the success you'll have with them. Never leave your invitation on the door knob: Tell the people about it face-to-face. Few people will have the flexibility of time and interest to attend all your events. That's why you do something different every time.

APRIL

- *Giveways.*   Rain hats (These were super successful for me.)
Car litter bag with spring motif
Forget-me-not flower seeds (or any seeds) for Mom
Cookie cutter: umbrella, boat or banana, arrow

- *Winning scripts.*   "Good morning. I'm Kathy Dibrell of Century 21. I wanted to stop by with this rain hat—maybe it'll come in handy to keep you dry. Have a great month, and thanks for talking to me. Don't forget—I'm here to serve all your real estate needs."

- *Scratch pad message.*   "Isn't spring great? Hope you get to enjoy the fresh outdoors when the sun is out. Real estate sales are soaring this spring. Remember me, your local area expert   Kathy."

- *Newsletter lead story.*   "Thinking of selling? There's no better time of year than summer."

- *Newsletter bottom lines.*
"April prepares her green traffic light and the world thinks Go."

—Christopher Morley

- *Farming technique.*   Complete your property catalog (see previous chapter) this month by asking questions as you work your way through the farm. Explain that you're compiling the catalog to better serve the community.

- *SUPER-promotion.*   Stage an Easter Egg Hunt at the local park or country club.

MAY

- *Giveaways.*   Mother's Day marigold plants
  Pencils imprinted with your name, phone, and slogan
  Cookie cutter: Mom (figure with skirt), hand, triangle

- *Winning scripts.*   "Hi. I'm Helen Early of RE/MAX. Here's a little remembrance for the holiday. . . . Thanks for talking to me, and if you have any questions about real estate, remember that I'm your local expert."

- *Scratch pad message.*   "Happy Mother's Day—and think of me if you need any real estate service—Helen."

- *Newsletter lead story.*   Write a profile of a good neighbor, a feature story about someone who lives in your farm and has contributed outstanding service to the community.

- *Newsletter bottom lines.*
  "A smile increases your face value."

  —Old Mohican Adage

  "May, with alle they floures and thy grene,
  Welcome be thou, faire, fresshe May."

  —Chaucer

- *Farming technique.*   Hand out plants or seeds the Friday or Saturday before Mother's Day. I advise against farming on that day.

- *SUPER-promotion.*   Treat your farm to a night of baseball. Rent a bus and take over a section of the ballpark.

JUNE

- *Giveaways.*   Barbecue apron for Dad
  Father's Day soft drink or beer holders
  Cookie cutter: Dad figure, auto, hexagon

- *Winning scripts.*   "Hi there, Mrs. _____. I'm Jim Andrews with Partners Realty. Here's a special holder for Dad for Father's Day. Enjoy it, and have a Happy Father's Day, and I hope you'll remember me any time you're thinking about real estate."

- *Scratch pad message.*   "Here's a special holder for Dad for Father's Day. If you need more room this summer, give me a ring and let's talk about it. Your old real estate buddy, Jim."

- *Newsletter lead story.*   "Our local athletes." (Be sure to mention *every* student in your farm who goes out for sports.)

- *Newsletter bottom lines.*
  "However small it is on the surface, it's four thousand miles deep, and that is a very handsome property."

  —C.D. Warner

- *Farming technique.* Hand out can holders or whatever the Friday and Saturday before Father's Day. I advise against farming on Father's Day.
- *SUPER-promotion.* Get the kids started off right on summer vacation by sending a free ice-cream truck around. Be sure you're standing there on the running board.

JULY

- *Giveaways.* Safety tips booklet
  Car game for kids
  Imprinted back scratcher
  Cookie cutter: flag, sunburst, star
- *Winning scripts.* ''Hi, Mrs. _____. I'm Karen Shepherd with Gallery of Homes. I specialize in this area, so if there's any real estate information you'd like, I hope you'll think of me. Here's a ____ and thanks for chatting with me.''
- *Scratch pad message.* ''Important enclosure—a safety tips booklet to hang in the kitchen. Enjoy the summer and call me for help on real estate problems—Karen.''
- *Newsletter lead story.* ''Homes are selling faster (slower) this year than last. Why?

    ''I'm an expert on real estate throughout Greenpretty Valley, but I specialize in the fine homes on Apple, Berry, Crab and Dukedom streets. In that area 32 homes were sold during the first half of last year, and 18 during the first half of this year. That's a startling increase (decrease) of _____. Why did it happen, and where is this selling surge (drop) going to take us?''
- *Newsletter bottom lines.*
  ''The house of everyone is to him as his castle and fortress, as well for his defense as for his repose.''

  —Sir Edward Coke, 1619
- *SUPER-promotion.* Watermelon feast for the kids. Stage it at a local park. (Get advance permission.) Give invitations out one week before the event that specify when the watermelon truck will get there. Be sure to emphasize that it's a ''First-come, first-served affair. Come late and you'll be sorry.'' Line up lots of mothers to help control the kids. Have plenty of plastic trash bags, napkins, plastic forks, etc. Think through the clean-up and disposal problem. Some trash disposal companies will deliver a small bin to a site and remove it the next day for a nominal charge. Events like this can be terrific if thoroughly planned and carefully executed. Arrange for someone in your office to cover for you that morning as though you were on vacation. You can't work with a last-minute buyer then, no matter what. Schedule this for mid-morning, not afternoon. Kids get impatient. And have a little something extra to give each

of them when it's over, so you can send them home happy. Balloons with your imprint on them are great for this.

- *Farming technique.* Wear your name, not your nametag. A T-shirt with your first name or nickname blazoned on it is a terrific farming tool. People will call you by name as you hand them a giveaway—and they'll be far more likely to remember you.

AUGUST

- *Giveaways.*   Coloring books for kids
                  Car games for kids
                  Cookie cutter: girl child, boy child, circle
- *Winning scripts.* "Hi. I'm Jeanne Cushing of Red Carpet Realty. If you'd like more detailed information about any aspect of real estate, please call me."
- *Scratch pad message.* "Here's something to keep the youngsters busy in the car. Have a nice summer—Jeanne."
- *Newsletter lead story.* "Ideas for inexpensive travel." Go to a local travel agency and offer them free publicity in return for some tips. You might acquire a good bird dog or two in this way.
- *Farming technique.* This is another good month to emphasize kids. Many mothers find summers especially difficult. You can win their gratitude by providing some diversion for the "There's nothing to do around here" element at their house.
- *SUPER-promotion.* Get together with some other agents, take over a local cinema for a morning, and put on a free movie for the children in all your farms. You'll be surprised how small the shared cost will be. Arrangements should be started at least six months in advance. Print invitations. Use them as a farm handout.

SEPTEMBER

- *Giveaways.*   Fall events calendar
                  Fall car litter bag
                  Cookie cutter: apple, mushroom, horse
- *Winning scripts.* "Hi, Mrs. _____. I'm Janis Van Dorn of McMillin & Co. Were Stevie and Susan glad to get back in school?" (Add a real estate reminder.) "Enjoy the fall season, and thanks for being so nice when I drop by."

- *Scratch pad message.* "With all the things to remember in September, I thought an extra pad would be handy. Your local real estate expert, Janis."

- *Newsletter lead story.* "Back to School Tips for Our Neighborhood."

   Call or visit your local store managers and list their specials and back-to-school sales. Ask what's selling best this year, and put that in. Then write your second story around the local housing market's performance over the summer just ended, and conclude with a prediction about what will happen to housing during the balance of the year.

- *Newsletter bottom lines.*

   "Eden is that old-fashioned House we dwell in every day without suspecting our abode until we drive away."

   —Emily Dickinson

- *SUPER-promotion.* Stage a moonlight hayride for the romantics in your farm. Your local riding stable may be able to handle this for you, or you may need to bus your people out into the country.

- *Farming technique.* Avoid farming the last few days before school starts. You'll find the mothers will be much more relaxed and talkative the day after school begins.

OCTOBER

- *Giveaways.* Trick-or-treat bags
   Stick-on decal that punches out and can be ironed on a T-shirt
   Halloween candy
   Cookie cutter: pumpkin, teepee, face (profile)

- *Winning scripts.* "Hi, don't be scared—it's really me, Meredith Osborn with Merrill Lynch Realty. I hope this _____ will make Halloween a bit more fun. I never did crazy things like this before I became a real estate expert . . . but it's a lot of fun."

- *Scratch pad message.* "Happy goblins! Call me if you have any questions for your local real estate expert—Meredith."

- *Newsletter lead story.* "Turkey drawing next month at the Gordon's house."

- *Newsletter bottom lines.*

   "I wouldn't join any club that would have me for a member."

   —Groucho Marx

- *Farming technique.* Wear a funny nose, witch's hat, or half-mask as you pass out the trick-or-treat bags or pumpkins.

- *SUPER-promotion.* Hire a truck and pass out pumpkins a few days before Halloween.

NOVEMBER

- *Giveaways.* Local and neighborhood directory (Compile this yourself. Include all the babysitters and yard-chore boys you can find in your farm, plus any other neighborhood services. Include emergency phone numbers, a list of nearby doctors and dentists, shoe and TV repairmen, and so on. Keep your imprint small, but readable.)
  Imprinted ball point pens
  Cookie cutter: turkey, cornucopia, cow

- *Winning scripts.* Talk about your lumineria promotion next month. Introduce yourself and remind them that you're the local real estate expert.

- *Scratch pad message.* "Happy Thanksgiving to you and yours. When I count my blessings I think of the people I represent in this neighborhood—Linda Malloy with Weichert Co.

- *Newsletter lead story.* "Join with your neighbors to create a special wonder this year at Christmas time. It's free and it's fun.

  "A local Realtor® (me, of course—I'm the local real estate expert who really cares about this neighborhood) is donating the materials for lumineria. Every homeowner who wants to join in producing this charming effect during Christmas week will be provided with three of these simple lamps. In old Mexico, villages glow at Christmas with a special soft loveliness that only lumineria can call into being. Let's do it here! It's free, it's lots of fun, and it takes less than five minutes each night to set them out. I'd love to tell you about it. Just give me a call any time, or I'll see you next month.

  "I hope you'll be heralding Christmas week this year in this gentle, heartwarming way."

- *Newsletter bottom lines.*
  "My house, my house, though thou art small, thou art to me the Escorial."
  —George Herbert, 1651

- *SUPER-promotion.* Give away a free Thanksgiving turkey.

- *Farming technique.* Hold your drawing at someone's house in the farm. This requires you to develop a friend there who'll stage this event for you. Women agents can have their friend put on a 10 A.M. coffee klatsch with prizes for the best cookies made with your cutters. (Appoint a committee to do the judging—don't make the decision yourself.) Also have several door prizes building up to the turkey drawing. Stick around for the clean-up, and give your hostess a nice gift. Men agents can have their wives handle this, and simply be present at the drawing, or schedule the event for the weekend when their hostess's husband is home.

DECEMBER

- *Giveaways.*   Holly trees
  A unique Christmas tree decoration that you order in quantity
  Cookie cutter: tree, Santa, bell

- *Winning scripts.*   "Hi, Mr. and Mrs. _____. Merry Christmas. I'm Danny Kennedy with Better Homes & Gardens. I hope you'll plant this holly tree and think of me as it grows. It reminds me of the way your property has grown in value. Have a wonderful season. Thanks for talking to me.''

- *Scratch pad message.*   "You're probably out Christmas shopping but I wanted to stop by and leave my holiday greetings. I'm hoping that you'll enjoy using this cookie cutter. Thanks for all your courtesy toward me this year—Danny.''

- *Newsletter lead story.*   You may prefer to send a hand-addressed "Am I lucky" letter like the one in Chapter 6 instead of your usual newsletter. Or you can summarize the year's events in finance and real estate as your lead story.

- *Newsletter bottom lines.*

  > *"And I am praying God on high,*
  > *And I am praying*
  > *Him night and day,*
  > *For a little house—a house of my own—*
  > *Out of the wind's and the rain's way."*
  > *—Padraic Colum*

- *Christmas cards.*   Yours will get lost in the deluge that descends on every home every year, except where you know the people quite well. Omit sending them to most of the people in your farm. You can save this money and time, and no one will know the difference.

- *SUPER-promotion.*   Light up your entire farm with lumineria.
  For about the cost of nice Christmas cards, you can create a very striking effect in your farm during the week prior to Christmas. Expect to spend some extra time encouraging the project along. The plus is that you'll be working with your farm people to enhance the quality of their lives, and you'll find that lumineria reflect well on you and your career. Be sure to call your local paper and tell them about it when your streets are glowing softly.
  The materials are simple: small candles, sand, and small white paper bags. The homeowners put the bags on their curb in the evening with the sand inside to hold both the bag and the lighted candle upright. Get sand by the

sack at your local building supply, arrange to buy bags and candles wholesale, and save lots of money. You'll find suppliers in the yellow pages.

- *Farming technique.*   Talk this project up in the daytime, and get people's permission to bring the lumineria at dusk so they can be lighted and put out on curbs immediately. Once you get this project started, it will grow on its own. Acquire the materials well in advance, and start actively promoting the idea early in December. Placing rows of lumineria at a few key locations, where people driving in and out can see them, will give the idea a big boost.

    Obviously this should not be done in fire-risk areas. Consult your local fire department first.

8

PROSPECTING

DEALING WITH THE FEARS

My finger pushes into the door chimes button. It's like pushing a fire alarm when you're ten years old—there's no fire and you're worried that you can't run away fast enough. Only now I can't run. So I just stand here, my adrenaline-charged blood pounding.

What can I say? "I'm Sally Tompkins, and if you wanna move fast, I'll be glad to help you?" That's terrible. She'll step on my corns. What makes me different from the two dozen other guys who've rung this doorbell before? Oh rats, I woke up her baby. Now I can hear her coming. She even walks like she's mad. I never realized before that footsteps could sound mad.

What do *you* want?''

"Can I use your phone? I'm so scared I need to call my shrink.''

Wouldn't that throw her? Somehow I have to throw her off the defensive; somehow I have to break through what separates her *she* from my *me*; somehow I have to get her shoes off so I can put them on.

Yes, I know about the fears of prospecting. I remember them well. In 1972, when I started in the business, the entire Board of Realtors® met in one spot for the weekly caravan. We'd all follow each other around and visit maybe 15 houses.

I was pregnant again—very much so—when I went on my first caravan. As I got in the car with two veterans of the business, these ladies gave me the evil eye. One of them said, "Just go home and have your baby." She laughed at me. "You don't have that much to lose in the next three months. Do you really think you have to do this?"

I felt terrible. I did go home. I cried and said, "I quit." Then, somehow, I pulled myself together and got back in there. No matter what that lady said, or anyone else thought, I knew I had plenty to lose by giving up three months: all the contacts I could make, all the knowledge and experience I could acquire, and all the much-needed fees I hoped to earn. I didn't need that lady's disapproval; I already had four beautiful reasons not to start work, and another on the way. But every today gives us reasons to put off paying the price of success, and every tomorrow brings more reasons for waiting—if we're looking for them. Instead of doing that, let's look for reasons why we *can* start, and start *now*, to pay the price of success.

There are lots of rationalizations for not prospecting.

"It's already been overdone."

"It doesn't have to be done."

"It isn't worth doing."

Prospecting is a proven method. It works. The only things that stop us are our fears. Yes, I've been stopped. I've gone home, beaten in heart and soul. I've tossed and turned through the night, and healed my wounds with tears. Then, after the healing, I went back to knocking on strange doors and phoning people I'd never met. I used every crutch I could find to boost my spirits—as long as those crutches didn't take up too much time, or stop me from working. The first 18 months of my real estate career, all my business came from prospecting and for-sale-by-owners. That's how it all started.

Prospecting is part of the dues in this business, part of the price you pay for success. Do it right, do it heavy, do it fast, and there'll come a time when you won't have time for it anymore. Long before that time comes, you will have banked lots of success.

Looking back, I know I was lucky. Circumstances forced me to go out and find business. At the time, I didn't feel so lucky that I had no floor time. I had to be my own one-woman advertising agency. The most logical place for me to start was on door-to-door canvassing. The very first time I went door-knocking, it rained. My first thought was, "I've got brains enough to come in out of the rain. I'll forget about door-knocking, put a log in the fireplace at home, and read a good book about selling real estate."

Fortunately, I had some freebie rain hats, and I realized there couldn't be a better time to give them out. So off I went to canvass in the wet, a raincoat wrapped around by big stomach.

I told the wives who answered my knock, "If you want to go out today, you might want to use this rain hat I brought you. Compliments of Danny Kennedy." It made an impression. There I was, dripping, a look of total honesty on my face, all eagerness to begin my new career. Several of the women asked me in for a cup of hot tea. Then they'd show me their new wallpaper and, pretty soon, they'd be saying, "Let me think. Do I know anyone around here who wants to sell? My neighbor next door may get a transfer." I would ask for the neighbor's name, and if I could mention to that neighbor how I found out they might move. It always seemed to help if I could say, "Marge sent me." I think people subconsciously approved of me because so-and-so approved of me. So much business came out of those rainy days that I was sorry to see our dry summer come. By the end of that first summer, I'd covered about seven hundred homes.

I really got to know the people. I wrote letters to them every month. In these letters I would give little tips about their property. If invited out to give an evaluation, I always put a handwritten thank-you note in the mail the next day. I felt more comfortable with personal stationery than company letterhead, so that's what I used. It worked.

I was trying to get across that I *cared*, and that, if they listed with me, they'd get something different. I didn't want to be the ordinary real estate agent. I wanted to be the person they could depend on. The person who cared. I've always felt that the difference in this world involves just one thing—*caring*. Either you do or you don't. And I did.

There's always a reason not to go canvassing. It's raining, it's too hot, too cold, too windy, too early, too late. I've heard all the little voices that talk inside every head that's thinking about going prospecting:

"I hate it. And I slept lousy last night. I wouldn't be any good out there today anyway."

"People are getting sick of me."

"All I'll get out of this today is sore feet."

"I think I'm catching cold. I better take it easy."

With a new baby at home, plus four more little ones, if I couldn't think of an excuse, they'd provide me with one. I was always struggling and fighting inside to make myself get out there. Now some people think I was immune to all these canvass diseases. But the truth is, I suffered with all of them more than most agents do because, every Friday afternoon and Saturday morning for more than three years, I pounded pavement and knocked on doors. That's a full year canvassing.

Slowly it gets easier. The fears fade away. There comes a time when you've ducked every punch too many times to be taken by surprise. You can handle it. But you don't love it. Never, ever, did I spring out of bed on a Saturday morning, quivering with joy that I could go out canvassing that morning. It's hard work. hard work that pays extraordinarily well when done right. And there are moments of great satisfaction in it too.

NONPUSH EXPRESSIONS

"Would you be offended if I _____?" Many heavy prospectors use this expression a lot. Put it in your quiver and it'll shoot a lot of birds down for you too.

When you ask people's permission to give them something, to meet them, or just to talk to them, it softens the blow. You have no hold on people in the prospecting situation, and you won't be able to work with any but the most submissive types unless you come on easy. You're calling them at their home to say they may need you. But their phone works both ways—if they were convinced that they needed to talk to an agent right at that moment, they'd call one. So show lots of deference when you disturb private people by dialing their number or knocking on their door. Convey this message to them by our manner: "Mr. or Mrs. Homeowner, you're in control here, I'm not pushing you." Better to exaggerate your deference than to come on too strong in cold calling or door-to-door canvassing.

- "Thanks for talking to me."
- "I hope I haven't interrupted you."
- "I hope I haven't offended you."

Their defenses start tumbling down when they realize they don't need defenses because you're not a pushy person. Then they're open to the idea that you're someone who has something to offer, and that you won't press them at an inconvenient time. Combine assertiveness with softness in such a way that you assert yourself without making people feel pushed. That means you're always ready to back off, always ready to try them again at some other time. There are more numbers in the phone book than you'll ever call. If rejection makes your gorge rise, if you take it as a challenge that must be beaten down, canvassing will give you a rough ride to nowhere.

- "Would you mind if—"
- "Could I have the pleasure of—"

Phrases like these enable us to softly and assertively sell our product.

PIDDLE THE PRIME AT YOUR PERIL

The best prospecting hours are few each week, and they go quickly. Don't piddle them away. Keep in touch with old clients at other times; prime time is for drumming up new clients. Organize beforehand to wrest the maximum performance from those golden hours. Chapter 24 has two items of interest for prospecting: a checklist of items to have at your elbow when you're calling, and the Fast Fact Grabber form.

Whether you use the Fast Fact Grabber or a plain notepad, start jotting down facts from the first moment you hear one from a prospect. Don't wait until you're certain you've struck pay dirt. If you do that, you'll lose many important details that can help cement your relationship with prospects who are slow to reveal an active interest in buying or selling soon. That's the usual case. Action-imminent people are cagey. They're afraid they'll have trouble getting rid of a strange agent if they let that person in on the big secret that they're about to move. So don't pounce if you sniff action. Accumulate facts, build rapport, and work up on the prospect slowly.

Gather facts on every call and you'll soon find yourself doing that automatically and effortlessly. Nothing is worse than talking intently with someone for half an hour and then, after finding the switch that turns them on at last, realizing that you've forgotten many of the vital details they've given you.

Immediately after completing each call, if the situation is worth pursuing, schedule a specific time to call that person back. The Fast Fact Grabber has space on the back for this purpose, or use my personal Danielle Kennedy Time Planner to organize your call-backs and appointments. But do it as soon as you hang up the phone.

You never know when you'll find the right key to their door. I've often said "Thanks for talking to me," after a rocky conversation, and started to hang up, when the prospect would say, "Wait a minute." And then he or she would spill it out: They're sweating out a transfer, or whatever. Remember, some people warm up slowly. That's okay. Every fee has a different price tag connected to it.

Skim over the notes you'll keep, and write out plainly any scribble you won't be able to decipher when your notes are cold. Complete all your notes and plans for that call right then, so you won't confuse one call with another, and then quickly get on with your next call.

KNOW YOUR TURF

Be on the lookout every waking hour for new happenings on your local scene that'll give you ammunition to fire when prospecting. You need reasons to call people repeatedly, and new information about the community provides you with something useful and free to give to the homeowner. Observe everything you can. Be active and visible. Go to your local college's library; see what services they offer the adult nonstudent. Make appearances at public events of all kinds. Your local papers are an excellent source for this sort of thing, especially the little throwaways.

Be a fountain of information about your area. Work at it. Talk to everyone you can (being always alert for opportunities to tell them you're a knowledgeable agent, and to give them your card, scratch pad, or flyer-packet).

Know what's going on in your area 24 hours a day. Whether or not you have the time and inclination for it yourself, some of your clients will want to know about the night life. So tune in, unless you want to limit the clientele you can work with.

PROSPECTING BY FOOT

Look Before You Knock

School yourself to be alert as you walk up to every door. Search for a sign reading, "Don't ring bell, baby sleeping," or "Daysleeper, don't disturb before 1 P.M." Notice things: toys left about, new landscaping improvements, the property's condition. Don't eavesdrop, but allow sounds to reach your ears of an argument going on inside, a child being disciplined, or any other clear indication that another time would be better for a farming contact. Avoid blundering into emotional situations. Try to get out of there quickly whenever your timing isn't good.

There need be no fear this will be used as an excuse not to make calls. Set a quota of actual contacts for each day's farming, and keep at it until you've actually talked to that many active occupants. When you realize, on reaching a doorstep, that the next house probably offers a better opportunity for a good farming contact right then, leave a scratch pad and hurry on your way.

Push your antennae out when you first head for a particular house, and start getting yourself in tune with those people. Have a dozen different opening lines so overlearned that you don't have to give a thought to yourself. Put all your attention on the house you're going to.

See if there's a fountain there, flowers, something these people have done to make the front of their house special. When they open the door, comment on it: "I really like your waterfall."

"My husband put that in. Took him a month."

Simple. But it's a rapport builder.

Knock, Don't Ring

Strangers and bill collectors ring doorbells, friends knock. Be a friend. Knock, step back, and turn your body and face to the side. If you don't look like you're going to leap on them the instant they open the door, you're more likely to pass the peephole inspection.

Chapters 6 and 7 have many tips and expressions for door-to-door canvassing; most of the telephone phrases and Winning Scripts in this chapter work beautifully on door-to-door situations.

PROSPECTING BY PHONE

Let's listen as Tony Dulvoyse sits down to prospect. We don't hear anything for half an hour except paper being moved and a chair creaking. Then Tony dials. The conversation is a bummer: It lasts on 27 seconds. Tony gets a cup of coffee, and talks for 19 minutes with another agent. They agree that the market is lousy. Tony returns to his desk and calls another name in the reverse directory. No answer. Encouraged by that, Tony immediately dials the next name. He reaches an ex-sailor who immediately switches the conversation to the Second World War, and relates his adventures on the *Yorktown* during the Battle of Midway. Half an hour later, with the battle still in doubt, the ex-sailor suddenly breaks off the conversation to answer the doorbell. Tony spends the next 15 minutes reconsidering the whole idea of phone prospecting. He finally decides to give it another try—next week sometime.

Psych Up, Not Down

Organize the items you'll need into a kit before you sit down to prospect. Organize several opening lines in your mind. Write down a goal for the number of calls you want to complete. Schedule a definite starting and stopping time. There's a purpose to all this: it's called psyching *up*. Throwing yourself into an activity you know you're unprepared for is psyching *down*, and that means a little voice in the back of your head will be crying, "You'll be sorry; this is going to be terrible; you don't know what you're doing." Shut that little voice up the only way you can: by preparing. The first time out, don't set yourself a staggering goal. Don't set yourself up to lose: Set yourself up to win. Schedule ten calls. Scribble notes during each call on any piece of paper and then review them right after the call to put them in good order. Or eliminate the rewrite by using the Fast Fact Grabber while you're on the phone. Be sure to write down any phrase you used that went well. Take the time to rejoice over any small victory you win, and further psych yourself up.

When you bungle a call (we all do now and then), look on that as a small win too. "I've learned something; I'll never say that again." Complete ten calls and then take a short break. Be alone. Walk around the block. Psych yourself up again. You've finished ten prospecting calls in one session: That's more calls than most people who take out real estate licenses will make during their entire careers. Congratulate yourself. You're a winner.

Now think about scheduling another phone session. What about making another ten calls, and then taking another short break? How about making that your regular prospecting program? Ten calls. Then get out of the office and stretch your legs. Let your mind go blank for a few moments. After that, you're ready to take a strain again.

Bang 'em Out (1)

I've watched successful prospectors work the phones, and I've seen dismal failures at the phone. Here's the main difference: Successful prospectors talk longer *and* they make more calls per hour. How can they do that?

They piddle away less time between calls.

Bang 'em Out (2)

Prospecting is a numbers game. You can't be successful at it unless you make a large number of calls. Think in terms of flipping off *no* a hundred times to get one good, solid *yes*. (Keep a tally; I think you'll do better than that.) You can't make a lot of calls unless you use your time wisely. That means organizing all the little details, staying at it, and closing the time between calls.

Bang 'em Out (3)

One hundred completed prospecting calls will always get you one immediate appointment to show property, or to visit a house that's going on the market soon. By averaging one call every 72 seconds, you can line up a firm appointment in two hours. Take an extra hour or two making those hundred calls so you can pursue all leads that develop, and after about three hours you'll have five or ten possible clients to follow up with in the future. This is how you develop your phone Prospecting Farm: File a 3 × 5 card on each person under the date you're to call them again. It's easy. All you need is one set of 1 to 31 date-file guides for the current months, and one set of January–December monthly file guides. If you don't use a 3 × 5 card system, try a Fast Fact Grabber log for each call and file them alphabetically in a three-ring notebook binder, or in your planner in the alphabet section.

Phone Technique

THE FEE WINNER
- Breaks off negative conversations quickly, courteously, and firmly.
- Builds rapport on small wins with prospects that show promise. Takes one step at a time. Progresses steadily toward obtaining an appointment.
- Loses little time between calls.
- Makes notes during prospecting calls to keep facts straight during each call, and to make future call-backs more effective.
- Speaks clearly,
- Uses common words and standard English to communicate with, and inform, prospects.
- Talks like a friend.
- Is relaxed and unhurried during prospecting calls.
- Wants results now, but also realizes that many situations can't be developed into active business now. Knows that next month will arrive right on schedule, that business will be needed then, that today's future client is tomorrow's hot buyer or seller. Works efficiently on future business without jeopardizing present business. Calls prospects back at the precise time they suggest. Is well organized for prospecting.

THE FEE LOSER
- Gets entangled in negative conversations. When finally off the phone, insists on telling the entire office what an idiot the other person was.

- Doesn't know how to build rapport. Makes one great leap for the appointment, finds the chasm too wide—yeeeeoooow. Splat.
- Is very busy doing nothing around the office between calls.
- Depends on memory. Forgets vital details. Doesn't use a Fast Fact Grabber.
- Mumbles.
- Uses real estate jargon, slang, and obscure references to impress prospects, but succeeds only in confusing and annoying them.
- Pushes like a salesperson.
- Hassles prospects with an impatient manner.
- Wants results *now*. Has no interest in, or capability of dealing with, future call-backs that can develop business later. Has never bothered to get organized for efficient prospecting and follow-up.

Can Discourage Encourage?

Can a discouraged-sounding voice encourage anyone to become your client? Think about that. Then read:

Variety, Clarity, and Speed

What your voice says to people goes far beyond the meaning contained in the words you speak. A second line of communication, more powerful than the words spoken, is set up by your voice. This second line is the variety and color of your tones, the clarity with which you pronounce your language's sounds, and the speed at which you talk.

Variety, clarity, and speed always reach the emotions of your listeners; your words sometimes reach only their ears. If you tell a prospect how knowledgeable, enthusiastic, and capable you are in a flat, monotonous, discouraged tone, with words carelessly slurred together and spoken with tiresome slowness, or excessive speed, your listener hears two conflicting witnesses. The first witness is your words, and your listener knows you direct them to further your own purposes. The second witness is variety, clarity, and speed. If these qualities testify against your words, your listener senses that they've escaped your control, and for that reason must be believed. Your words are found guilty of perjury, and you are sentenced to oblivion as far as that person is concerned.

Within the words, and the other sounds you make, are other witnesses who can also swear against you. Too many uh's, too many interminable sentences, too much slang and jargon (or too little, if you're talking to a trendy type), irritating repetition, too many vague terms—all these can testify. All these unprejudiced messages are more readily believed than your words.

Pull your act together. Convert all the other witnesses in your voice to your cause. Set your portable cassette tape recorder by your phone when you prospect.

For faster auditing of your phone mannerisms, record only your end of the conversation. Record when you talk, press the Pause button when they talk.

Listen to that cassette and you'll discover improvements you can make in your prospecting techniques. Practice your improvements. Record and play them back. Get together with another enthusiastic and upwardly mobile agent to critique each other's taped performances on actual prospecting calls.

The Best Times to Prospect

The best times to prospect depend on local laws and customs, climate, and season. The prime and no-no times given next are valid in many areas. Determine which hours are best and which are to be avoided in your area by inquiry, and by checking the results of your effort in the field.

Prime Time

Here are my best phone prospecting times, least effective first, most effective last.

- 10 A.M. to noon, weekdays
- 3 to 4:30 weekday afternoons
- 7 to 8:30 weekday evenings
- Noon to 5 P.M. Saturday
- 3 to 6 P.M. Sunday
- 3 to 6 P.M. Friday (Everyone's in a good mood.)

Note that the two best phone prospecting times are also the best times for open house. Why not do both? See *20/20/20, Go Like 60* in the next chapter.

No-No Times

Never prospect, either by foot or phone at these times:

- Before 9 A.M. on weekdays.
- Before noon on weekends, unless you see unmistakable signs as you walk by, that they're not sleeping late.
- Between 5 and 7 P.M. any evening, because people are usually eating dinner then, and interruptions irritate them.
- After 8:30 P.M. For many people, this is getting late to hear from strangers. And there are lots of early-to-bed, early-to-rise folks around.
- Whenever there's a major sports event on TV.

- And, of course, never prospect on religious and important national or local holidays.

Using the Crisscross

If your office has a by-street directory, you have access to an invaluable prospecting tool. When I used prospecting, I called any names I faintly recognized first. Do that to build confidence. Calling people I know slightly, or who are friends of someone I know, usually gives me something to work into later conversations with the people I don't know at all. By doing that, I'm going to hit a friendly conversation or two. Those wins will boost my morale, and they'll encourage me to call the strangers on the page.

For example: In the crisscross, I see the name Dabney on the street I'm calling. I don't know the Dabneys personally, but I do know Mary Jackson, and that Mary plays tennis with Mrs. Dabney. So, when she answers my call, I say:

"Hi, Mrs. Dabney. I hope I'm not catching you at a bad time." Leave just a short pause here, but don't give her too much time to think up reasons for not talking to you. "I'm Danny Kennedy with Sell Fast Realty, and I think we have a mutual friend."

"Who's that?"

"I understand you play tennis with Mary Jackson."

"Yes, quite often."

"Mary and I have known each other for a couple of years through our church group. I just thought I'd call to remind you that I'm with Sell Fast Realty, and that I keep quite actively involved in real estate sales and listing in your neighborhood— and also with general community affairs. Do you know of anyone who may be interested in making a move in the near future?"

"Offhand, I can't think of anybody."

"Thank you for trying. If someone does come to mind, or even if you folks are considering a move, I hope you'll think about using me to assist you."

"Okay."

Pause. Give her just a brief moment to volunteer something. If she doesn't, say: "Thank you for talking to me, Mrs. Dabney. Goodbye."

You're looking for immediate results when you cold canvass—but never overlook an opportunity to build the pool of people who know of, and respect, your abilities in your chosen field. So I'll send Mrs. Dabney a thank-you note that same day: "Thanks for talking to me on the phone today." I'll slip a reminder of our mutual friend into the note, too: "Please say hello to Mary for me when you see her."

The impression made by a brief phone call is very slight, and Mrs. Dabney wouldn't remember me by that alone. But the phone call followed by a thank-you note (it must be mailed that same day) has a good chance of causing Mrs. Dabney to mention me to Mary. If Mary responds with some favorable comment about me—

and I'd never use Mary's name unless I was sure she would—I've made three strong impressions on Mrs. Dabney. By dropping her address in my send-newsletter-quarterly file, I'll be able to keep building my reputation in Mrs. Dabney's mind four times a year with tiny effort on my part because I'm working with flexible and efficient systems.

Use the just mentioned discourse when you *don't* have a mutual friend, by beginning your call with, ''I keep quite actively involved in—''
Now you're making the true cold canvass calls. Without encouragement, linger not.

Stage a Telethon

One of the greatest ways to get shy agents rolling on the telephone—and have a lot of fun at the same time—is to stage a Tuesday Night (or any night) Telethon. Ask your broker for permission to organize one with your fellow agents or, if you're a broker, why not organize one for your associates?
Here's the plan: Pick the hours between 6:30 and 8:30. All the salespeople can chip in and buy nutritious snacks. (No eating while phoning, please.) Notify the staff at your regular office meeting that a week from Tuesday you're having a Telethon. Pass around a sign-up sheet to see how many promise to participate. Then divide up the calling areas by page number in the standard phone book, by street in crisscross directory, or by farm areas. Have prizes for whoever makes the most cold calls that convert into specific appointments (perhaps a facial at the local salon, or a free haircut and style at the barbershop).
Here's what each person needs for the telethon:

- A mirror set by the phone (Use it to monitor your expression. If your face frowns, your voice will too.)
- A small cassette recorder if you want to tape yourself, or others.
- A grabber to write down facts about the people called.
- Your appointments book and my Time Planner to record an appointment you might acquire from the call.
- Your own inventory book and the Multiple Listing Book in case the conversation turns into property inquiries.
- Your comparable file. (Be careful not to give them too much information over the phone. Do that in person with a Guidelines to Market Value form.)

Here are some samples of powerful phraseology that you can use at the telethon:

"Good evening. This is Danny Kennedy with Sell Fast Realty. Are you Mr. Walter Frankel?" Pause (Be very businesslike and confident. Ask this because crisscross directories are often wrong.)

"Yeah, why?"

"Well, Mr. Frankel, my company is conducting a special telethon tonight to update our records of people living in the community. We wanted to be sure that you still live there. Our job is to know that, in order to be sure the right people know where to contact a good real estate agent if they need one."

"I don't need one."

"Well, that means you're happy where you are. But, may I ask, have you noticed our signs and activity in your area?"

"Yeah, so what?"

"Well, what do you think? Does it look like we are doing the job? We're part of this community like you are, and we want to do the right things. Have you heard any negatives?"

"No, but you *are* bothering me now."

"Well, I'm glad you haven't heard anything bad. Thank you. I'm sorry for the interruption, but I know something now I didn't know before I talked to you." Pause.

"What's that?"

"Walter Frankel doesn't think Sell Fast Realty is all bad. And I thank you for that. Goodnight, and the best of everything."

"Good luck, kid."

On calls into any street where your firm has recently sold a house, use this approach:

"Good evening, Mr. Jones. Danny Kennedy with Sell Fast Realty here. I'm just making a quick call to tell you about your new neighbors. Have you met them?"

"What are you talking about?"

"Well, the Schaefers, who lived right down the street from you, have just moved to Denver. We marketed their home for them in 20 days to a lovely family with school-age children. Do you have any youngsters in elementary school?"

"No. So you're the guys who sold the Schaefers' house, huh? What did they get?"

"Well, that transaction has closed, so I can give you the information." (If it hasn't closed: "I'm not at liberty to give out that information over the phone because the transaction hasn't closed yet, but if you're really interested in neighborhood values, let me prepare a Guidelines to Market Value for you in your home.")

Additional scripts that are effective on telethons and in regular prospecting are given later in this chapter. Your best scripts, probably, will be those you create yourself. The key is to always have a reason for calling and to use that reason as a catchy, *take 'em off guard* opener.

Here are some winning cues for your scripts:

- Our signs and activity in the area.
- Recent sales.
- Voting night: The night before elections, have a telethon and kill two birds with one stone. Remind people to vote (the volunteers at the polls, who are also homeowners in your farm area, will love you) and remind them about the tax proposition, or any such issues that affect them as homeowners. Caution: Don't try to impose your own political views on the people you call.
- Cultural events: "Hi. I'm Danny Kennedy with Sell Fast Realty. Just making a call to remind you of the spring home tour tomorrow that's sponsored by our company. Have you ever thought about selling your own beautiful home?"

There are as many openers as there are people. When you put a group of enthusiastic agents into one room for a telethon, creativity flies. Learn from each other and have fun.

WINNING SCRIPTS

Twelve Opening Lines

These are just starters. Take five minutes now and write out another dozen that fit your climate, your region's special idiom, your personality. Always identify yourself first.

1 "Hope I haven't interrupted, but—"

2 "Good morning. I hope this rain hasn't got you down. Here's a rain bonnet—"

3 "Hello there! Can I take a minute of your time?" (Point to your watch.) "Just time me. I'm _____ of _____ Realty."

4 "Hi. I'm _____ with _____. May I leave this scratch pad with you as a token of my appreciation for your smiling at me this morning?"

5 (After noticing a freshly cut lawn) "Good morning! Look's like someone's been busy sprucing up. Would you consider coming over to my house and doing the same?"

6 "Hi, Mother.—Well, how does it feel to have the kiddies back in school! Here's a memo pad for September to remind you of things to get done after summer vacation."

7 "I'm _____ of _____ stopping by to say hello, and to distribute another set of cookie cutters, compliments of our company."

8 "Hi, there, Mrs. _____. I'm Nellie Neat of Reliable Realty. Are you as happy here as you look?" . . . "Great. Well, if you know of anyone who can't stick around and enjoy this lovely block, could I ask a favor? Mention my name. They may not know a top-flight real estate agent."

9 "I've got something to tell you." Relate some news item about a store opening, a house sold and a new family moving in—anything except juicy neighborhood gossip.

10 "Guess who's back with a smile, a newsletter, and a _____." (Name whatever you've got in your hand to give away.)

11 "It's me—your old buddy from around the corner who helps move folks around."

12 "I'm just stopping by to say hello, and to give you _____."

PROSPECTING FROM OPEN HOUSE

Winning Scripts Calling Everyone from Open House

"Hello. I'm Matt Butler with Seven Pines Realty—calling you from just down the street—where I'm holding an open house for one of your neighbors right now."

Pause now, and they will often ask you which house. If they do, chat about the house, and invite them over to see it. Tell them the time you'll be there, and then say, "My sellers here are very sorry to be leaving this beautiful neighborhood, and I certainly understand why. Do you share their enthusiasm for this area?"

Answers to that question will fall into three groups.

1 *"We like it here."*

Respond with, "I was sure you'd say that. Do you happen to have any friends or relatives who'd like to move in here and share this wonderful neighborhood with you?"

"No."

"Perhaps someone at work?"

2 *"We don't like it here."*

This may indicate a desire, or need, to move. Don't pounce. Let the conversation develop naturally:

"I'm sorry to hear that. Would you be offended if I ask you why? I'd be very interested to know." Be very careful to ask this question sympathetically. You don't want them on the defensive, and you don't want to pant with eagerness to move them out.

3 *"It's okay. I guess we're neutral about it."*

With some low-key people, this is equivalent to "I hate it," or "I love it." Here are eight tacks you can take to develop how they really feel:

"Do you think we're too close to the city?" (—too far from the beach? the mountains? the city?)

"Is this area convenient to your work?"

"Do you enjoy living in this state?"

"Does the aroma of the glue works bother you?" Every area has at least one minor negative you can exaggerate and use here. Smog. Congestion. Summer heat. Winter cold. Or both. Frequent brush fires. Morning fog. Anywhere in California you can always ask, "Are you concerned about earthquakes?" and get a response. The purpose is to get them talking.

"How long have you lived here?"

"What do you think of our schools?"

"Do you think the shopping is good around here?"

"What do you think about the restaurants in this area?"

When you pick up a hint they may be moving, or if you've simply had a friendly conversation, conclude with: "I've enjoyed talking with you. I hope I haven't taken too much of your time. Would you be offended if I dropped off one of my handy scratch pads for you after my open house?" Don't pause. "I can't stay more than a minute because I have a commitment" (you can truthfully say that even if your commitment is to walk your dog) "but I'd like to meet you while I'm right here in your neighborhood. Would that be all right? About five?"

Then add this prospect to your people-I-know farm so you can routinely keep in touch and efficiently build your credibility as a real estate expert with this new person over a period of time.

Calling Expired Listings from Open House

Many listings will be passed around from office to office until finally, after a year or more, the sellers agree to a price and terms that, in all likelihood, the first agent advised them to go with. Work expired listings. Call them from open houses. Be especially alert for present fizzbos who were listed by some other office in the past.

In the future, success will go to the agents who use their time effectively to work with more people. Here's a general opening line for expireds:

"Hi. This is Danny Kennedy with Sell Fast Realty. I'm just updating my listing book and I was wondering if your property is still available."

Notice that I did *not* say, "Is it still for sale?" or "Has your house sold yet?" Those questions remind them of their failure; mine reminds them of their opportunity. And it gives them a chance to say yes instead of no. If they have already renewed or listed with another broker, asking if their property is available doesn't create problems with your competition.

When they do say yes, which is most of the time, you've created an opening for, and put them more in the mood for, making an appointment with you to hear your listing presentation. Lead into that by asking them another question: "Can I show it?"

COLD CANVASSING BY FOOT OR PHONE

"Hi, I'm Alex Hawthorn with Helena Homes, and I'm calling to ask your help. We just sold a lovely home in your area, and we need another home to sell there because we're working with a lot of buyers in this office. Do you know of anyone who's thinking of selling?"

"I specialize in selling homes in your neighborhood. No one in this world knows more about the real estate between Elm and Birch than I do."

After a good phone call, drop by their house an hour or two later, hand them your scratch pad, and tell the person: "I just had to meet you after our great talk on the phone this afternoon. I've got to run to an appointment now but I just wanted to say thanks so much for your courtesy."

Always finish by repeating your name and affiliation: "I'm Alex Hawthorn with Helena Homes. I specialize in your area."

9

OPEN HOUSE— BRING YOUR OWN BANANA, AND PROSPER

The Odds • Hold the Right Houses Open for the Right Reasons • Twig or Berry? • Productive Open Houses Must Be Planned in Advance • Invite Success • Hand Out Flyer-Packets • Before an Open House • Use Low-Cost Automatic Selling Devices • 11 More Moneymaking Open House Ideas • During Open House • Winning Scripts • Capturable Customers and Clients • Lock Up and Turn Off the Lights • Bring Your Own Banana

THE ODDS

The odds are at least 250 to 1 that any given person or couple walking into an open house won't buy it. Yet big money is made by agents who understand this promotional method. These agents do a good job of showing the house they're holding open because that's an essential element in their success with the method. They take good care of their sellers' interests *and* effectively work the other five reasons for holding houses open.

If you have difficulty believing those 250 to 1 odds, you're probably equating *visitors* to open houses with present-time buyers. Looking at houses is a minor or a major hobby with millions of people. Most of those millions will buy somewhere, sometime. But somewhere may be a thousand miles away, and sometime nine years off.

Many agents throw themselves into trying to capture every walk-through as a client or customer, and suffer great frustration at their inevitable failure. Others react to the public with dull indifference. Successful agents meet all visitors with relaxed alertness and a pleasant, helpful attitude.

Check out the financing in advance. Know for certain whether there's a prepayment penalty. Have at least one loan source tentatively lined up.

Have a list of any special conditions, no-go items, things the seller has agreed to correct, amenities outside the home that a prospective buyer might overlook (a nearby walkthrough to the elementary school, for example).

Have your Guidelines to Market Value and Buyer's Closing Costs on that listing filled out and handy, along with forms for writing up offers and a calculator. Be ready to do business. Opportunity has a light knock and a short attention span, so be ready to seize the moment.

HOLD THE RIGHT HOUSES OPEN
FOR THE RIGHT REASONS

The right houses are

1 Located where arrows can bring good traffic
2 Priced at the market
3 Suited to the weather
4 Attractive from the curb

The right reasons are

1 To capture a present-time buyer for the house held open
2 To capture present-time buyers for your other listings
3 To capture present-time buyers for any property
4 To make contacts with present-time sellers that will lead to listings
5 To contact future buyers
6 To contact future sellers

TWIG OR BERRY?

The people who come into any open house can be divided into twigs and berries. The twigs are

• Spies for your seller,
• No-dough dreamers,

- Sellers, already listed with another agent, checking their property's competition,
- Owners of similar houses looking for decorating and landscaping ideas,
- Recent buyers of the same type of home worrying whether they got a good deal, or
- Simply curious time-killers of all kinds and descriptions.

There are three varieties of berries:

- Seller or buyers moving up, sideways, or down within your sales area;
- Buyers moving in; or
- Sellers moving out.

Berries come through your open house in various stages of maturity:

- *Ripe:* The need-to-move-now people who are pushed by outside forces or internal emotion.
- *Semi-Ripe:* Interested and able folks who aren't pushed yet.
- *Green:* People facing a possible change of circumstance, and people who want to move now, but believe they can't act yet because of real or imaginary obstacles.

Many twigs will be candid and thoughtful: "I just listed my house with Dick Ewell of Port Republic Realty. He said I ought to look at this one."

"Sure," you respond, "I know Dick. He's a nice guy and a fine agent. You're in good hands." Then show Mr. Honest-feller through with the utmost courtesy. Maybe it'll get back to Dick and he'll do the same for you. In any event, you behaved professionally and helped the cause. You've had a chance to practice your sales speech on a live one, and that's all you can take out of that situation.

Some twigs will never admit the real reason they came in. Don't fall into the trap of thinking you've failed miserably every time visitors won't give you their names. Don't beat yourself down trying desperately to find the key, or say the magic word, that'll turn a twig into a client. It can't be done.

I'm not advocating that you hang back, watching suspiciously, until the newcomers declare themselves. Between that posture and the hard-sell pounce, there's plenty of room for a variety of relaxed and friendly approaches, suited to your personality, that'll open up most people. Keep your house presentation lowkey and nondominating. Put gentle pressure on them to talk and reveal themselves by generous pauses. That is, keep your mouth shut a lot. Don't beat them down with words. When your mouth is on, your ears are off. What *they* say is more important to you than what *you* say. Ask cordial questions in a relaxed and nonthreatening way. If you watch and listen carefully, they'll soon tell you, by words or action, whether they're twigs or berries.

Once you know they're twigs, of course you remain cordial. Practice your good stuff on them if you feel like it, or save your energy. The point is, you can truly relax and use the opportunity as you wish. It's no defeat to miss a twig— there's just no juice there. Stay friendly, enjoy the conversation, and remember that any twig might be in touch with a berry. Above all, protect your enthusiasm. Keep it bright and sharp for when you need it to pluck the berries. When that time comes, you don't want your enthusiasm dull and sticky from overuse and discouragement chopping twigs. Your most effective afternoon-long approach will depend on your personality and energy level that day. Bubble over with all the twigs if that's your nature—but dive not into the pit of despair when people leave without responding. You were simply chewing a dry twig, not a juicy berry. No harm done. That is, there's no harm done unless frustrations with twigs make you do a hard-sell pounce that drives off a genuine, ripe berry.

Hang loose. Think of funny things. Stay up. Mr. and Mrs. Gottamoovnau are coming through that door any minute. Be relaxed and ready to charm them.

PRODUCTIVE OPEN HOUSES MUST BE PLANNED IN ADVANCE

The secret of the top producer is this validation (see Chapter 27): "I do the most productive thing possible at every given moment."

You're on open house: "Okay, I'm eating cookies, I'm drinking pop, I'm sitting here with my feet up, the music's playing, and I'm waiting. Somebody, anybody! Come in here and buy this house from me!"

If there's a dog in the garage, you're hoping it'll bark when someone drives up, so you can jump up, brush the cookie crumbs away, and look busy before the people get in there. That's doing the most productive thing every available moment?

Say to yourself, "What can I do right *now* to generate business?" That's better, but not good enough. Say to yourself the *Monday before* open house, "How can I generate business while I'm holding that house open this coming weekend?" Then you can prepare. You can have the neighbors' phone numbers and names from the crisscross, your list of expireds, your copy of the local papers with the fizzbo ads. Even if you don't have your farm file completed yet, you can work up enough of it to keep busy calling this next weekend.

Location, the Number One Ingredient of Successful Open Houses

Hard-to-find houses are sold by escorting buyers to them, not by holding zero-traffic open houses there. Avoid inconveniencing your sellers without purpose; avoid wasting your time: Hold only those houses open that can easily be found. Not more than four arrows should be required to guide house hunters to your open house by the most direct route from a main thoroughfare. If five or more arrows are necessary, reconsider your other choices—you can probably pick another that will generate more traffic.

Choose a Well-Priced Listing

It's counterproductive to hold open house on clearly overpriced properties. Stoppers get the wrong idea about your area. Neighbors come in and think:

"If the professionals expect to sell this place for *that* much—wow! My creampuff's worth at least $10,000 more than this dump. Maybe we should—"

You're in a bad position. You can't knock the price because it's your listing (not that you ever should) and you're talking to a neighbor who may report what you say to your seller. The price is too high, you know that all too well, but you're forced into defending it. This can lead to an expanding set of priced-out-of-the-market, and therefore unsalable, listings that'll cost you money and maim your enthusiasm.

Unless your ambition is to work hard and earn little, give properties with at-the-market prices first call on your open house time.

What if My Choice Is Between Price and Location?

This weekend you can hold Greedy Street or Hidden Hollow open. Greedy Street, on a well-traveled and easily-flagged corner, is joltingly overpriced; Hidden Hollow, so hard to find people swear it isn't there, is priced snap-up. Which should you hold open?

Do the bounce-off.   Team with another agent for a Greedy to Hidden play. Take the walk-ins alternately. Keep your cars nearby, all warmed up for a fast run to Hidden Hollow with your new prospects. How do you avoid knocking Greedy's price?

A prospect: "How much are they asking?"

You tell him. He staggers, then gasps, "Are they serious? I mean, how much bargaining pad is packed into that price?"

You: "I'd be happy to assist you in finding that out. The only way that can be done is by making an offer."

"No, I was just asking. I had no idea property was that high here."

You: "A premium location like this one isn't what everyone is looking for, of course. We have another fine home on Hidden Hollow listed for—" You name the price. "Unless you see that house, you won't know the fine values available here in Greenpretty Valley. I can take you and Mrs. Bysmartz to view that lovely home in a jiffy. We can be back here in less than fifteen minutes. Would you like to see it now, or after—"

Both agents should work Greedy Street together, rather than have one waiting it out at Hidden Hollow. There are four reasons for this:

1 One agent always stays at Greedy Street, to keep that house open and well-looked-after, while the second agent takes prospects to the other property. Never close down an open house during the hours you've asked the owners to be away. This is a direct injury to their interests, for which they will be properly resentful. And you can't capture more customers there if it's closed up.

2 The rapport that one agent builds with prospects is largely lost if they're sent to another agent.

3 Many of the prospects will never reach Hidden Hollow on their own.

4 Working bounce-off together causes less fee-sharing dissatisfaction than working at separate houses.

Weatherwise Is Saleswise

It's July. Ninety degrees in the shade. Your open house doesn't have air conditioning, but people are driving up in air-conditioned cars to look at it. They walk into your oven—and right out again. Even if they'd stay, would they think about the floor plan? Would they want to buy it? Hardly. While you're standing there, hot and sticky, how good are your chances of capturing them as customers to look at other, cooler properties?

Not too good.

When it's hot, hold air-conditioned homes open. When it's cold, pick one with a nice hearth, a big family room, and lots of homey appeal. Get the owner's permission to build a fire in the fireplace, turn on cheerful music, and fill the air with the good old smells of baking.

INVITE SUCCESS

Call the seller Tuesday. Mail the invitations Wednesday. On Tuesday say, "Mrs. Johnson, would an open house this Saturday be convenient for you?"

"Sure."

"Would it be okay if I send out some invitations?" This comment is effective with sellers who have difficulty sticking with plans to be gone:

"I have quite a program of mailing invitations to my own list of buyers. The advantage is that we greatly increase our chances of finding a buyer fast; the disadvantage is that we can't postpone the open house after the invitations go out."

The good old 3 × 5 card file makes the fastest-working, easiest-to-update, mailing list. Build up your list to include all present and past clients, all drop-ins from your guest log of previous open houses, and the personnel directors of all companies within commuting distance.

Local hotels and motels, where people thinking about moving into the area might be staying, are also excellent places to send your invitations. Ask them to display it at the registration desk, or by the coffee shop cash register. The hotel clerk may let you drop a flyer in each guest's mail slot at the front desk.

And don't overlook the neighbors, any of whom may have friends or relatives interested in the area. A crisscross telephone directory makes it easy to locate everyone living near your listing.

Use Your Client's Phone

Ask their permission to use it for local calls. This item should be on your checklist for making open house appointments.

"I'll be the person representing you at the property while you're gone Sunday. Would you be offended if perhaps I made some phone calls?—when no one else is in your home, of course. They'll all be local calls. I'd be very careful to charge any toll calls to our office phone."

The owners may call in to tell you something, to see if there are any messages for them (but certainly *not* to check up on whether you're actually there!). A busy signal may upset them if they're not forewarned. If you don't get a chance to clear the phone situation with them beforehand, on the note you always leave after an open house write something like, "Dear Jim and Betty: Three couples came through today. Their general response was that . . . Thanks so much for setting the stage so nicely. I hope you don't mind, I used the phone to return some pertinent messages today, and to drum up more visitors to see your house. They were all local, nontoll calls. I appreciate the opportunity to work at your home from 1 to 5 this afternoon.

Sincerely,"

Remind Sellers to Keep the Stage Set

During the listing presentation, you educated the sellers on setting the stage properly. (See "Danny's Dozen that Brings Your Sellers More Money" in Chapter 12.) When you hold it open Saturday, be sure to remind them about stage-setting in your note, so they'll take care of it right for your Sunday open house: "You've done a beautiful job of keeping your home sharp and bright. This effort will pay off for you."

For emergency cases, when they won't leave, here's how to get the sellers gone, gracefully.

Get the Sellers Gone, Gracefully

When you come to open the house, either you or the sellers must leave.

While you're making the appointment on *Tuesday,* if they aren't enthusiastic about clearing out, explain that for people to reach the decision to buy, they must first become emotionally involved in the house. Buyers must see themselves, in imagination, doing their own thing, surrounded by their own furniture.

"If you're there, Mr. and Mrs. McComb, or if you leave Granny and the kids, the feeling that they're intruding into someone else's space, instead of standing in their own future home, overpowers them. Let buyers dream a little, Mr. and Mrs. McComb. They've got to. That's the process that sells. Let's put that powerful process to work for us.

"People coming through open houses often ask me right off: 'Is this your home, or are you an agent?' They're always relieved when I say I'm an agent, because then they know they can relax, react as buyers, and say what they think without offending anyone."

If your sellers persist in wanting to stay home, ask why. Press for answers in a courteous manner. "It's vital that we understand each other, because you have a lot at stake here. Are you concerned that something valuable might be damaged or taken?" If they say yes, suggest putting the precious items in storage.

"Are you uncertain whether I know all the features of your home well enough to show it to best advantage?" If they hesitate here, ask them to go over every detail with you again. With people of this sort, you should already have notes. Check them again. Add copious detail if necessary. Exhaust your sellers.

If all fails, suggest that they are not emotionally ready for an open house yet. In negative moves resulting from illness, divorce, death, unwanted transfer, or money problems, this must be handled with great sympathy and tact. Even when the move is generally a positive one, and they are happy about where they are going, there often is regret about friends and activities being left behind. The last thing you want is despondent or anxious sellers hanging about, charging the air with tension.

"It's not worth the emotional stress you'll go through, Mr. and Mrs. Mc-Comb. We'll wait a couple of weeks and let you both get used to the idea. Then we'll talk about an open house again."

"But we can't afford to wait two weeks. We want our house sold now."

"The purpose of open houses is to find buyers. People rarely buy the first house they walk in to. So, actually, all our open houses help sell yours."

"You've already told me that. I still want *our* house held open."

Now, with strong conviction in your voice (Think, "I'm in control.") say, "Fine. And thanks for your cooperation. I really appreciate it. I know it's not easy at a time like this. Now, which afternoon will be most convenient for you to be away?"

"Well—Saturday, I guess."

Add This to Your Operating Theories
Regarding Open Houses

"I can't expect someone to walk in and buy the house I'm sitting on more than once a year. That means I have to hold a hundred open houses to get one sale—unless I *make more happen*. I won't accept one sale for one hundred days' work. I'm going to earn a lot more, so:

"I'll prepare effectively. I'll hold the right houses open. While I'm there, I'll work efficiently to make good things happen. It's up to me, not luck."

When and if you make the above decisions, you've taken the *second* most important step to making open house pay off big for you.

What's *first* in importance?

Action.

Great ideas are inspiring, but completed action is bankable.

Fish Where the Fish Are

You catch more that way. Open houses don't placate sellers, sales placate sellers. The best way to get agents to notice your listings is to sell one of theirs. Hold houses open to *capture new customers*. Select them and act with that objective in mind.

Organize Backup Before Need

Mr. and Mrs. Hotbuyer walk in. You relate well to them. They want to see houses now, because they're catching a plane back to Comingfromville at 8 P.M. They're tired of fooling around; they want to buy now.

It'll never happen? Don't you believe it. I've had buyers like that walk in on me several times. The fee is there, just waiting to be grabbed—if you're ready.

If you have a good grip on the inventory.

If you've done your homework on qualifying, financing, and closing.

All you need now is someone to take over your open house or floor time. Lining up an agent to do that for you is a lot easier to arrange if you work it out beforehand. Here's where close cooperation within your office pays. Be part of that close cooperation; the only way you can get it is to give it.

Write Ads for the Open House Yourself

As the listing agent, you should show the ads to the seller for approval on Wednesday, or call them up and read it to them over the phone. "How's this sound? Does this sound good?" Read it out loud and then laugh "Ain't it great!" Have fun. Sizzle with life. "Does this sound good?" Keep them enthusiastic. Keep their spirits up. Every time you do something to sell that house, involve them in it if possible. If not, keep them informed.

When you write the ad for the open house, always write an ad aimed at a certain kind of buyer. A two-bedroom house appeals to retired or newly married couples. Make that the theme: "Open house this weekend, all newlyweds, all retired people." To gear into what the market appeal is for that house, think of broad groups of buyers. But check with your manager first. One person may be in charge of coordinating ads.

Screen Walk-ins Carefully

I used to give flyers on the house I was holding open to everybody who came through. I'd say, "Feel free to go through and I'll be happy to answer any questions you may have." Then I realized that I was as important to the buyer as he or she was to me. They need to pick my brain—why should I put everything on a silver platter for them so they can say, "Thank you, goodbye."

So now I follow the winning scripts in this chapter; when they ask if a flyer is available at the door, I'm likely to say, "We can sure dig one up while you're previewing the property." Then I proceed with the script and demonstrate the features of that home to them.

It's often better not to have a flyer on the property you're holding open. This works out well because then you can say, "Let me do a personalized work sheet for you with all the pertinent financial information." Having your *easy-way-out* flyers on the house you're sitting on often makes it too easy for an excellent prospect to get through the door too fast for you to make any connection. Make yourself work a little harder—and make a lot more money—by having all the details on that house memorized, not printed.

HAND OUT FLYER-PACKETS

Your card goes on top; stapled behind are flyers for all your other listings. The packet should have at least six house flyers, preferably with a price spread that indicates the range available in your sales area. Whenever you have less than six listings, exchange flyers with other agents in your office.

The last page of the packet is titled "Profile of a Champion." It promotes you. Chapter 13 tells you how to write one about yourself fast.

A company wrapper covers your packet with an air of competence, but if your office doesn't furnish one, don't let that keep you from putting your flyer packet together.

Fizzbos, dissatisfied sellers whose listing with another office is about to expire, and homeowners just reaching the decision to sell will be impressed by this graphic display of your advanced marketing methods. Buyers interested in a future move to your area are more likely to keep your packet, and call you later, than any one of the dozen business cards they've picked up on their fast swing through your area. You've demonstrated competence, professionalism, and local knowledge very effectively to the need-now buyers we're all looking for.

Material promoting your area has no place in the flyer-packet. It adds bulk, diffuses your purpose, and renders fuzzy what otherwise would be the sharp image of an exceptionally competent agent. Make area promotion a separate handout and give it only to the deserving.

Promote Your Area with a Giveaway Package

Chambers of Commerce, land developers, banks, city and county governments, and special districts often will give you a supply of brochures extolling your area. You'll probably acquire a variety of folders and documents from these sources that would be awkward in stapled-packet form. If so, pull them together with a highlights flyer and give yourself another plug. Put it all in a glassine envelope, with your highlights flyer on top so it'll be visible from the outside.

HIGHLIGHTS OF GREENPRETTY VALLEY

Greenpretty is growing. New jobs, new businesses are coming.
All about Lake Lotsafishnfun.
Greenpretty's schools score high statewide.
List of local churches.
Cultural activities.
Leisure time in Greenpretty Valley.
Sports are a way of life here.
Chamber of Commerce roundup of facts and figures.
Late Flash—Zap Corporation to build research center in
Greenpretty Valley and employ 500 engineers.

Gathered for Your Convenience
by John Magruder
Quaker Road Realty

Serving all of Greenpretty Valley
with friendly professionalism.
Let's talk about the good living here . . .
No obligation, of course.
Office 987-6543   Home 123-4567

BEFORE AN OPEN HOUSE

Visit the property. Make up a list of features and extras, of what stays and goes. Find out how kids get to all levels of school from there, and where the schools are. Drive the neighborhood and familiarize yourself with what's nearby: parks, churches, shops—good points and bad. Know all the houses for sale in the immediate area, including fizzbos—what they are, their condition, price, and features.

USE LOW-COST AUTOMATIC SELLING DEVICES

Low-cost automatic selling devices can hold a buyer for you if you happen to be momentarily busy with someone else. On a slow open house it can impress a prospect with your professionalism enough to swing another listing or sale your way. Buy four inexpensive, lightweight wood easels from an artists' materials store. Have them cut illustration boards (the double-weight kind won't quickly warp) to desired size for your easels. When you paste your items on the board, use white paper cement, not rubber cement that soon stains through. Use a square and ruler to position your items neatly.

On easel 1. Good: Your "Profile of a PRO" flyer.

Better: Typed sales story along the lines given next.

Best: Sales story typed by a commercial art shop on reproduction paper to look like printing.

Use this model to draft your own sales story:

"Orange County's Saddleback Valley has six distinct communities, each with its own unique advantages:

- El Toro
- Laguna Hills
- Laguna Niguel
- Lake Forest
- Mission Viejo
- San Juan Capistrano

"Between 1 and 2,000 houses and condominiums are usually for sale here in the valley. Finding your best home in this vast inventory is no easy task. Knowledgeable professional service will save you time, effort, and money perhaps a substantial amount of money. Our business is knowing where the values are.

"I've qualified myself to give you that professional service by . . ." [here you briefly list your professional awards and accomplishments] " . . . intensive training, and constant study of our local housing market.

"Let's talk about your needs. I'm a full-service Multiple Listing agent, ready to ably represent you in the purchase of any real estate in the Saddleback Valley. There's no cost or obligation, of course. I'm here to serve you."

Add a small (about 4″ × 5″ maximum size) *recent* portrait of yourself to the illustration board. Why, if you're in the house? Because there may be several people milling around, and a prospect might not know who you are, hesitate to ask, and walk out.

On easel 2. Mount an illustration board that says in large, neat letters: "For you." Arrange on that board in peg-board pockets, or on shelves: flyer-packets, business cards, buyer-catcher maps.

On easel 3. Place this legend: "Welcome. Thank you for coming in. I'm proud to present this outstanding property.

"On the kitchen table is more information about Saddleback Valley and real estate values here. Please give me an opportunity to answer all your questions."

(your signed first name)

Will your sellers object that you're selling other properties, not theirs? Explain to them that no one buys without believing they are getting good value for their money.

"The sooner I can educate your buyer, Mr. McComb, the quicker your sale is made."

Easel 4. Use it to illustrate an informal story lesson about your area. Add boards one at a time, as you develop or find interesting material to paste on them. Leave this easel empty, with a stack of story boards lying against one of its legs. People will ask, "What are they? Can we see them?" That's your signal to launch into your talk. A pointer is handy to direct attention to details. Start with orientation maps that highlight the main traffic routes, relate the various communities to each other, and locate points of interest. Keep each board simple. Put your name (no slogans or phone numbers) on each board in clear, easily read letters. After the maps, add other boards that show aerial, panoramic, or sunset views of your area; schools, recreational facilities, shopping centers, parks; prevailing wind patterns; outstanding homes; historical photos; charts of seasonal temperatures, construction trends, average prices—the possibilities this method provides to subtly establish yourself as *the agent with the expertise* are endless. Stay alert to prospect reaction to your story lesson and you'll soon find yourself developing some boards that will always get a laugh, and take you light-years closer to winning your listeners as customers.

Sometimes (Glory be!) an open house really jumps. Several parties show up at once, and the heavy traffic keeps on coming. It starts suddenly, for no apparent reason, and just as suddenly stops. While it lasts, you're on your own. Only what's already in your head, and what's sitting around the house, can help you.

Prepare for heavy action. It pays.

11 MORE MONEY-MAKING OPEN HOUSE IDEAS

(1) Hold Vacant Properties Open

Vacant dwellings that are in good condition and well located for traffic flow make terrific open houses. Why? Because you can capture customers there and take off— to show other property more in line with their needs—with no worries about owner backlash. Your sellers aren't inconvenienced by having to stay away or spiff the place up.

Several days before holding a vacant house open, check it out.

Flush every toilet. If there's an overflow problem, get it fixed before a home-looker's kid comes squishing out on a Sunday afternoon.

Make sure the utilities are on. Make this your rule: No lights, no water—no open house. And, if the weather requires heat or cooling, insist on having that functioning too.

Consider installing a phone for your own use if the owner agrees and you can protect it from unauthorized use. Buy a phone lock from an office supply store, or have the phone installed in a lockable closet. Unless you can bang out those calls, the house must be exceptionally well located to justify your losing touch with the world during the most important hours of the week.

Leave a card table and three chairs at the vacant house so that you can work effectively while you're alone, and also offer seats to a house-seeking couple. How long will people stick around if they have to stand? Many won't for very long.

(2) Professionals' Day

Doctors and dentists often take Wednesday or Thursday off, as do other professional and business people. In many areas those two days will outdraw Monday, Tuesday, and Friday.

Don't expect many stops during a midweek open house, but what traffic you do get (other than curious locals) will often be high quality, ready and able to buy now. People moving into the area from distant points usually look for a home without regard to the calendar; you stand a better chance of picking up these hot buyers midweek than on weekends when there's so much more competition.

A vacant house that's well located and easily flagged makes the best midweek open house because your schedule remains flexible. At the last minute you can skip the open house and show property to the buyer who just phoned in. Guard that flexibility: Don't advertise the midweek open house, and don't definitely commit to it with your seller.

(3) Use Giveaways

Have a supply of scratch pads with your name on them to use as coffee coasters. When you give walk-throughs a scratch pad, say, "Here, take notes on any houses you see this afternoon that you like." They'll be doing it on your scratch pad, with your phone number and picture on it.

(4) Bake Cookies?

Why not, men? Your supermarket has the prepared kind. All you do is slice, lay on a cookie sheet, pop them in the oven, and the house is filled with the fresh fragrance of home cooking.

Get your sellers' permission, of course.

If you're contemplating your original venture into the oven, have a trial bake at home. During open house, keep your sellers' kitchen shipshape, and leave it spotless.

For the most fragrance with the least fuss, put a few drops of vanilla on a tin plate and bake in the oven.

(5) Make Up *Sold* Door-Hangers During Open House

This is important. Will you have time right after selling this house to sit down and fill in its address on three hundred *Sold* door-hangers? Activity tends to come in bunches. You may be swamped then. If you have those *Sold* cards already made up and ready to hang, you'll find time to hustle around your farm with them—and take a few bows from the people you meet while you're hanging them.

But, if you don't have the door-hangers made up, that tedious chore *and* the effort of hanging them is staring you in the face. It's easy to put it off until tomorrow—next week—then another week slips by—and you realize that your sale isn't news anymore, that you're not going to put those door hangers out, that you've lost a powerful boost to your momentum, and you decide not to think about it anymore.

Don't lose that powerful boost: Knock this job out of the way on your first open house.

- It increases your commitment to selling the house.
- Having the house numbers of all your houses memorized makes you look very with-it, very professional. You'll remember—after writing the number 393 times.
- Most important—those door hangers will get hung promptly—when they're news—when they'll do you the most good.

Do you leave them out as you work? Certainly. What if someone comes through and sees this stack of *Sold* door-hangers?

"Yes," you say, "I *am* confident this house will sell soon. It's a very sound value, and—" Off you go—you've got a great lead-in for your sales speech. People like enthusiasm and confidence. And among the neighbors you've invited to the open house and the other walk-throughs are some people thinking about selling, not buying. Impressing them with your energy and spirit won't hurt your chances of listing their property.

There's another reason for making these *Sold* signs up in advance: if you don't get them hung fast, someone else may beat you to it. What's to prevent the guy at Sellzip Realty from telling the people in your farm about the sale you just made via one of *his Just Sold* door-hangers? It's the truth: The house has been sold, and he isn't saying that he sold it.

Then you come along later with a similar door-hanger announcing the sale of your listing. Guess who looks like they're trying to ride someone else's accomplishment? The number two person does, and that's you. There's no way to salvage the win if you're second; a flyer that explains and complains will look petty.

The residents of many areas don't recognize street names only a block or two from them. The impact of *Sold* door-hangers is greatest on the people who live on the same street, less on people who travel the street on which the sale occurred, and very little on people who fail to see any connection between their interests and the sale of a house that, for all they know, might be located on the other side of town.

Get those door-hangers out fast, especially along the same street. I suggest hanging them first thing the morning after the sale, when you go back there to put your *Sold* rider on the property's *For Sale* sign.

That afternoon, run a flyer with a sketched map of several nearby streets. By stapling that flyer to more *Just Sold* door-hangers, you can greatly expand the area in which the news of your sale will have strong impact.

Keep your sketch simple so people will instantly see that the just-sold property is nearby.

(6) Put a Hook on Your Maps

Maps can be prospect-catchers too. Write something like this across your sales area maps (do it legibly—people won't take time to decipher code):

"For knowledgeable help in locating your dream home, and for skilled assistance negotiating the best possible terms for purchasing it, call [your name] at [draw an arrow to your office's phone number printed on the map]. Home Phone 123-4567. Don't hesitate to call if you're just looking. No obligation, of course."

The last two sentences are important: They take the pressure off the prospect. Otherwise it comes across as, "Don't bother me unless your furniture is already in the moving van."

Also staple one of your business cards to the map. Sure, it's likely to get torn off—that's why you write your message on the map—but sometimes a prospect will take your card off and file it.

(7) Take Your Fizzbo File

And take the local papers where fizzbos advertise. Saturday and Sunday afternoons are great times to call for-sale-by-owners—the ones you don't have time to see later. They're home. They're thinking, "Buyer, where are you?" They'd probably like to talk to someone—anyone.

Give them the phone number you're at. Offer to consult over the phone should they have any uncertainty about handling something with a possible buyer.

Keep your call brief, unless they hold onto you. Identify yourself first, then ask if you're interrupting someone who's there looking at the house.

See Chapter 5 for the full discussion on working with fizzbos.

(8) Take Your Farm File to Every Open House

With no other preparation than the moment it takes to put your farm file in your car, you're ready for an effective day, even if traffic is light on your open house.

With your farm file you can make dozens of brief, image-building calls into your farm, inviting people to your open house. To those people in your farm that you don't know yet, make cold canvass calls, looking for people interested in buying the house you're sitting on, buying any house, or listing any house.

(9) Call Expired Listings from Open House

Open house afternoons are great for calling expireds. Now and then you'll hit expireds who are disappointed that their former agent didn't hold open house for them.

What an opening! Explain that you're calling from an open house with the client's permission. Invite your expired over to see how you work open houses. Tell him about your flyer-packet, your giveaways, all your neat action.

"I get *buyers* from open houses. It's a great tool. I use it all the time."

You don't have to say one word against his former agent. Don't be drawn into discussing anyone's failures. Not only might the other agent be the expired's friend or relative, that's dangerous ground ethically. You can't strike at another agent without harming the industry's image, and your own image is interlaced with the industry's.

Since they probably won't come, hit that lightly and try for an appointment to see them later. If you get a no, mail your flyers with a note. Then a few days later, call them again. And again. And again.

(10) Call Neighbors from Your Open House, Using the Crisscross Directory

Month in, month out, there's probably no better time to prospect, to make cold canvass calls, than Saturday and Sunday afternoons. That also happens to be the prime open-house time in many areas. So why not do both? Don't just sit there. Take the crisscross directory and work the immediate neighborhood by streets.

(11) Targeting Cold Calls from Your Open House

Upgraders are an important source of real estate transactions. These rising families have received the promotions, built up the equities, or otherwise acquired the funds that'll enable them to move up.

Whenever you get a listing, consider where, within economical phoning distance, trade-ups for that particular house might come from. Then take your crisscross directory to that open house and bang out a hundred calls seeking a trade-up. This technique is most effective when you call into an area that you serve, so that you might acquire listings as well as buyers.

"Hello, Mrs. Smith?"

"Yeah."

"I'm Kathy McComb with Cedar Run Realty. I'm calling you from an open house we're holding today in a beautiful view home. Do you happen to know anyone who'd be interested in a large 3-bedroom home with a nice-sized family room and a lovely covered patio?"

"No."

"I'd like to invite you to visit our open house. It's on Via San Pedro. Just follow the signs off Marguerite."

"We're not interested."

"I won't keep you, Mrs. Smith. Thanks for talking to me." Be sure to pause at this point, or you'll always miss out on the goodies.

"Uh, you're in real estate?"

"I sure am—Kathy McComb with Cedar Run Realty."

"Do you ever do anything in El Toro, Kathy?"

"I'm over there nearly every day."

"Well, we're thinking of selling. Jack wants to go south."

Something like that will happen at least once every hundred calls. Once every twenty, more likely. The above conversation took about 40 seconds. Making a hundred cold canvass calls takes time and it's hard work. But it gets easier; the first hundred calls are the hardest.

DURING OPEN HOUSE

The 20/20/20 Go Like 60 Goal Plan

When warm bodies walk in the front door, your cold call plans slip out the back. Obviously. Your primary aim at any open house is to capture all capturable clients and customers who stop there. On light traffic open houses, be careful not to get so involved in secondary activities that you're not thoroughly prepared to do a superlative job showing the property and picking up customers when people do walk in.

But don't be nervous about being on the phone when someone walks in. It's easily handled. If you're talking, you simply say, "Someone just walked in—I'll call you right back, thanks, goodbye." Gentle click. Get off the phone fast. Don't give them a chance to tell you not to call back.

Saturday and Sunday afternoons are the week's most valuable hours: Don't default on them by doing nothing but keep-busy paperwork then. Fizzbos are home. Just-transferreds are home. Movers-up are home. And the people who know who's doing what are home too.

Call them. Prospect. Drum up traffic for your open house. Fertilize your farm with phone calls. Develop your own plan for getting the most out of those golden hours. Use your plan on every open house. Refine the details as you go. Here, for starters, is a schedule for an open house advertised for 1 to 5 P.M.

11:45   Have a quiet, high-energy lunch that'll carry you through a busy afternoon and into early evening.

12:30   Set arrows and flags.

12:40   Say goodbye to owners. Open up the house. Set the stage. Lights on. Drapes open. Put your prospect-catchers on the kitchen table.

1:00   Tour the property. Review out loud all the neat stuff you're planning to say to prospects.

1:10   Slide a sheet of cookies into the oven and brew some coffee.

1:20   Call 20 neighbors from the crisscross directory. Invite them to drop by and munch a cookie, sip some coffee, and see the house.

2:20   Call 20 people in your farm. (If you work eight open houses a month and do this every time, you can cover a 320 house farm *six times a year* this way, without putting in any more time than you now are.) Note that you have to reach 20 active people in your farm; indigent relatives, kids, maids, and no-answers count zero toward 20.

3:20   Eat one cookie. Relax 5 minutes. Start your note to your sellers. Then call fizzbos until you have an appointment after open house, or until you've reached 20 of them.

4:20   Take these 40 minutes to complete any calling you couldn't do before.

5:30   You're still here. In summer, 5 to 5:30—or even 6—is often the best time of the day for stops. But don't schedule your open houses that late. Preserve flexibility. If your owners return, leave. If you have a fizzbo appointment at 5:30, close promptly at 5:00 so you can recover your flags and take time to lock up properly, and to psych yourself up properly.

        Close up methodically. Give close attention to this task. The fine impression you've made on your seller by how you handled the open house can be spoiled now by a moment's inattention, by forgetting to lock or turn something off.

        Complete your note to your sellers. Keep it upbeat, friendly—and honest. "Thanks for allowing me the pleasure of playing hostess here today. We had 3 stops . . . I appreciate the opportunity to serve you."

Sixish: Recover all your flags and signs. Be careful not to leave them sagging out there, irritating the neighborhood.

Finally: Head for the appointment(s) you lined up with your 20/20/20 calls.

When making that fizzbo appointment, be sure to cover yourself—in case someone stops by and delays you right at closing—by telling your fizzbo that could happen, that of course they'd want you to work with those people, who might turn out to be buyers for the fizzbo's house.

This schedule, followed faithfully, with calls made in a bright, friendly, and confident manner, will give your career and income a tremendous boost. Resolve now to put those golden hours of quiet, open house time to work.

Shoot Arrows with Care

Always ask permission before you put a directional sign on someone's property. Not only is it common courtesy, not only does it build rapport for you, your firm, and the industry, not only might you make, or renew a contact that could lead to a listing, but you avoid having an irritated homeowner turn your sign around or lay it down.

Remember that you're intruding into someone's territory. Kids sometimes feel this more strongly than do their parents.

Never have the sign in your hand when you ask permission to put it up. I did this until I was turned down a couple of times. Some people can't handle that kind of presumption except by saying *no*. Be modest and pleasant. Say, "May I have your permission—" Then, after getting their okay, go to your car and get the sign. This may seem like a small thing—until you're refused by someone who controls a corner that's vital to directing traffic to your open house. And don't use too many arrows and flags because that shouts, "Beware—this is a hard-sell guy."

Here I Sit

Here I sit alone on a Sunday afternoon, in this strange but familiar house. They think my open house sign is magic, that it will bring the perfect buyer and his precious pocketbook floating down into my arms and make him buy. I know better. While I wait for perfect buyer to float, I phone. And phone. And phone.

It's amazing how working that phone hard makes the time fly on even the slowest open house. And digs up business too.

An Open Door Says, "Come in"

Whenever weather and insects permit, leave the front door open during your open house, especially if it can be seen from the street. An open door says, "Come on in. You can walk right out again if you don't like the situation inside."

A closed door means they have to ring the door bell and stand there like dummies until someone comes. Or should they walk right into a strange house, and risk making a social mistake? Decisions, decisions. "What lies behind that closed door?"

You may say, "If a little thing like that will stop them, they can't be serious buyers."

Not necessarily. Many people head straight for a Realtor® to save themselves the stress of blundering up to strange doors, unexpected and unescorted. Shy people need homes too, and they often make your most loyal customers once the ice is broken.

If it's too hot, cold, or windy to leave the front door open, stake out a sign that reads:

WELCOME
WE'RE EXPECTING YOU TO
WALK RIGHT IN—PLEASE DO

On the back of that sign, where your house hunters will read it as they leave, drop your name on them one more time under the legend, "Thank you for stopping."

What's the First Thing to Do After the Signs Are Up and the Stage Is Set?

Role-play. Talk to an imaginary prospect. You're alone—you can do it without embarrassment. There's nothing like practice to put customer-capturing phrases, and house-selling tie-downs, on the tip of your tongue.

"Is this your first visit to Grand Junction?"

"Isn't this a pleasant patio?"

"You can almost sniff the aroma of steaks cooking on the barbecue, can't you?"

"Wouldn't this be a cozy room to spend a rainy night in?"

Make notes of all your good stuff. Review it two or three times during the afternoon. Keep those notes so you can quickly get them fresh in your mind the next time you work that open house.

Use Your Guest Log Right

Guest logs hurt more new agents than they help. One sure way to turn them into a small disaster is to make a big thing of trying to get everyone who comes through the door to sign it. Relax. A guest log is a minor tool that occasionally will be useful, and that's all it is.

Leave it out in a conspicuous place, preferably on an eating bar, where it's easy to write in. Jot down a couple of names at the top of the page because no one likes to be first to write on a blank page.

And never ask anyone to *sign* it. That's an alarm-ringing word. Use these phrases instead:

"Would you mind leaving your name in our guest log?"

"Could we have your name here to remember you by?"

"Would you be offended if I asked you to enter your name in our guest book?"

"We'd be proud to have you registered with us."

"If you'll leave your name in the guest book, I'll *mail* [emphasize that you'll mail to them, not call] flyers to you now and then on outstanding properties in this area."

Use every other line of the log for remarks. After the first name you fill in, write something like, "Might move here next fall. Wants my newsletters. Add to mailing list." Under the next name write, "May be interested in 3-bedroom lake view. Send info re: the Brown house. Not in hurry."

It reads nonthreatening. Things are going to be *mailed*. No heavy phone calls. Leave your guest log out where it can be seen. It's one more way to convey this idea: "I'm a busy professional who's too busy to bug anyone. But I can be of real service if you need my expertise."

Remember: Rapport first, then you go for their name. If you can't build rapport, don't shove the log at them: That marks you as a fumbler.

Have a list of items you can mail to prospects: a brochure on the country club, a new map, your newsletter giving prices and local events. As you talk with the people, stay alert for something you can mail them tonight. Enclose a short note, "Here's that brochure on the lake we were talking about this afternoon. . . ."

This gives you a perfect excuse to call them in three days to make sure they received your flyer on your area's schools, or whatever. No bugging. Just a friendly call. That call will often be an essential step toward earning a fee.

Floor-time Walk-ins and Open House Walk-throughs Are Different Animals—Keep That Difference in Mind

Office walk-ins say, in louder-than-words action, "We want to work with an agent. Solve our housing problem without making us mad and you've earned a fee."

Open house walk-throughs (those who are newcomers seeking a home) make the opposite statement: "We drove past twenty realty offices getting here. If we wanted to work with an agent now, we'd be with one now. We're just looking. On our own. We want to size up this area, see if we want to live here, maybe find out what the for-sale-by-owners are doing. Perhaps we can't afford this neighborhood; maybe we can afford a better one; possibly we can't qualify for anything right now. That's our business. At this time, we're just sniffing around—"

There's often a final kicker to this unspoken speech: "—unless some real sharp agent handles us just right."

With the office walk-in, you move directly into the qualifying phase. Your company's image and location dropped a golden nugget in your lap. Not so with the open house walk-through: There you've been given just one swing at the ball—and the pitcher is tough on the unprepared.

Be Security Conscious

When they walk in the door, they're strangers. Strike the happy medium here. You want to know where they're going, from room to room, to make sure they're not picking up anything that belongs to the owners, but you also want them to feel comfortable. What I like to do at an open house is to take the hostess approach by standing at the door and saying something like: "Welcome to our open house. If you have any questions I can help you with, feel free to ask. I'll stay about ten steps behind you so you can look at your own pace."

If the people look hesitant as they come in, suggest:

"If you'll step this way, I'll be happy to show you through the property."

A lot of them will just follow because they're not sure of how the house flows. If they have any questions, they'll ask you. Keep your eye on what they're doing—in a relaxed, casual manner—because they're people you don't know, and you're guarding that house that day. You don't want to smother the people when they walk into an open house. Let them know you're there, but don't overwhelm them.

Never Leave an Occupied Open House

If someone comes in and says, "I want to see property right now," and you've qualified them and know they're a hot prospect, call the office and get someone to take over for you, or make another appointment. This is hard to do, but you have an obligation to the owners of that house you're holding open. If they come home an hour early and the place is locked up, or the neighbor spy sees you go, it's very embarrassing, and it might prove to be disastrous.

Beware of Sellers and Neighbors
Disguised as Buyers

It happens all the time. You're being watched. It will be subtle and unobtrusive in most cases. How you handle that open house is important for future listings in your farm area. If you're not in your farm, how you conduct yourself will have a lot of bearing on your company's image. How you answer key questions about that homeowner's property will be remembered and repeated back to your seller.

Tune in on a conversation between a neighbor and your seller a few hours after an open house:

"You should've seen it—she was doing a bad job—cookie junk all over the place—she wasn't keeping it nice and cleaned up—and she was telling people more about that house three blocks down than she was about yours. And get this: The first thing she said when we walked in was, 'They're soft on the price'."

WINNING SCRIPTS

The Buyer's Analysis for Better Service questions in Chapter 15 and the Winning Scripts in Chapter 8 all have series of questions that are powerful on open house.

Your tone and manner must be friendly, relaxed, and interested. Before you get into what a walk-through couple can afford, be sure to cover what they like and want. Establish rapport first, then ease into qualification. If you press too soon, without first taking time to develop rapport, your chances of gaining them as a customer are poor.

Most people looking at open houses want to be left alone. They want you to answer questions when they ask them, and that's it.

The best way to handle the people coming through is to *not* fight their desire to be left alone. Here's an introductory script that'll meet that and allow you to work with them:

"Hi folks. I've found that the best way for you to preview this property is on your own. Feel free to go through by yourselves."

"Aha," they think, "just what we wanted—to be left alone."

Then you say, "But before you do, I would like to point out just one thing." And then you demonstrate the house.

I can hear you saying, "Hold on—I thought you told me to let them go through alone." No—that's what you tell them. But if you let them do it alone, you won't reach your goals. How can you build rapport when you don't talk to them?

For this to work, you have to learn how to demonstrate that house. Get there early. Find out everything special about that house so you can point out things that aren't obvious. It's worse than worthless to trail them around saying, "This, of course, is a bedroom."

For example, showing them one unique thing can take you through several items and then to the back yard. There you can say something like, "It looks like this property ends at the fence, but it goes down this gentle slope and includes those flowering peach trees."

If they have any interest in the property, they'll ask about that. "How many trees are there?"

"Fourteen. And they all bear fruit, the owner tells me."

Anything like this will cause them to perk up and help get the conversation flowing. Continue demonstrating and weighing their responses. Remember not to get so wrapped up in your demonstration that you fail to interact with them—your whole purpose in making the demo is to interact with them.

It's a two-step process—demonstrate, pause; demonstrate, pause.

At an open house when the buyer looks like he would want a much cheaper home than the one you're working, preface the price by saying, "We have many lovely neighborhoods in this area where prices start at $96,000. They go all the way up to $400,000. This one I just happen to be holding open today is $145,500."

"Are you presently working with another broker?" I always ask this. If the prospects are working with someone else, and they feel loyalty to that other agent, I want to honor that loyalty whether it's to someone in my company or not. I also want to save my time for prospects who show me a better chance of earning a fee.

When they say, "Yes, we're working with another Realtor®," respond pleasantly with:

"Fine. I'll be glad to give your agent all the information about this property that I can."

There are three situations here:

1 They're interested in the property you're holding open and it's your listing.

2 They don't like the open house, so it doesn't matter whether it's your listing or not.

3 They like the house and you're working another agent's listing.

Here's how to cope with these three different circumstances:

1 Cooperate with their agent. Offer to call him or her, to deliver information. Don't try for both ends of the fee when they've told you they've worked with another agent and it's your listing: You can't do that without seeming greedy.

2 If they're not interested in that house, tell them about your other listings. If you strike no spark, switch your emphasis to selling your community. The more people who move into your area, the better it is for you.

Avoid pressuring them. Flow with their indicated interests and establish yourself in their minds as an area expert, not only on its houses, but also on its amenities and opportunities. Suppose their loyalty is to an out-of-area agent, and they're looking here in your area without that salesperson along. The chances are good that should they decide to buy here, some agent in your area will capture them as customers. That agent might as well be you.

Build rapport before you ask whether their broker specializes in another area. If they're trying to get out the door without being rude, let them go. But if they're hanging around, go for an appointment to show property.

In this situation it's essential that you have a feeling of solid rapport with them and establish that they'll work through you if you find what they want. Be friendly and candid. Explain that your time is your stock in trade. Don't set yourself up to spend a week showing property and then have someone's cousin or fraternity brother come in to present the offer and collect the fee.

3 Most people, even those who've bought several houses, don't have a clear idea how the real estate business works. They assume, because you're holding the house open, that you must be the listing agent, or that you'll get a portion of the fee—or else they aren't thinking about that at all and just want an agent they feel confidence in to represent them, and them only, in the transaction.

Therefore, when they walk into an open house, it's with the idea that, should the house interest them, they'll bring in another agent for the purchase negotiations. Loyalty isn't involved.

When you see buying signs and it's not your listing, make sure the prospect knows that. Explain carefully how you'll look out for their interests with dedication and skill. Emphasize that in-house transactions, where the sellers' and buyers' agents both work out of the same office, account for about half your company's business. Convince them that the in-house transaction's feeling of mutual confidence, and the speed with which paperwork can be handled, puts them and you in a stronger position, rather than a weaker one, to negotiate the best possible terms for them.

"Do you know anyone who lives or works near here? Maybe we have a mutual friend."

Drill yourself on all your area's activities, especially those involving children, so you can zing in things like, "Your children look very athletic. Did you know that we have a very strong [name the sport] program here? Last year our boys' [girls'] team was in the play-offs, and—"

"Have you seen Lake Mission Viejo yet? It's 124 acres big, and has great fishing, boating, and swimming. Are any of you excited about these sports?"

Know the crafts, the playgrounds—everything that offers opportunities for leisure-time activities in your area. Be ready to talk about the activities with mass appeal *and the more specialized interests: the photography, chess, curling, skating, and square-dancing associations; the drag-racing, skate-boarding, and ice-fishing places.*

CAPTURABLE CUSTOMERS AND CLIENTS

Seven Statements You Should Make

Seven statements you should make to every serious prospect who comes through your open house door—provided that they're true:

1 "I'm a full-service Multiple Listing agent."

    I say that because a lot of people, particularly first-time buyers, don't realize that agents will research their needs, and take them around to see a lot of houses, completely without charge. Some of them have the idea that, because Green Gulch Realty's sign is on a property, they have to call Green Gulch to see it. It sounds very basic, but some of the buying public does not understand how the Multiple works. To make this statement, you must belong to an organization that is authorized to use the Multiple Listing MLS trademark.

2 "I'm a hard worker. I understand how important a real estate decision is to you, and I do everything possible to make sure you get the finest of service."

3 "I want to prove myself to you. You deserve the best in professional representation. Real estate is a person's soundest lifetime security."

4 "I'll make every moment count. I know your time is precious."

5 "I'm a pioneer here." (Say this if it applies, as it often does in the newer neighborhoods and communities. Newcomers like to associate with pioneers because pioneers are believers in that environment and know it well. In mature communities, say "I've been here a long time." Be sure to declare it if you have. Your prospects will be impressed and pleased.)

6 "Let me give you the royal tour of our community."

7 "I feel a responsibility to do right by you. So I hope you'll consider me a prime resource for the solid information and hard work it takes to find exactly what you want."

Take One Step at a Time: Leaps Scare Off Capturable Prospects

Suggest to the lookers, "Let me make up a list of houses that might meet your needs."

"Okay. Then we'll drive by and see if we like any of them."

This is a counterstroke. They're not ready to commit to an appointment yet. You don't need to press for an appointment—what you need is a way back to them.

"Terrific. Should I phone the list to you, or mail it?"

"I'll call you—I've got your card."

"Sounds great." Let him off the hook. They aren't ready for action yet. What you want to do is hang in with them, yet lose the least amount of time. Talk a little. Then say, "I know of three houses you might want to drive by." (Here's where your Quick-Speak Inventory pays one of its many dividends.) "Let me just jot something down so you can run by them on your way home."

Pull out one of your Show List forms and jot down the addresses and a few other details. Two of the houses aren't your listings. Tell them you can represent them to obtain the best possible price—and go on to say that you're a full-service Multiple Listing Agent. Try again for their name, "so I can put it together if you see something you like and want to call me back."

Phone Phrases for Upping Attendance

Identify yourself as soon as they answer, and then say:

• "I hope I haven't interrupted your Sunday, but if you're in the mood for looking at houses, please stop by and see me. I'm holding a home open two blocks north of your house, just over on Magnolia."

- "I represent your neighbors, Frank and Clarissa Armstrong. Do you happen to know them?"

When you've made courteous reply to their answer, go on with, "I'm the special agent" (*special* rather than *listing agent*) "servicing their property. They're leaving us, unfortunately. Do you enjoy this neighborhood as much as the Armstrongs have?" After their reply, go on with, "Well, good. Do you know of anyone who might want to invest in this fine area? The reason I ask is because I *am* holding the Armstrong property open today and I'd be glad to contact anyone you think might be interested in living here in our wonderful community."

Build Your Clientele with a Note-taking Habit

Immediately after each couple leaves your open house, jot down everything you can remember about them. Better yet, dictate everything you recall into your portable cassette player-recorder. Using a tape recorder will encourage you to recall more things about the people, to visualize them more clearly, and that process will intensify your remembrance of them.

Prospects want you to remember what they like and don't like. They're insulted and diminished when you forget, flattered and made to feel important when you remember. Retaining many of the little details they drop about themselves helps you to understand what they'll like in a house, and what will turn them off. It adds up to an impressive statement of "You are important to me."

Finding Your Way Back to the Hesitant Prospect

Here's where your questioning techniques and note-taking habits really pay off. A couple comes in to your open house and, in your relaxed manner, you draw information out of them. The man is elusive, doesn't want to be pinned down. Not until late in the conversation do you learn that he's being transferred into your county. At that point, their baby starts crying and they quickly leave.

You immediately jot down all you know about them:

"M/M Field. Chuck and Marcie. One child, new baby, Laura. He's slender, thinning blond hair, glasses, nice big toothy smile. Doesn't say much, voice soft. Marcie, short, red hair and freckles—she does the talking."

As you write that, you're visualizing this couple and impressing their distinguishing characteristics on your mind. You add, "Chuck is an electrical engineer, being transferred in by Sparks Corp. She's a nurse, not working now."

You add a number of other details, what colors she likes and so on. They came in at 4 P.M. on Sunday, took one of your flyers, and you doubt you'll ever hear from them again unless you do something about it. You don't know where they're staying, or where they're coming from except that it's out-of-state.

Monday morning you call Sparks Corporation. Their receptionist says she's never heard of Charles Field. You ask for Personnel and identify yourself. "Yes, Mr. Field is scheduled to start work here on the 15th."

"He's interested in a house I was holding open yesterday. Could I send you some information about that house so you could forward it to him?"

You don't ask for his address and give Personnel the perfect opening to get rid of you fast and feel righteous about it: "We're-not-allowed-to-give-out-that-information-sorry-I-couldn't-help-you-goodbye." Zap. You're dead.

Instead, she's thinking, "I don't want to be bothered with this." So she says, "Mail it to him direct, that way he'll get it sooner. His address is—"

Write the Fields, ". . . enjoyed talking with you last Sunday very much . . ." Of course you don't relate how you got their home address. There's no need; you identified yourself to his company and stated your legitimate business. By the time the Fields get your letter on Wednesday, they'll assume that one of them gave you their address. Chances are, you're the only agent who got back to them. You've scored points with the Fields by making them feel important. Follow up your letter with long-distance phone calls. You have a clear course now. Fly it, and the next time they come to town you'll have an appointment to meet them at the airport and show them property.

Two Separate Parties Walk In. What Do I Do?

Your "Quick Overview of Greenpretty Valley" notebook, your "Popular Floor Plans and Price Ranges" notebook, your flyer packets, and your storyboards and self-advertisements on the four easels (described earlier in this chapter) will keep the overflow people busy while you talk with the first ones in. Say to your first couple, "This is a 4-bedroom home with bonus room and view, priced at $210,000. Is that in line with your needs?"

They answer, "No, we don't need that much room."

"Well, I don't know, we're just looking."

"Maybe."

You say, "Fine, I've developed this compact presentation of the most popular floor plans here in Greenpretty Valley. Price information is in there too. Would you like to look at this for a moment while I greet these other people?"

They answer, "We didn't want to go over $150,000."

You say, "Terrific. We have several lovely properties in that range. Take a look at my compact presentation while I greet these other fine people for a moment."

They answer, "Yeah this place really turns me on."

You say, "Wonderful. Make yourselves at home. Feel free to look around. I'll check with you in a moment, after I've greeted these other fine people."

You do. Then make your decision, based on your immediate perception of what's best for you, of who to stick with, or whether you should keep moving back and forth between the two groups. Don't allow the decision to be made for you by whoever happens to be the gabbiest or the pushiest. Simply break in, smiling, and say, ''Excuse me. I'll get back to you in a moment,'' if your attention is being monopolized by a chatterbox.

Don't Allow a Multiple Listing Book to Be Seen

You impress prospects by what you know, not by what you dig out of the MLS while they stand there, drumming their fingers, wondering why they're wasting time with an agent who doesn't care enough, or know enough, to be properly prepared for prospects.

LOCK UP AND TURN OFF THE LIGHTS

Another basic, obvious detail. But if you, as an owner, were to come home after being away for the day because of an open house and find closing-up details neglected, you'd be on the phone fast too. Be careful about closing up. Don't rush. And don't have your mind on getting home, or on working with a buyer, until you've finished your open house properly. Closing down your seller's home is important; it deserves a few minutes of your undivided attention.

BRING YOUR OWN BANANA

The first open house I worked started off poorly and then got worse. At the last minute I thought about signs. By the time I'd rushed around borrowing them, I was late.

The owners gave me dirty looks and drove off. I walked inside. The tension didn't go away. Finally I realized that I was trembling with hunger. I'd passed up breakfast for lunch, and then missed lunch. Not only was I hungry, I had nothing to do. I'd brought only a pad of deposit receipts.

All through that long, dispirited, weak afternoon, I sat there. Only two couples, neither very interested in the house or my services, came through.

It was a small house. Nothing to read. Nothing to eat either, except four big beautiful bananas on the kitchen table.

I didn't dare look squarely at those bananas. My will wouldn't have been able to handle it. I kept telling myself, ''Eating a client's food is stealing.''

Playing it safe, I stayed in the living room—but I couldn't stop thinking about those luscious bananas. Four bananas. But the owners had two kids of banana-eating age. A banana would be missed for sure. At 4 o'clock I was shaky blue with boredom and hunger, but I knew there was no way I'd let myself touch those bananas.

Until about 4:15.

Suddenly my resolve melted. I crept up on the kitchen table like a Comanche, seized one of the bananas, ripped off its end—and stared at wax.

Since then, I've always brought my own banana. That idea soon expanded to include bringing everything I'd need to effectively work an open house. Then I took it a big step further. Before every kind of appointment, I began taking a moment to visualize the coming situation. I thought about preparing mentally, about psyching up when that was called for, about gathering the necessary gear to be productive when I got there.

Sometimes it takes a lot of forethought. But it's worth it. Take that moment to visualize where you'll be, what you'll be doing, what attitude and items you'll need. Take that moment early, while there's still time to prepare.

Always bring your own banana.

And prosper.

10

UP-TIME

You're Up • The Best Opener • Winning Scripts for Ad and Sign Calls • Spotting Phony Numbers • When You Have to Put Someone on Hold • Spirited Teams Make More Money • Create an Environment • What Walk-ins Fear • Tea Cart, Be-back Book, and Sign-out Sheet • Winning Scripts for Walk-ins • Up-Time is Opportunity Time

YOU'RE UP

The phone rings. Even though you've already taken a hundred calls from and for other agents today, you still answer pleasantly.

And briefly.

Some people answer the phone with a speech: "Good morning. Thank you for calling Eagercluck Realty Company in beautiful Greenpretty Valley. This is Rosemarie Eagercluck speaking. How can I be of service to you on this glorious spring day?"

"By shutting up, and letting me tell you what I want," your caller feels like saying.

Other agents think they sound busy and important if they answer the phone with a grunt, or a growled hello. Already the caller is sorry he called. Grunts and growls on a business phone are often taken to mean, "I'm in no shape to handle new business."

THE BEST OPENER

"Sell Fast Realty, this is Mary."

That simple statement of your company's name, followed by your own, is the best opening line you can use. Saying those few words pleasantly conveys a great deal: You're brisk, businesslike, and friendly; your caller has reached the office he wanted to reach; he's talking to a person important enough to be known by name. And your straight-to-it manner has subtly said, "It's okay to get directly into the reason for your call. In fact, I'd rather you would."

An up-call is any call from a prospect the up-person can legitimately try to bring in as his own customer. When people call in asking for another agent, it's larceny to try and take them over. These things get back, and they cause trouble. Play square. Make supporters instead of enemies in your office; foster cooperation instead of score settling.

Your purpose when you take an up-call is to make an appointment, not to help that person eliminate the property he's called about. Bear in mind that it's often not possible, so make your try with determination—and a light heart. Your caller may be checking to see how his own listing is being handled, or killing time waiting for the agent he's already decided to work with.

Converting calls to appointments—that's where the money is, and the only place it is, on up-time. Those calls will come in sandwiched between all manner of routine calls. When they do, it's your duty—to yourself and your company—to concentrate on getting that appointment to the exclusion of all else.

Your backup person should be quick to pick up the phone when you wave your hand in the air to show that you're occupied. It takes concentration to convert a prospecting call into an appointment.

Here is how it's done.

WINNING SCRIPTS FOR AD AND SIGN CALLS

1. Many agents give the buyer immediate control. Whenever possible, don't give out the price.   The following introduction is a winning script to use on all ad calls:

"Stones River Realty, this is Liz McCleary."

"I'm calling about your ad—the one that says, 'Rainbow's end.' Can you give me the price?"

"Certainly. I'll put you on hold for just a moment while I get that information."

Come back on the line in no more than 15 seconds and say, "Another agent has that file right now. Will you be where you are now for another five minutes?"

Usually they'll respond with something like, "I can be."

"Fine. If you'll give me the privilege of knowing your name and number, I'll call you right back."

Some of them won't tell you what their name and number is, which is a practical way to separate the calls that are worth your time from those that aren't.

When you call back to those who do tell you, you're in a far stronger position. You know their name and number, and they've asked you to call them—so the first threads of a relationship are in place. Now you have a good chance of arranging a meeting with them. Had you simply given them the price when they asked for it, the odds are about eighty to one against your ever hearing from them again.

2. If your ads tell everything, you won't get many calls.   Whatever basic fact (price, address, terms) the ad doesn't give, that will be the thing most callers want to get out of you. They'll want to do that fast so they can get off the phone with you and go about their business. Here are three ways of coping with this problem. Note that these responses work whether they're trying to get the price, the address, or any other bit of information out of you.

A. "Thank you, Mrs. Summers. I'd *love* to give you the facts on that property. In fact, I'll be happy to drop off a copy of the property fact sheet. Would you be there at two this afternoon, or would you rather come over here now and pick it up?"

B. "Thank you, Mr. Turner. I'd *love* to give you the facts on that property. May I ask, have you ever looked for property and been frustrated because everything you looked at wasn't to your liking? Or perhaps when selling your own property, you've been frustrated because everybody who came through wasn't right for your home? Well, we don't do things like that here. You and our homeowners are too important. We promised them that we'd interview everyone prior to showing their property because time is important both to you and to them. So, could you stop by our office in the next hour, or would you rather I'd meet you somewhere else early this afternoon?"

C. When they won't let you off the hook, answer in one breath, "Two-hundred-forty-thousand—that's-the-range-you-had-in-mind?"

"I didn't want to go over one-fifty." He sounds wounded.

"Terrific," you say, with en*thus*iasm. "We've got several beautiful properties at that price."

If you allow the faintest hint of disappointment or condescension to creep into your voice, you've lost the caller. You can trade a bit of free enthusiasm for a fee here.

3. You've held your prospect past the price problem.   Continue with: "I know I have just the right property for you, but I'm going to ask you a few questions—you don't mind, do you?"

With the caller's permission, ask, "How many are there in your family?"

Use this roundabout way instead of asking directly how many children they have. Through tragedy or disappointment, *how many children* may be a very sore point. If they give you any number over two, after telling you they're married, fill in your knowledge of their basic housing needs. Suppose your caller says there are five people in his family. Say to him:

"Are the other three all children, or do you and your wife have some adults living with you?"

"Our three children live with us."

"So that I'll understand your needs correctly, what are your children's ages?"

Usually they'll volunteer the sex of their children along with their ages. If they don't, ask.

"Is your six-year-old a boy or a girl?"

It doesn't matter at the moment what his family's pattern is, but don't make the mistake of letting his answers fly through your head. Keep notes of what your caller tells you. If you've forgotten the answers you're trying his patience to get now, you'll lose more credibility than you can afford to lose when you meet him. Use a Fast Fact Grabber form as shown in Chapter 24 to organize this information, or design your own form.

As soon as you have the answers to your questions about the caller's family, you have to make a fast decision. This is the earliest that you can take the next step without sounding insincere, but it would be better if you knew more about their likes and dislikes as to house style, interior colors, and amenities. But if your caller is getting impatient, another round of questions now may get you the "I gotta go, goodbye" shutoff. There's no defense against that. Unless it's an easy flowing conversation, and you're hitting it off well with the caller, go with what you have now.

4. Tell your caller: "I saw a terrific property yesterday that might be exactly what you're looking for. I believe it's just come on the market, so it's not on the Multiple Listing yet." (Don't you always know of such a property?) "Let me check out the particulars and call you back. Will you be where you are now for the next 30 minutes?"

"I can be."

"Great. What's the number there?"

5. Getting the phone number on an up-call is a midsize win. Once you have the number, they'll readily give you their name. Go with that, and call them back in ten minutes. You know his price range, the number of bedrooms he needs, and something of his preference from the house he called about originally. From your Quick-Speak Inventory, you'll be able to jot down at least three houses on your show list that should be of interest to your prospect. But, before you ring off, you have two more things to do. Your caller has told you his name is Tom Jordan.

"Mr. Jordan, I know you've circled other ads in the paper (—looked at other properties in the area—if he called from a sign)—and I'd love to help you with them. Which ones interest you?"

If he gives you that information, you'll be able to learn more than he can about those houses by calling the listing offices and telling them, quite properly, that you have a customer who is interested in one of their offerings.

The second thing you must now do is make sure Tom Jordan gave you his real phone number. The method of doing so is given later in this chapter.

6. You struck out on questions 3 and 4. But your caller hasn't hung up on you, so keep whacking away with the following string of questions. Any one of them may open up a new line of discussion that will guide you in to an appointment close.

"What was it about the ad that interested you most?"
"What's causing you to think of moving this way?"
"Do you own your home now, or do you rent?"
"Will you keep your present home as an investment, or will you sell?"

   OR

"Is it necessary to sell your present home before you buy another?"
"Are you calling from your home, or are you already out looking?"
"Have you seen any houses in this area yet?"
"How long have you been looking?"
"Have you seen anything you like?"
"What area do your friends live in?"

7. If you're flying high with the prospect, really hitting it off well, don't go on too long before you press for a name and phone number.   Be frank about it. There's no better technique than reality. Use it whenever you can.

"We've been talking for a few minutes now." (Even if it's been half an hour, never say it's been a *long* time.) "I feel confident that I can serve all your real estate needs. In case our conversation gets cut off unexpectedly, let's stop right now and arrange an appointment. Which hours do you prefer—daytime or evening?"

Now be quiet. If your caller isn't playing games, he'll make the appointment with you. If he or she is playing, and weaving away from the appointment, thank them kindly for calling, and ask them to call again if they'd like to work with you. Now go for the name and number. "One o'clock today? Great. Please spell your last name, and give me your current phone number."

8. You've made the appointment.   They're coming in. If it's happening fast—before you're off floor duty, have your backup take over. While you wait for your new customers, work as close to the door as you can. They said they'd be there at one o'clock. It's now one o'clock. The door opens. A couple you've never seen before comes in, so you take the initiative.

"You must be Mr. and Mrs. O'Brien. I'm delighted to have the chance to meet you. I introduced myself on the phone. I'm _____. [Repeat your name now because they may have forgotten it and, as you do so, hand them one of your cards.] It's a privilege to have the opportunity to serve you."

Now follow the coffee and qualifying routine given in Chapter 15 in Winning Scripts.

SPOTTING PHONY NUMBERS

"By the way, I want to make sure I have the right number." Repeat the number they gave you, but transpose two digits: they said 123-7654, you repeat back 123-7645. If they correct you, it's a good call. If they don't correct you, they've probably given you a phony number. But you're not certain yet. So play along with them to the end of the call. Then think of a reason to call them back: a question you forgot to ask, or you just got a message postponing your afternoon appointment, so you could meet with them right away after all. Have a plausible reason for phoning back because they might answer. They might've given you their right number, and simply have been too preoccupied to notice your intentional transposition when you repeated it back. But, if they didn't correct you, the odds are they gave you a wrong number. Checking it out will save you the trouble of getting ready for them.

WHEN YOU HAVE TO PUT SOMEONE ON HOLD

"Thank you for waiting. I really appreciate your patience." Get back to them often if they're holding for another agent in the office. Make sure all callers realize they've reached a superior office where the people really care about giving service.

SPIRITED TEAMS MAKE MORE MONEY

Playing square with your comrades in the office builds a team spirit that clients and customers feel, appreciate, and value. Every time you're tempted by a gray area, put yourself behind the other agent's eyes, and imagine how you'd like it if you were on the other end of the same situation. It takes the whole team to build team spirit. You can start a rebirth of the team spirit in your office. You don't have to be Goodie Shined Shoes to do it; simply set a good example of fairness, of leaning to the other guy when the case isn't clear cut, and tell the other agents that you're acting with enlightened self-interest—which is exactly what you are doing. Working in an office where strong team spirit has built mutual trust and respect among the associates is not only more satisfying, it's also financially more rewarding.

Some agents need more time than others to learn that they can't expect their office mates to take good messages for them if they don't take good messages for their office mates. Unrecorded or wrongly recorded messages can lose big money, or cause big trouble. Take messages with care.

Never tell a caller, "He's not in." Those are mean little words when used by themselves. Many agents say that with a *Go-away-I'm-busy* note in their voice as though they want to discourage the caller from bothering them with a message. Saying, "Not in," often makes the caller ask, "Do you know where I can reach him?"

Some thoughtless salespeople create problems by volunteering information in this situation. They create problems for the other agent and for themselves too; callers often report such things with great glee when they finally get through to the person they're calling. Here's a sampling of trouble-making phrases:

• "I haven't heard from him all day. He's just part time here, you know."
• "I think he took off for the beach."

- "He's out of town somewhere—maybe on vacation. I don't know when we're going to hear from him again." (Translation: "If you're in a hurry, you better get yourself another agent.")

People who want to work in an office that has an uplifting spirit and money-making ways say something like:
"Dranesville Realty, this is Karen."
"John Forney, please," says the caller.
"He's out in the field, but I'll hear from him soon. May I have your name and number? I'll make sure he gets your message as soon as possible."

CREATE AN ENVIRONMENT

Create an environment that inspires confidence in your integrity, stability, and competence. It's enormously easier to deal with people who trust you. And people will trust you if you don't jangle their alarm bells. Many people who buy houses equate cleanliness and order with honesty and competence. Maintenance of the building is management's responsibility, but the nighttime cleaning crew can't pick up during the day after trash-unconscious associates. Dispose of plastic cups and fast food clutter swiftly. Don't let newspapers and cigarette butts accumulate. Do your part. Your office's image is inseparable from your own.

Not only the surroundings we work in, but the way we dress and our personal grooming, our eye contact and body language, our manner and tone of voice, our entire posture and attitude, are part of the environment in which our customers' confidence will bloom—or wither.

Your Aerie

You never get a second chance to make a first impression, and if you have a desk that indicates finding a pen would be difficult, they'll wonder how you'll ever find them a house. Have things on your clean and orderly desk like an amortization book, legal size pad, and net sheets.

Display your real estate trophies and certificates around your desk. People like to know they're dealing with a winner.

And have a family photo there to show that you're something besides an agent, that you're a human being too. "Oh, he's got a family. Maybe he isn't such a bad guy after all," they'll think, though not in those exact words. But they'll absorb the fact and feel more comfortable with you. Have you ever gone into a doctor's inner office and noticed, with a twinge of surprise, the family photos on his desk? Reassuring, wasn't it, to realize that, instead of appearing out of nowhere in a white coat each morning to do whatever he does to people, your doctor has a family, and his concerns are similar to yours. Let your personality and interests show. But just let the tip of the iceberg be seen (or talked about) because your customers are far more interested in themselves than in you.

WHAT WALK-INS FEAR

People have their defenses raised when they walk into a real estate office to announce their desire to buy or sell. The fear that they're saying, "Here I am— dump on me," walks in with them. Remember that. Never put the thought in a walk-in's mind that he's doing something odd. Never allow a walk-in to feel he doesn't belong, or isn't welcome. And never let him think coming into your office was a mistake. All too often, after being ignored for two endless minutes by people who continue to talk on the phone without showing a flicker of interest in him, he's thinking along those lines. He doesn't know the system. He doesn't know the up-gal went out for doughnuts, and the backup-guy went to the bathroom without telling anyone to take over the floor. He doesn't know that everyone else has taken him for the man Mac called to fix something. Another walk-in, another walk-out.

Other offices do the scramble. Let's hit one. Inside the front door is the usual row of desks. Looking like a prosperous couple from out of state, we walk in. Instantly, thickets of eyes stare at us, and panic grips the air.

"Yikes—who's up?"
"I think Jack is."
"But the dang fool just went downtown."
"That's Jack for you. Gimme that schedule. There it is, Wednesday morning. You're up, Jean."
"I was up yesterday. This is Thursday."
"Oh, my God. *I'm* up."

There should be an up-desk or a secretary's desk at the front of the office, if the room is large. When someone walks in, the up-person or the secretary immediately gives them a pleasant, "Good morning. May I help you?"

If no secretary is on duty, the up-person should be seated close to the entry area. Everything needed for the qualifying interview should be handy, along with his or her sales and listing kits.

TEA CART, BE-BACK BOOK, AND SIGN-OUT SHEET

Floor time can be efficiently organized on a tea cart. On its top and a shelf or two, there'll be plenty of space for

• Your office's master inventory file of listings.

- A notebook or file containing copies of all current ads.
- 3 × 5 file box, with dividers for each salesperson, so it's easy to check for their messages.
- Call record book in duplicate, such as Aico Utility Forms 50-176. After a message is recorded, the original is torn out and filed behind the divider of the salesperson called, and the duplicate remains in the book to insure that no messages are lost.
- Sign-out sheet. A page for each day provides a place for every agent in the office to leave instructions to the up-person as to how their messages are to be handled at that particular time, and when they'll call in or return to the office.
- Be-back book, or a page in the listing and ad notebook, provides a place for the up-person to record the name of any prospect, walk-in or call-in, who might return later. Whenever that happens (in offices using this procedure) the current up-person advises the agent who recorded the prospects's name that his customer or client has come back to work with him.

When a buyer walks in, the up-person greets him, and then signals for the backup person to take over the floor. As unobtrusively as possible, the backup person comes forward and takes over the up-desk, or wheels the cart back to his own desk. This allows the up-person to concentrate on converting the walk-in to a client or customer.

Warm welcomes kick those conversion attempts straight at the goal. But if your walk-in had to face twelve eyes in a staring contest, and then had to ask before being recognized, the game's nearly lost. Why start from behind? This is not the time when silence is golden. This is not the time to make your walk-in feel isolated.

Ideally, windows will allow one of the staff to see people coming before they reach the door. The secretary, or whoever sees them, should say in a calm voice, "Someone's coming in."

The up-person, if seated in the back, should immediately come forward and act as the host or hostess. The prospects walk in the door and there's no time lag; Someone immediately gives them a friendly, "Welcome to Quarles Realty. May I help you?"

"I need a map."

"Fine. I'll get you a map." He hands it to the walk-in—who then walks out. That's it. That prospect is never seen again. The up-person didn't say one word that could've caught the golden nugget, and started it toward his bank account.

Let's try it again.

WINNING SCRIPTS FOR WALK-INS

Cultivate a bright and cheery manner, and an enthusiastic but businesslike tone whether you're face-to-face or on the phone.

9. Your office has a sign out offering free maps.   A man comes in and says, ''I need a map.''

''You've come to the right place, sir. Are you new in this area?''

''No, I'm looking for a friend's barbecue party, and I'm having trouble finding their home.''

''Hey, have a good time at the barbecue. Here's your map—and a scratch pad and my card. If you ever need any real estate services, or more maps—or even if you're just in the neighborhood—drop in and say hello. Bye—nice talking to you.''

Make that person feel glad he went in your office. He might get transferred tomorrow. Or find out at the party about a friend who's just decided to sell. He's in your office. You've got an instant to make an impression. Be sure he goes away with the feeling that your office's reason for being open is to serve *him*. That kind of a feeling isn't forgotten.

10. A confident-looking couple on an area-scouting expedition come in.   ''You've come to the right place for a map, folks. I'll be glad to get you one. Is this your first trip to the valley?''

''Yes, we're looking here for the first time today. But, quite frankly, we haven't decided to work with an agent yet. We want to take a map, drive the area, stop at some open houses—and see the new model homes. We just don't want any pressure right now.''

''Fine. If you don't find what you're looking for at the model homes, we have several resales of the same quality. Many of our sellers here in Greenpretty Valley have taken great pride in home ownership, and buying one of their homes is like buying a model. Sometimes it's a lot better, because everything's done. And our availability might be greater than what they have in new home sales. So, please, before you make your final decision on a new home, come back and see me afterwards—if you have the chance. You might be very pleased that you did.''

Then hand them one of your prospect-catcher maps that you have ready.

''And, just to give you an idea of what's available on the resale market, here's some information on several outstanding properties we represent in this office.'' Here's another place to use the flyer-packets we told you about in Chapter 9.

11. If they're not running for the door, now is the time to try for their name.   ''By the way, I'm Jim Carleton of Mesilla Realty—?'' This and a friendly smile will usually draw their name from them.

''Uh, I'm Harry Lookwell.''

If they come back, it will probably be after you're off floor duty. Your office should have a ''Be-Back Book'' (A page in the up-book will do it.) ''M/M Harry Lookwell—Jim Carleton.'' If the Lookwells come back, whoever's on the floor should then call Jim Carleton and say, ''That gentleman you talked to while you were on the floor—the one you put in the Be-Back Book—he's here now. He'd like to give you the opportunity to work with him a little bit.''

So, it's important, when you hand them the map, to say, ''Here's my card. I'm with Kelly Realty, and I'm here to serve you. May I ask your name?''

"John Pelham, but I'm going to the models."

"Fine, Mr. Pelham. If you want to, feel free to stop back later today. Maybe we can help you get more familiarized with resale homes. It's a big-dollar decision, and lots of people want to make sure they've seen everything of interest before making it. Have a nice day."

12. A man and woman walk in.   They look unsure of themselves.

Up-Person: "Welcome to [name of your company]. May I help you? [No pause here.] My name is _____?" [Remind them to tell you their names by saying yours as a question.]

[After giving their names] "We want to look at houses."

"You've certainly come to the right place, Mr. and Mrs. _____. We're one of the fastest-moving real estate offices in this area, and we're here to serve you. May I ask how you heard about us?"

[They say something.]

"Thank you so much for choosing our firm. It's a privilege to meet both of you, and hopefully we'll have the opportunity to work together until your housing needs are filled. The first thing I'd like to do is invite you to be seated at my desk," or, "—to join me in our conference room. Perhaps both of you would enjoy a cup of coffee."

[Walk them back to your desk or the conference room and pull out the chairs.] "Make yourselves at home. Please excuse me while I prepare a bit of coffee for you both." [Bring two of your imprinted scratch pads back to the conference table.] "Here you go. You might want to use these scratch pads for a coaster, and then make notes on them while we're out touring property."

13. House hunters sometimes find it more convenient to walk in than to phone,   after seeing one of your company's signs on a property, or reading one of your ads.

Again, the up-person should be in the front third of the office and on the alert. "Welcome. I'm Liz McCleary with Stones River Realty. Can I help you today?"

"We saw your sign over on Vista del Lago and we'd like to look at that property."

"Wonderful. Would you like a cup of coffee while I call for an appointment to show that home?" Take them back into the conference room, sit them down with their coffee and, after building rapport for a few moments, get into the qualifying interview. Use the buyers analysis for better service form. Chapter 15 covers this crucial step in detail. Qualify them. Work in the light, not in the dark.

UP-TIME IS OPPORTUNITY TIME

Up-time is rightly called opportunity time—but don't rely on it for your income. Consider any business you acquire through working the floor as a bonus, and organize yourself to use the quiet moments while you're up constructively. The business is out in the field, not in the office.

11

How Listings Are Won—And Priced to Sell

Strong Listers Have the Best Protection • Before the Listing Presentation Appointment • The Listing Presentation Manual • LPM Preparation • The Listing Presentation • Listing the Caseys, a Role Play in One Act • Winning Scripts

Before you can be a strong lister, you must have a strong listing philosophy. Much more than the desire to make a lot of money is required. You must believe in yourself, in your ability and determination to promote and negotiate the large issues, and in your willingness to follow through on the smallest detail. You must be fully aware that, although the money is there, it isn't there merely for the taking—it has to be earned with timely and effective work.

Three factors determine salability: price, condition, and location. If condition and location are favorable, price then becomes the key factor.

STRONG LISTERS HAVE THE BEST PROTECTION

Each day, all available real estate in the nation calls for bids in a vast, silent, slow-paced auction. In the process, Montana's cattle ranches compete for mortgage funds with Florida's condos. Most buyers are limited by their roots or work, and consider only the properties available within a small area. But, each year, more buyers widen their horizons and compare Maui to Miami before buying in either place.

With few exceptions, effective demand comes down to two things: The will to own now, and the ability to deliver the necessary cash, whether borrowed or owned. Every real estate transaction involves impermanent people in semipermanent decisions. Circumstances are changing for the buyers while they wait for their transactions to close. Will-to-own-now is the sum of many emotions held together by anything from a thread to a chain of logic. In a stable market, individual decisions to sell roughly match individual decisions to buy. When either supply or demand exceeds the other, conditions are ripe for the herd instinct to aggregate the emotions of millions, and create price pressures too great to be long maintained. The reaction, the countermovement, must come. It always does. We know this. So why should a sudden shift in effective demand ever take us by surprise?

During my sales career the money market was constantly changing, just like it is now. I especially remember one 12-month period when the mortgage market fell into a sorry state. People couldn't buy a resale home in California with new conventional financing unless they could make an initial investment of 40 percent. That year my volume was four million dollars. The trick was, I took 92 listings during that 12-month period. Many of them had assumable loans, and many of my sellers were willing to take back second mortgages for part of their equity. While I was working frantically to keep up with my opportunities, I heard on every side how pointless it was to take listings because who could find buyers with enough money to plunk 40 percent down?

I couldn't find many 40-percenters either, but I certainly located, and closed, lots of assumers. Strong listers have the best protection against the market's whims if they adapt to its changing conditions. Listings taken and listings sold are the heart of this business. The more listings you take during periods of high demand, the more you'll be able to take when demand drops off. By concentrating on obtaining and marketing listings that will sell in the tightened situation, the strong listers insulate themselves from the worst of a cold market's chill.

The only way you can protect yourself is to think ahead and prepare for the next change. Wherever your market is now on the cycle—rising, falling, or stable—it's preparing to change. It will probably do so sooner than you now expect. We tend to live in last week and tomorrow. Successful listing agents look beyond next week, and pass their foresight on to their sellers.

Your listing goals and methods should be very different in the rapidly rising market, the falling market, and the stable market. Bear in mind that some parts of your marketing area, or some types of houses within it, can be falling while other parts or types are rising.

BEFORE THE LISTING PRESENTATION APPOINTMENT

Careful preparation makes or breaks the listing presentation. Before you go out on a listing presentation, be sure to

• Drive the area

- Compile a Guidelines to Market Value (GMV)
- Note overimprovements

Drive the area. Look for properties that don't show up in the record: FSBOs, exclusive listings, new listings, recent sales. Research all activity you find. Knock on the FSBO doors, or call the listing agents, to get any information not in the record.

There's a good chance that two things just happened: (1) another house nearby just sold; and (2) your prospective listees have learned of it.

Here's how it works. You come in for a listing appointment with the Smiths and the first thing Mr. Smith says is, "How much did the Halls get?"

The best way to handle this is to name the price the Halls sold their home for (if the sale has been recorded), and then firmly steer the conversation away from pricing. You don't want to talk money until you reach your game plan's time for working on this crucial and touchy matter.

But you can't go that way because you don't know what the Halls sold for. In fact, you don't know what house Mr. Smith is talking about, or even whether a family named Hall lives in your farm. If you knew all the family names in your farm, you could now say with assurance, "No family named Hall lives in my area of specialization, so that sale was elsewhere. What street—"

That confident statement also conveys, "I know this locality extremely well; I really am *the* expert on the property here."

But you have to answer Mr. Smith's question. As you realize it's been two weeks since you've driven your entire farm, cold sweat trickles off your armpits. You know that a lot could've happened during those two weeks.

Now all you can do is throw a rock at the bear: "You must be talking about the 4-bedroom house at West and Elm. It sold for $216,500. I'm not sure the name was Hall though. By the way, I love your living room paneling. Did you put it in yourself?"

You made a good try, but Smith won't let you off the hook. He says, "Dick and Nancy Anderson sold the place at Elm and West. Haven't you seen the Hall's house?"

When in trouble, speak confidently, give pertinent information if possible, and ask a subject-changing question. You could minimize the damage if you could now say, "Sure. It's the two-story stonefront. Nice house. Must've just sold. I'll call right now and find out what it went for."

You could do that if you knew the house. But you don't know fact one about it. All you can say is, "Duh, I'll find out what Hall sold for and get back to you."

"Well, I hope so," Mrs. Smith says. "The Hall's place is just like ours, and it sold fast. I'm surprised you don't know about it. Anderson's was on the market for ages. Gus, is there any point in talking with this *person* until we know how much the Halls sold for?" As you slink out, Mr. Smith mutters, just loud enough for you to hear, "Some expert."

Picture that happening to you. Imagine it vividly. Then you'll never forget to drive the area before a listing presentation. It doesn't matter whether your appointment is in your farm. Sellers usually don't know or care about the farming concept. Are you an expert on the real estate around here, or aren't you? It's that simple to them. So drive the first few streets around a listing appointment. Allow yourself time for checking when your search turns up activity you didn't know about.

Compile a Guidelines to Market Value (GMV). Select and enter on this form (Chapter 24 has a sample) those sales, expired listings, and current listings that are most like the property you hope to list.

Most like the property in what way?

In all ways. In location, number and size of rooms, floor plan, condition, age, and lot size. In amenities, in the presence or absence of any important advantage or disadvantage.

Where do I get this information?

By visiting the properties involved. If you can't get inside, drive past. Then gather more data from

- Your personal comparables file, your office's comp file, your Multiple Listing Service's records,
- Title insurance companies in some states,
- Computer or microfilm services where available,
- Or from the county assessor's office.

Have the information fresh in your mind, and concisely written on a Guidelines to Market Value form, when you keep your listing appointment.

What if there are no comparables? Particularly in areas with older homes constructed by many builders, this can be a problem. Here are two ways to deal with this:

1 Widen the area you can draw comparables from by establishing price differentials between your locality and other localities. Do this by comparing average prices *paid* (ignore asking price, of course) per square foot. Call a friendly Realtor® in the other locality for the information you need. With just that bit of research, you can determine that houses in Westport, where you operate, sell for 8 percent more per square foot than similar houses in Eastport, a town just outside your board's jurisdiction. Armed with this price differential, you can use with conviction comparable sales in Eastport to establish value in Westport by the simple process of adding 8 percent to the price paid.

2 Contact a loan representative and discuss the property you need to establish value on—its location, lot size, age, condition, and so on—and get his opinion as to the loan that property would carry for a qualified buyer.

Note overimprovements. Many people put a great deal of money or personal labor into improving their homes. Unless they're knowledgeable in these matters, or have been well advised, these improvements installed to their own taste and for their own pleasure won't add what they cost to the value of the property. I've had clients who felt they should get three dollars back for every one they spent on improvements—when in fact their expensive decorating experiments had lowered the value of their property.

When you walk in for a listing appointment and see room additions, costly wallpaper, exotic details, and many expensive extras, make careful notes—and get in a good frame of mind to fight that when it comes to pricing. Sellers don't understand that quality doesn't mean a whole lot to appraisers from lending institutions. It's important to the sellers and their pride, but we still have to look to the market and contend with its realities. We can go only so far in recovering the cost of these overimprovements if the house is to sell. Generally, this won't be as far as the sellers expect to go.

Recognize how emotionally into the overimprovements the sellers are as you tour the property. Acknowledge the sellers' comments with interest. Be sincere with your compliments. "It's a pleasure to tour a home as lovely as yours." As you work with them and the Guidelines to Market Value form, be very sensitive. The seller's pocketbook is sensitive, and his hands with their blisters are sensitive! You'll find effective phrases for this situation in this chapter's Winning Scripts.

Always carry a Listing Presentation Manual (LPM) when you keep listing appointments. Here's why you should, and how to create an effective one.

THE LISTING PRESENTATION MANUAL

Objectives of the Listing Presentation Manual

- To build the sellers' confidence in the salesperson and in the company that agent is associated with,
- To build the salesperson's confidence in himself,
- To break barriers with client prospects,
- To improve presentation quality, and
- **To Win More Listings.**

Some agents are tense, and grope for words, during the listing presentation. By so doing, these agents transfer their uncertainty and tension to the prospects. Having a manual organizes the agent's thoughts and keeps the interview moving.

Your listing presentation manual will repay many times the concentrated effort necessary to create a good one—and to practice using it effectively.

Creating an LPM focuses your mind on developing a superlative presentation. Before you're there in reality, it projects you into the listing situation in your imagination so you can practice your lines, perfect your manual, and then go out and close more listings.

How to Create a Listing Presentation Manual

Do you realize that communication is 80 percent eyes and only 20 percent ears? Think about that as you plan your LPM.

Before you start putting it together, ask yourself these questions:

- Why do sellers need an agent? What can a broker do for them that they can't do for themselves?
- What makes my company better than other companies?
- Why should the sellers select me?

You begin by selling the industry, go on to selling your company, and end up concentrating on your own value to them. They don't need you if they don't need an agent; they don't need you if they don't need your company's services; so sell them on those two concepts before narrowing it down. Fill the stage with scenery before you bring on the star: yourself.

There are two points of special impact in any presentation, the beginning and the end. The end is the more effective of the two because it's closer to decision time.

For this reason, end on yourself. There's another reason for orchestrating your presentation this way: If your accomplishments and general greatness are the opening number, many people will think you're taking an ego trip on their time, and they'll be offended. Save yourself, not for the finale, but until the mood's set and your audience is warming up. But, with your competent manner and control, sell yourself all the time. The reality is that it'll be you and the sellers all the way for 90 days. You're the one they're thinking about working with on a day-by-day basis. You're the one who'll represent them as the hammer strikes the anvil when an offer comes in. They must have faith in your professional abilities or they won't list with you. Make sure that your presentation doesn't simply sell the industry and your company. Sell yourself. Do that with finesse, subtlety, and conviction.

Put together the best LPM you can today. Then build on that nucleus. The items needed for your Listing Presentation Manual are given in effective working sequence in Chapter 24. Presenting phrases for use with the manual appear in this chapter's winning scripts.

LPM PREPARATION

Keep Your LPM Speech Out of the Can

Memorizing a listing presentation speech from beginning to end is disastrous. Doing that means you'll give the same speech to the just-promoted and the just-fired, the angry divorcee and the devastated widower, the sophisticated and the naive. That's saying, "You're all the same to me, all you people I give this pitch to." Prospects catch that put-down and remain prospects until another agent, who is willing to recognize their uniqueness, comes along.

If you're irritated by interruptions and have to get back on the track before you can continue, you've canned your presentation speech. That's going to hurt you. Change the sequence. Practice the parts, not the whole. The Listing Presentation Manual is only a guide. Always personalize your speech to your prospects' situation. Skip over the parts that don't apply, or whenever your listeners fidget and show boredom because you're covering familiar material or going into unnecessary detail.

Encourage them to ask questions. Give full answers, and linger a little in the areas that interest the sellers. Talk with them, not at them. Keep these people involved. Get lots of feedback by relating the items in your LPM directly to their lives, the house they want to sell, and where they're going.

Photos in your LPM of you holding a *Sold* sign, and shaking hands with other sellers, provide many opportunities for happy and effective talk:

"That's Fanny and Jack Gordon. They needed a bigger house just like you folks do—and I was able to find them a beauty. By the way, they're skiers too—maybe you'd like to meet them someday."

Determine the Sellers' Motivation

If possible, without pressing too hard, find out why they're selling before you have your evening meeting with the husband and wife.

Unless you know why, you can't give them the best possible service. Unfortunately, many sellers believe otherwise. Their line of reaction runs something like this: "If we let the agents know we've got to sell in 60 days, they're going to gang up on us and beat down our price. By keeping them in the dark, we can get several thousand more dollars for our house." Many a wife (or husband) has received strict orders from a fearful spouse to withhold the truth.

This usually results in disaster for the sellers. The agent goes along with unrealistic pricing, and the sellers think they've won an important battle. Time passes. No action. Then the sellers panic. Who gets trampled in that panic? The seller *and* the unwary listing agent. The listing expires or is cancelled and the house sells through another office in a week at thousands under market. Ignorance of how the real estate market works, and the first agent's failure to gain the sellers' trust, lead to these fiascoes.

Variations on this theme are played constantly in real estate. The best defense against price games-playing is a genuine concern for your clients' welfare, sensitive alertness, and a frank attitude toward and thorough knowledge of pricing.

Other sellers are reluctant to discuss their true motivations for understandable personal reasons. Where a family is breaking up, serious illness threatens, or careers and financial security are jeopardized, revealing true motivations may be too painful an experience for your sellers. Be empathetic. Credit them with more than unreasoning greed. Financial or personal problems may make them feel desperate, or such a large decision as a house sale may simply have distorted their ordinary personalities.

Sometimes it's easy to forget that we're dealing with people, especially if we've been in real estate for quite some time. Everyone is different. They come from different backgrounds; they're bound for different destinations; they'll travel different routes to get there.

Someone calls me and says, "Come over and list the house." Not until I get there does it come out about the divorce. They've been married 5—maybe 25—years. When I come in for that listing, I'm the guy who's going to put the *For Sale* sign up in front of their house; I'm the guy who's chopping at their roots; I'm the symbol of what's happening to them. Where's the empathy if I hustle in there bubbling with enthusiasm, success, and good cheer?

"Wow, the market's really going great! I'm having a terrific year, folks! Yeah. Now let's take a look at the rest of this sweet little home of yours. Gee, it's neat. I like what you did with the wallpaper. I *love* this carpet."

Don't chirp on and on at deeply wounded people. Don't bubble at all when you take a listing where there's a death, divorce, or other grievous problem. Try to understand what they're going through. Do the job as quickly and professionally as you can, and then get out.

Why is it so important to know why they're selling as soon as possible? Because it'll tell you how to act during your meetings with them—it'll even tell you how fast to walk while you're touring the property, and whether to be relaxed and jolly, or crisp and businesslike, during the listing interview.

The Prospects Are Talking to Other Brokers, But You Haven't Presented Yet

If they're considering three, the ideal thing is to make your presentation third. I usually win out when I'm last, if only because they're tired by that time. But if you're first, and then they're going to talk to Tom Green, and after that to Sara Rice, it's "Who was the first gal? Oh well, let's go with Sara—she's here."

So, if you think you can pick your position on their schedule, try to find out who the competition will be. "Hm, I already have an appointment early this evening—who else is coming over tonight?"

Their answer, and your judgment on the two *how heavy* questions below, provide the basis for your decision on what course to fly now. This decision has an important bearing on your success ratio and it must be made instantly, so think through every aspect of it that you can in advance.

- How heavy is the competition I'm facing for this particular listing? That is, can any of them close powerfully?
- How heavy an impression have I made so far on these prospects?

When you're competing against a strong closer (it only takes one to do you in) but you haven't already made a strong impression on the prospects, your best chance is to strike before the strong closer does. When sellers are ready to make a decision (and scheduling appointments with three agents certainly indicates they could be at that point) the first guy up can always get the listing. Then you're likely to get a call from that agent canceling your appointment with the prospects who are now his clients. They've laid that on me too.

When you're competing against agents whose closing abilities you doubt, and you believe you've already made a strong impression with the prospects, shoot for the last spot. Be sure to say, "Now, you won't list with one of those other agents before I get there, will you? I'd be so disappointed if you didn't give me a chance to serve you."

Use your other appointment to maneuver yourself into the spot you want for the listing presentation. "I'll work it out with them—I *know* I can do that." (Don't leave any uncertainty here or the sellers may lose you in the night's scramble.)

Tips on closing listings are given under *Five Excuses* in this chapter's Winning Scripts.

Aim for the Kitchen Table Before You Head for Their House

Going in loaded down with gear for your presentation intimidates people. Right away they're worried about hard sell, and that you'll be there all night unless hustled along. Travel light. Have what you'll definitely need in your hand, and leave everything else in your car.

How will I carry all my listing materials into the house?

Will I stagger in with ungainly packages under both arms and in each hand? What do I need to have with me?

1 Listing folder (See the role play in this chapter.)
2 Calculator

3 Clipboard

4 Multiple Listing book

5 My Listing Presentation Manual

If you'll be more comfortable walking in with everything neatly in place in an attaché case, then select an LPM format that'll fit inside one. Think about that situation at the front door. You want to feel cool, relaxed, and friendly. You also want to look, and be, efficient. Organize so you'll have all those qualities going for you.

It's important to get in sync with the seller—if they're meticulous, you be the same. Be sensitive to their needs and ways of doing things.

The rehearsal and research phases are over when you walk in their door. You're on stage. Now you perform. Will you walk out to a standing ovation—that is, with the listing? Whether or not you do depends on preparation more than performance.

You can muff a line, smile, and try again. Without damaging your chances, you can say, "I didn't put that well. What I mean is—" You can correct minor flaws in your performance as you go along if you have to, but you can't remedy lack of preparation after the meeting starts.

THE LISTING PRESENTATION

You Can't Get a Second Chance

You can't get a second chance to make a first impression. The first 15 seconds are critical. Be relaxed, alert, and friendly. Above all, be on time. Demonstrate by action that you regard the meeting as important. "Mr. and Mrs. Smith, this is a pleasure—"

Never light up a cigarette, or carry one lit. Use their names a lot so they know you know them, and because it makes them feel important.

Rapport

Build it from the moment they open their front door. Keep on building rapport while you're still standing in the entry meeting everyone. Build rapport not only for yourself, but also for the company you represent. The reason you're there—because of what you've done or who you know, or because you took a come-list-me call on floor time—doesn't alter your need to build rapport for both yourself and your company. They're not considering employing just you; they're also considering employing your company's name, know-how, connections, prestige, advertising, office location, and entire staff. So build rapport for yourself and your company, especially during the early moments of the contact.

Tour the Property

After you've met everyone and chit chatted briefly, say to the homeowners, "I'd really love to see your home. It'll help me a lot to have a thorough understanding of all your property's features. Can we do that now?"

If you haven't already determined their true motivation to sell, keep alert for openings to talk about it, or clues to the reason that may develop during the property tour.

Adjust your tour manner and pace to their mood and reason for leaving. When it's a move brought on by divorce, someone's passing, or other tragedy, don't linger and exclaim over their plaques, trophies, and family mementos. Walk through with your clipboard, make quick notes, and move on. Be reserved, professional, and respectful.

Your attitude should be completely different in the happy situations. Don't try to hurry when Daddy laid every brick in the walks, planted every shrub in the yard, and stuck up every roll of wallpaper in the house. Daddy is going to tell you about every brick, dig, and glue bucket, and about all the hours and all the days he spent doing it, and how much little Stevie helped him. Share his enthusiasm—unless you want him to find someone else who will. The property tour is short or long, as determined by the sellers' motivation, not your mood or schedule.

Organize the items you walk in with for easy carrying. Then, as you go through the kitchen on the property tour, say something like, "Mind if I leave some of these things here for a bit?" and set everything except your clipboard on the kitchen table. That table, of course, is where you want to be sitting when the tour's over and you get down to business. Kitchens are friendly places where families gather; living rooms are formal chambers where tense people sit back and stare at strangers.

Now You're at the Kitchen Table

Keep in mind that sellers want:

- More money,
- Less trouble,
- And fast action.

"Sure, we want all the money we can get. But I don't want to fix that cracked sink. And I want our sale to go fast, too." Sound familiar?

Be aware of something else your sellers want: peace of mind. They want to feel safe with you. So conduct yourself with integrity and win their trust.

As soon as you're all sitting at the kitchen table, give them the listing presentation by going through the manual. During that presentation, tell them about yourself, tell them about your great company, compliment them on their house, and then get down to the bare facts: money. Exact figures. That's the time to roll out the Guidelines to Market Value. This form is often called "competitive market analysis," a term many proud homeowners find insulting.

Score When You Explain Financing

Explaining this complex subject gives you another opportunity to score points—or to anger people. Rattling off a quick rundown of the available financing methods, while using as much confusing jargon as possible, is showing off. They'll know you're trying to look indispensable by making them feel stupid. Demonstrating disrespect for their feelings is no way to build trust.

It's not necessary to make a dazzling display of financing knowledge; that will come out naturally as you make your simplified explanations. The clients will have questions that'll give you ample opportunity to display your professional expertise. As you do that, keep this thought uppermost: Never make a client feel stupid.

Start with the existing loan on the property. Review how they bought, and then explain how a similar loan would be written today, what interest rate, term, and down payment would be involved, and how much income a buyer would need. Discuss whether their loan could be assumed by a buyer, or if the property could be sold subject to the existing loan. Then pass on to the other financing methods appropriate and available for the price range of their offering.

Don't lecture. Keep it a three-way conversation between you, the wife, and the husband. Drop in good things like:

"I know it seems complicated, but that's just because you don't work with it every day like I do."

Preoccupation Is Everyone's Pet Peeve

Having eye contact with people when they talk to you is vital. A glassy stare focused above their heads is not eye contact. Look them in the eyes most of the time.

Not being preoccupied with other matters is also vital. If you've got things on your mind when someone is telling you something important about their property, they'll see your mind and eyes drift away. That client will then drift away from you. Don't flatter yourself that you can hide your preoccupation, that you can think your faraway thoughts, nodding wisely while they prattle, without offending them.

We brokers and managers are often guilty of this with our sales associates. They come to us, all excited and happy, and we're so bogged down with urgent but petty details that our hearts and minds aren't really there with them. They see that, it kills their enthusiasm, and they leave us alone. Having messed up the important part of our managerial function, we're now free to get back to squashing grasshoppers.

Be very careful on a listing presentation to be 100 percent with your clients. Leave your problems at home or in the office. Before you head for the appointment, start psyching yourself up for it. The first step is to put everything else out of your mind.

Specific Listing Form Tips

All facts must be accurate. The buyers' agent will rely on the information in the listing and pass it on to the buyers, who can then claim they based their purchase decision on that information.

Don't state the house's square footage, the lot size, or any other quantity unless you've verified the information and are prepared to rest your case on its accuracy. Buyers who think they've bought 1,800 square feet, and then measure only 1,672 after moving in, get very upset. If you stated in the listing that the house is 1,800 square feet, and the price the buyers paid works out to $50 a foot, they're going to feel cheated by $6,400—and a court may agree.

"NT." Some agents write square footage as "1,800 NT," meaning "1800 square feet, not taped." What they're really saying with that cryptic symbol is something like this: "Somebody told me the house is about 1,800 square feet, but I didn't measure it myself. I'd like you to think you're getting 1,800 square feet, because that sounds like a lot, but if the house is actually smaller, don't blame me." They will blame you, and you'll find that "NT" really means, "New Trouble."

Pools are another source of trouble. Pool builders sometimes round the inches to the next higher foot—and they often measure to the outside of the coping. Homeowners will say and believe that their pool is 20 feet wide when the water width is only 16 feet, 6 inches. Measure it, or simply state that there's a swimming pool. Call it stunning, shimmering, fun-filled, exotic, custom, free-form, delightful, large—but don't get specific unless you know your facts.

Keep the fluff out of the facts, and the facts out of the fluff. There's a sharp line between the opinions you express in the remarks section and the specific facts called for by the listing form's spaces and boxes. If you add facts in the remarks section, keep them concise and accurate; when you express opinions there, keep them generalized and descriptive. "Large ranch home with pleasant, well-lit rooms," announces itself as opinion; "1,800-square-foot ranch home with imported Italian ceramic tile entry and top-of-the-line Great-stuff carpet," states facts. If the carpet falls apart and the buyers call in a floor man, who tells them that not only is the carpet the cheapest made, the tile is local nonceramic, they're going to send you the replacement bill. Will you lose a sale because your description reads, "Large ranch home with gorgeous tile entry and carpet"?

Don't bind your sellers to a specific move-out date on the listing by stating, "Possession on August 30, 19____". Tie the possession date to the day the transaction closes (settles). That makes it move with the time the property is on the market.

Working with the Guidelines to Market Value Form

How we use this market analysis technique often determines whether or not we get the listing. When you're sitting at the kitchen table in a prospect's home, don't look over the form and say, "Well, now, this house on Pine Street is a little nicer than yours." You can use a market analysis so beautifully—if you guard well what you say. See *Guidelines* in Winning Scripts.

Use a range. Let's consider a four-bedroom house with five comparables listed on the Guidelines to Market Value (GMV) form. Same house, same square footage, roughly the same kind of property; some have pools, some have views. I see a range from $210,000 to $225,000. Write across the top of the GMV: "Range—$210,000 to $225,000," and say to the seller, "This is what the market will bear on this particular kind of property right now, based on whether or not it's got a pool or a view."

Make it clear that you didn't put the range on these properties. The public did. While you're doing this, your sellers are sitting there thinking, "Okay, somewhere in that range is where we sit. $220,000? Well, that one had a pool and a view. Ours doesn't. But the $210,000 doesn't have a view either. Hm."

Already, you've got him framed in. That's what you want to do, frame him into a reasonable market value price.

Don't compare their home to someone else's. Don't do it at all, even if they bring it up. They'll say to you, "Well, you know, we saw the Clarks' house down the street and quite frankly, ours is a lot sharper."

Answer like this, "Yes, I've seen it. Some things there appeal to certain buyers, but there are things about your house that definitely appeal to certain other buyers."

Take a negative and turn it into a positive, but don't compare. Comparing gets you in trouble.

Seller's net sheet. Wait to do a seller's net sheet until after you've chewed over the GMV with your prospects. After you've looked at all the prices and have seen what's sold and for how much, after you've discussed what's expired, what's listed, and how many days these various properties have been on the market, you're ready to face setting the price. Now they know one sold for $215,000 with no pool, and one sold for $218,000 with a pool. Another house with no pool has been on the market at $216,000 for 190 days. We say something like this to the seller: "Looks like that one is too high; the market just won't pull its price."

Study the GMV at the kitchen table. Analyze it. Watch your body language then. You're concentrating on that Guidelines to Market Value. You may have every figure on that form memorized, but when you're sitting there with your sellers, you're studying it as deeply as they are, as though it was the first time you'd seen the information.

What the Salesperson Must Keep in Mind to Price It Right

Once you have the range established, you can start to zero in on the right price, the magic figure that will encourage offers without being a giveaway. At this point, the sellers are going to say, "Okay, what do you think my house is worth?" Let's think about these things before we get into the final decision:

Location.   Does this house back up to busy highway? What's the market activity in the immediate three or four blocks? Are there a dozen or more properties already for sale here? Or only two or three? None? Does this location carry a prestige premium?—Or a prestige discount?

Condition.   Be thinking, "What do I have to tell this couple to help them get their offering into proper market condition. How can I say what has to be said diplomatically?"

Price.   Will the seller stay within the range? You should know by now, based on their reaction to the Guidelines to Market Value. You've gone over the guidelines and he's said, "Well, the house on Maple Street had a pool and it sold for $215,000. We don't have a pool, but I can tell you something—our view makes up for their pool!"

How can a view make up for the lack of a pool? You can't swim in the air. This problem is not peculiar to areas that have pools. Sellers everywhere say, "This makes up for that." They'll try to equalize any condition: "Sure, our street is dangerous out front, but we've got the biggest backyard in this end of town. That makes up for our front problems."

Comments like this from the sellers, as you grind on the GMV together, tell you that you'll have to fight the price. You'll fight more effectively by taking side cuts. If the missing amenity is a pool, don't talk about pools. Make your point without hitting that hard. Tell a story about something none of the houses on the Guidelines has. See *Horse Lots* in Winning Scripts.

Terms.   What financing is available? Tell them about this in as much detail as they'll accept. Are 80-percent loans available? What points will a buyer have to pay as a loan origination fee? Don't assume that professional people know financing. Doctors have no special reason to know about real estate. Many lawyers are too busy with their specialized practices to keep current on real estate financing. Get down to basics with all your people and explain everything.

The sellers' motivation.   The sellers' reason for moving, their needs, and their emotional makeup are going to determine how their house gets priced.

If they've bought a new house that won't be ready for six months, and they think the market's going up $10,000 during that time, they'll set their price that much higher than anyone else. "We've got plenty of time," they'll think, unaware of the yearly buying pattern in your area.

People who've been transferred act very differently. Many companies pay the brokerage on the sale of their transferee's present home, and take care of moving costs. People who change homes frequently to take new assignments often have a realistic view of house pricing.

Are they gamblers or worriers? Some sellers need to carry a house vacant for several months before they can get realistic. Others feel overextended and want to get out from under fast.

You need to know these things. Pick them up during the afternoon preview and the evening presentation. You've got to, or you'll never get them to okay that magic figure.

"I Like the Number"

"I like the number," my seller said, explaining how he set his price $10,000 too high. Other sellers add in their airfare from across the country, their monthly mortgage payments, what they paid their gardener. The oddball "cost" items that show up in a house's price aren't limited by reason.

That entire approach to price setting is very *un*—*un*businesslike, *un*realistic, and *un*necessary. The sellers are entitled to all they can net out of their house. No justification is required; what their costs were is irrelevant to the issue of what the market will now pay for their property.

But some sellers actually believe that their costs set the price their property will sell for. We are, of course, talking about a "normal market" here, not one in which buyers are driving up prices by frantic bidding.

Many people flip their switch from "buy mode" to "sell mode" with no carryover insight into how a buyer of their property will feel, even though they've just bought a house—and felt absolutely no interest in the problems and goals of the persons who sold it to them. Not only do many people compartmentalize their buyer-seller feelings the same day or week, some can do it in the same breath. With their sellers' hat on, they have an amazing ability to totally block out the simple facts that govern buyers:

1 Buyers won't knowingly pay too much.

2 Buyers want to get a good deal.

3 Buyers aren't interested in paying for sellers' mistakes.

4 Buyers couldn't care less how much money the seller needs for an initial investment on the seller's next house, to start the seller's new business, or whatever the seller has in mind.

5 Buyers actually check to see what other properties are available, and compare values.

The sellers who block out these universal buyer's rules aren't too dense to see the truth; they simply don't want to. You'll generally have little difficulty explaining, and getting agreement to, the first four rules. It's the fifth that will give you the most trouble because most sellers—even those offering a common, drab house in need of care—think theirs is a unique and highly desirable prize that's far superior to similar properties. Tread softly here. Such sellers sail a dreamboat on a pond of delusion. It works something like this: "If buyers are shrewd, my dreamboat won't float. Therefore, buyers are stupid. And anyway, I only need one buyer—just one guy smart enough to have the money to buy this house, and too dumb to know it's overpriced."

Overpriced Listing Tactics. Come in Third and Walk Off with All the Money

This discussion applies only when there are comparable houses available at the lower value set by market action. Don't use these ideas unless the market has clearly established values, and the overpricing is extreme.

But what is extreme overpricing? Where there are many comparable properties with few differences, the salable price range will be narrow; where there are few comparables and many differences, the salable price range will be broad. No simple rule of thumb will fit all cases.

I've carried listings as long as 13 months before finally selling them. That involved constant consultation with, and step-by-step education of, sellers too headstrong to listen. I hate to let go, but sometimes it's the best thing. When the sellers know you disagree with the pricing, they're tempted to search for an agent who does agree. Then, 9 months later, the house sells at the price you said it would 270 days earlier. You've lost that one fee, but how many more did you make during that period with the time saved?

What is the most profitable way to operate? You need to keep asking yourself this vital question. Measure the opportunity in hand against those you could acquire with the time and emotional energy that servicing your overpriced listing preempts. If you can hang in there with small loss of time, that's the most profitable way to go. But if you are a high-volume salesperson, that listing may be costing you too much in time and enthusiasm. Perhaps a less-active agent will have the patience to work through the pain and education process that difficult, overpriced sellers require. As a new salesperson, I tended to hold on until my sellers saw things the market's way, no matter how long that took. Then, as my volume increased, working with seriously overpriced people began to take too much time away from servicing reasonably priced clients who would listen to me.

Many agents start strong by writing a number of overpriced listings and for a few weeks think they're taking over their farms. Then the listings start to expire; the word goes out that they never sell anything, and, before long, their signs have all disappeared. Suddenly they discover that newsletters, door-knocking, clever giveaways, and close personal contact avail nothing. They decide that farming is passé, that working with buyers is the key to quick success.

Except for one small detail, they did everything right on their farms. Unfortunately, into that one small detail is packed most of the real estate profession's problems. When that detail explodes into a clutch of angry, haven't-sold sellers and expired listings, it becomes painfully obvious how large a detail price is in the scheme of things.

Many agents feel they have no choice. They must take overpriced listings. If they don't, someone else will. But will that other agent gain an advantage by letting his sign sag for 90 days on Tewhi Terrace?

What's your game plan? To take every listing you can, regardless of price, and hope for the best?

Or do you take an overpriced listing only when there's an understanding that the price will be reconsidered unless the seller's price is validated by offers within an agreed time?

Your problem may arise from confusion on the sellers' part. They may believe that an agent's function is to sell property for more than its worth, that it's easy to get market price, that doing so is "giving my house away." That emotion may be too deeply rooted for words to wash it away. Try. But don't be crushed if you can't do it. If you fail at first, back off and allow time's pressure to push them into reality. When the overpriced listing with Eagercluck Realty expires, go back in for it with redoubled confidence that you'll add to your readily salable inventory.

Sellers need to sell, and they won't unless they price realistically. If you never push sellers hard to make their price realistic, you're failing to protect their interests. It's a serious failure, one that can destroy you as a listing agent.

Aim for that second or third listing where the money is. With very obstinate sellers, payoff might be delayed until the fourth or fifth time that house is listed. It may seem too risky to decline the listing in hopes of catching it at a more realistic price after it expires, but you're certain to save energy, time, and money for more promising opportunities by not promoting the unsalable.

Instead of thinking about the fee you'd earn if a one-in-a-million buyer comes along who has no regard for value but does have all cash, or the huge initial investment it'll take to get the appraisal past a loan committee, think about the buyers you'll face with that price. Think about the cost of flyers, the pressure to hold the house open, the phone calls about why it didn't sell—all the listing service time.

Outside your farm, you have only time and trouble versus opportunity to consider. You can be quicker to take an overpriced listing in hopes of price reductions later. Outside your farm, your presence is unlikely to be felt—or missed. But, if the property is in your farm, consider how it'll look to have your sign fade and sag there for months and then, when the seller is furious with you and finally ready to accept market price, your sign comes down, another office's goes up, and the property sells within days. That's not the right scenario for your fast takeover of that farm.

How much better for you if those nonsolds drive past the signs of your activity—especially your *Sold* riders—as they come and go. Some gray morning it'll hit them. "If we'd only listened to that bird who's selling all the houses around here, we'd be long gone by now." That's when you get a come-list-me call.

Of course, if you can get a firm agreement that the price will be reduced to a realistic figure after a limited market-testing period, it's always best to take the overpriced listing. The situation is a firm demonstration of effective control of your farm. Decide in advance what your tactics will be when faced with an overpriced listing. There is no perfect solution that will work in every instance, and you may be successful with methods that fail another agent.

Your decision is complicated by the season. Allow for that in your discussion with the client. Lay the groundwork for your return by asking them to consider what will happen if your forecast is correct and they list with another firm for 90 days at what you believe is $20,000 over market. After 60 days, you think they might reduce their price $5,000, and when their first listing expires, go to a second office, again for 90 days, and still $15,000 over market price. After six months, where will they be in relation to your area's usual peak selling season?

After six months—after just 60 days—will they remember you? They should, if they live in your farm and you're in effective control there.

Don't always take overpriced listings. Don't always walk away from them either.

Market Forecast

After you've toured the property, and worked through your Listing Presentation Manual, tell them what the market's like. Say (if it's true that day), "You know, the marketing time lately has been running 90 to 180 days. It used to be that you could sell your house in 20 days around here. No more." Tell them what the market's like *now*.

Collect articles from the business and realty sections of magazines and newspapers that bear out what you're saying. Put these articles in your listing presentation manual. Homeowners usually don't have this information; they rely on you for it.

Overpromises

People think you mean them. If you tell someone, "I'll get you the moon for this property," they'll expect the moon. "That so-called agent of mine, Betty Bignews, convinced us she was going to sell our house for $159,500. So we signed a 90-day listing. Now she wants us to extend her listing—even though she's never brought us an offer. It'll snow in Panama before I renew with her."

Agents don't control what their listings sell for—unless they buy them. You're an agent, not a buyer; talk like an agent, not a buyer.

Take Command of Listing Remarks

If you run off your sparkling sales blurb without regard for the space limitations of your Multiple Listing book, you'll force someone else to make decisions that only you and the seller should make. Save time and trouble, and look professional, by doing the job right the first time.

The following "remarks" were taken from a recent entry in the Multiple Listing book issued by my board:

> $500 BNUS TO S/O W/FULL PRC OFR. OVER 2,100 SF LXRS LK LVG W/FNTSTIC LK/MTN VU, PRSTGS LOC, QIET CDS NOTE UPGDS: CERM NTRY, NWX FLRS, PLSH CPT, WTBR, CERM CTRS, TRSH COMP, INDR LNDRY, & *MW*.SM LNDR SV PPP

How many busy Realtors® have time to decode that cryptogram? I called the listing agent for a translation. Here's what he meant:

> $500 BONUS TO SELLING OFFICE WITH FULL PRICE OFFER. OVER 2,100 SQUARE FEET OF LUXURIOUS LAKE LIVING WITH FANTAS-TIC LAKE AND MOUNTAIN VIEW. PRESTIGIOUS LOCATION ON A QUIET CUL DE SAC. NOTE UPGRADES: CERAMIC TILE ENTRY, NO-WAX KITCHEN AND BATHROOM FLOORING, PLUSH CARPET ELSEWHERE, WET BAR, CERAMIC COUNTERTOPS, TRASH COM-PACTOR, INDOOR LAUNDRY, AND MIRRORED WARDROBES IN MASTER BEDROOM. PLEASE STAY WITH SAME LENDER TO SAVE PREPAYMENT PENALTY. DON'T LET THE SMALL DOGS OUT.

Note that the board typist, who did a superb job of compressing nine lines into four, had to give up on the last sentence. Unfortunately, that was the most important one to the sellers. The agent told me they were furious because their precious poodles had been ignored. You can try to blame things like this on the board, but your sellers will hold you responsible—as they should in this case.

Such problems are easily avoided. First, find out exactly how much space you have by counting the number of spaces your Multiple Listing book allows per line of remarks. Then write your remarks to fit, and run off a few copies of this note:

"Board Secretary: Please type the remarks exactly as shown. They will fit.

Thanks,"_____

Pin one of these notes to each one of your listings when you submit them to the board.

Writing effective remarks fast. Before you write your throbbing description, list everything that has to be said. As the sellers reel off four times as much

Page 186, Chapter 11

stuff as you have space for, list them in two columns: *must go* and *if possible*. The if-possibles will never make it, but you don't have to tell the sellers that.

Once you've written all the must-gos in the shortest form busy agents will understand, count the spaces used, deduct them from the total available, and the remainder is what your *selling remarks* are limited to. Don't waste time writing and polishing 100 words when you only have room for 35.

The Delicate Art

"How much for our home?" they ask, their faces pokering the soft distress that only their eyes betray.

But who can put a price on love, warmth, security? Sure, it's windows and walls and rugs and grass. I've seen thousands, sold hundreds. But the numbers game is gone when you're sitting across from two people and their hopes, dreams, joys, sorrows. He paneled the den; she papered the kitchen. Here they argued, and there they made up. The cause of the quarrel is forgotten, only the sweetness of its settlement is remembered. The master bedroom—a private place to hold one another, make love, laugh, cry. Each room evokes special memories—and marks many paths that can't be trodden again.

And now come I, the stranger, to tell them the worth of this prized place of their caring, to set a value on this nest of their yesterdays. I'm to say what the highest bidder will pay for the priceless—for this dwelling hallowed by a time that's now to end for them. "We've been happy here," they say.

Yes, but the thing must be done. They tell me so. Then let me do it—with intuition—with understanding of their next move—with empathy for their new dream—with a sharing of their bright dawning hope. Let me be firm. Let me be strong. But, oh, please, let me be *deli*cate.

LISTING THE CASEYS, A ROLE PLAY IN ONE ACT

Cast: Your manager
        Danny, the agent
        Harry Casey
        Martha Casey

Designed to be read by four people at an office meeting, this role play trains the agents who participate and the other agents present at the meeting who form the audience. The person playing Danny, the agent, should read the play before hand and prepare for the ad-libs. No other rehearsal is required if all four members of the cast have their own copy of this book.

The manager or broker conducting the meeting reads the manager's part (all of which is directed to the audience). Volunteers play the other three parts. The agent may be a man or woman associate.

Props required: three chairs, three coffee cups, a table (a desk will do). Danny carries a clipboard and Listing Presentation Manual.

(Lines that are to be spoken to the audience are given in parentheses like these.)

[Stage directions are enclosed in brackets like these.]

Manager: (Our play this morning is *Listing the Caseys.* _____ and _____ have consented to play Mr. and Mrs. Casey, and our agent, Danny, will be played by _____. The time is a Saturday afternoon in football season. The scene is the Caseys' front door in our town. We're about to observe our agent arrive for a listing presentation. He/she has done this dozens of times, and his/her odds are terrific. But there's a reason for his/her good batting average, as you'll see. Besides what you observe, remember that Danny has an impressive inventory of houses on Quick-Speak, keeps excellent records, and drives the area thoroughly prior to an appointment. Our agent comes in knowing all his/her lines. We all know that the key to any successful performance is preparation.)

Danny: Good afternoon, Mrs. Casey, I'm Danny _____ and we have a two o'clock appointment. Am I right on time? I sure tried to be.

(Of course, I wouldn't say that if I wasn't on time.)

Martha: Yes you are. Do come in, Danny. We were expecting you. Let me go get Harry. He's in the back watching football.

[Walks away.]

Danny: (Aha! Football. There's nothing that makes a man madder than someone intruding on his Saturday football. I better do something quick.)

[Harry enters.]

Danny: Hi, Harry, I'm really sorry. I make it a policy never to interfere with clients watching football games. Can I return at a more convenient time?

[Looks at audience.]

(I'm dead serious about this. It's inconvenient to come back, but not as inconvenient as losing the listing.)

Harry: Gosh, you're the first agent who's appreciated how much I like football. But Danny, we've got to get this show on the road, and I have two more agents coming in later. We better get on with it. If you notice me running to the TV from time to time, don't be offended.

Danny: Heck, no. I'm a real Rams' fan myself. Harry and Martha, do you think we could do two things at this time? Number one, give me a cook's tour of your property and, number two, can I set my things down on the kitchen table for our meeting after the tour?

Martha: Be my guest.

[Danny sets the Listing Presentation Manual on the table, and retains the clipboard.]

Manager: (Notice how Danny takes control here after finding out that Harry's attention can be taken away from football. But, had Harry been unwilling to hear the presentation, Danny would make another appointment to come back and give it later. No sense wasting time.)

Danny: Harry, do you mind if Martha gives me the tour? Then you can watch the game until we get back here to the kitchen. Unless, of course, there's something you want to show off.

Harry: Great idea. I'll just watch the old tube and let you two do your thing. Martha, I like Danny. He (she) isn't trying to cut me out of seeing the game.

Martha: Well, Harry, are you going to play me or trade me?

Harry: Very funny.

Danny: Okay, Martha, let's see this lovely home of yours.

Manager: (Martha and Danny take the tour. Harry bursts in every now and then to point out the brick fence he built himself, and the mirrored wardrobe in the bedroom.)

[As the manager talks, Danny and Martha go in one direction, Harry in another. Martha points, and Danny looks, scribbling furiously on the clipboard.]

Danny: You certainly have a lovely home, Martha. Let's go back to the kitchen now. Perhaps you and Harry and I can talk about how your property fits into the local real estate front.

[Martha waves Danny to a seat at the table, pulls out the three coffee cups, and pours as Harry comes in. They all sit down.]

Danny: How're the Rams doing, Harry?

Harry: Lousy.

Danny: Then let's get on a better topic, Harry. You have a lovely home. I certainly feel that you and Martha have done a lot to enhance this neighborhood. How do you feel about leaving?

Manager: (This is an important question. Danny knows that if the reason for leaving is good, his/her marketing and pricing of the property will be easier. Generally, distraught sellers—those who move for reasons beyond their control—are tougher to work with. Examples are: a split-up where one party doesn't want the divorce, a lateral move in a company to another part of the country, a pair of empty-nesters moving to a smaller house because their children are grown up. All these people have long thoughts about leaving their cherished homes.)

Harry: Well, I've just been promoted to Sioux City, and we're pretty excited about the job and pay raise. But there *is* one problem. I just got back from Sioux City, and I find I can't get as much house there as we have in River City.

Danny: Harry, the thing we must remember is that we can't compare apples to oranges. All we can do is try for the top dollar here, and not compare this market with Sioux City. But I can understand how that would be a disappointment to you.

Harry: Yeah, but the promotion is good. So what's this area like right now?

Manager: (Danny must maintain good eye contact now with both of them.)

Danny: Interest rates are running about _____ percent.

[Locks eyes with one of the Caseys for a few seconds, then turns head to eye-lock with the other while speaking.]

The average number of days a house in on the local market here, before being sold, is 72 at this time. Considering the season, our market action is brisk, and weekly sales this year are running about 5 percent ahead of last year. Generally, the market is bright at this moment.

But we have to remember the season. We're coming up on the holidays, and that usually starts slowing the market down about now.

Manager: (Danny adapts that market evaluation to the current situation each time he/she gives it. The market evaluation is a powerful display of expertise, and belongs in every listing presentation.)

Harry: After the holidays, what do you think the market will do? Take off?

Danny: I don't expect it to take off, but I do think it'll continue to be brisk, and keep on running about 5 percent ahead of the year-ago figures.

Martha: Wow, things look good then.

Danny: In general, yes they do, Martha. May I ask, how did you hear about me?

Harry: Yeah, the owner of the corner gas station says you come in there all the time, and really seem to be a busy one. Plus your picture is always in the paper.

Danny: I work hard at being a true professional.

Harry: Yeah, it shows. But I have two other hotshots coming over later.

Danny: Great. Now, let's get back to the business at hand. I'd like to tell you a little bit about my company, our philosophy, and myself. May I demonstrate my Listing Presentation Manual to you?

Harry: Okay, but will you wait one second? I gotta check that score.

[Harry runs out, then trots back and sits down again. Danny flows with this naturally, smiling and leaning back in the chair.]

Danny: [When Harry is back.] First off, let me tell you a little bit about our company—

[Ad-libs a sales speech about your company: how long it's been operating; how many people are on the staff; if you're in the top six, where your office ranks on the board in volume; what the relocation connection is; what the advertising program is; how impressive the office decor or location is. Harry and Martha may interrupt several times to ask questions or comment.]

Harry: Okay, Danny, let's get down to bare facts. What can we get for this place?

Danny: Well, you mentioned that you have other agents coming in. Do me one favor. Please don't choose a broker based on pricing. We all have the same facts of record and, quite frankly, I hope you'll make your choice based on ability, integrity, and track record. Will you do that for me?

Harry: Sure. But what will I get for this place?

Danny: First, Harry and Martha, let me take out my Guidelines to Market Value form. Heaven knows, I don't want to compare your home to others because it's so special.

Manager: (Danny's pauses and sincere manner make an important contribution to rapport at this point.)

Danny: You both have really done an outstanding job here. But the appraisers from the lending institution that we'll be working with after the sale always come back to me and want the facts of record.

Martha: Who are they?

Danny: Well, when the property sells, the buyer needs to qualify for a new loan, and so does the property. Qualifying the property means that we have to get an appraisal on the property that's high enough to carry that new loan. Of course, the appraisal has to reflect the values in the neighborhood. Shall we look at the Guidelines to Market Value?

Manager: (Before they look at it, Danny always talks about the Guidelines to Market Value form so that the sellers understand its purpose.)

Harry: Okay, shoot.

Manager: (Note the agent's concentration on both sellers to pick up their body language, and any defensiveness they might show.)

Danny: [Points with pencil.] Notice this property about two blocks from here. It sold 10 days ago for $289,500. Very similar to yours. I believe the carpet was installed just prior to marketing the property.

Harry: Yeah, but did they have a block wall? My carpet is only six years old—and it looks good.

Danny: [Calmly.] I definitely am not trying to compare your property. I'm just trying to establish value. No, they had a wood fence, but I just want you to know what's out there, and what sold.

Harry: I know this one, Martha. That's where your stupid friend, Rosie, lived. She cleans like Phyllis Diller. Every two years she lights the top of her stove to burn off the grease. Can you believe she got $289,500 for that pit?

Martha: Honey, you're right, she's a messy housekeeper.

Danny: That particular property sold for a higher price because its owners were willing to sell "subject to" their existing loan.

Harry: What?

Danny: Well, the seller didn't need a lot of cash, and the buyer didn't have much. So the sellers carried back a lot of the paper, instead of getting paid off in cash. The buyers took the property over subject to the seller's present loan. Do you want to consider something like that?

Martha: Heck, no. We need all our cash for Sioux City. And we want this loan paid off, right, Harry?

Harry: Right.

Danny: Well, just keep in mind then that those special financing arrangements made Rosie's house marketable to a certain type of buyer. And that it has value too, even though she wasn't the housekeeper you are, Martha.

Harry: There certainly are a lot of special circumstances in this real estate business, aren't there?

Danny: That's for sure, Harry.

Manager: (We'll skip over their review of four more properties.)

Danny: Now that we've looked over the Guidelines to Market Value, I'm going to write the range right here. In the sold houses, it's $286,500 to $289,500. On the listings, $286,900 to $292,999. Harry and Martha, do you see yourself in that range?

Manager: (Danny isn't afraid of silence. Right now is one of those times when the ability to keep quiet is of vital importance.)

[Harry, Martha, and Danny sit looking at each other, without speaking, for several seconds. Danny doesn't move, Harry and Martha fidget.]

Harry: You tell me, Danny. My contact at the gas pump tells me you're the one who has the real estate brains.

Danny: Well, Harry, I appreciate that. But please keep in mind that when we list a house, we've only heard from its owners. They can set the price wherever they like. But for that property to sell, we also have to hear from a buyer. And, for the sale to be completed, the property has to have sufficient value *that an appraiser can document* to qualify for the new loan. It boils down to a willing seller and a willing buyer getting together on a price that's good for both of them. So the market values are set by folks like yourselves, together with buyers who are interested, emotionally and physically, in your home. I'm just the mediator. But here's what I'd like to do—

[Pauses, staring at the guidelines form.]

—How about if I prepare a seller's net sheet for you at this point? I'll pull a figure out of my hat off your Guidelines to Market Value form here. That'll give you an idea of what you'd net—in dollars and cents to you—at the closing. That's if you sell at a number in the general vicinity of what I'm going to put down.

Harry: Okay.

[Danny pulls out a seller's net sheet form and works quickly at entering amounts on it.]

Manager: (Danny will figure the price at $287,500, knowing full well that it's on the low end of the range, based on the comparables. Our agent wants to get Harry and Martha used to the scale of value they're in, and frame them in on a salable price. It takes guts to pull a figure out and put it on the net sheet with a critical seller, but it has to start some place, and the logical time comes right after the Guidelines to Market Value form is studied.)

Danny: Let me explain each of the charges on this net sheet, Harry and Martha.

Manager: (Everything down the line is explained, including prepayment privileges. The sellers should be impressed with the agent's thorough knowledge of the net sheet.)

Danny: Harry and Martha, please add up these figures to be sure I didn't make a mistake on this net sheet. I don't want to give you any false information.

[Harry and Martha study the net sheet intently.]

Manager: (Danny knows the figures are right. The point is to involve them.)

Harry: So this means we come out with $232,600?

Danny: Yes, approximately, barring any miscalculation you may have given me on your loan balance, or anything like that.

Martha: Harry, we were hoping for $234,000.

Harry: Yeah, especially when I think of Sioux City's prices.

Manager: (Danny doesn't say a word while they're talking to each other.)

Martha: Yeah, but remember, Danny said we can't count that, honey.

Harry: What do you mean? If it's money, it counts.

Danny: Oh, I agree, Harry. Please keep in mind that no one wants to see you get more for your property than I do. But, the thing is, if I'm not honest with you, you won't appreciate my stroking after it takes too long to market your home. Then a new, and more honest, agent might come along, list it at market value, and sell it quick.

Martha: You're honest, Danny. But do you think we could get, or maybe even list at $289,000?

Manager: (Danny originally gave the low-end target price of $287,500 in order to have room to come up to a higher asking price.)

Danny: I'd suggest a maximum list price of $288,900. That hundred dollars under makes a big difference in the buyer's head. I'd figure that allows $900 to $1,900 for a negotiating pad. Am I in line?

Harry: Danny, I do want to get some other opinions.

Danny: I appreciate that, but may I tell you about some of the deadlines that we Realtors® are up against? In order to get your home on next week's caravan, your listing has to be in the board office by _____. Also, if you give me the opportunity to work for you, I'll personally greet everyone at your open house by serving a progressive Mexican lunch. The finest agents in our town are my friends, so I'll send out special invitations to all of them. Plus I'll send a sharp photographer out to shoot both the interior and exterior, and then I'll personally make up a special brochure of your home.

Martha: Harry, let's do it. Remember, you and I wanted to go up to the city tomorrow to see Mary and Dick, and I hate having to interview more agents.

Harry: Well, I don't know.

Danny: I could work an open house for you tomorrow, and get the ball rolling, if you weren't going to be here. I love writing ad copy, so I could shoot an ad into today's late edition if there's time.

Harry: Yeah, but what about your cousin's friend—the agent guy.

Martha: Oh, yeah, maybe we better talk to him.

Danny: Who is your cousin's friend?

Harry: Howard Jensen.

Danny: Oh, yes. He's with Vibration Realty. Nice guy. He's a Multiple Listing agent like we are. He could still sell it, you know.

Martha: He could?

Danny: Sure, I would be exclusively representing you as your listing agent on all offers, but I cooperate with all other agents who bring in a buyer besides myself.

Harry: Well, aren't you going to sell it?

Danny: I certainly am going to try, but the neat thing about a Multiple Listing agent is that you have a team of _____ [ad-libs the total number of agents on your board] on your side. I get along very well with Howard and most agents in the board.

Martha: Well, Harry, I think Danny's pretty thorough. Let's just cancel the other appointments.

Harry: Well, okay, but now I'm going to tell you why, Danny. You didn't try to take me away from my football.

WINNING SCRIPTS

The front door opens where you're to give a listing presentation. If they're both standing at the door, focus eye contact on each of them in turn. If not, zero in on the second person as soon as you see him or her.

"Hi, Mr. Shepley. I'm _____ with _____ and I really appreciate your letting me stop by." Pause at the entry hall and look in all four corners of the living room ahead of you. If you're properly psyched up, your alertness and intensity will create a presence, a feeling of subdued excitement, a mood that something good and important is going to happen now that the expert is here. Your presence commands respect, and allows you to exert control.

If this is a referral appointment, say:

"I'm very happy that the Prestons recommended me when you told them you needed a market evaluation on your home."

"Aha," thinks Mr. Shepley, who wasn't listening when his wife reminded him, "This is the fireball real estate agent Jack was telling us about." Having so identified you, several of Mr. Shepley's defense barriers fall flat. Always mention your referral connection in front of both of them, at a time when you have their full attention, because one of the couple may never have been told that you were recommended. (And remind them early, so you benefit throughout the interview from the greatly expanded credibility that a recommendation gives you.)

"I represent Palfrey Realty, now one of the top four brokers in the area. I'm really proud to be a part of that team. I wonder if I might ask you a favor? [Don't wait for an answer.] "Can both of you give me the grand tour of your home now? I need to walk through so that I can appreciate what you've done before I can counsel you."

Five Excuses Sellers Frequently Give for Not Employing You, and the Five Ways You Convince Them to Do Just That

Many situations require that you choose a course and stick to it, win or lose. So you can't always convince them. But you don't have to win them all (which is lucky, because that's impossible). Go with your hunches. You can't develop intuition unless you listen to its first whisperings. If you don't get a hunch, play the odds. If you don't know the odds, act with confidence. Always move and act with confidence. Expect to fail more often than you succeed. Accept that, be comfortable with it, because that's how the numbers work out, especially at first.

1. **"I'll sell it myself and save the fee."** That's the for-sale-by-owner's whole trick. Chapter 5 tells you how to train this tiger.

2. **"I'll think it over."** When they tell me that after my listing presentation, I always ask, "Have you definitely decided to make a move now?"

If they answer, "Oh, yeah, we've decided that. In fact, we're already talking to some other brokers," I say:

"Is there something I've missed? Are there questions in your mind? Something I haven't told you or covered? Is there a barrier between us that I can overcome and break through?"

Be frank and honest with these people. They're just human beings. That encourages them to be frank and honest with you. Find out why you don't have a signed listing in front of you.

If they say, "We want to sleep on it; we want to talk to someone else," and they come up with a bona fide reason, "This is the first time we've ever sold a home; we'd really prefer to get two or three other opinions," honor that. Pressure only goes so far.

If they have an appointment at 2 o'clock the next day with another broker, tell them, "Before you make a final decision, give me one more chance to see if there's something I can do for you that maybe someone else has told you they can do. Just give me one more chance." Always end on that note. Then try to make another appointment with them after they've talked to the other brokers.

3. "We want to buy a new house before we list." I don't feel bad about this if their new house won't be ready for several months. But if they're talking about purchasing a resale home before they list, say to them: "If you plan to make an offer on another house before yours is on the market, does that mean you have the necessary funds to close on the new house before selling your present home?"

"Oh, yeah. We've got the money in a savings account."

If they have the money, fine. If not, tell them now about the problems they can have trying to buy their next home *contingent* on their present home selling.

If they're leaving your sales area, you have a worthwhile chance at a referral fee by lining up a broker for them in the region they're moving to. If they're staying in your sales area, they're probably not committed to another agent regarding the house they'll buy, or they wouldn't be talking to you about listing the one they'll sell—unless they're building, or planning to buy a new house from a developer.

Be alert for these opportunities. Many people won't volunteer this information; they'd just as soon let the more alert and effective agents pry it out of them. In many cases, they aren't sure precisely how to proceed. It's a big decision; in this case it's two big decisions—with lots of things to worry about in the wee hours of morn. So people often take the long way around when meeting their wants or needs, especially when the decisions are easily postponed.

Just don't let the dollar signs flash in your eyes when you discover they're in the local market for a house. Be relaxed, cordial, and interested. Let them be comfortable with you. Try for a small commitment first, a relaxed, "Let's see what's available" trip of an hour or two. Then thoroughly prepare and give these people the highest priority on your time. The odds are you're working for two fees here, or none.

If their answer to your question, ". . . does that mean you have the necessary funds to close on the new house before selling your present home?" is negative, you'll learn a lot from the exact way they phrase it.

"Well, isn't there some way we could be sure of where we're going before we let go of this place?" These people need help. Talk basics.

"Oh, no. We'll make our offer contingent on this house selling." This couple is more sophisticated about real estate. Use a little jargon on them.

"I don't want to wind up owning two houses and making two payments. But we've got to have a place to live. I can't see spending a fortune storing my furniture and living in a motel in my home town, and I darn sure don't want double payments." This man believes that timing his sale to fit his purchase is a difficult problem fraught with unknown perils that can break out unexpectedly. (He's right.) The important thing is what he's just revealed to you, probably unintentionally: He'd welcome a strong agent taking charge of coordinating both the sale of his present home and the purchase of his new one. The only way to work with him is to earn two fees. Spend a little time telling him you're an expert and that you can handle it; then go out and find him the house he wants while you're lining up a buyer for his place. He's told you where his shoes are. Put them on. He wants to be sure of owning one house, no more and no less, all the time. Assure this man you'll protect him from a double move. He'll probably flex a little pricewise, on either end, and he'll probably bend a little on what he wants his new home to be like too, just so he can be sure of a roof over his head without risking owning two homes at once.

Most people don't worry much about all this until the last few hours. They just assume it'll all work out okay, as it usually does—by the sweat of an agent's brow.

If you haven't had experience with contingent offers, Chapter 23 tells how to develop a sales dialogue explaining this subject to your clients.

4. "If I list, I'll list with my friend."   "Consider me your friend."

Smile and go on. "You know, close friends can't be detached about each other. Isn't this what friendship is: a sort of agreement to filter out imperfections so the good things shine brighter? That's great for friendship, but it's poor for business. Being realistic is the best policy when you're selling real estate, and it's hard for anyone to be both close to, and impartial about, the same person. That puts too heavy a burden on friendship. You have a great friend in the business, and I respect that, but keep in mind that you want professional service and opinions here, and even though your friend says, 'I'll be realistic with you,' it's almost impossible because of the rose-colored glasses a friend wears."

5. "Another broker told me our house was worth $5,000 more."   "Mr. and Mrs. Sellers, don't choose a broker based on price."

Nearly every time I used to go out on a listing presentation, they'd say, "Well, after we're through talking to you, we're going to call in two or three other brokers." After you've toured the property, gained empathy, moved in with their mood, worked the sellers' net and the Guidelines to Market Value, after you've run the full 26 miles giving the whole listing presentation, you should look at them and say,

"Please do me and, more importantly, yourselves, a great big favor by not selecting a broker based on who comes in here with the highest price. Please remember that we're talking about your asking price, not our bid. An agent coming in here with a price higher than the market will pull isn't offering to buy at that price. All of us have the same records; we're all Multiple Listing brokers. If you decide not to follow the market and price your house higher, I can do that too. And

I'll back you 100 percent. I may not want to do it because I want to solve your problem. You have a need to sell here, so I may fight you a little bit on price. But please don't choose me based on pricing. Choose your broker for professionalism, for integrity, for willingness to work.'' Tell them that, right up front.

A real estate friend of mine recently said, ''When I give a seller a price that's lower than another broker's, the other broker always gets the listing because he put more money on it.''

Talking further with her, I discovered that she wasn't facing the issue squarely. She was treating it as an unmentionable. It is--but you've still got to talk about it with your sellers.

''Choose me for my know-how and my honesty—and the pricing we can work out.''

Guidelines to Market Value

Appraisers

''The reason I brought this Guideline to Market Value with me today was *not* to compare your home to others because, Lord knows, we can't compare anybody's house with anybody else's. We can't compare anyone's kids with anyone else's. We're all unique; we're all originals—every single one of us—'' We've got to get this point across to the seller.

''—but the reason I brought it is those darn appraisers. You know, we can set a price, and sell it for that price, but then the appraiser comes out from the bank, and he says, 'How did you arrive at this price? Can you substantiate it?' Then we've got to go back to the records and prove that the value is here.'' You must explain all this to the seller, because he doesn't know that.

Horse Lots

''It's like 'horse lots.' Are you familiar with that term? There are places out in the country where riding horses can be stabled on certain properties called horse lots. A family walks into a real estate office in an area like that and the husband says, 'We want a house on a horse lot. We're all riders. We love horses. That's our sport. Let's go look at the horse lots you've got.'

''The agent says, 'I know a place you'll love. Can't have horses there, but it's got a terrific tennis court. So you swat tennis balls instead of horse flies. Same difference.' Obviously, the horse-loving family will walk out on that agent, and go to one who'll show them what they want. Any time your property omits something that's important to certain buyers, you eliminate those buyers. And you don't add others unless that omission is reflected in the price of the property.''

Defining Price

Have you ever said to them, "Well, Mr. and Mrs. Jenkins, what do you want to get for your house? Do you have an idea in mind?"

They're going to look at you and say, "You tell us. You're the expert, the pro, the champ. You're the best. Now you tell us."

Reply with, "Thanks for the compliment. But you and the mystery buyer will become the experts. *Market price* is created by willing buyers and willing sellers, not real estate agents. That's why you should not choose a real estate agent based on price. We all have the same facts of record. These facts are used by appraisers when your house is sold and a new loan is placed on it."

You've got to tell the sellers that. They think you're pricing their house like an appraiser. You're not an appraiser; you're the third party who creates a channel to new owners for the property they no longer need. You're the mediator, the negotiator; not the czar of price. Don't let them get upset with you for following what the market, the law, and the whole environment has brought about. Don't let them confuse you with the problem you're there to help them solve; don't let them blame you for things you're not responsible for.

Bailing Out

I've found it helpful to discuss pricing along these lines.

"You're entitled to every penny you can get for your house. That's our system. Owners of an investment that increases in value make money when they sell; those whose investment has decreased in value lose money when they sell. You don't need to make excuses for taking a profit because nobody would cover your loss if you were to have one.

"A lot of forces are at work determining what the selling value is: supply-demand ratio and timing are the two important ones.

"The market makes prices. Not sellers acting alone, because they're all competing against each other for the buyers in the marketplace *at that time*. And not buyers acting alone, because they too are competing—against the other buyers in the marketplace *at that time*—for the most desirable, best priced properties, the properties that offer the buyer the most value for the least money.

"In setting your price, please don't fall into the very common error of approaching it from the standpoint of your costs. If you want to sell *now*, determine what price range the market will *pay now*.

"I have never talked to a buyer who had the slightest interest in bailing a seller out, or in paying more than market price. Buyers want to buy right. Of course they sometimes get emotional, they sometimes pay a little more for something that really turns them on, but they do it to satisfy their own whim, not the seller's need.

"Now, let's talk about what the market says is a fair price for your house today."

Put Them Eyeball to Eyeball with Truth

"Let's figure out how much it would cost you to buy your own home at the price you're thinking of asking, $125,000. The most common arrangement is 20 percent down, and the current interest rate is 10 percent, so your monthly investment would be $877.58, plus property tax and homeowners' insurance. So, at that price, we're looking at a housing cost of a thousand dollars a month. If you decide to go that high with your asking price, I'm with you 100 percent, but I'm going to have you take responsibility for that price. Maybe we can re-evaluate it after we get some buyer response.

"Now let's talk about the appraiser. The lender tells him, 'We're looking at a risk of $100,000 here, so this property darn well better be worth it now, and after the economy's taken a hard bump too. We're loaning our depositors' money, so we've got to be careful.' That appraiser will take the lot size and your house's square footage into consideration as he compares it to other properties that have sold recently in this same neighborhood. But he'll simply lump the upgrades into one category: excellent, good, or poor. That's rough on you and me, but that's the way they do this, and we have to be aware of the realities.

"When we come into the book and appear on the caravan sheet with your four-bedroom home, the other agents—the sharp ones who do all the business—will know quite a bit about your house just from its location. If they feel it's overpriced, they won't show it. They won't even preview it because they're always pressed for time. And they don't want to irritate their buyers by showing them overpriced properties, so why should they take time to see a house they believe is too overpriced to sell?"

I constantly ask things like, "How do you feel about this?" Questions give the sellers a chance to confide in me.

"Do you agree?"

"Does that sound reasonable?"

"Are you satisfied on that point?"

"Do you see what I'm saying here?"

You have to make your points, and the only way you can know you're doing that is to get them to talk, to voice their objections, to air their gripes about the system and to speak of their true feelings. You need to say the right phrases, but you need to listen to them even more.

One of the winningest scripts is the gold-grabbing silence of the superb listener. Such listening takes every bit as much energy and attention as does delivering an effective sales talk.

Make the sellers aware that they are not to come back at you if there's no activity, that if they get their price no one will be happier for them than you will be, and that a price re-evaluation will be in order in a couple of weeks.

Take Overpriced Listings Very Carefully

Take overpriced listings entirely cautiously. Don't let yourself be pulled into carrying overpriced listings in a buyer's market by wishful thinking about getting the prices down later, especially if the seller is never going to be that motivated to move.

Deadlines Are Closes

But they can close you *out*, if you're timing is bad, instead of closing you *in* on a new listing. Here's how it works: You've made a strong listing presentation and feel you're almost there—but they want to wait. You're the last of three agents they've heard. They can't quite make up their minds and want to think it over. Your office caravan is Tuesday; the Thursday board caravan deadline is 5 P.M. Tuesday; the following week's Multiple Listing book deadline is Friday at 5 P.M. Here's what you say:

"I know how you feel. You're thinking. 'We can wait a few days; we're not quite ready emotionally to take the final step.' It *is* a big decision. But, actually, you've already made the big decision [to take that job a thousand miles away, to buy the new house, whatever] and now you're doing a very understandable thing: catching your breath for a few hours."

Smile understandingly. "A few hours delay can't make much difference, can it?" Pause briefly. Whether they say anything or not, continue with, "Well, let's talk about that. Let's make sure that waiting those few hours isn't going to cost you a bundle. First of all, our office caravan is every Tuesday morning. Tomorrow. We have a hard-driving team, and all of them are working with buyers. So, a few hours delay wipes out showing your home to our office for a whole week. Then comes the next deadline. Five P.M. tomorrow is the cutoff for getting on Thursday's caravan. So we miss that for a week. Well, you may say, 'What's a week?' "

Your next lines will depend on what the market's doing, and the season. (Any facts that you give now must, of course, be true at the time.) "Sales have dropped every week for the past four weeks. That's not much of a change—but every week the activity is a little less than it was the week before. When we have a condition like this, the buyers sense that the market is going down and wait for better prices. This action cuts sales further and increases the downward pressure. That's why we have these up and down cycles in real estate and, frankly, I think two months ago would've been a better time to have your house on the market. We can't roll the calendar back, but we can make sure that no more time gets away from us.

"Next week, probably 70 couples will buy here. That's what we're all telling each other. But the market often moves with suddenness, and turns yesterday's sound assumptions into tomorrow's wishful thinking. You want to sell. Considering the season, we can forget about the market taking off during the next few months. But we can't forget about it getting worse. You're going to give someone the assignment to sell your property soon. Why make it tougher on yourselves by waiting? It's not that it'll be tougher on me to sell your house next week, because I'm going to be selling houses next year, and the year after that. I'm thinking about your situation.

"You should have your house listed in the next issue of the Multiple book. It should be on Thursday's caravan. Our office should come through here tomorrow morning, and start comparing it to their buyers' needs. All I need to get this aggressive sales program moving is your approval right here." Slide the listing form over to them. "Shall we proceed?"

Rising Market

But what do you say if the market is rising? You're sitting in their home in February, at the beginning of your heavy selling season.

"Mr. Seller, the four top selling months here are March, April, May, and June. Sales peak in June, hold constant or slide off slowly through August, and then drop sharply to the off-season lows. Those folks who are fortunate enough to market their home now, at the beginning of our heavy selling season, can expect top dollar and minimum selling time—*if* their conditions and location are right. In that situation, we can project a bit of appreciation into our listing price. But remember that a price too much over the market will discourage showings and offers.

"Let's see, $285,500 is the top market figure right now for a comparable sale of this size home in your neighborhood. That sale occurred just 10 days ago. Prior to that, the figures were $282,000 and $283,500. I'd suggest a spring maximum list price of $287,900. This gives us a projected cushion, and it's still believable in the marketplace. The spring forecast is good, and sales are beginning right on schedule to make their slow climb to the peak, so I feel comfortable with $287,900 at this time.

Nonrising Market

If you don't expect the market to rise this spring, use this dialogue:

"Mr. Seller, it's true that March through June is our most active selling period, but last year's rapid appreciation drained off all chance of further spiraling prices this spring. So I believe that our sales prices will remain constant for another 6 to 12 months. Until demand catches up with supply, and rising income brings the buyers' ability to qualify up to higher levels, I don't see an economic base that'll support higher prices. Last year's rapid appreciation has hurt us, and brought on the correction period we're in now. Please bear this in mind when we agree on price."

Such speeches are highly effective when they flow smoothly out of your mouth. You'll find the material for them in your ongoing study of published economic figures and forecasts. Your public library will have copies of *Forbes*, *Fortune*, *The Wall Street Journal*, *Barron's Weekly*, and other prestigious financial publications.

Make your own forecast of future sales activity and price levels in your sales area. Write down your predictions. Refer to them after the facts are in, and see whether you can figure out why you were right—or wrong. The more careful and thorough your predictions are, the smoother and more convincing your sales speeches giving them will be.

Overimprovements

They have a 2,200 square foot, four-bedroom home. "I've compiled the data on all the four-bedroom homes within a six-block radius that are on the market now, and I've also compiled the list of similar four-bedroom homes sold within the past two months. I've also shown the expired listings that were on the market and didn't sell."

Break it down and tell them why each expired didn't sell. "This listing was higher than the market could bear." (You're not blaming the agent or the seller—it's the market functioning in its mysterious manner that's to blame.)

Get a range for selling. "Is this somewhere in your frame of reference, Mr. Seller?" Usually, the sellers will now give you the sales price they've been thinking of.

If the seller says, "Those properties don't have the improvements we have," pause, look at your guidelines to market value with great concentration, and say, "$225,000." I talk to myself a lot in front of an overimproved seller.

Give the seller a track record of the market. An agent must read newspapers, go to seminars, and be in the thick of the market in order to speak with authority in this situation.

"Your home is really beautiful. This is my area, and I've sold many homes here, so I know that yours is one of the nicest. I hate to do what I have to do next, but you know that I'm a licensed real estate agent, that to get licensed I had to go through certain training. And in order to practice real estate, there are certain codes of ethics and procedures that I have to follow.

"So, at this point, I need to do something out of obligation to you. I'm not comparing your home to any other because it's special, but my problem is that you're so close to this house, and there are so many good memories for you here—and everything you've done is the best—that it's hard for you to be as objective as I am.

"I deal with people every day and I know how the people who'll be coming in here think. I know they'll appreciate your home, but no matter how well beauty and art and loving care are appreciated, they still have to be backed up with facts.

"Quite frankly, if we don't discuss this, later on you'll be upset with me. You've put a lot into this house, and it shows a strong sense of responsibility to be such a good homeowner. Now, if I get the opportunity to be your representative, I feel we should go over these facts."

Agree on Pricing

If you're not honest with that homeowner, later on somebody else will be. That's why I say to sellers complaining about the information I've presented: "If I don't give you the real facts and figures, someone else will, and I'll have failed to act responsibly toward you. The asking price is your decision, but a selling price takes three: you, a buyer, and a lending committee."

If they still want to go with a high price, say to them, "Okay, I'll go along with this price, and from here on out, I'm behind you 100 percent. But do two things for me: First, give me the chance to come back in two weeks to re-evaluate the price, based on public reaction. Secondly, be aware that I'm not taking responsibility for this price. You set the price on this house, not me."

If you don't make that clear up front, they'll say later, "Well, you told us we could get $255,00 for our house." But you never said that. To ward off this evil, during the listing interview write on the seller's net sheet how the price was arrived at. Jot down something like, "Mr. and Mrs. Shepley feel their house is worth $255,000, but my analysis indicates, and I recommended to them, a price of $239,000 to sell in this market." Make a copy for your file, initial the note, and give it to the sellers.

Then, if your sellers seek to blame the nonsale of their home on you later, tactfully remind them of the recommendation you made when taking their listing. Never do this angrily. Mention your recommendation and sympathize with their need and desire to take all the money they can out of their house. But stand clear— keep yourself separated from the market. "It's the market. The market simply won't put that number on your house today. It's the old law of supply and demand."

Tell Them Your Marketing Program

"I'm going to advertise your property once a month in my own personal ad that I run in the _____."

"Our company's advertising program will feature your house on _____."

"I'm going to bring our office staff through on our special office caravan next Tuesday. As I said before, our team is strong. Year in and year out, we sell _____ percent of our own listings."

"I'm going to bring the board caravan through here next Thursday. The entire board will be invited to see your home." If you'd like to serve refreshments on board caravan day, now is the time to discuss this with your sellers and get their permission."

"The Multiple Listing Service will have this property in the new book that comes out a week from Wednesday."

"I'm going to make up a temporary flyer to have for next Thursday's caravan."

"Then I'll make up a brochure with three pictures and a printed description. I'll leave a stack of them here for people coming through, and distribute them to the other offices. I've got my own list of out-of-area buyers and brokers that I'll send your flyer to, and, of course, it'll go in the flyer packet I give all the agents and prospects I contact wherever I go."

Explain How Advertising Works

One of the mistakes agents make with sellers is to assume they understand how the process works. They don't. It's no wonder sellers get so upset when they don't see their house advertised—no one has corrected their erroneous ideas. Sellers think a newspaper ad, with a photo of their house and a few lines of type, will cause a buyer to dial the real estate company and say, "I can tell from the picture that I've found my dream house. I just know that's the one I'm going to buy." Sight unseen, they've gone wild.

We have more modest goals when we advertise, don't we? We don't expect to sell a house with a classified ad; we just try to make the phone ring. That's all the ad can do—give our up-person a chance to make an appointment. We know there's a long, hard road to travel between that phone call and a completed sale. But many a successful trip down that road begins with the ad-generated phone call.

So I like to say, "Number one, Mr. Seller, all properties advertised with our company can sell your home. It doesn't matter whether your house is advertised or not. You see, they may call us on a three-bedroom home priced at $159,000—they don't know the price yet because we're going to give that to them on the phone— and we find out that they need four bedrooms for not more than $209,000. Then I'm going to tell them about your house—after I qualify them in the office, of course. But first I have to get them in. What I'm going to say when they call in on the ad is, 'Yes, this particular property is $159,000. It's a three-bedroom home, and it's lovely. Does that sound in line with what you're looking for?' They'll say something like, 'Oh, no, not at all.'

"Then, Mr. Seller, I come back with, 'We have some terrific properties in several price ranges,' and I'm off and running to convert them to your property. Just because you don't see your house advertised in the *Bugle* every morning doesn't mean we're not working. Our phones are ringing! Every single day."

Explain that to your sellers. Otherwise, you'll be hearing, "I want my house advertised every day. I want my house held open every day for two weeks. *Every* day." Sellers don't understand how this business works. We have to explain it to them.

If ads aren't the main source of buyers in your company, explain why they aren't. Maybe your firm has researched the matter, and determined that classified ads just don't bring in enough business to justify their cost. "The unique advantages that brought you to this area, Mr. and Mrs. Sellers, are the very reasons why classified advertising doesn't make the phone ring here. It's because we're so close to the city—the people just drive out. It's because we're so far from the city, people come out for the weekend. Because of the lake—the college—because we're so much like a resort.'' Give them a reason that applies in your locality.

Then tell your sellers, ''The sign we'll put in front of your house is a 24-hour billboard that really does make the phone ring in this area. You see, people aren't afraid to call a Realtor® and ask about a property. They don't hesitate to tell us, 'That's too high,' or 'I need more bedrooms than that house has,' or even, 'I'm looking for a steal.' They know they won't be talking to the owner, and maybe get put down hard. That's what makes the phone ring around here, the 24-hour billboard. And our sign is a particularly effective one.''

''Nationwide, this has been proved: Effective broker house-signs make the phone ring more than all other kinds of advertising combined.'' Then tell them about the other things your firm does, and you do, to gain the business that comes from ads in other areas. If you belong to a national relocation referral network, tell them how that makes the phone ring and brings in customers.

The 1-percent-edge Approach to Holding or Raising Your Fee

This is an effective method with all motivated sellers, but especially with expired listings and property that's been on the market for a long time. Here's what you say:

''You have many options as a homeowner to get your property marketed. A very important part of selling your home is motivating the [state the number] agents in our Board of Realtors® to see your home and then interest their buyers in it.

''In a market such as this, the homeowner suffers and so do agents. As an extra incentive, let's offer this property at a fee that's 1 percent higher to the selling agent than is customary.''

People who are transferred or are otherwise motivated for a fast sale often see the value of taking this approach. When you are working with someone you think will try to grind you down, the 1-percent-edge approach often allows you to at least take the listing at the customary fee. To make this work, you usually have to bring the fee up before they do.

Here's another version:

''Mr. and Mrs. Brillson, I understand from what you've told me that you're interested in a fast sale, but you also need to sell your home at the top of the market in order to have the funds necessary to buy your next home.''

Wait for them to answer—they'll always say, ''That's right.''

''Well, I have a plan that has proved to be very successful in the past with people in your position. Mr. Brillson, if you said to me, 'I want you to handle the total sale of my home; I don't want it on the Multiple Listing Service; I want all offers to come through you.' If you told me that, I'd be hard-pressed to help you sell your house. What I'm saying is this. I work very closely with other agents, not only in my office but also in other offices. I've worked hard to develop a reputation as an honest person who is easy for other agents to work with.

''What we need to do is excite those other agents because that tremendously increases the number of buyers who will be exposed to your home. What I suggest is this: instead of placing your home on the market at $250,000, let's increase the price by 1 percent and put it on at $252,500. At the same time, we'll increase the brokerage fee to the selling agent by 1 percent.

''Now this doesn't guarantee that your house will sell, but it does insure that your property will be shown to far more of the qualified buyers coming into this area than would otherwise be the case. Your property will be a favorite listing in all the offices here—and the icing on the cake is that it doesn't cost you anything to get all the agents here on our side.''

Fighting the Fee-cutters

In many cases, a demand for a lower than customary fee will come up before you've had the opportunity to establish sufficient rapport to bring it up yourself. Here's an effective response in these cases:

''It's funny you should ask that, Mr. Cassidy. A lot of people feel that this is something I can approve. But my broker believes that when you play favorites, you cheat the rest of our clients. You see, we have many homeowners committed, in writing, to us at _____ percent. Our company considers it highly unethical to have a special arrangement with only a few homeowners that isn't disclosed to all our clients.

''This attitude on our part is extremely important to you—if we'd conceal a special arrangement with you from our other clients, what guarantee do you have that we wouldn't do the same thing to you? When we talk about the price of your home we're talking big dollars—and it's vital to you to associate yourself with people you can trust.''

On higher-priced homes, you can often dispose of this question by saying:

''When marketing your home, Mr. and Mrs. Collingsworth, we want to appeal not only to the new and inexperienced agents—we also want to reach the top producers. I'm referring to the highly successful agents who are earning in excess of $100,000 per year. These are the people who sell most of the properties, and they are always working with buyers—but they just will not show any property that carries a reduced fee. In other words, going with a reduced fee means you've reduced your chances of selling drastically. Are you prepared to do that in this market?''

12

SERVICING LISTINGS

Start Servicing Fast • Advanced Caravan Technique • Give Them What They Want • Call Every Monday Morning • Never Wing It • Getting the Price Down Less Painfully • The Not-so-Neaters • Danny's Dozen to Bring My Sellers More Money • The Thorough Stage-Setting Program • Beware of Overnight Panic • Avoid Possession Hassles • Winning Scripts

The problems related to servicing listings fall into two distinct categories; you pass from one to the other every time you cross your sellers' property lines. The first problem area is the rest of the world from which the buyers must come, and the next six chapters treat various aspects of that category. This chapter concentrates on the second problem area: the sellers, your relations with them, the property itself, and its price. As has often been said, correctly priced listings require no servicing because they sell fast. This is a great and profound truth that real estate agents should think long and hard about, but they must also face the fact that most listings cannot be brought in at quick-sale prices. Therefore, to be a successful listing agent, one must study the skills of servicing listings, and learn how to motivate sellers so that they will do what must be done to get the property sold—within the time limit of their patience.

START SERVICING FAST

Sometimes we work so hard getting a listing, we feel it's all over when they finally sign. But that's only the beginning. You've been hired! Now you get to do the job: Sell that house. Don't let any time go by while you rest up from your labors; do all the servicing you can that night. Before you leave them

- *Prepare the sellers* for the reality of the marketing process. Forewarn them, so they'll know what to expect. Inform them how it actually will work, so they'll be cordial, resigned, and cooperative, not startled, angry, and on the phone to you complaining about people you have no power to control.

* *Convince them to leave* when the property is shown.
* *Convince them that the stage must be set.*
* *Convince them to banish the negatives.*

The words that'll do all that are given in Winning Scripts at the end of this chapter.

The seller is the most important person in our real estate world. Somebody must have cast a spell on me a long time ago because until a listing of mine sold, I used to go through terrible pain. I'd hold their house open if they wanted me to, but I don't believe that sold them. Price and terms sell property. If all the sellers I've ever worked with had listened to my advice at the onset of their listings, there would have been no pain. But few of them did. You see, I was involved in something very personal: their home.

To establish value, I did two things. First, I considered the financing that was available for that property. If the only houses currently being sold are owner-carrybacks at extremely favorable terms, you can't justify investing your time in a listing that must have a new conventional loan.

Second, you look at similar houses in their neighborhood and at the prices those properties sold for. You have to, because the buyers will. The new lender—if there is to be one—will, too. Unless the sales price conforms to their value formulas, no sale. But the sellers hated it when I compared their house to others. In their minds, nothing compares.

I didn't want the sellers to think I was indifferent to their house, and would "give it away" if they'd let me. Usually they don't know about market cycles, or understand that they can set asking prices, but only a buyer—by buying—can set a selling price. Many sellers are unrealistic. I didn't want to alienate them and lose the listing, nor did I want to take it so high that we'd never (within the longest period I could hope to stretch the listing out for) get within negotiating range of what the market would pay. I wanted to compromise—on a reasonable figure.

Servicing listings that are priced right demands skill, knowledge, and close attention, but these are the happy situations. There's lots of action. Your sellers stay excited. A low offer comes in and you can prove their asking price is right. Before long you've brought buyer and seller together and the property is sold. Now you're off working on other opportunities instead of burning time and energy trying to explain to unrealistic sellers what they find unexplainable: why their property hasn't sold.

Never forget that if the price isn't realistic, you can do everything else right— you can work very hard, you can spend lots of money promoting the property—and earn nothing. In the last chapter, we talked about overpriced listings and what to do with them. That's still with us here—your number one service item is adjusting the price to a level that's realistic for the value offered and realistic to the sellers' timing.

ADVANCED CARAVAN TECHNIQUE

Your office should have its own caravan each week before the regular board caravan for all offices. The office caravan takes place immediately after the weekly office meeting. It's an important tool for our listing agents; often the sight of their kitchen table carpeted with our staff's business cards is the final push that gets the listing. Yes, we caravan houses before the listing is nailed down, when requested.

Empathize with your sellers. The lady will go through a lot of trouble to glitter up her house. Then the salespeople will go whish-woosh, in and out, and they're gone. The poor owner will think, "All that work—and they weren't here ten minutes." Tell her beforehand that she's working with professionals who know what to look for, and they see a lot fast. There's something else you can do. We've found it makes a terrific impression, and we've never had a complaint about our caravaning speed since we started doing it some time ago:

Leave a rose.

Your florist will put the roses in vases for you, and deliver them to your office during the meeting. Also leave a short note along the lines given next, if the sellers aren't there. Write your note before caravan so you can give all your time to showing the house to your staff while they're on the scene.

"Dear Diane and Mark: You did a beautiful job setting the stage. I hope this is the start of a very happy transaction between you and Sell Fast Realty—Helen."

Now we'll assume you're working with a realistically priced property, not a throwaway, mind you, but a fair, at-the-market price. That means much effort, skill, and knowledge is still required to create a sale. An important part of that effort involves securing the sellers' wholehearted participation in what must be a cooperative venture if the best price is to be obtained quickly.

GIVE THEM WHAT THEY WANT

Keep in touch with your sellers. Update them constantly with every significant development: sales, new listings, changes in financing, the general market—everything that bears directly on the salability of their house. Do this and they'll never blame you if the property doesn't sell; they'll blame the marketplace.

My longest listing was 13 months, but I told him what was going on every single Monday morning. That house had bad problems. My seller hung in there with me, and I was able to hang in there with him, only because I kept talking to him. I didn't keep him in the dark. That's all they want—to be loved, like everyone else in this whole wide world.

And, they want a sale.

CALL EVERY MONDAY MORNING

Failing to keep in touch has cost more listings than any other single cause. You can't let an unrealistic seller stew in overpriced isolation, and at the same time build the credibility that'll allow you to get a reduction to salable levels. Their house isn't getting shown. If they aren't hearing from you, they'll think that whatever you work at isn't connected with getting their house sold. And maybe they'll be right.

When you call a seller and he says, "I haven't heard from you in a couple of weeks."

You can reply, "Well, I've tried to get you, but your line was always busy," or "—but no one ever answered." Great lines—if true. If not, can you blame your sellers for getting upset when their largest asset languishes on the market without a flicker of interest from the public, or even from their agent?

They're right in thinking. "No one is too busy to give me a call once a week. I'm not gone that much; my phone isn't busy that much. Selling our house just doesn't rate very high with my agent."

At the very least, call all your sellers every Monday morning. If you're too crowded by clients that morning, do it Monday afternoon, Monday night, or Tuesday. Without fail, the first of every week, call every listing you have. Tell your sellers what's happened to similar properties in the marketplace, and report on any activity on their listing.

What about sellers whose phones really are always tied up? On the back of one of your letterheads, jot down every time you call:

    7/19   9 A.M. Busy
               9:15 A.M. Busy
               9:35 A.M. Busy
              11:05 A.M. Busy

At this point, flip over the page and write them a pleasant note. Mention your calls noted on the reverse side, and add, "Thought I'd better write, in case I couldn't get through to you on the phone." Some people don't realize how much they (or the children) keep their phone busy. Don't let a minor item such as this damage your relationship. Build a case if their phone really is busy. The burden of proof is on you. Dropping by for a fast and friendly update might be in order here.

Make Promises You Can Keep

If you tell them you're going to call every Monday morning, call them every Monday morning. If you say, "I spend Wednesdays with my family, but I'm on duty most weekends," then be active on the weekends and make sure they know it. Tell them, "I can't be reached on Wednesdays, but I'll call you every Friday between 4 and 6." Then do as you said you would, and you'll save yourself a lot of trouble. Make promises you can keep. Then keep them.

One of my sellers asked me to join his family in prayer about the listing before he would sign it. The house was a wreck. Two weeks later he gave me a hard time because his house hadn't sold, and suggested that I cooperate with God. I told him that he should do likewise, that God means for us to help ourselves, so would he please clean up his house and give us both a better chance. That didn't go too well, so I reminded him that God was interested in the welfare of the buyers too, and this devout man finally saw the point. The next time I visited them, cleanliness was next to Godliness, and their house sold soon after that.

NEVER WING IT

You've proclaimed yourself the local area expert, and a competent professional in the general practice of residential real estate. That doesn't mean you have the answer to every conceivable question. Never put yourself in the position of talking with clients about subjects you aren't qualified to discuss. Don't hesitate to say, "That's outside my area of specialization." When the conversation strays from your area of expertise, an occasional "I don't know" dispels any suspicion that you're a tiresome know-it-all.

GETTING THE PRICE DOWN LESS PAINFULLY

Sunday night, after some weekends of open houses, is a good time to get a price reduction, if that's indicated. Your sellers are feeling down and out. They may not have been willing to listen to you before, but now you've gotten the public's response. You may be able to sit down with them and say, "Now, we've had four weekends of open houses. Based on the Guidelines to Market Value I brought out a month ago, it looks like the public is telling us the same thing. Let's think about this a little bit—"

They're going to be more receptive to realistic pricing after the public has validated your opinion.

Caution: Don't wait too long. Stay in tune with your sellers. If you're slow in seeking a price cut, they may blame you for their house not selling.

THE NOT-SO-NEATERS

Wait Them Out

With not-so-neaters who are moving away on a certain date whether their house sells or not, bring in a cleaning crew when that house is vacant. Clean-up labor goes further when there's no furniture in the way, and it lasts longer in unoccupied houses.

Think ahead. Consider the seasonal buying patterns, the length of your listing, how well you relate to the people, and how realistic their price is. Can you hold the listing long enough to make this work? If there's a good chance you can, you'll often be better off to ride them easy about their poor housekeeping.

Build Curb Appeal

A few hours labor and very little money will often increase curb appeal enormously. I'm always amazed when people put a house on the market for over $200,000 and let their kids keep on digging holes in their front yard.

Part of your job is to put some pressure on, so they'll think. "If my agent sees that, he'll be right on our necks about it." So they yell at little Hector and keep him in line. You've got to keep the pressure on with some people, and that means doing it carefully so it doesn't blow back in your face. Always come on with a firm but considerate manner. "I'm sorry to mention this, but I'm afraid of the front yard now. The way it works, an agent drives up with some buyers, and they've already seen ten houses. They're a little tired. Your house might be just what they're looking for. But when they drive up and see those big holes in your front slope, one of them says, 'I don't even want to see the inside. Go on to the next one.' And that's it. Off the buyers drive. That kind of thing happens all the time. Please understand that I'm not trying to interfere. If it weren't my job to get your house sold, I wouldn't say anything because I know you've got a lot on your mind right now, but that slope needs a little attention."

Another seller had a houseful of pets. You went through the entry sideways because of the rabbit hutch. The living room was a zoo. Every little creature made his own daily contribution to the unusual aroma in that house. I suggested to them that they do one of two things: reduce their price by $20,000, or move the zoo. They moved the zoo. But it still smelled like a zoo—to everyone except the owners. They wouldn't accept the fact that scent is our most easily fatigued sense. We simply can't smell an odor that we are exposed to for several hours a day as keenly as someone who isn't accustomed to it does. So they didn't quite believe my delicate comments that Essence de Barnum was driving off buyers. They were getting restless. Then their new home was completed and they moved into it. This time the zoo had its own shed. I closed their old home up tight, let it steam for a July week, and then took them back for a sniff. They got the point.

"What should be done?" they said. The walls were painted early Tarzan; the carpet, being different in every room, matched Tarzans' every mood.

I told them: "Get a crew in here and rip out the carpet. Rent a couple of large fans and let them blow a lot of air through while another crew repaints the whole house off-white. After that's done, put down honey-colored carpet throughout. One color. Every day bake vanilla in your oven. Do all this and you'll be able to recover your fix-up cost in the price—and it'll sell promptly too."

They did, and it did.

If you're a new salesperson and are slightly unsure of yourself, if you really can't come out with the "paint the inside, cut the grass, de-junk the place" bit to your sellers, make up a flyer along the lines of the following "Danny's Dozen to Bring My Sellers More Money." Then hand a copy of this flyer to each of your sellers. (Put one in your Listing Presentation Manual too.) It's a crutch, but don't hesitate to use crutches until your legs are strong enough to run on. I never hesitated to, or failed to grow out of any. You won't either.

Use your name instead of mine, of course. Call your flyer:

- Arnie's Assortment of Ideas to Bring My Sellers More Money—
- Betty's Bundle of—Bag of—
- Carl's Collection of—Clara's Carton of Clues to—
- Ellen's Emeralds for Selling Your Home for More—
- Frank's Famous Ideas for—
- Gerta's Group of—
- Hank's Hard-hitting Tips that—
- Helen's Heap of Helps for—
- Ida's Ideas that—
- Jack's Gems that—
- Karen's Keys to—
- Larry's List of—
- Mary's Methods of—
- Ned's Neatest Twelve for—
- Opal's Sale-openers that Bring—
- Pat's Package of Twelve Ideas that—Pile of—Program for—
- Quill's Quota of—
- Ruth's Rollcall of—
- Sam's Selling System for Getting More—
- Tawna's Twelve Tips for—

- Urban's Price Upturners that Bring—
- Vicky's Vital Views on—
- Wally's Wonderful—
- Xavier's Zingers—
- Yolanda's Yummy Tips for Upping the Yield
- Zack's Stack of Zippy Tips for—

A touch of lightheartedness here relieves the tension when you ask your sellers to put their shoulders to the wheel and grunt to get their house sold.

DANNY'S DOZEN TO BRING MY SELLERS MORE MONEY

1 **Cultivate curb charisma.** Some of the best buyers are the most impatient because they need to make a decision fast. If the view of your house from the street turns them off, they might not even stop. Shape up your front yard.

2 **Take a critical look at your house's front side.** If it's weathered looking, or if anything that needs repair can be seen, eliminate these problems. Don't turn your buyers off before the inside can turn them on.

3 **Never stay in your house with house hunters.** Let the agent handle it, and remove yourself if you possibly can. Remember, that agent has worked for many hours with these people, and knows what they're looking for, and how to work with them. Let him or her do the job without interference.

    You may feel that an agent isn't showing the important features of your house to people, but the agent knows people aren't sold by details until they've become emotionally involved with the big picture of your house. The presence of any member of the sellers' family can't help, always unnerves possible buyers, and often prevents a sale. Don't put this obstacle in your path: Leave when buyers are coming.

4 **Give your dogs and cats a vacation.** They need it. So does your pocketbook. Having pets (especially aggressive dogs) around when you're selling your home can be incredibly expensive. Many people are acutely uncomfortable around some animals, and simply can't think *buy* when their minds are on *bye*.

5 **You can't find a better investment** when you're selling a house than a few cans of paint and putty to brighten up its interior.

6 **Drips do worse than run up your water bill.** They make possible buyers worry about your house's entire plumbing system. Fix these little problems before they cost you a sale.

7 **Squeaking doors and creaking floors,** torn or missing screens, cracked glass, and anything in need of repair dampens the house hunter's enthusiasm. Many of them believe there'll always be ten problems they haven't noticed for every one they do see.

8 **Hide (or neatly arrange) everything that looks like work:** lawnmowers, hoses, vacuum cleaners, all the gear you used to fix up the house. Accent everything that looks like fun: stereos, skis, toys in the kids' rooms.

9 **De-clutter.** Repack compactly, dispose of unneeded items, or rent a mini-storage room and move out as much material as you can. Your home's storage space can't look adequate to a buyer if you've got it jampacked.

10 **Turn up the shelter.** If it's hot, cool it; if it's cold, light a crackling fire.

11 **Harmonize the elements.** FM radio or stereo on softly, TV off. All lights on, day or night. Drapes open in the daytime.

12 **You can sell pride of ownership faster and for more money.** It's called cleanliness, and cleanliness has more buyers than used dirt. Put sparkle into your bathrooms and kitchen, and you'll take lots more silver out.

Sometimes the decor makes a house unsalable even when it's priced under the market. A friend of mine took a listing from a collector of medieval weaponry. Swords covered every wall; from every ceiling-suspended lamp a nasty head banger was hung. Buyers laughed at first and then felt oppressed. No offers were received until the house was demilitarized because the owners moved away with their obsolete arsenal. Then it sold promptly.

After you've discussed de-junking, cleaning up, and fixing up with your new clients, you should explain:

THE THOROUGH STAGE-SETTING PROGRAM

This should be run through every day buyers may appear. Compile a checklist that suits your area, and go over that checklist with each of your sellers as soon as possible after securing their listing. Here are some points to discuss with them:

Watering

Little drops all over the plants and lawn give a delightful, fresh feeling in summer, and all year long in dry, warm climates. Suggest that your sellers time their sprinkling so that the dewy effect remains when the buyers are likely to appear. Hosing down the walks also adds sparkle. But leaving hoses strung around, and gardening tools lying about, looks tacky and spoils the dream by reminding househunters of chores instead of the good life.

Lawns and Grounds

Explain to your sellers how important it is for the yards to look appealing and well cared for. When the work's done, it looks easy; when it's undone, it seems formidable.

Lawns should be mowed and edged, hedges cut, trees trimmed, weeds eliminated. If possible, bare ground should be covered by gravel or bark; at the very least it should be raked and kept moist.

Lawns that have patches of dead grass can be greatly improved in appearance by buying a few square feet of sod from the local nursery. It's surprisingly cheap, and anyone can successfully install it. This is all it takes: notch out the old with a spade or trowel, cut the new sod to fit, and stomp it into place. What a difference it makes!

Drapes and Window Coverings

Consider each window and room separately. Is the view pleasant, or do you see the neighbor's trash cans? Are the window frames attractive when exposed? Are the drapes themselves more striking when opened or closed? Does the room show better by sunlight or lamplight? When not certain, opt for sunlight. Buyers want to see, and light encourages them.

What you're doing here is showing your product to its best advantage, not concealing defects. The buyers can open the drapes and see the trash cans, but they're still reassured that there are drapes to hide this from their own guests. You are working here on effect more than substance, on emotion more than fact. Keep that in mind as you direct them in setting the stage for the first time.

Lighting

Tell your sellers to switch on every single lamp and light in the entire house every time they prepare it for a showing or go out.

Music, Maestro

What's the mood of the house? Select what enhances that mood, rather than what happens to be your, or your sellers', favorite. Loud country music playing in a stately home furnished with antiques is as out of place as one of Bach's fugues playing in a family room paneled with knotty pine. Soft and romantic is the choice for that place just made for two. When in doubt, go with something current, snappy, and not too loud.

You're selling lifestyle along with walls and floors, so harmonize all the elements. Have your sellers leave the radio on to a station playing music that suits the house each day they leave. For a specific showing, the right selection on the tape deck can be a powerful mood-setting influence. Tell your sellers to make that part of their house-show drill.

Set the Stage.

SET THE STAGE

SET THE STAGE!!

Lights on. Drapes open. Music playing quietly. Fireplace going on a cold day, air conditioning going on a hot day.

Sellers away.

Beds made. Kitchen sparkling. Everything in its place. Pets at grandmother's. Windows cleaned to invisibility. Lawns mowed. Hedges trimmed. Tools in the garage.

Sellers not home.

The buyers come. They linger. "I don't know what it is about this one, but I feel good here. You know—it's like home," the wife says.

"Looks like an easy place to take care of," replies the husband. "There isn't anything we'll have to do. The company'll move us in, and I can hit the job the next day."

Ring. Ring. Ring. That's the agent calling you. "I've got an offer for you. Say, you know, that house sure showed well."

When Is the Stage to Be Set?

Every day. Selling a house is a continuous, ongoing, daily performance. Use the analogy of a stage play to dramatize your enthusiasm; sellers like it. Specifically, the stage is to be set:

- For your office caravan,
- For your board caravan,
- Whenever the house is shown,
- Whenever open house is held there,
- Whenever your sellers leave the house during the day and, especially, on weekends.

They should keep their house showable—clean at all times, and be ready every day of the week to go through the whole stage-setting process, and *then leave*. Not all sellers will give you this kind of cooperation. If they're overpriced, the market is slow, and you don't expect many showings, you may be well advised to conserve their patience and energy during that Let's-test-the-market-with-a-high-price phase so many of them insist on going through. Then, when they've become realistic and more in the mood to cooperate, come on strong about constant stage setting.

Home Is a House that Shelters Us

On a raw, overcast day with a cutting wind, an agent brings two shivering people into a cold, dark house that's empty and silent. The buyers walk quickly through, and then hurry back to the warm car. They drive on to one of your listings. This house is also empty, but the lights are on, and it's warm inside. Soft music shuts out the sound of the wind. In the fireplace a cheery fire is crackling behind a screen. This time the buyers don't hurry back to the agent's warm car. They take their time, look the place over carefully, and mentally move in. This house feels like home. It's already sheltered them once, and the idea of making the arrangement permanent is entrancing. They sit down at the kitchen table with their agent and write up an offer.

That offer, which your sellers accept, came about because you persuaded them to light a fire and then leave, as part of a thorough setting-the-stage program. Their property has sold quickly because you've promoted it well, and because they've done their part by setting the stage whenever a phone call told them their house would be shown.

Furnished or Vacant, Which Sells Better?

There's no hard-and-fast rule. But it's good to have some patter organized in case you're asked. In most cases the sellers don't have much choice, they either have to stay until it sells, or they're under considerable pressure to move before it does. If you're dealing with a situation where they have no choice, make them feel good about whatever they have to do.

There are buyers who love to look at vacant houses, and others who are uncomfortable in them. There are buyers who can't stand anyone else's taste in furnishings, and spend most of their time reacting to the decoration rather than to the floor plan. Most buyers, however, will be somewhat more comfortable looking at furnished houses that are neat and clean, where the furnishings are suitable and don't crowd the rooms and make them look tiny.

If your sellers are living in a small house they've jammed with furniture while preparing for a larger house, tell them, "Move some of these lovely pieces of furniture to storage; the fees you'll pay will come back to you many times over in selling this house sooner and for more money."

It's not a serious sales problem if smaller homes, those under 1,700 feet, are vacant. As the size increases, it becomes more and more important that the houses be furnished, or at least partly furnished. Large empty houses, those over 3,000 feet, seem like acres of empty space if left totally unfurnished.

BEWARE OF OVERNIGHT PANIC

People can swing from hanging tough to panic overnight. Never forget that. Keep in close touch with your sellers; keep yourself aware of how they're feeling; never let them feel abandoned. Keep them posted on what the market is doing. If it's tightening, stay ahead of it and them. Be quick to tell the most obstinate hang-toughs to make a serious price cut now, before the market drops even further under their price. Note in your file when you told them to cut, and how much. Collect the facts that'll enable you to defend your competence in a firm, confident, and convincing manner. With this type of seller, you'll often have to do just that. They'd much rather blame their high price on your advice, and change agents when they lower that price to where you told them it should be from the first. Since they're the judge, prosecutor, and jury on this question, you've got to have your facts straight and solid or you'll lose their case.

Less Now, or More Later—Maybe

(What follows applies primarily to the stable or falling market. It has little application to a sellers' market.)

A point that skewers many a seller considering an offer is, "Maybe I can get more." That same point skewers many an agent too, because offers rejected by the seller have a way of looking better and better as time passes if no other offers are forthcoming. Sellers are natural history-revisionists. After a few weeks they often turn your quiet urgings of acceptance into damnation of the offer by faint praise.

If you believe an offer on your listing is realistic, come on strong with the sellers. Tell them, "In my professional opinion, this offer should be accepted." Make clear that, while you'll loyally support any decision they make, such loyalty doesn't show any lack of conviction on your part that the offer should be accepted.

Dwell on this. Make sure they won't ever claim you didn't urge them strongly enough to accept the offer.

Suppose a higher offer comes in a day or two later? If you've done a thorough job with your Guidelines to Market Value, it's unlikely that another offer from a different buyer will immediately come in more than 2 or 3 percent above the price you've already urged them to accept. Not a large possibility but it does happen, and it's happened to me. Your sellers then tell you, "Lucky we didn't listen to you. If we had, we would've lost 4,200 tax-sheltered dollars."

You reply, "I'm really happy it worked out the way it did. Sure, there's egg on my face, but better sweet than rotten egg. I'm really happy for you guys that an emotional buyer happened to come along—a best buyer, we call them—ready and willing to pay your price. And what timing! Great. I wanted to play the odds—and they're about 99 to 1 that you wouldn't have seen an offer like this before the one you turned down started to look real good—but you took the risk, and won! Terrific. Just don't check out the details of how it happened—of how those folks happened to show up right when they did. It'll scare you how chancy it was. Not inevitable at all. But, the important thing is—''

Et cetera. But you pocket the listing fee. For that, accept the egg on your face in good grace.

In the far more common situation, where the offer is rejected and there's no second offer, you remain the unpaid listing agent of an unsold property—for the remainder of your listing contract. If you came on strong for accepting that offer, you're in an immeasurably stronger position to fend off the seller's natural tendency to gripe at you because the house hasn't sold. Be careful, of course, not to say ''I told you so.'' Much better to make sympathetic noises whenever the subject comes up. ''I understand—that was a difficult decision. Next time, we'll be forewarned.'' Not, ''Next time we'll know better.''

Suppose there's another party who's interested in the house but won't make an offer. All closing techniques fail. Yet they continue to make buying sounds while your seller is considering an offer he really doesn't want to take.

What you have is a garbage can banger, not a buyer. Tell your sellers so. What someone might do tomorrow, next month, in the year 2084, all lies in the uncertain future. There's only one kind of buyer—the for real, now kind. All others are future-maybes, whose eventual buy is dependent on fate's favor, and on their changeable plans, tastes, and prospects.

A prospective buyer who signs a purchase contract, and puts deposit money behind it, pays your seller a substantial compliment if, in the opinion of a competent listing agent like yourself, the offer is realistic. Much professional effort and marketing expense were required to secure that offer. You should not allow your sellers to brush it aside lightly—*they'll* hold it against you if you do.

AVOID POSSESSION HASSLES

Binding your sellers to a specific move-out date on the listing (for example, ''possession on August 30, _____'') exposes them to possible legal problems. Instead of the specific date, tie the day that the buyers will take possession to the settlement date.

When the offer comes in, again be sure that possession is based on the day title changes hands—that it is not named as a specific date. Unless you do this, a last-minute paperwork problem that delays the close may put your sellers in the position of having agreed to give the buyers possession before settlement.

You can then be caught between the buyers' insistence on moving in on the *agreed* possession date, and your sellers' refusal to move out before they have the money in their hands. This can be time consuming for you, and expensive (also for you) if the buyers are living in a hotel and their furniture arrives by van that day.

The time to negotiate possession date is when the offer comes in. During the weeks or months that pass between the day the sellers list and the day they consider an offer, the circumstances that govern the exact timing of their move can change drastically. There's no better time to get this established than when the sellers are considering the offer. They can't realistically do it when they list; they don't know when they'll get an offer, or how much more time must pass after they accept an offer before settlement will occur. But when the offer is being considered, this timing is an important part of the offer. Urge your sellers to make their move-out decisions before they accept the offer.

Can they be out on settlement day? Do they want one, two, or three days more? Will the buyers agree to allow them to stay that long after settlement (close of escrow)? Make this part of the accepted purchase offer. If necessary, use a counteroffer just for this. And make sure your sellers understand exactly what they're agreeing to on this point. It doesn't seem too important when everyone is thinking about selling price and money, when moving day is a month or three away. Then moving day suddenly arrives. Your sellers turn balky because they haven't made the arrangements.

Avoid that sticky mess by showing a friendly interest in their moving preparations as the transaction progresses from offer to settlement. "Well, I guess you're all set to move. You didn't have any trouble lining up a mover, did you? Someone was telling me that the movers are sort of busy right now."

WINNING SCRIPTS

Prepare the Sellers for the Market Process

Tell them what will happen, how things will really work. Doing a thorough job of this can fend off complaint calls about things you can't prevent. Tell them:

"Other brokers will call at 1:30 and say they want to show the house at 2. You rush around and set the stage beautifully. It's not convenient, but you leave anyway. You're gone two hours, come home, and a moment later the doorbell rings. It's that same agent, and he has his buyers with him. You'll probably let them in, but you'll maybe think, 'Why couldn't this person be more considerate?'

"Please remember that agents can't make their buyers arrive on time—or arrive at all. Buyers make appointments and expect to go right out to see property. If the agent waits until the buyers actually arrive, then he'll have even less warning to give you. Buyers who are late for appointments buy houses too, so we want to work with them. And maybe the buyers were unavoidably delayed.

"You might get a call ten minutes before the agent wants to bring people through. Sometimes they come to the door with buyers in the car. They shouldn't—but some prospects won't conform to a schedule. Many helter-skelter buyers are that way because they've got to make a decision fast." Explain that to your sellers. "These situations can be aggravating, but they can pay off with a quick sale for you, too."

The Sign Is Out Front

Tell your sellers, "A stranger may come to the door and say, 'Can I see your home? I noticed the for sale sign out front and I might be interested.' " Forewarn your people that this can happen. Here's what you tell them to do:

"Don't let anyone in who doesn't have an agent with them. Here are three of my business cards. Keep them handy by your front door. Unless they have a real estate professional with them, tell anybody who wants to see your home, 'This is the agent who's handling my property. You can call their office for an appointment, or if you want to see the house right now, I'll ask you to excuse me for a moment. I'll call the office and get an agent to bring you through.'

"That person will be a stranger. Let us find out who he is. That's our job."

Convince Them to Leave When the Property Is Shown

Tell them, "I'm really doing this to protect you emotionally, too. Because I know you love this house, and I know every brick that went into this place went into it with love. When some guy comes in here and says something like, 'This brick job is sure bad,' or 'The drapes aren't right with the window,' your feelings are going to be hurt. House-lookers say things like that when something doesn't suit their particular taste. That doesn't mean their taste is any better than yours—it's just different. Sometimes they say stuff like that to drive a better bargain by pretending they don't like your house.

"Or they might say, 'Oh, I love this place. It's my dream house! I'm going to run back to the office right now and we're going to make an offer!' You don't know, Mr. Seller, that they say that about every house they see. I want to save you from that emotional mish-mash. I don't want to see you go through it all. So, just leave, and we'll tell you what the response is."

Convince Them that the Stage Must Be Set

"You know, selling a house creates an abnormal situation. It's not normal to have strangers walking in and out of your house. You want to get that process behind you as soon as possible, and the way to do that is to think of your home as a theatre. From now on, you're putting on a performance. It's like staging a play.

"Buyers don't get into the buying spirit unless the scenery's right. They need to dream a little to imagine the exciting new lifestyle they can live here. Let's set the stage right and make it easy for them to get into the buying mood."

If your sellers both work outside their home, tell them to turn on all the lights that will show off their house every morning when they leave for work:

"I know your electric bill's going to be a little high for about a month, but that's okay—it'll be worth it to you many times over.

"Imagine an agent coming into your house with a buyer when it's dark inside. That agent may have seen your house on caravan, but he was concentrating on the floor plan and the amenities, not on where the light switches are. So all of them come in and stumble around. Finally the agent finds a light switch, and then runs over to open the drapes. He can't find the pull cords right away. While he's hunting around the buyers get impatient. 'Oh, forget it,' they say, and walk out. Everything about your house might have been marvelous for them. If they'd taken time to see the whole floor plan, they might've bought it. But the stage wasn't set, and they didn't have the patience to set it for themselves. Most buyers won't. We've got to do that for them.''

There are two steps to setting the stage: fix-up and turn-on. It isn't hard to get people to switch the lights on and open the drapes, but fix-up can strain your diplomacy if the house needs work, and overstrain it if the place is dirty. Telling people their home is unclean, or that it needs work, risks making enemies; not talking them into doing the cleanup and fix-up makes enemies because you can't sell their unsalable property. The first is a risk and the second is a certainty; so take the risk and avoid certain disaster. Ideas for working with these difficult problems follow.

Convince Them to Banish the Negatives

Fixer-uppers can be sold—at fix-em-up-and-make-a-bundle prices. That's workable, if the sellers can accept that their home falls into this category. They usually prefer to think it doesn't. When you list a house that's in bad condition, use this approach:

"I want to see you get the best, the absolute best, market price for your home. I want people to come in here and be excited. So you've got to help me. I can't do it without you, and gosh, I know—hey, I've got finger marks on my walls too. Those darn little kids! You know, you gotta keep repainting every year. But, I think we better paint the walls.''

In the kitchen, the dishwasher is very tired. Open it a crack and it falls apart. Take the problem back on your shoulders. "Oh, I know, I've used my dishwasher so much—" Be nice to them but get the point across: buyers will be turned off if the house is shown in its present condition. Replace the dishwasher, repaint the walls, trim the hedge. "This home needs work—but I understand. Okay? I really understand.''

Cover everything you can think of. "I hate to tell you this, lady, but we've got to clean the oven. Here's why: Some women today want to see what the oven looks like because they're very meticulous, and they feel that if the oven is dirty, maybe none of the appliances will work as well as they should.''

If the seller says, "I don't know if our water heater will make it to the close of escrow (settlement date), but I'm not about to spend the money to replace it. I'll never get it out of the house.''

Tell them, "Let's think about this. I know how you feel. It's not a new house, and it didn't have a new water heater when you bought it. But the heater was working, wasn't it?''

"Yeah, sure."

Put your seller back in his buyer shoes: "When you moved in, you assumed that when you finished putting things away, you could take a hot shower. Right? You would have been pretty upset if there wasn't any hot water. So right away you'd be on the phone. 'What are my rights?' Well, the buyer has the right to presume appliances are in working order. [State laws vary. Check yours.] I don't want you to have a legal problem or a last minute hang-up that delays the settlement. You'll save money by avoiding the hassle. If I were you, I'd replace that water heater right away."

Making this point often helps: "Most of the value of a home, of course, is in the land, the location, and the structure—that's the iceberg. But what affects buyers just as much is the tip of the iceberg: cosmetics like fresh paint, and elbow-grease items like trimmed hedges and shiny bathroom fixtures. Nothing adds more value for less money than cleanup, shine-up, and paint-over. I know how busy you are. I understand what you're going through right now [add something here about their new baby, his long commute, whatever] but your house will sell faster and for more money if you'll—" [tell them what needs to be fixed up].

More Dirty-House Dialogues

Make an appointment to show them the "competition." You may have to use a little pressure, because they may suspect—many times without even admitting it to themselves—what you're about. Show them just one or two perfectly kept homes that are for sale in roughly their price range. Pick houses that are not noticeably newer, or the lesson will be lost.

Talk money to them. Everybody understands money. "I don't know how this woman finds time to keep her kitchen so spotless. Look at that—" Point to something that gleams. "My housekeeping certainly doesn't match hers—except when I put my house on the market. She probably didn't keep this place this sharp month in and month out either—but she'll get an extra $5,000 for it. Oh, yes, squeaky-clean houses sell for $5,000 more around here in this market. And they sell faster, too. Much faster."

If your seller doesn't seem to get the point, you may need to repeat your "see the shine" tour with her once a week or twice a month until she does. Of course, the person responsible for the dirty house may be a him, not a her. That doesn't matter; what matters is whipping the place into shape so it'll sell.

By this time you should have a clear idea whether they're unconscious, lazy, or both. The person who's aware of the problem will make excuses: "I know this place is a bit yucky, but I just can't seem to get it together—"

"I know how that is. Don't I ever! I really understand. Why don't you let me swing a cleaning crew in here for you? I've seen clients get a dollar back for every two cents they spent on a cleaning crew."

"Really? You think it can make that much difference."

"Absolutely."

"My husband would have a fit if I even mentioned it. He'd tell me to do it myself."

"Maybe you just have to put it to him in the right way. I don't know—but we're talking about a lot of money here. And it's not only money that's at stake; the house could sell much sooner if we brighten it up. Cleaning crew or you, it needs to be done, and the sooner the better. I'll call you tomorrow and see what you think then."

The Intruder Theory

When you have a listing that's too jammed or junked up to show well, say to your people:

"You know, when prospective buyers go into someone else's home with the idea of buying it and living there, they have serious problems seeing themselves in that new house. Some people tell me they'd rather look at vacant houses, because then they can visualize how their furniture will fit into the rooms. And—I don't think they want to mention it—but the fact is, a lot of people feel uncomfortable in the role of buyers. It's like they're pushing someone out of their home—or they're intruding. A lot of people really have a thing about not intruding. That's why it's so important that the owners not be there, so the prospective buyers can feel as relaxed as possible. But, if there's so much physical presence of the family, if the place is crowded with furniture, the walls are covered with family photos and awards and hung with their hobbies and interests, a lot of buyers are overwhelmed by this feeling of not belonging.

"I think that's what we've got here. You've made great use of this house; you've really lived here and made it your own. That's as it should be—until you decide to sell. As things are, it's tough for buyers to put themselves in here mentally. And they have to move in mentally before they'll sign the papers that'll let them do it physically. The quickest way for you to take your money out of this house and get on with your lives is to make your ownership less powerfully felt. It's really going to make money for you, speed things up, and cut down the number of times you'll have to get your house ready to show, if you'll put a lot of this stuff into storage.

"Here's a card from Save-Most Storage on Fabricante. You can rent space by the month there. Believe me, you'll make more money if you store—[specify what]—until you move."

Trash and Clutter

"Rent a big bin from the local city dump and clean out your garage, side yard, attics, closets, drawers, nooks, and crannies. Literally move out and in again. Half the things we save we won't use again during this lifetime. Keep trash cans stored on the side or in the garage. On garbage pickup day, be sure to put those cans out of sight immediately after the trash men empty them.

"It's a real shock to house hunters if they step out of an agent's car and see empty trash cans rolling around on the lawn. It might happen all the time at their old home, but they don't think about that. When they're buyers, people are in a much more finicky mood than usual.

"All bikes, trikes, big wheels, papers, candy wrappers, and what-not should be *out of sight* at all times when you're living in the house-showing fish bowl. I know one lady whose eight-year-old had a thing about wadding up paper and throwing it around. She was otherwise an immaculate housekeeper, but she'd given up on the boy's paper. We never could get that house sold until the kid went off to camp—those wads of paper lying around made the whole place look junky."

Talking Sense to Mr. Sellhigh

Most sellers want to base their price on what they need, or on how much they've spent. Sellers are prone to think that buyers are emotional folk who don't much care what they pay as long as they get what they want. Sellers don't care much about the interest rate the buyers will have to pay, or how large the buyers' monthly payments will be. They'd like to sell their house at next year's prices.

Buyers, on the other hand, feel the strong position money takes when it talks. They tend to think that buyers compare prices and values carefully, and will compromise on their wants to drive a hard bargain. Buyers have no interest at all in paying over market. In fact, they'd like to buy at last year's prices.

You have to explain this to many sellers. The conflicting buyer-seller viewpoints provide many of the reasons why agents are needed: to bring the principals together at today's prices. Prepare to do so. Memorize the following speech. Then compose two or three more ways of saying much the same thing in different words. You'll find such speeches profitable and time saving.

"The market is made by willing buyers and willing sellers [call them by name here]. I know your needs are important. I empathize with your needs—but we have to be realistic if we're going to make anything happen for you. We can't put a price on this house that just validates your next move. That price also has to validate the market, or no buyer will buy. If you wait for the buyer who won't look at any property except yours, you'll wait a long time. Not one buyer in a thousand will do that. People shop carefully for houses, and even if they didn't, appraisers appraise carefully. If the loan isn't approved, we can't close the transaction and cash you out.

"You want a sale, and you want that sale soon. So let's not lose sight of the basic element that'll make or break our chances of a sale—correct pricing. Buyers want to buy right. They're determined not to pay more than what they see as market value, and in the market we have today, with [insert the number of listings available now on your Multiple Listing] properties available for them to choose from, they know they're in a strong position. Today's buyers know they have a wide range of choice.

"I can't control the marketplace. I am legally bound to present all offers. I am behind you 100 percent as far as not gossiping about the pricing of your property behind your back, but I must tell you now that I am giving you full responsibility for rejecting this offer that is right at the prevailing market price.

"If we allow this offer to die, and then, sometime in the future, wish we had accepted it, I want it understood—and remembered then—that I recommended accepting it. I understand your problems, and I feel for your needs, but we must always be realistic."

Then make a note on the communication log in the file: "Agent highly recommended acceptance of other broker offer on 9/15/___ ."

Winning a Listing Extension

Here's our new letter to persuade sellers to extend their listing with us. The first time out, it won an extension that was long enough to allow one of my associates to sell a realistically priced house. This agent had kept in close touch with the sellers throughout the listing period, but the final extra touch that brought in the extension was this letter.

Dear Max and Corinne:

We know that you are upset because your house has not sold—we are too! We work very hard for our clients and you are top priority on our list.

Let us tell you what we are planning on doing to successfully market your house in the future:

- $500 bonus out of our pocket to the selling agent.
- Handwritten notes to the top producers of all the real estate companies in the area.
- Recaravan the property with refreshments for the area agents
- New flyers to remind agents again about the price and of your willingness to participate in financing the sale.

All we are asking for is time. Granted we have had it for six months but, as you know, we are going through a low swing in the real estate cycle. Now that the "good" season is approaching, let us have a chance to prove to you that no other agent can do more for you or work harder than I do.

Please give me this opportunity to continue to serve you. It means a great deal to me.

Sincerely,

PROMOTION

Real Estate Writing Tips • Style • Getting Newsletters Out Fast • Writing Your Profile of a PRO • Profile of a PRO • Plugs Sell Listings • Listing Remarks • Your Name Is Your Trademark • Your Product • Imprinted Scratch Pads: Your Most Effective, Year-round Farming Tool • A Cornucopia of Ideas

The most effective promotion in a given situation may be a few timely words spoken quietly to the right person, or it may be 20-foot high words towed across the sky by an airplane. Successful promotion communicates. It reaches people. It causes them to do something they would not otherwise have done. It causes them to phone you, to go see your listings, to remember you at the right time.

Somebody gets the message. That's promotion. That's all it is. The message in real estate is simple. The whole of it can be said with fifteen words: "I am the agent you should work with. This is the property you should buy." Everything else is mere elaboration of these two points.

But elaborate we must. Some very successful agents will vehemently deny that they promote. "None of that Hollywood stuff for me. All I do is talk to people." Many agents have built a thriving business doing just that—the tennis player in Chapter 6 is one of them. Yet that tennis player is promoting himself very effectively every time he calls a new member with an invitation to an early morning game, and he's getting the message across by introducing that new member over the net to one of his satisfied clients. In many cases, the most effective promotion is the lowest keyed.

The farming almanac in Chapter 7 has ideas for farm promotions you can create yourself, find locally, or buy through the mail. The most successful real estaters match their promotion methods to the sales goal they wish to accomplish, not to their own personal preferences. They realize that their own taste is not an infallible guide to what's effective in promotion. They constantly seek feedback from the public as to what messages are getting through and what messages are being ignored. They think long thoughts about the answers and act on them. The common fabric of their promotions is verve, persistence, and innovation.

Avoid stereotyping yourself as an orange picker, or business will be slow for you when all the oranges are crated and only apples are ripe on the trees. Learn to pick apples too. More important, let the world know you pick apples. The person with a flair for the flamboyant can work effectively on soft sell merely by picking up the phone. The faceless soft seller, who is unknown to anyone beyond his or her circle, can divert an entirely new flow of opportunities with a single spectacular promotion. If you suspect your image is a bit stodgy in spite of considerable success, hire an elephant and trainer to give your customers and their kids a ride. Then send them up in a hot-air balloon, or drive them around town in a double-deck London bus. People who never could remember your name will start saying they've known you a long time. Everyone will think you're just a little bit crazy—in an exciting, entertaining way—and they'll give you that large helping of extra respect such persons command. Being ignored is the most expensive state there is in real estate. You can't afford it.

Promoting yourself, promoting listings, and promoting buyers are the three legs of promotion's success tripod. All three are attached to each other. Newspapers charge the same whether your ad pulls many phones calls or none at all; printers charge the same whether your flyer is a winner or a dud. Which is cheaper: a $26 ad that produces nothing, or a $52 ad that puts you in contact with a buyer who drops an $1,865 fee in your pocket? Doubling the size of your ads isn't necessarily the solution; doubling the thought you put into your advertising is.

"Effective promotion produces income. I do as much of it as I can afford." If you can validate that statement to yourself without qualms, you're ready to make big money through promotion. But if you consider promotion to be an expense of dubious value that should be avoided whenever possible, you will gain nothing from it. Money is only one-fourth of the price you must pay for a successful promotion. The other three-fourths are enthusiasm, effort, and insight. Unless you are enthusiastic about your promotion, unless you complete the work on time that's required to carry if off, unless you direct the entire operation thoughtfully, your money will be wasted. No amount of money can make a promotion successful that is not timely, well thought out, and accurately aimed. Nothing blends this mix better and stretches dollars further than liberal doses of your own excitement and punch. Here are five thoughts for successful promotion.

1. If You Aren't Enthusiastic About Your Promotion, Can Anyone Else Be?

Stop concentrating on the costs of advertising; start thinking about the earnings from advertising and promotion of all kinds. "Sounds great," you say, "until I have to file for bankruptcy." You're thinking about costs again. Fine. It's important to budget carefully so that you can complete any plan you start. And there's a limit to how fast you can afford to increase your income; promotion can be effective only when it's balanced against the other demands on your time, energy, and money. But remember, effective promotion can only make money for you if you're capable of handling more business when it's rapping on your desk.

2. Give Promotion First Call on Your Most Creative Time

You may easily afford the expense of promotions that fail, but are you willing to give up all the income that well-managed promotion would bring you? No work in real estate is more demanding of your best thought and follow-through than promotion. No work in real estate returns greater rewards for effective effort than promotion.

3. Work Well Ahead of Deadlines

Last-minute-rushitis is the most common plague that afflicts promotional activities with failure.

4. Always Tell People Who You Are, Where You Are, and What You Do

Even on one-shot, get-business-now ads and promotions, never miss a chance to build your image. If you miss the one-shot, you'll still benefit from the long-term image-building effect.

5. Be Careful of Your Money Until You Discover What's Effective

Devise ways to gauge what response you're really getting from your promotions. This is more difficult than it sounds, but it's vital to success.

REAL ESTATE WRITING TIPS

Gather the specific details you'll need on a fact sheet, and make the decisions that have to be made. You can't complete the writing of an ad until you know all the facts you're going to give and how much space you'll pay for. Since real estate moves so fast, don't waste time writing anything you don't have the complete facts on. By the time you get the last detail, the house may be sold.

When writing flyers, it's usually best to put your second-strongest point in your lead-off sentence. Your third most important point goes somewhere in the middle to sustain interest. The strongest point comes last, so your send-off will sing. That's the bottom line, the time when they decide to act on your flyer or forget it. So put the power there.

In between the lead and the end, enter all your other points in a natural order of smooth progress. The direction will be dictated by your opening sentence. If you're starting with the gorgeous carpet, don't jump outside for point two and write about the hedge in front. Having begun inside, run through all the interior features about the home before you mention location, landscaping, or exterior style.

As you work your way through the points, keep more paper handy to jot down any bright phrases and fresh ways of saying things that occur to you.

If your flyer says that the kitchen is huge, the backyard is huge, and the living room's fireplace is huge, your readers will be bored by all this hugeness. People don't want to look at boring houses. One of these huges could be bonus-sized and another extra-large, if big and large aren't powerful enough for you. Or they could be enormous, gigantic, mammoth, immense, king-sized, vast, ample, colossal, extensive, generous, giant-sized, imposing, large-scale, lavish, massive, capacious, or even wide and deep. *Sisson's Synonyms* lists 40 words under *huge* and more under *large* that can give your expressions of size a pleasant variety. *Roget's International Thesaurus* classifies synonyms but is slightly slower to use. But neither of these books gives the best term to describe a large kitchen. So develop your own list of synonyms in your important information notebook.

STYLE

Avoid using abbreviations on printed business forms, flyers, and brochures. It looks tacky and commercial. Unless your company is known by its initials or abbreviated form, spell the name out in full. And give the full, nonshortened address in small type, including the zip code. Giving all this information on your scratch pads allows people to tear off a sheet and send it to a friend with a note written on it that says something like, "This is the sharp agent I was telling you about." And there it all is: your name, address, phone number, the business you're in, and your photo.

Show your phone numbers like this:

Office	714/770-0211
Home	000/123-4567

That's dignified, clean, and clear. Avoid abbreviations before phone numbers such as:

Off:	Off with what?
Res:	Is that a bug killer? And why do you want to call your home a residence anyway? Why sound pretentious?

Bus: Do you drive a bus, or call that number for a bus, or is it
        short for "Don't call me unless you mean business"?

GETTING NEWSLETTERS OUT FAST

The secret is to set up a format and stick to it. Then you know exactly what you
need. Your big job is automatically broken down into several small ones. Have a
lead story of interest to the community (Chapter 7 gives one for every month), and
then drop in a joke or a quote. That's the program. Now comes the commercial: a
brief item of real estate news. Give a few facts. Where do you get facts? From
experts. Everyone knows that. So give them real estate facts in every issue, and
you'll find that your newsletters are working harder for you. Tell them the average
number of days homes were on the market before selling, the average price of
houses sold, compare last month to the same month last year.

Keep it simple. Type it on your letterhead—the one with your photo printed
on it. Then drop it off at the local quick printer.

And always get in this message: "I am the real estate expert for your
neighborhood. If you want more information about real estate, please call me." Say
it in different words each month, but say it.

In your lead story, don't try to compete with *Time* Magazine, *Vogue*, and *The
Wall Street Journal*. Do what they can't do: Tell what's going on inside your farm.
Print the news about the good things: the babies born, the promotions, the vaca-
tions, and who won the local bridge club's tournament.

WRITING YOUR PROFILE OF A PRO

It's simple. Just substitute information about yourself for the details given here
about Kate Bancroft. Type it on your portrait-imprinted letterhead. Get copies and
staple them as the final sheet on the packets of listing flyers you give to open house
walk-ins.

PROFILE OF A PRO
Kate Bancroft

Born in Small Pond, Arkansas. Graduated from Pathfinder High School,
Denver; attended UCLA, Westwood, California. Her husband, John Bancroft, is a
mechanical engineer.

The Bancrofts have a ten-year-old son, Sean, who is active in soccer. Family
activities include backpacking, tennis, and camping.

Kate specializes in the Meadowlark area, but keeps fully informed on all real
estate offerings in the entire Greenpretty Valley.

For knowledgeable, understanding care of your real estate needs, call a professional: Kate Bancroft. Office phone 123-4567; home phone 765-4321.

You can write something like that about yourself the first day you are in real estate. You're a professional the moment *you* decide you'll do those things that distinguish the pros from the piddlers and losers, and you're not obliged to beat the fact that you're new into the heads of every prospect you contact.

Later on, you can put things like this into your profile:

"Kate added five families to her list of satisfied customers by selling five houses last month. Continuing the training that has enabled her to solve the housing problems of 31 couples last year, Kate studied advanced real estate practice at _____."

PLUGS SELL LISTINGS

One of the best ways to promote your listings is by plugging them at the monthly meetings of your professional association. A plug is a short talk that's designed to make your fellow agents aware of your listing. The more aware they are of it, the more likely they are to show it to their buyers. The more buyers that see it, the more likely it is that your listing will sell.

If plugs for listings aren't being given now, call the president and ask that they be included in future meetings. Point out that plug sessions provide greater value to the membership at no extra cost.

Some boards have developed a plug procedure that works smoothly. Here it is:

- A *plug sign-up sheet* is kept at the door of our monthly meetings. Only the first ten members to put their names on that sheet are allowed to plug their listings that month.

- When the plug session is called, the pluggers are asked to line up near the podium in the order that they signed up. They then proceed to give their plugs in turn at the microphone.

- Each plug is allowed one minute. The board secretary has a horn and stop watch, and if the plugger is still talking after 60 seconds, the horn goes off and stops him or her. This might seem harsh, but the strict enforcement of this rule is essential if plugging is to be a success. The horn won't have to be used often, but the threat of it makes the pluggers organize their thoughts, keep up a brisk pace, and make the session interesting.

The plug session will be a highlight of the meeting if originality and humor are encouraged. To this end, the clock is stopped whenever a funny plugger has to wait for the audience to stop laughing before he or she can continue.

- The elected officers at the meeting give scores to the pluggers, and a winner of *The Plug Award* is quickly announced. This award is a prize donated by an affiliate member. A free ad in a local newspaper or a real estate book is a suitable prize. The winner is also mentioned in the following week's Multiple Listing Book. But the greatest reward is the attention your fellow agents will give to your listings.

- The point system used in the scoring is:

Effectiveness of description	25 points
Creativity	25 points
Giving your name	10 points
Giving your office's name	10 points
Giving your listing's address	10 points
Giving your listing's price	10 points
Escaping the time's-up horn	10 points

- If that week's caravan takes place after your monthly meeting, the plug session is an even more powerful selling tool.

Put Showmanship into Your Plugs

Effective plugs can be given straight, that is, with facts and figures stated simply and clearly. If your listing is really an outstanding value, or has some very special features, the straight plug can be very successful. But if your listing is neither unique nor bargain-priced, as is usually the case, showmanship and humor can supply the sparkly that'll make agents remember your listing. These plug scripts are award winners. Use them as is, or use them to ignite your own creativity.

Hat Plug

Props: Three different hats.

Opening: The agent giving the plug wears a huge sombrero to the podium, and carries two other hats.

Script: "I'm Scrappy Smith with Magnificent Mansions. We agents wear many hats in real estate. Here's a listing that'll knock yours off."

[Brushes sombrero off head, and gives price, address, and a brief description of the house being plugged. Then puts on a chef's hat.]

"You're all invited to join me for lunch today. I'm serving homemade chili there with all the trimmings. That address again is 12345 Adios."

[Whips off chef's hat and replaces it with a motorcycle crash helmet. Taped to the helmet are paper horns or some other weird device, and a placard reading, in large letters, *BUY NOW*.]

"This is my real estate hat. I'm on a crash program to get this house sold fast.

So please come see it, enjoy lunch, and help me get my clients moved. Thank you."

A stovepipe hat, a fez, a pith helmet, and oddball headgear will do for your lead-off prop. Chef's hats are paper; a local restaurant will give you one. And a bike shop will lend you a crash helmet.

Valentine Plug for February Meeting

Props: Heart-shaped red and white box tied with big white ribbon. Inside are various articles that tie in with the property.

Opening: Agent takes box to podium and starts taking out the articles.

Script: "I'm Zippy Brown with Dwellings That'll Delight You. How sweet it is! Let's see what special treats are inside."

[Takes out a large paper key.]

"Here's the key to my lovable listing at 4567 Honeymoon Hollow, priced at $140,000."

[Takes out a large piece of cheese.]

"To slice on the built-in chopping block in its fantastic gourmet kitchen."

[Takes out bathing cap.]

"For splashing around in the gorgeous swimming pool."

How to Create Winning Plugs Fast

Ideas are everywhere. Most good plug ideas can be adapted to any house. So keep on the lookout for them throughout the month as you watch TV, read, and talk with people. When you get a good thought for a plug, jot it down and start collecting your props. It's amazing what can be done with rags, paper, cardboard, a spray can of paint, and a little effort. Do it early, so you won't be up till 3 A.M. the night before your meeting.

The actual speech is the easiest part. Make a list of the essential points. Then practice your talk, timing yourself as you do so. If you're working against a 60-second time limit, trim your plug to no more than 30 seconds when you say it at a normal rate of speech. If you have trouble getting it down that short, write it out and cut unnecessary words. One minute is plenty of time.

If you're nervous, practice your speech until you can say it in your sleep. And remember, you'll have your notes and props to help carry the freight. Prepare carefully and it'll go beautifully.

And be sure to get there early enough to get on the list.

LISTING REMARKS

Don't burden your listing remarks with scrubby details like the new dishwasher unless your Multiple Listing book gives you lots of space. If you only have a line or two left after putting in what has to be said, write something bright that'll make agents want to see the house. Here are some ideas:

- "Your clients will give you rave notices for showing this lovely _____."
- "Strictly top-drawer describes this elegant _____."
- "She'll love you forever, sir, if you purchase this _____."
- "Be a love-bug and snap onto this cozy _____."
- "No blarney here, just happy loving in this 7-bedroom stylish _____."
- "Don't just keep up with the Joneses, pass them. Move into this fantastic _____."
- "No-mow lawn—it's that kind of house."
- "Mom will love cooking in this gourmet kitchen while the whole clan lives it up in the adjoining family room that's complete with _____."
- "This colonial castle features a special _____."
- "Zowie—your own private spa. Think of the possibilities."

YOUR NAME IS YOUR TRADEMARK

People won't call you if they don't remember your name. Make it easy for them. Difficult names aren't necessarily a disadvantage, but blurred ones are. Harold L. "Hal" Sturgis isn't a real estater's trademark, it's a confusion. Hal Sturgis is crisp and memorable, and that's the way Hal should print it on his letterheads and business cards if he wants maximum impact.

Zoltanovich X. Buttersnichel doesn't need the "X" as much as John R. Hall needs the "R," but it's surprising how often the Halls of this world drop their middle initials, and the Buttersnichels slap theirs on everything.

Give some thought to how good a trademark your complete legal name makes. When it's longer than people will use in ordinary conversation, it's too long to be your most effective, money-making trademark. If you feel comfortable with the idea, consider using the shorter version of your name that you actually go by on business cards, flyers, and letterheads. Sign your full name only on legal documents. If you don't like your given name, or find your last name annoyingly long, why not perform plastic surgery on them? Zoltanovich X. Buttersnichel becomes Zolly Butter simply by telling everyone that that's his label, and by using it exclusively whenever he orders something with his name printed on it.

Before you start your next big promotional campaign, consider whether a more colorful and shorter name will be remembered better. Sometimes that's all it takes to swing another fee or two your way. A name that sticks in people's minds is money in the bank.

YOUR PRODUCT

In the area of promotion, the opportunity you have as a real estate agent is much like that of a product manager. A person with that title is in charge of marketing a brand of soap, cigarettes, or sailboats for a large corporation. Successful product managers win public recognition for their products by endlessly repeating the same trademarks, slogans, themes, and colors. Over long periods of time they maintain a family resemblance as one advertising campaign succeeds another. When necessary, they update their advertising to remain fresh and current. They change—yet they remain the same. These managers build on, instead of waste, their past efforts; they carefully select their new pattern from what is consistent with their old pattern. Instead of scattering their efforts, astute product managers concentrate their efforts on consistency—and achieve impact even with a small budget.

How does all this apply to a sales associate making the rounds of a farm? Very closely. The photo on your imprinted scratch pads should be a recent one. It should show you as you usually look when working real estate, not as you dress for Mardi Gras night. Use that same photo, the same slogan, and the same style of type on your business cards, letterheads and newsletters. Maintain the same complete visual package as closely as possible on all your giveaways. Follow it as much as you can on display advertising.

If you're flashily dressed when first bouncing through your farm in December, then are sloppily dressed when dragging back through January, and finally achieve a conservative well-dressed appearance when prospecting briskly in February, can you expect people to remember they've seen you before? They won't remember Flashy or Sloppy either; they'll just think that about four agents have been calling on them.

Select a suitable mode of business clothing and stick with that mode, changing gradually with the styles but not switching wildly from day to day. Don't wear the same dress or suit every time you farm, but do think about presenting a consistent image of dependable professionalism when selecting your farming and working wardrobe. Think about the same things when selecting and developing all your farming and working tools, whether the item in question is an automobile, or a flyer about your new listing.

Consistency counts. A bright, brisk, businesslike manner counts. Confidence counts—if it doesn't come off as arrogance. All these things count heavily when your identity score is suddenly totaled up, as it is every time someone on your farm decides to sell.

You have a product to manage: yourself and your marketable services.

Manage your product's advertising astutely: Concentrate on consistent repetition—
and achieve impact even with a small budget.

IMPRINTED SCRATCH PADS: YOUR MOST EFFECTIVE, YEAR-ROUND FARMING TOOL

Here's what goes on your scratch pads:

- Your company's name, address, and phone number,
- Your name, photo, and home phone number,
- Your slogan if it's brief (about half a dozen words at the most),
- Plenty of space for your clients and customers to write on,
- And emergency phone numbers (fire, police, and so on).

Two cost-effective sizes are:

- One-half of a regular sheet of typewriter paper, 5-1/2 × 8-1/2".
- One-third of that 8-1/2 × 11" typewriter paper, 3-5/8 × 8-1/2".

In the smaller size, the emergency numbers are lightly printed so that they can
be written over. It costs a little extra, but it's well worth the money to have special
final pages printed that add: "This is the last page! Time to call [your first name] for
another scratch pad."

A CORNUCOPIA OF IDEAS

Where to Buy Giveaways

The giveaways you need for farming and other promotional use can be bought from
the companies listed under *Advertising Specialties* in the yellow pages of your
telephone directory. If you live in a small town, your local telephone company
office or public library will have the yellow pages from the nearest large city.

All giveaways must be imprinted. If it's impossible to imprint the item itself,
imprint the packaging. Keep the imprint as simple as possible, and avoid crowding
in several slogans.

Have a commercial artist paste up your imprint with set type, and tell him or
her to make a dozen "repro proofs" that you can send to your various giveaway
suppliers. The repros are also handy when you run display advertising. Have the
artist select bold type (if that's in keeping with the style of your letterhead and
business card) so the imprint can be reduced in size and still be easily read. If your

company name doesn't clearly specify that it's engaged in real estate, add, "Serving Your Real Estate Needs" below your name. If you don't do that, a good many people will associate you with insurance, automobiles, or tulip sales.

Hard-selling but Soft Words for Your Brochures

For many, the gorgeous spa off the master suite is the outstanding feature of this fine home; for others, it's the panoramic view—or the secluded rear yard. All will agree that the tastefully decorated interior complements the thoughtfully developed grounds, that the whole is a delightful meld of ample family living space with private and party-time entertainment amenities.

Extensively customized with care and artistry . . . the distinctive fireplace recalls old Taos, the patio evokes new Maui . . . the grounds blend desert, flower, and turf into a unique, pleasing whole that's set off by view-enhancing stucco fences . . . framed by planter walls, the patio is housewide, covered, and has its own entertainment dining served by a pass-through from the kitchen . . . built-in buffet, wired to conceal a TV, enables the family room to swiftly convert for spacious, elegant dining . . . a louvered closet nearby has wires for stereo components . . . Franciscan ceramic tile kitchen, Italian ceramic tile entry, fully finished garage with multiple extras . . . .
We could go on,
   and on.
   But why?
      THIS ONE YOU MUST SEE!!!

Newsletter Idea

Each month, print your newsletter on one side of a sheet of paper, and a calendar–appointment record on the other. Any printer can do this for you. The first month you deliver your newsletters, supply a magnet on a 1½" plastic button to hold these sheets on a refrigerator door. Advertising specialty firms can supply you with the inexpensive magnet-ads—the 1½" size allows plenty of room for your name, phone, slogan, and company name.

For Swifty House Flyers

1234 ANY STREET
OFFERED AT $275,000

Located on a quiet cul-de-sac, this home exemplifies one of the finest values in the Prestige Pines area. With 3,000 sq. ft. of versatile and flexible living, it offers excellent schools and shopping in a pride-of-ownership area. The land is fee simple and encompasses almost ⅓ acre, beautifully arranged for a tennis court or pool. Many fine features as listed below:

- DECORATOR DRAPES
- UPGRADED CARPETING AND PAD
- FULLY INSULATED WALLS
- MIRRORED WARDROBE CLOSET DOORS
- CERAMIC TILE ENTRY
- BUILT-IN SHELVING IN LIVING ROOM
- PROFESSIONALLY FINISHED UPSTAIRS
- ADDED FREEFORM PATIO OFF LIVING ROOM
- BLOCKWALL FENCING
- SPRINKLER SYSTEM
- CUSTOM LAVA FOUNTAIN IN REAR YARD
- PROFESSIONALLY LANDSCAPED WITH EXOTIC PLANTINGS
- PRICE INCLUDES BUILT-IN WET BAR IN UPSTAIRS GAME ROOM

- LIVING ROOM 13′ × 20′
- MASTER BEDROOM 14′ × 17′
- UPSTAIRS LIVING AREA CONTAINS 1,300 SQ. FT.

14

THE SUBTLE AND LEARNABLE ART OF CAPTURING CUSTOMERS

Revving Up for Relo Action • New People • The Essence of Client-Capture • Buyers' Beguine • The Proof-of-Competence Phase • Equality of Looks • Tune in Emotionally • Shoot Your Best Shot and Don't Worry About Competition • Lonely Charlie • Smile Mysteriously • Lunching with Buyers • Expanded Folk Wisdom • Another Window • Don't Tell Them You're New • Use Your Buyers File Constantly • The Hungry Breath • Winning Scripts • Lender Qualifyer

REVVING UP FOR RELO ACTION

In many areas, national relocation firms have become an important factor in real estate sales. Relocation firms work with large organizations that frequently transfer employees from one part of the country to another. When the transferred family sells their home, these large employers often pay the brokerage fee and, through the relocation firm, recommend a real estate office in the area their employee is moving to.

This means that national relocation firms provide a flow of buyers coming in and sellers going out—qualified, right-now buyers, and sellers with no time or interest in going fizzbo. Since relocation firms provide some of the finest clients and customers around, it's vital that they get the finest service—or they'll take their considerable business elsewhere.

Making sure that the finest service is given to the relocation begins with an organized system for working with their referrals from the first phone call. This means that the key person who handles referrals in your office must be prepared to do two things anytime he or she picks up the phone: (1) provide accurate information about the area; and (2) ask the right questions about a family being referred.

The well-prepared relo specialist in your office would say something like this to whoever calls in from a relocation firm:

"Thank you so much for giving us the opportunity to serve your client or customer. Here at Sell Fast Realty we pride ourselves on the thorough and professional way we counsel the people you send us. In order for me to do this in the most beneficial way, I need some details about them."

"How many are in the family?"

"Where are they relocating from?"

"How long have they lived there?"

"What size home do they now have, and what is its value?"

"How much equity do they have in it?"

"Do they have to sell their present home before they can buy here?"

"Is the company purchasing their present home?"

"How many times has this family been transferred in the last ten years?" (If they've been moved frequently, plan on using a great deal of empathy with the wife.)

"Do both the husband and the wife work outside the home?"

"Are they happy about the move?"

"Do they have any special requirements, such as being near their church?"

"What is the new position of the person being transferred?"

"Is this transfer a step up or sideways for them?" (Is it a promotion or a lateral move?)

"Will they come out to look together, or will one of them come alone?" (If one will come first, find out which one, the wife or the husband.)

And, of course, ask all the obvious questions—their name, phone number, address, ages of children.

Follow up the relocation lead by immediately calling the transferring family:

"Hi. I'm Danny Kennedy with Sell Fast Realty in Greenpretty Valley. [Mention your connection with the relocation company.] I'm looking forward to doing everything possible to make your move here pleasant."

Give them an opportunity to respond. Then continue with, "Do you have any questions about Greenpretty Valley that you'd like to ask?"

After you've offered to answer their questions, they'll be more receptive to answering yours. "I was given some information about you and your family to help me serve your needs better, but I'd like to check some of those facts."

Then go through the list of questions you asked the relo firm and verify the facts they gave you. The information you already have on that family will allow you to phrase your questions to them tactfully and avoid sensitive areas. As you talk with them, get more details about their likes and dislikes, and note down what they tell you in the file you're building on them. Ask as many questions as you can about their present lifestyle without seeming nosy.

Discover, if possible, what they're hoping to find in your area. With many people, you learn most by letting them talk—use questions such as, ''Is your son interested in sports?'' Few mothers can resist talking about their children. After you've found out about the children's activities, it will seem very natural for the wife to start talking about how she and her husband spend their leisure time.

Your purpose is to have them feeling that they'll be meeting an intelligent, concerned, and knowledgeable friend. As you approach setting an appointment, you may want to leave the exact time loose and have them call you when they arrive. If they're flying out for a quick house-hunting trip, they may not rent a car, and instead will rely on you for transportation.

When you set out with them for the first time, give them an overview of your area. Have a route worked out in your mind for a quick tour to show them the points of interest; introduce them to the various communities and neighborhoods they should be considering. As you drive, reel off your prepared scripts, the sales dialogues described in Chapter 23. Hand them both a simplified map of your area (a sketch you've had duplicated works great for this purpose) so that they will get oriented rapidly.

Remember, the quicker you can make them feel that they know the area, the quicker they'll be willing to make a decision. As you cruise the various communities with them, keep verifying your assumptions—and change your plans when you realize you're somewhat off the mark in what you thought they'd want in a house. First, zero in on the community they feel comfortable in; then start showing houses. If you have a large Quick-Speak Inventory, you'll have no problem switching directions quickly. Many times people coming to a new area change their requirements when they see, for the first time, what's available.

Always keep in mind that the transferee faces many problems. Let's talk about the traditional situation where the husband is the one who's been transferred. He might be getting a $5,000 raise—but his wife might be leaving a $20,000 job that isn't available in your area. So it's costing them $15,000 a year to take his promotion. The lender qualifyer (at the end of this chapter) must be introduced and explained.

Perhaps you'll be called on to help the wife find a job in order to firm up their move and make the house sale on your end. Every case is different. Get a head start on the second income aspect of transfers by learning all you can in your initial phone conversation with them. Many times I've called hospitals for incoming nurses and schools for incoming teachers to find out about licensing to help the wife get started on qualifying for a job sooner. It's all part of the services a real estate practitioner provides.

This question often comes up: ''Should every agent in the office be allowed to handle the referrals your company receives through its relocation affiliation?''

My answer is a loud ''No.'' Only the active agents—the ones who work the field, find prospects on their own, and bring business in—should be rewarded with agency referrals. The sit-around agents—the ones who get all their sales from floor time and ad calls—shouldn't be rewarded for being part of the problem instead of part of the solution. Only companies with a tremendous competitive advantage can survive with agents who depend entirely on company-generated business. The rest of the industry must have agents who knock on doors, work FSBOs, and generate fees independently—or we go out of business. It's as simple as that.

The individual who gets the relocation agency referrals must have a patient personality. Some agents are not good with out-of-state referrals. Working with them means many trips to show property. Sometimes months go by before the sale is made—the first step might involve finding them a rental for six months. In other cases, pictures of property need to be taken and then mailed, along with detailed information about such things as schools. The person you choose to get the referral business not only must be knowledgeable and well-prepared agent, but also he or she must be detail-oriented and organized to handle it all. Many pros have secretaries who can do much of the follow-up work, leaving the agent free to work with more people.

The agent or agents you select to handle relocation agency business must be committed to you and to giving good service—that one agent can lose the whole account for you. I've had people say, "Forget that relocation business. The people are too picky, and for the commission you get, it isn't worth it."

My experience has been that relocation agencies prefer to work with one person in each office who will then funnel the referrals to a few outstanding agents. The manager is the ideal middle person to do this. If too many people get involved, confusion reigns—and the agency account is in jeopardy. Most relocation groups have certain forms that they want filled out and sent back. Also be sure to use a communications log for every relocation prospect. (A suitable form for this purpose is illustrated in Chapter 24.) Keep the relocation people informed every step of the way. The follow-up and detail work is a critical part of ensuring that they will want to continue doing business with your company.

On listings you take through relo agencies, be sure to find out what to do when the homeowners move out. Some companies want you to have the utilities billed to your office, and then be reimbursed by them. When the employer intends to buy a transferred employee's house and move them out, the relocation agency will ask you to give a "market evaluation." Your market evaluation will then be put together with one or two appraisals they pay a fee for. Be honest and conservative with the relocation people—they need *realistic* prices.

In some parts of the country, even owner-occupied personal residences have been bought and sold primarily as investments with the hope of rapid appreciation. This doesn't work in difficult markets when faith in the inevitability of appreciation has disappeared. We have to realize that real estate is a commodity—its true value rests on the uses to which it can be put in the present, not on what its price may be at some time in the future. Like the current price of any other useful thing, the price of real estate is based on the relationship between supply and demand—but it's value to any given person, couple, or family depends on their needs at that particular time in their lives.

In past decades, people decided that real estate was hotter than any game in Las Vegas. They stopped investing and started gambling, and for a while every bet won. The boom in real estate prices generated ever higher prices. The game was to buy a place, hold it for the short time it took to double your equity, sell it, and then move up to a larger place. At that larger place your equity was working harder, enabling you to use more OPN (other people's money) in search of more gain. But other people's money costs three or four times as much as it did 30 years ago; now it's not so easy to make money with other people's money because there's no one coming along behind willing and able to play the same game.

In some cases, relocation firms and major corporations have large inventories of properties they can't get their money out of—transferred employees' homes they purchased at phenomenal prices when the market was still rising. These problem properties are haunting the brokers involved in the transactions.

Relocation is competitive. Many firms are vying for the business. Remember that big brother is always watching when you're involved in relocation. But, if you're professional, and if you treat the company's money as if it were your own, you won't go wrong.

Create a relocation packet—a collection of data about your area that's organized so that incoming people can quickly find what they want. Type up a table of contents, on your letterhead, to use as the first page. The relo packet should contain the following items.

- Simplified map of the area's communities.
- School district information. (Include a Lender Qualifyer.)
- Recreational opportunities available in your town.
- List of churches. (Omit addresses. Show them where their church is when they're in your car.)
- List of shopping centers. (Again, plan to show them when they arrive.)
- Brief discussion of climate.
- Map showing access to airports, to where they'll be working, to points of interest.
- List of several places they can reach on a weekend for recreation.
- Financing information. (Include a Lender Qualifyer.)
- Your company brochure.
- Several house flyers.

Having a relo packet stamps you as a professional. When you start working on yours, check what your local Chamber of Commerce and library have that you can use. Make up several relo packets before you need them. This will allow you to mail one to prospects the same day you get the referral, or hand it to a prospect coming in with no prior notice other than the phone call from the relocation center.

NEW PEOPLE

Active real estate agents constantly meet new people. Successful real estate agents not only meet *more* new people, they meet them *better*. In the vital meeting situations that must result either in the gain or loss of a new client or customer, the successful agent has a high success ratio.

Much of that success is determined in the critical first 15 seconds of each meeting with new people. What can happen in just 15 seconds?

Time yourself with your watch. Get up, walk to a window, look out, walk back to your chair, and sit down again. The chances are, you can do all that in 15 seconds. A fourth of a minute is long enough for an enormous amount of nonverbal communication, plus a considerable amount of talk; time enough to say 50 or 60 words without hurry. It's time enough to get preoccupied, to show irritation that the new people have interrupted you, to stare at them with obvious suspicion that they'll be a waste of effort. It's time enough to demonstrate that you're friendly, ready, and eager to work with someone new, and that you're pleasant to be with, too.

Some agents don't warm up to new people quickly. Sometimes this stems from an unwillingness to accept the role that a salesperson must: be the first-mover, first-smiler, first-greeter. Sometimes the slow warm-up mirrors their behavior in purely social meetings, or is a defense against feelings of inferiority in the customer-agent relationship. What's vital to believe and feel here is that social equality or inequality between agent and prospect isn't involved; it is a professional, not a social, relationship. Agents who greet newcomers with hesitancy and suspicion must be unaware of how badly they're wounding themselves in this way. Monitor yourself; knowing that you have this problem solves it.

When they first walk in, do you run up to them and put your hand out, or do you watch for their signals? Does their arm go up a little bit?

If it does, catch on. Reach out and shake hands.

Some people don't like to touch right away. They seem to be saying, ''Don't invade my personal space.''

Then don't. Build up slowly, slowly.

Some people walk in and hug you. That's fine, you know. It's their built-in reaction.

But, be careful. Don't crowd people who can't handle it.

THE ESSENCE OF CUSTOMER-CAPTURE

Bait the hook with knowledge. Depend on knowledge for the power, and on your winning personality and charming smile only for the assist.

During your first face-to-face encounter, what you can tell them about your area and what you can learn about their needs without offending them by seeming to pry, are all-important.

Flow with Their Stroke

Fit your attitude and your schedule to their moods, personalities, and time plans.

Product Knowledge Is Serious Business

You'll wither unless you know the inventory of available housing thoroughly; you'll flourish if you do. Only top-flight real estate people take product knowledge as seriously as it should be taken. (Chapter 3 discussed how you can rapidly gain a large and detailed knowledge of your inventory.)

Listen, Really Listen

Top producers invariably are intent listeners (at least to prospects); low producers tend to be sloppy listeners. When you listen, listen actively—with your ears *and* your eyes. Keep asking yourself things like: Exactly what does she mean by that? Why didn't he finish that sentence? Do they really mean that? Listen and watch for hints to follow up.

And keep them talking about their feelings. Treat what they say as important. Prove you think it's important by remembering what they tell you.

Be an Expert

On financing. On the right things to say. On all phases of residential real estate practice. Prospects know they'll be spending large dollars with you; they also know they're worth large service.

BUYERS' BEGUINE

''Put your left foot forward, and your right foot out, and head in the direction where the buyers hang out!'' All we need is a great melody and we've got a sensational new dance—for three. You and a pair of buyers. Even without the beat, some agents get the steps down pat, and others end up doing the hokey-pokey all the time. But the buyers' beguine, like all dances, can be learned if you've got rhythm in your head and desire in your soul. When done well, the dance is smooth, graceful, and flowing. That takes practice, practice, practice. Once you get the steps on quick-foot, watchers can hardly tell who's leading and who's following. But you and I know who's controlling the movements—your trusted friend and mine, the real estate agent.

You can learn the steps before, but the complete performance must be polished on the dance floor. In real estate, as in dancing, some people dance well together and others never keep the beat too well. But, with a strong and subtle lead and quick responses, we can have our clumsiest partners thinking they're dancing *Swan Lake*—all the way to homeownership.

THE PROOF-OF-COMPETENCE PHASE

All the demanding work of promotion, phone and mail prospecting, door-knocking, holding houses open, and floor time has but one object: contact with a buyer or seller. Once you have that contact, the search phase is over, and you are thrust abruptly into the proof-of-competence phase.

"Wait a minute," you say. "What about building rapport? Don't I have to show that I'm genuinely interested in solving their housing problem, that I regard them as unique and important individuals, that they'll like doing business with me? Don't I have to create trust, confidence, and friendly feelings before I can take the next step?"

Not with action-imminent buyers or sellers, you don't. They're not looking for Smiley Jokester or Sally Sincere; they're searching for a capable expert who is socially acceptable.

In actual practice, you'll meld competence demonstration with rapport building as the situation dictates. Agents who've made their Breakaway will demonstrate their competence with the relaxed alertness that wins prospects, by

- Responding to comments made by prospects with references to specific properties whenever possible. These responses reveal the agent's depth of knowledge while they develop useful information:

    "You'd prefer a larger dining room? I know of a lovely home with an impressive dining room that's available now. The carpet there is powder blue. Do you like that color?"

- Asking the right questions at the right time with the right words. To a quiet couple who say nothing of consequence after your initial greetings: "Is this your first visit here?"

- Speaking in an informed way about any phase of real estate that comes up.

- Sliding one, or several, of their sales dialogues smoothly into the conversation, tailoring them to fit the prospect's needs and tastes. Once you gain a prospect's attention—even momentarily—you have an opportunity to demonstrate, without brag or bluster and without knocking other agents or misrepresenting what you can do, that you are a real estate expert, that you can help them get the house they want for the least amount of money possible, or sell their house advantageously.

You don't tell them, "I'm a hotshot agent." You don't overwhelm them with real estater's jargon; you simply respond with casual competence to whatever questions they have with the confidence born of knowledge. Then you guide the interview in the channels you want it to go, remaining always alert to the direction they want to go.

The problem is to let them know you're hot stuff without directly saying so. You do this by drilling yourself on Quick-Speak.

EQUALITY OF LOOKS

If the salesperson is a woman (there are lots of pretty women in real estate), and she only looks at the male half of the buyer pair, and the afternoon wears on with just those two looking at each other—there's trouble in Sales City. That saleswoman is operating as though the man will make the decision, which is always a risky assumption to place all your bets on.

While all this he-and-she looking is going on, the wife is thinking, "We're going to buy a house from her? *No way*. I've got an *ugly* girlfriend in real estate, and that's who we're buying from."

Or the salesperson is a man who, making the same assumption, only looks at the husband. All day long they're talking man-to-man, while the wife is saying to herself, "This twit of an agent thinks I'm too stupid to be involved in a big decision like the choice of my own home. I'll show him. Tomorrow, we'll find an agent who'll involve me too, and then we'll get serious about buying."

Look at them both equally. Speak to them both equally. Sometimes that's difficult, and often it's the wife who is forward and talky, and the husband who is quiet and withdrawn. Make a continuous, strong effort to include them both in all the minor decisions and discussions that lead up to the one big decision. Even if you can't treat them equally because one spouse is so dominant, the less-aggressive half will recognize what you're trying to do and appreciate it greatly. Very often it's that quiet one who, though refusing to say much in public, will cast the decisive vote in private. Operate on the theory that, to capture either of them as customers, you have to capture them both. Two birds in hand are worth more than one on your shoulder and another in flight.

TUNE IN EMOTIONALLY

Ask yourself, Who am I dealing with? In handling buyers, you must listen, and watch, and *think* if you want to understand human nature. Always keep in mind that there are many kinds of people. Be sensitive to the emotional level of your prospect. Meet it and build from there. Maybe you're naturally outgoing and flamboyant. Tone that down when working with an engineer type who is analytical and calculating. You must become a numbers nut for this person. You must show this individual that his or her concerns are your concerns. When you are working with an extrovert who is warm and understanding like yourself, but his wife keeps the books and is suspicious, you have to appeal to her more conservative ways and still be warm.

SHOOT YOUR BEST SHOT AND DON'T WORRY ABOUT COMPETITION

Kitty Jamison had an experience that illustrates this point. An out-of-state referral, a single woman, gave explicit requirements and said she was seeing houses with another agent on Tuesday, but would be available to look with Kitty on Wednesday. Kitty knew there were only about half a dozen properties in Mission Viejo that would meet the lady's requirements. After a thorough review of the MLS book, she found a seventh. Certain that the other agent would show all seven of those houses to the buyer on Tuesday, Kitty called every active agent she could, trying to find some new or pocket listings to add to the seven. No luck. Time ran out.

Exuding a confidence that was all sham, Kitty met the buyer and drove her to the first stop. The lady looked glum when she saw the house. After prowling through it silently, she said, "Now this is more like it."

"You haven't already seen this home?" Kitty gasped.

"I didn't see anything yesterday that came anywhere near this close to what I want."

"I've lined up six more that are even closer," Kitty said.

"If you have, I'll buy one of them from you."

And she did. The other agent hadn't shown a single one of the seven houses that fitted the buyer's requirements, even though all seven were in the book. Why didn't she? The answer to that question might go far toward explaining why 20 percent of the agents do 80 percent of the business in most real estate offices.

Over a period of time, the top 20 percent doesn't work harder than the middle 20 percent, but they work smarter, and they make productive use of the time and energy that others spend complaining and discouraging themselves. And the top producers in any sales organization have made the initial all-out effort that success demands of us all.

LONELY CHARLIE

Not all husbands looking for their next house, while their wives remain back home, are Lonely Charlies. Men with a heavy travel schedule, outside salesmen and regional executives, for example, are used to being away from home. Most of them have learned how to handle it.

But Lonely Charlie hasn't. Every day before his transfer he worked at the same desk with the same people. Every day he bantered at the same coffee urn with the same office friends. Every day he drove to work at the same time, parked in the same space, and drove home by the same route. Evenings and weekends he spent with his family in even more familiar surroundings.

Then the transfer jerked Charlie out of his comfortable rut. His wife must stay behind until their old house sells, or until the kids finish school. Suddenly Charlie's world is gone: no wife, family, home, personal friends, familiar work routine—no grass to mow, no albums to paste stamps in, no kids to yell at. The streets are strange and the climate is off-key. He has to learn which light switches do what all over again. His new job helps—during the day. But his evenings are grim: four motel walls closing in on him. And his weekends are endless.

No wonder Lonely Charlie looks at houses—and looks, and looks. And who with? A friendly, attractive saleswoman. He's in no hurry. His house hasn't sold yet. And, as soon as he makes his choice, there's no reason for her to spend time with him anymore. So—even if Lonely Charlie doesn't have trouble on his mind—he does need a socially acceptable, and cheap, way to fill all those lonely hours. Maybe Lonely Charlie doesn't admit even to himself what he's doing—but consciously or not, he'll waste as much of your time as he can.

Charlie is a needful person during this lost interlude between the secure home-office situation he's left behind, and the secure home-office situation he'll create as soon as he possibly can. Meanwhile, he's hurting. A saleswoman needs to be very professional when working with Lonely Charlie, and she must set limits on how much time she'll spend with him. The longer she works with Charlie, the more the wife back home hears about her, and the less likely it is that the wife will permit the purchase to be made through the long-suffering agent.

Even without this complication, there's rough air to fly through here. Lonely Charlie is the easiest customer-capture around for the saleswoman—and the hardest to close. Like impossible with the true L.C. Before you invest a huge amount of time, pretty lady, investigate. Ask to call his wife, no matter where she is. A long distance call will cost a fraction of what the time you can put into him is worth. Tell him you want to talk colors, and such. If he squirms at the idea of your calling his wife (no matter how plausible his reasons sound) he's a full-blown Lonely Charlie. Or, if you do get the chance to phone his wife and she's suspicious and unfriendly, you're not going to get the business anyway, so forget it.

SMILE MYSTERIOUSLY

A number of buyers have told me, "We came to you because we hear you've got properties no one else knows are for sale."

I smile mysteriously and say, "I've had a little luck along that line."

Of course I have. Every active agent knows half a dozen fizzbos or expireds who'll go for a one-party show, or people who've said, "I'm going to list with you in a couple of months, but if you get some hot buyers for a house like this in the meantime, bring them around."

And an active lister usually knows, at any given moment, one or two people who can't make up their minds who to list with, or when. But this kind of thing isn't what made my reputation for knowing more properties than anyone else. What did? Knowing the inventory in the Multiple Listing Service's book better than anyone else. How did I do that? By working hard, smart, and alone, by keyviewing and reviewing the inventory until I had everything in my area of specialization on Quick-Speak.

You can do that too by spending every spare hour during the entire week studying houses. That means you cut off the whoopee-time caravaning. When your crowd from the office piles into one car and laughs their way through a few houses, firing zingers at each other and telling funny stories all the way, it's great fun. You see half as many houses as you would traveling alone, and you remember none.

I liked whoopee-time caravaning as much as anyone. If I was losing touch with the people in the office, or getting punchy from the pace and needed the camaraderie, I'd go with the crowd and have some fun too. But if you make it a habit rather than an exceptional treat, ha-ha caravaning will cost you more than a new Mercedes.

LUNCHING WITH BUYERS

You can't save a lost sale by taking the buyers to lunch, although you often can make amends with a lunch for an inconvenience that you've inadvertently inflicted. Except for special circumstances such as that, save your lunch money for buyers you have great rapport with, for the times when you're on the verge of getting an offer and need to review with them what you've seen together. But make very sure that they really want to have lunch with you. Tell them, "I'd be pleased (flattered, honored, happy) to join you for lunch now, but I hope you'll be candid with me. You're about to make an important decision, and if you need the time to talk privately, I certainly think that's more important than my pleasure at this moment. So you tell me. The vital thing is to solve your housing problem."

When I use to show property from 9:30 or so and it was about 11:30, I'd say something like, "Let's maybe take a break now—maybe you all would like to get a bite to eat. I'll give you two a chance to be alone, and talk about the houses we saw this morning, and would you like to meet at one o'clock?"

Ask yourself, was it an ad or a sign call that brought these people to me or a solid referral? Be selective. If you're a new salesperson, you should conserve your funds. There are people around who'll not only waste your time, they'll happily let you spend your money on them too.

Should a saleswoman, showing houses to a married man looking without his wife, ask him to lunch?

Unless he's an old friend, she knows the wife well, and is on a solid footing with her, no. Say to him, "Have a nice lunch. Let's get back together at one o'clock and resume our tour."

Should she accept lunch from him?

For the same reasons, no. She should tell him, "I want to devote as much time as possible to you because I know you need to find a home for you and your wife, and you need to have me available to assist you, so I'd like to use the lunch hour to catch up on phone messages at the office."

Obviously, if you've already told him that he's your first customer, and you don't have *anything* else to do, you've put yourself in line for Lonesome Charlie's full trip.

The first time out with people, it's usually best to avoid taking them to lunch. You can say, "I'd better make a few quick phone calls and grab a sandwich. I'll see you at one o'clock."

But, if you've been out with them two or three times and they're very close to making a decision, then put it like this: "Would you two like the opportunity to be alone during lunch so you can discuss what we've seen this morning—because I know you've seen a couple of houses that you really like?—Or may I have the pleasure of taking you to lunch?"

If you're going to pay for the lunch, say it right up front. Make it very clear. You've got to do that before lunch. Otherwise, you're going through the whole lunch and everybody's nervous.

This should happen only when you're on the verge of closing the sale—and only if *they* want to be with *you.* Don't let your ego get involved here; they may want to be alone and, if so, your chances of closing a sale (that the people won't back out of later) are much better if you do let them be alone.

A sales*man,* working with a wife looking alone, should show the same degree of professionalism. Even with couples, unless they're friends of the family, repeat customers, or something of that sort, going to lunch with prospective buyers hurts rather than helps in most cases. Use the time to plan your next move with them, to scout out new houses to show them, perhaps just to think over what they've said and not said, and to reflect on whether you've missed something. That lunch hour away from them will often give you the unpressured time to step back, look at the situation, and figure out how to keep their interest up. Use that time well. Don't fritter it away in chit chat. Then you can charge back after lunch and guide them to purchasing the home they need.

In light of what you've learned about them that morning, the chances are you'll find some additional houses in the Multiple Listing book you'll now realize they should see. Perhaps questions have been asked (or you're afraid certain questions will be asked in the afternoon) that you couldn't answer. Here's your chance to get the answers.

EXPANDED FOLK WISDOM

It's not what you say but how you say it. Let's expand that compressed bit of folklore into four specifics for real estate.

1 *Never present negative information with*
  • An enthusiastic, "Isn't this just peachy-keen?" manner that rings false because it is false. With most prospects, once your credibility is cracked it can never be mended.
  • An arrogant, "Take it or drop dead," attitude.
  • An inflexible, "This is how it's got to be," stance unless you've tried all the softer approaches first.
  • A hand-wringing, "You're going to kick the furniture apart about this," posture that tells them they're expected to throw a tantrum. Many people can't resist that opportunity.

2 *State negative information clearly and directly, with few words and no excuses.*

Sympathetic half-smiles and small gestures are often better softeners of hard facts than words. Watch your customers closely while you're talking: Allow them just long enough to understand the negative (a split second may do it) and then say something upbeat, or ask a positive question.

3 *When you've handled a situation poorly.*

Summarize the situation in a brief written paragraph at your first opportunity and decide how you could handle the same circumstances better the next time. Write down the smooth phrases you think up after the event, and practice saying them so you'll be ready next time.

4 *Acknowledge every statement by a customer.*

"I understand," is a good phrase for this. Allow a second to pass before you change the subject, if that's your intention. And take time to understand what your customer is telling you. If you keep on saying "I understand" while you're thinking about what's on your mind, the customer will soon realize that your mouth is on automatic pilot.

ANOTHER WINDOW

Another window to an understanding of your customers' emotions is this: Consider how large the sum of money involved in the house purchase looks when it's compared to the sums of money they deal with in their daily work.

The wheeler-dealers who make decisions involving millions are at one extreme; the hourly workers who make no money decisions at all in their regular work are at the other extreme.

These people will have vastly different attitudes. The hourly worker may be humble or antagonistic; in any case he's sensitive to being condescended to. So be careful not to big-deal the hourly worker. He's vulnerable. He's especially vulnerable in front of his wife. You can wound him by showing him up as being ignorant. He already has problems with that. Guard his ego. If he snaps out "I know that," respond with a cheerful:

"Great! I see you're much better informed than most of my customers are." That'll get him on your side.

DON'T TELL THEM YOU'RE NEW

When I was new, people would ask, "How long have you been in the business?"

If it was someone referred to me by a personal friend, I'd say, "I'm green but I'm growing." Everyone else I'd tell, "I entered the profession this past year." The last 12 months are the past year, right?

If you started in December and it's January, you can honestly say, "I'm working my second year in real estate."

But don't let it drop there. What they've really said is, "Are you competent to handle our business? This is an important matter to us. We don't mind helping you get started, but we don't want to pay for a beginner's mistakes."

They need reassurance. Give it to them. "I've been very fortunate so far." Say that firmly, with a tone that indicates you've made lots of money because you know what you're doing. Then continue with, "I don't expect to ever stop learning; that's one of the things that makes this business so exciting. But if I don't have an answer, I know where to get it fast." Then ask them a question about their requirements and get on with finding them a house.

Some new agents are so defensive about being new that they overcompensate by trying to prove they know it all. That turns people off because, most of the time, they've heard or can tell that you're fairly new. Do your homework, know your job, and you won't have trouble with people worrying that you're new.

USE YOUR BUYERS FILE CONSTANTLY

Fools rush in. Do you call your buyer prospects without first reviewing everything you know about them, everything you've carefully jotted down in your buyers file? You won't do this if you're calling them every day, but if several have gone by, the chances that you'll forget something they've told you (something they'll remember telling you) are too great to ignore.

When you forget how many children they have, that they like a corner lot, or want a big garage, your act of forgetting is taken by them as if you'd said, "I didn't care enough to remember."

Capture customers by caring enough to recall their uniqueness.

THE HUNGRY BREATH

Long time, no commission. I'm beginning to doubt, and it's beginning to show. It's no longer the comfortable, "Would you like to buy?" look. Now it's the hungry "You gotta buy" look. It's the old, "Don't waste my time unless your suitcase is ready" pitch. The hungry breath of a salesman casts an odor. No one comes near. Somebody give me a breath freshener. I smell terrible! Avoid this problem by working my 3 circle formula in Chapter 1.

WINNING SCRIPTS

"We're large enough to serve you, and small enough to care."

"We are members of the Multiple Listing Service. Although we are *very* active listers in this area [it's important for buyers to know that you and your office control a lot of listings], we also keep current on all the other brokers' properties on the Multiple Listing Service. Do you have any specific ads highlighted today that you'd like me to inquire about for you?"

During the first few minutes after they come in, build on the common denominators. If it's a referral situation, mention the people who referred you right up front in the conversation. Here's why: They may have been referred to three other agents by various friends, and now they can't remember who you are. So you say to them, "Mr. and Mrs. Palmer, it's so nice to talk to you. I've heard a lot of nice things about you from Mary and Bill."

"Oh, yeah," they think, "This is the gal that helped Mary and Bill get that neat place of theirs on North Drive—Okay." Their defenses come down a bit.

"Are you presently working with another broker?"

I always ask this. If prospects are already working with someone they feel loyalty to, I want to honor that loyalty whether it's to an agent in my company or not. I also want to save my time for prospects I have a better chance of earning a fee with.

During my first meeting with buyers I always say, "When I look for a house for my own family, nothing bothers me more than the idea that I might be missing something. It's maddening to house-hunt with an agent you know isn't on top of everything that's available. The one house he doesn't know about might be the perfect home for you, and a good buy too. Believe me, I've been there. I know the feeling. That's what keeps me constantly hustling all over this town making sure I'm familiar with everything on the market. I know my prospects don't want to miss anything. That's why I know all these properties like I know my children's birthdays."

LENDER QUALIFYER

The next chapter tells you how to integrate effective qualifying technique into your sales system. Use the following lender qualifyer with the customer early in the interview. Have them fill it out. Determine your house selections from this information.

LENDER QUALIFYER - A FORM BUYER FILLS OUT AT FIRST INTERVIEW

EXAMPLE:

For a family with gross annual income of $42,000 and monthly long-term obligations of $400 (installment debt, auto loans, credit cards, child support, etc.)

A. Gross Annual Income $42,000
(Before Taxes)

B. Gross Monthly Income $3,500
$42,000 divided by 12

C. Monthly Allowable Housing $1,260
Expense and Long-Term
Obligations
$3,500 multiplied by .36 (36% of gross monthly income is usually allocated for principal, interest, taxes, insurance *and* monthly long-term obligations.)

D. Monthly Allowable Housing Expense $860
$1,260 minus $400 (Subtract monthly long-term obligations from line C. Remainder is allowable principal, interest, taxes and insurance payment.)

> NOTE: Monthly Allowable Housing Expense on line D should not exceed 28% of Gross Monthly Income on line B. If it does, enter the lesser amount on line D and continue.

E. Monthly Principal $774
and Interest Payment
$860 multiplied by .90 (90% is the amount of the monthly allowable housing expense usually allocated to principal and interest payment only, *excluding* taxes and insurance.)

F. Estimated Mortgage Amount* $96,100
$774 divided by 8.05 multiplied by $1,000 (8.05 is the factor for a 9% loan amortized over a 30-year term. Factors for other interest rates and terms - consult a lender.)

G. Estimated Affordable Price Range $120,125
$96,100 divided by .80 (80% is the mortgage loan amount, assuming a 20% down payment. Use .90 for a 10% down payment.)

ACTUAL:

A. Gross Annual Income $ _____
(Before Taxes)

B. Gross Monthly Income $ _____
Line A divided by 12

C. Monthly Allowable Housing $ _____
Expense and Long-Term
Obligations
Line B multiplied by 36

D. Monthly Allowable Housing $ _____
Expense
Line C minus long-term obligations or line B multiplied by .28, whichever is less

E. Monthly Principal $ _____
and Interest
Line D multiplied by .90

F. Estimated Mortgage $ _____
Amount*
Line E divided by the appropriate factor from the interest rate chart and multiplied by 1,000

G. Estimated Affordable $ _____
Price Range
Line F divided by .80 or .90 depending on down payment

> Should you select an adjustable rate loan, your Sales Associate can also show you how to use this Worksheet and Interest Rate Factor Chart to determine your affordable price range and monthly payments.

This material is intended for example purposes only and is not a commitment for financing.

This work sheet is intended for use on primary residences. Your mortgage amount and price range will vary depending on the size of your down payment, the specific terms of your loan, other monthly obligations and the amount of association fees, if applicable.

*Rounded to the nearest $100.

15

QUALIFYING

Why Do It? • Backstroke with Style • Rosebuds • Privacy • Set Up the Close When You Qualify • Silence is Never More Golden • General Maintenance • Winning Tactics in the Qualifying Interview • Winning Scripts

WHY DO IT?

Agents often skip the qualifying interview when working with buyers for the first time. Some do this in the mistaken belief that it's easier to delay doing so, and many fear they'll offend the buyers. Other agents, in their eagerness to show property, charge out of the office with whoever comes in, and hopes it'll all pay off, somehow, somewhere down the road.

But, by omitting the qualifying session, agents raise more barriers between themselves and a collected fee. Showing people houses they can't afford creates awkward situations that drive prospects away; working with people who can't buy makes you unavailable for people who can; getting an offer accepted for someone who can't obtain a loan won't feed a parakeet. Curb your hunger: You'll get to the feast quicker if you know where it is.

There's a lot more to effective qualification than simply finding out how much they make. After a properly conducted qualifying interview you also have a clear idea of what your buyers want in their next home; you've learned much about working smoothly with them and about where the power lies between wife and husband; you know where they're coming from, why and when.

It's just as important to understand your people's motivation when they're buyers as it is when they're sellers. *Why do they want to move?* And do they both want to move, or do you have a split: the wife wants to stay, the husband wants to move (or vice versa). If so, the move may be months or years away.

If they have a house to sell, discuss interim financing with them, and the problems of making offers contingent on the sale of their house. Explain that, whether it's in the offer or not, from a practical standpoint they can only make an offer contingent on their own house selling if that has to happen before they'll have the money to complete the purchase of their next home. Most people don't understand these things; that's one of the reasons they need you.

You won't be able to start the process of moving the people you hope are buyers into a house until they're willing to reveal their reasons for wanting to move, and their capability of doing so. Unless they will reveal this information, the odds are they are concealing the fact that they're not ready to move yet. If so, they are lookielews and, while such people often become active customers in the future, you can't afford to work with them when doing so prevents you from working with present-time buyers. The active agent must constantly make these decisions. You'll rarely go wrong giving priority to people who trust you with information about themselves over those who won't.

When I began, I hated to qualify. Perhaps I was so afraid to qualify people because, when I was a little kid, my mother always told me, "Never discuss your father's income, or anybody's income, with anybody. It's nobody's business; money is personal." Then, suddenly, I'm in real estate; suddenly it's critical that I say to these people sitting in front of me, "Can you give me an idea of the income you're earning per month, so I can better serve your needs?"

I couldn't do it.

If you can't do it either, your fall-out rate will be fierce, because you'll be dancing around mansions with people who can't buy a shanty unless they stretch. Three weeks later you sell them Default Villa and a lender connects you with reality. Bang, pow, ouch.

We've got to get this fear of qualifying behind us. We've got to develop the hardheadedness to back away from hopeless situations. I was a strong lister who couldn't sell except by accident until I learned to qualify. Don't make the same mistake—it'll save you so much heartache. Use the lender qualifyer in Chapter 14 early on.

Show me a salesperson who continually faces cancellations and I will show you a salesperson who is a poor qualifier. In Chapter 24, we have included the Buyer's Analysis Form. Use it with your prospects and you'll see great results in keeping everything together until closing. That form gives you the exact sequence of questions to ask on the qualifying interview; it's an efficient tool for new salespersons who fear being direct with their people. The Lender Qualifyer gives them something to fill out after you use the Buyer's Analysis.

BACKSTROKE WITH STYLE

The more qualifying interviews you conduct, the more aspirations you'll shave with the sharp razor of reality. Do that with courtesy and style. It costs no more, and it'll bring prospects back to you in the future. You'll find things like this happening:

The couple found their dream house on their own, and then came to see you about making an offer on it. In the qualifying interview you find out that they don't qualify. They don't even come close. Should you wilt them with a contemptuous smile and say, "Guys, let's face it, this house is too rich for your blood."

Or try a little joke: "I've done some creative financing in my time, but this is ridiculous."

Take that extra moment to be empathetic. "We all want to buy as much house as we can. I know what you're thinking: 'It'll be tight for a while, but our income will be higher before long, and then we can handle this house easily.' I understand, I sympathize with that. Believe me, I've been there—"

Pause. Make helpless gestures. "—But we have to put this through a lender's loan committee. They only look at today's numbers—"

Fix a firm, sympathetic look on them. "—And our problem is that today's numbers just don't work out right for us." If the people can't afford to buy *any*thing, go into a pleasant farewell speech and tell them, "I hope to see you again soon."

With people qualified to buy a less-expensive house, get right into solving their housing problem: "—Today's numbers don't work on that particular house, but we have a lot of terrific properties where your numbers will absolutely *fly* through a loan committee. Let me tell you about this really neat place over on—"

Make an obvious effort to be especially cordial to these people you've had to bump from first-class to tourist accommodations. Refuse to be embarrassed—for them or for yourself—and demonstrate by your courtesy that you value them no less as customers. You're dealing with prickly pride and bruised egos now, so be up, be enthusiastic, and don't refer to the bumpdown again if you can possibly avoid it. Also, be equally careful not to treat them as though they've done something socially unacceptable in trying to buy beyond their means.

What about the people who can't afford anything in your sales area? Why bother with involved diplomacy with such folk? Why not get rid of these time wasters fast with a few blunt words?

Because today's can't-buys have a way of becoming tomorrow's buyers. People get promotions, inheritances, substantial aid from parents, or they join with another couple to buy a house. They also get calls to advise friends who are buying now. In real estate, as in life, courteous concern for others returns good things, and arrogant action paves the road ahead with troubles.

ROSEBUDS

I love big, full, long-stemmed yellow roses. But they aren't big or full when they're delivered: They come in a box as tiny, tightly folded buds. Some people are like that when we first meet them in real estate—they hold onto themselves, their arms folded tight, their eyes fixed on the floor—or on your throat. You can almost hear their inner voices saying, "This agent's just out to sell me any old house, whether I want it or not. But I'm not going for it! I won't smile, move, or talk. I'm not giving this salesperson any opening to get at me."

We have a job to do when the rosebuds arrive, and when we encounter these people. The buds we put in a water-filled vase, and the vase in a window's sunlight. Then we see the miracle of roses unfolding into full bloom. Think of those tight-lipped customers of yours in the same way. Like the rosebuds, they're protecting themselves until conditions are right for them to open up.

If they weren't softies deep down inside, they wouldn't be so fearful. If you try to open a rosebud by pulling at its petals, you'll destroy it, But, if you create the right environment, if you provide the warmth and light, it will open itself.

Create that right environment for your tense prospects so they can open up and smile pretty too. That's what they really want to do, but they've been hurt, cheated, and hassled in the past until they can't—without your gentle and compassionate help. They really want to open up and become your customers, but they don't know that yet. They won't know until it happens—and it'll happen just as soon as you beam the warmth and the light on them that they're seeking.

PRIVACY

New sales people are ill at ease when qualifying a prospect in front of their associates. They're concerned about having their performance critiqued. Managers should be careful *not* to listen; they should be especially careful not to go in and take over the qualifying interview because they think they'll do a better job of it than the new agent can. Unless their aid is called for, they must keep out of it, or they'll find themselves unable to build a capable staff.

And, often, the buyer hates being interviewed about very personal business where several strange people may or may not be listening. Respect that and, if at all possible, conduct the qualifying interview in private. If you have to do it at your desk, speak very softly unless your buyer acts like he wants to tell the world his business.

SET UP THE CLOSE WHEN YOU QUALIFY

The point of qualifying is to find out what (if anything) you can close them on. Use the qualifying interview to accustom them to the closing room. Of course, you never let them hear that term; it's always the "conference room." Even in the natural close that I advocate, there's the tension of large decision making to contend with. So it helps to take them back to a room they've been in before. We're all more comfortable in familiar surroundings. And, on their second trip into the conference room, your prospects understand that business is conducted there.

However, if the jet stream of desire for a home is driving the people you're talking to on open house, qualify them there. Or at a coffee shop booth in the hotel where you meet out-of-state referrals. Be prepared to qualify anywhere that's reasonably private and free of interruptions. But avoid unseemly haste to get at business. Offer them coffee or other refreshments, invite them to sit down and make themselves comfortable, and exchange a brief bit of small talk first.

SILENCE IS NEVER MORE GOLDEN

Silence is never more golden than in the qualifying interview—and when you're showing property, closing customers, and negotiating offers for them. Silence, beautiful silence, you're golden because you're the least offensive way known to man or womankind of saying *no; this is the way it has to be; that's our best offer; we really mean it; if you want this agreement, you'll have to improve your offer; I'm willing to wait you out, but you'll never get a better offer from us.*

Yes, silence is amazingly communicative, so much so that we should really say that *silence talks.* How else can one say, "I'm firm, I'm strong, I'm confident. You need me more than I need you. If you don't do something to save it, this transaction won't transact." Given the right situation, silence will say any or all of that for you, without committing you, without giving offense.

Silence. It's such a powerful tool—why are we so afraid of it when we're with people? When silence settles in, we don't think, we panic: "It's so quiet in here, I could hear an ant sing. I'm going crazy. I gotta think of something to *say.* Anything. This tension is killing me."

Whenever you feel silence-cramps coming on, quietly take in a deep breath, hold it, and see how high you can count before your customer starts talking or you have to breathe again. Recite the alphabet *backwards* in your thoughts. Relive your first date, relive any other first that will relax you while you remain confidently alert. Do any sort of mental gymnastics, but don't talk, and don't bang the tangibles around just to vibrate some sound waves.

Remember all the things the prospects have to think about during this high-pressure time for them. Remember that you're in for about 2 percent and they're in for about 100 percent. You've asked them penetrating questions, or you've pushed them hard against a huge decision; they need time to accommodate to the implications of it all. So let there be little quiet times along the way. Be generous with silences, not afraid of them.

As you become more relaxed in the qualifying interview, you'll notice the customers becoming more relaxed. They're thinking, "I'm okay! I'm with someone who's capable and confident: I'm in good hands."

But, if the salesperson is nervous, the customers are thinking, "I wonder if this agent can really do the job. And why is he/she so uptight? I wonder if someone's trying to pull a fast one on me—and's afraid I'll catch on." When they start to doubt, when all the negative stuff starts creeping in, your difficulties escalate.

GENERAL MAINTENANCE

When folks walk into an office, no matter whose customer it is, they look at the overall picture: coffee cups all over the place, trash that hasn't been emptied, filled ash trays. Don't be one of these salespeople who says, "Well, it's not my mess. Why should I have to clean it up?" Work together with team spirit; tomorrow somebody may have to clean up *your* mess.

WINNING TACTICS IN THE QUALIFYING INTERVIEW

Watch to see who is the leader between the husband and the wife, or whether it is an equal opportunity situation. The loudest, or the quickest to speak, isn't necessarily the leader. You can miss this if you're not watching closely.

Gear your remarks to the level of each individual, but be careful not to talk down to anyone. Pay a lot of respect to the man where he has the full responsibility for providing income to the family but, especially if you're a saleswoman, be careful not to make the wife defensive about not having a job outside the home.

Give full attention to the buyers. You can't do this and search for property on maps. If you must do that, go to the back room after the qualifying interview is over. Give your full attention to those buyers in the interview, and don't introduce interruptions.

When working with a couple where the husband is submissive, try to draw him out without making his dominant wife angry. If you're a saleswoman, be very feminine and warm, and find out what the husband, as well as the wife, likes. Always pull people up and make them feel good about themselves. When you do that, you'll make your sales much more easily. The button that starts this engine is the ability to convince people that you really care about their welfare on the gut level. Call it heart power. You have it. When you can express and demonstrate it sincerely, and have it accepted without embarassment, there'll be no limit to your success.

Your job is to help people achieve what they want in housing; if achieving what they want isn't practical at this time, it's also your job to tell them so with honesty and graciousness.

When buyers tell you they want a four-bedroom view home, find out during the qualifying interview what their price range is. With your inventory knowledge, you'll then be able to give them a quick overview of what they can expect to find in the way of square footage, lot size, and amenities in four-bedroom view homes within their price range. Do it then: Why show them ten houses that will just disappoint them? They'll tend to translate their disappointment in housing prices into dissatisfaction with you—and rightly so. By giving them an overview before you left the office, you could have saved them, and yourself, a day of dismay.

If they're serious about a house in your sales area, but want more house than they can afford (the buyers' usual dilemma), the sooner you start guiding them toward practical compromises, the better are your chances of closing them on an offer before heart and foot aches close their minds. Of course, don't refuse to show them specific houses they want to see, even if you know those houses will disappoint them. Just don't show them such houses exclusively, or even primarily. Be sensitive. Probe for the weak items in their list of requirements. If they want a pool, and it's out of their price range in the smallest house they'll accept, then point out recreation facilities nearby. Our job is to give the buyers alternatives in housing if they can't find everything they want. This calls for creative thinking on our part. It's important to constantly throw problem-solving questions to the buyers like a true counselor. Get them to look into all alternatives. We have to see things objectively, and guide them, because they can't be objective and find their way without our help.

Sometimes it takes two or three meetings for buyers to open up. I never showed them a lot of homes until they opened up to me with their needs and their capabilities so I could know their price range.

WINNING SCRIPTS

Here's how to introduce the Buyer's Analysis for Better Service form and the Lender Qualifyer after your preliminary remarks are made, some chit chat is exchanged (be careful not to prolong it), and the coffee is on the table:

Agent: "It's very important to me to serve you courteously *and* productively, Mr. and Mrs. _____. I know you are busy people. [Make lots of statements that emphasize their importance.] So many times, people will randomly look at houses with an agent, not really knowing what they want. The agent just does some guesswork and, when their time together is over, everyone is frustrated. I pride myself on my ability to make every minute count with people. But, before I can do that, I need your permission for something."

Customers: "What's that?"

Agent: "Well, our company has compiled a questionnaire called the Buyer's Analysis for Better Service and the Lender Qualifyer. With the aid of these forms, we interview our people before we look at property so that our time together today will be more meaningful. Would you be offended if I ask you some of the questions on this form?" [When you've acquired the confidence to work without the form, omit all reference to it by saying instead: "Would you be offended if I asked you some questions so I'll know how to make our time together meaningful?"]

Customers: They agree.

Agent: "Thank you both. I assure you that this is done in your best interests. We really do want to serve you well."

Make lots of affirmative statements in an enthusiastic tone throughout your entire time with customers. This can be overdone, of course, but more often its underdone—or left entirely undone. Reinforce the rapport you've already instilled into your agent-customer relationship by affirming your determination to serve them well whenever you have a natural opportunity to do so.

Flashdeck These Questions

Flashdeck these questions from the Buyer's Analysis for Better Service form and become a qualifying pro in a hurry. Make runs through this flashdeck twice daily until you can roll these questions off perfectly any time you're with people. When you can do that, you'll have stepped into the top 5 percent of salespeople with respect to this vital skill. Make no mistake about it, if you can't qualify effectively you can't be a strong producer. Here are some questions:

- "Is this your first visit to our community?" (Or name your town.)
- "Where are you folks from?"
- "How long have you been looking for a home?"
- "How many are in your family?"
- "Then you have _____ children?"
- "May I ask their names and ages?"
- "Where do you live now?"
- "How long have you lived there?"
- "Are you investing in your present home, or do you rent?"
- "How is the resale market in your area?"
- "May I ask, Mr. and Mrs. _____, where are you employed?"
- "How long have you been there?"

- "Have you seen any homes you really like?"
- "What prevented you from owning that home?"

Urgency Questions

"How soon had you thought of making a move after you've found the right home?"

"How much time will you have to see homes today?"

"How many bedrooms will suit you best?"

If They Own Now

"How much do you feel you will realize from the sale of your home?"

"Will it be necessary to sell your present home to purchase the new one?"

"Will you be converting any of your other investments to cash in order to complete the purchase of your next home?"

"If we are fortunate enough to find the right home today, will you be in a position to make a decision to proceed?"

"Not to be personal, but to do a better job for you, may I ask, how much of your savings do you wish to invest in your home?"

"What price range have you been considering? Better yet, since most people are concerned with their monthly outgo, how much do you feel you could comfortably invest each month in your new home, including everything?"

"Please take a few minutes to fill out this 'Lender Qualifyer.' It's a perfect guide."

Use on Lower-Price-Range Properties

"A rule of thumb most lenders use is that the monthly allowable housing expense and long-term obligations should be approximately 36 percent of gross monthly income. (This would include principal, interest, taxes, insurance, and monthly long-term obligations.) Are we in line here?"

"Please take a moment, Mrs. _____, to describe your present home to me, including all your likes and dislikes."

"What are your special requirements for your next home?"

"Are there any other special requirements that I haven't noted yet, such as _____ [suggest some of the popular amenities available in your inventory] that you'd like to see in your next home?"

Then Make the Following Statement

(Memorize this one.)

"I have several properties pictured in my mind that I think you might like. Please do me a favor—I'll set up the appointments so we can view these homes— but if my first houses are out of line with what *you* are picturing in *your* mind, promise me you'll tell me so. I won't be hurt—I'll promise you that in return—and, because I know the inventory so well, I can change my game plan on a minute's notice to what you *are* picturing and hoping to see. Will you do that for me?—tell me if I'm off on the wrong tangent?" (—tell me if I'm not hitting the nail on the head?" —if I'm playing rock when you want to hear Bach?")

Use whatever metaphor suits you and the situation, but get a commitment from them that they'll tell you about it if you're not showing them what they want to see. Otherwise, they'll grumble to each other behind your back, and you'll never know why you couldn't solve their housing problem.

Have the inventory sheet next to the qualifying form, and glance at the housing listings as you qualify them. Keep trying to mentally place them in some of the houses that fit into their price range. If your inventory sheet is arranged by price, lowest to highest, you can gear into the price range where they belong and avoid scanning the entire inventory.

Remember that your customers are under a lot of tension, and that makes most people impatient. During this interview they watch to see how quickly and brightly you respond. Short words and quick movements are vital now; keep the pace fast so your people won't start wishing and planning to be someplace else. And keep a sharp eye on their reactions; don't frighten them by going too fast, either.

Take a show list form and fill in the properties you intend to visit with them. While you make the appointments, ask them if they'd like to use the rest room or have another cup of coffee.

By knowing the inventory and the qualifying questions, you're in control; you've had a favorable impact on them. They are impressed with your competence, and you have set a high standard that few other agents can match, should those prospects work with someone else for an afternoon. When you smoothly and confidently ask the right questions, you get the needed answers.

Giving Commands to Customers

Success here isn't as difficult as you might think, if you know the limits and how to do it. A command to a customer must always tell them to do something they want to do, something that clearly furthers their interests. And that command must be softened with a polite preface:

> "What we should do now is—"
> "Would you mind—"
> "May I ask you to—"
> "After you."
> "May I urge that we—"
> "May I suggest that we—"
> "The most important thing for us to do now is—"
> "The next step is for us to—"
> "To accomplish *your* purpose, what we must do now is—"
> "I know it's an annoyance, but the lenders insist on—"

Such "commands" get things done.

P.S.—The Lender Qualifyer

The lender qualifyer is a new time saving tool for agents and prospects. Use it consistently. It may not be necessary if a lender is interviewing your buyer in conjunction with your first meeting with them. This is common practice to involve the lender early these days. A great way to eliminate time waste.

16

SHOWING PROPERTY—
AND SELLING IT

The Secret of Successful Showing • Danny K's 23 Ways to More Paydays • Potpourri • L.A. to Seattle, and the Loyalty of Buyers • Selling the Williamses: A Role Play in One Act • Winning Scripts

THE SECRET OF SUCCESSFUL SHOWING

Eenie, meanie, mynie, moe,
I've got twenty homes to show.
Why show this one, why show that,
When I know not bird from bat?

That's not the way.

The secret of successful showing is effective preparation. The secret of effective preparation is doing it intensely, on a daily basis, for all buyers you may encounter. You do it for all buyers because the precise opportunities that may be yours before any day ends cannot be known in advance. So you must prepare for a range of opportunities.

Intense, daily preparation means that you

- Use the Quick-Speak concept and keyview regularly,
- Develop sales speeches and a property catalog,
- Train yourself on your area's streets until getting disoriented there is an impossibility,

- Watch the local and national financial situation,
- Keep current on general real estate and business trends,
- Know your board's sales and listings for last week, month, and year,
- Know your area's appreciation rate, average days on market, and average prices paid,
- Know your community's events, opportunities, schools, and shopping.

Yes, it takes all this knowledge, plus fine showing and selling technique, to attain the high success ratio that top producers enjoy. You don't start on top, of course. You climb there rung by rung. As you acquire the product knowledge, practice the techniques that follow on as many live buyers as possible.

DANNY K'S 23 WAYS TO MORE PAYDAYS

1. Show Your People Houses They Can Afford

Chapter 15 told you how to qualify your buyers. Thorough qualifying is the key to successful showing, closing, and fee collecting. You can't win a thing by selling people houses they can't buy.

2. Respect Your Buyers' Stated Top Limit

Do that even when the figure they've named is well below what they can qualify for. Let them make that decision. Bend every effort to satisfy their needs within their comfort zone as to price.

You qualify the Rufus Kings to purchase a $130,000 house. Mr. King tells you, "I don't want to go over $100,000." Don't show them any house that costs more than $100,000. It's astonishing how many agents will take a stated top limit as a challenge and, working with the Kings, immediately begin showing houses in the $125,000 to $135,000 range.

Work for your buyers, not against them. Show them the best properties available within their stated top limit. Let them decide how much of their income they'll put into housing. If you find something the Kings like at $99,000, you're doing great. Four times out of five, the Kings will only live in that $99,000 house for a year. Then they'll come back to you, if you've handled them right, wanting to move up. At that time you'll list their present $99,000 home, and also sell them their next home for $130,000. Three transactions for you—none for the agent who made the Kings mad by showing them $125,000 houses in the beginning. Referral business doesn't just happen: it's built—by service that's tuned to the customers' wavelengths.

Now they're here, I have no choice.
Could I claim I've lost my voice?
Off we go till sun does set.
You must know how far I'll get.

3. Ask House-eliminating Questions

As you gain skill in qualifying, and learn how to probe deeper into your buyers' likes and dislikes in the qualifying interview, and as your Quick-Speak Inventory increases, you'll find yourself narrowing down your show list to fewer and fewer houses. Your ability to match buyers to houses will grow rapidly; and the time it takes you to sell each set of buyers will drop dramatically. The key is (a) thorough knowledge of the inventory; and (b) developing an effective list of house-eliminating questions and an easy manner of asking them so your buyers feel comfortable answering them. This list of questions will be dictated by the housing available in your area.

Be alert for the house-eliminating questions that arise naturally as you show property to buyers. When you ask one, make a mental note of it, and add it to your list.

You're showing property to the Cosbys. You've asked them a number of questions, but haven't thought to check about back yards yet. At one house, you get into the back yard and it's small. All concrete and pool. You don't know if they want a big yard or a small yard. So you say, "George, I don't know whether yard work really thrills you, but this is definitely low maintenance."

He may say, "Oh, no—I travel a lot. I don't have time to work on a yard. This is perfect."

Or perhaps one of them will say, "This is too much concrete. I need running room."

"Aha," you think, "another house-eliminating question. I'll just add that gem to my list of HEQs. Next time, I'll ask something like that in the qualifying session."

Showing houses is an ongoing discovery process between you, your customers, and the available housing. With many buyers, you'll be able to gain a very clear picture of what they want and take them right to it—when you know well what's available and what to ask.

With some people, their aspirations so far outrun their pocketbooks that selling them is primarily an exercise in reconciling them to what they can afford. But even with them, possession of a good set of house-eliminating questions will enable you to cut through the confusion, and focus on their achievable needs, in the shortest possible time. Develop your list of questions whose answers reveal what buyers like and don't like. Avoid asking these questions at a time or in a way that will get you a yes, no, or grunt for an answer. Phrase your questions to elicit a broader reply from your buyers.

4. Analyze What They Tell You About Their Likes and Dislikes

It will sometimes be conflicting, even from the same person (the man wants a large, lush backyard, but he doesn't want to do the maintenance work or pay a gardener).

When you hear such conflicts, don't take them too seriously at first. Point out the conflict sympathetically, and ask for directions. If they seem stuck on dead center, suggest that the question will resolve itself, and request permission to show property that lies on both sides of the conflict.

Usually, careful analysis of what they're saying will guide you straight to what they want—if you're willing to listen closely, and carefully weigh their words.

Huffing, bluffing, till day is done,
I'll swear is hardly that much fun.
I wish I'd previewed every one,
'Stead of taken looks at none.

5. Listen, Really Listen, When Your Buyers Talk About What They Want

Ask about their likes and dislikes. Listen to the answers. Remember the answers. Make, and use, notes.

Some agents remember to ask, but don't bother to tune in for the replies, much less memorize that information as it's given to them. Agents who don't remember what the customers say are easy to spot: They're the ones standing around the office complaining that buyers have no loyalty.

6. Don't Show Houses You Haven't Previewed

You can't fake this. People will tell you, "I hate blue carpet and I can't stand dark-paneled rooms; I want a large dining room, and we need a huge back yard."

How are you going to avoid showing them houses that don't have their negatives, but do have their positives, unless you have a large Quick-Speak Inventory?

Now they're angry, grumpy, sore—
'Spected me to know the score.
Realty is such a great big bore
Unless you know the in ven tore.

7. Show Buyers What They Want to See

No, we're not insulting your intelligence. We're hammering on a point some agents find difficult to act on. If your buyers tell you they like simple, clean lines and can't stand gingerbread, don't show them a provincial for any of these reasons: (a) you know of one in their price range; (b) it has a $1,000 bonus to the selling office; (c) you promised the listing agent you'd show the house; (d) it's your listing; (e) you think it's cute; (f) it's on the way; (g) showing them the provincial will kill some time; (h) the provincial is one of the few for-sales that you can drive to without getting lost.

If you can only show three houses that meet their general specifications, do that, and try for a later appointment with them when you'll be better prepared. Plead other pressing business. That won't anger them, as wasting their time with the wrong kind of houses surely will if they've stated their preferences clearly.

Tell me, have I nipped my greatest chance
On the easy closing to advance?
Oh, when all I want is just the fee,
Why so unreasonable must they be?

8. Parking Technique

Whenever you keyview a property, decide then how you'll park if you bring customers to see it. When showing houses with good curb appeal, don't park right in front, or pull into the driveway. An important part of such a property's emotional impact is the prestige its street view conveys. Usually, the best vantage point to absorb that impact is from across the street. Approach the house from a direction that makes it natural to park across the street. Then sit in the car for a moment, looking at the house. Ask your buyers to pause, if they're about to scramble out, and look too. If the front view isn't inspiring, park right out front. If it's really bad, pull into the driveway.

Winning Scripts has effective phrases for these situations.

9. Learn When to Use (and Not to Use) the Demonstration Technique

The demonstration of unique features must be a key element in your presentation—if you're selling can openers or computers. But, if you're solving housing problems for customers, don't insist on demonstrating a house's details to buyers who aren't excited about its floor plan or location.

Beyond the basics of shelter and indoor plumbing, a house's most sales-worthy functions are in the emotional sphere, where they relate to prestige, refuge, and territory. You can show every inch of wallpaper, and push a hound through every pet door, but unless that house taps the buyers' feelings, there's little chance it'll become their home. Demonstrating the cutsie little goodies of properties that fail to make your buyers emote simply delays the house-finding process—and irritates most buyers dangerously. Fees are not won by such methods. But if the basic house ignites their interest, then the skillful demonstration of neat details can fan that flame into a red hot offer.

Of course, some buyers are slow browsers. For them, crank every gimcrack in every house you show. Never mind your own impatience. If your buyers browse like cows, help them chew all the grass. Try that with the fast-moving folk, though, and you'll soon find yourself back at the office wondering as they drive off whether her headache was the real thing.

And there are buyers who expect to be led like sheep. For the sheep and the cows, you must know the demonstration technique. Just don't try it on the geese, on the fidgeters and the scamperers, or you'll have a conflict that you can lose by winning, or lose by losing, but can't gain from. Flow with the buyers, adapt to their idiosyncrasies, dance to their rhythm instead of trying to make them polka to your tune. Customers who want you to take a strong lead will say so, or will indicate that desire by sticking close instead of trotting off in every direction.

Here's how to assume the control necessary to demonstrate features.

When entering a house, suddenly take a few quick steps ahead, turn to face your customers, spread your hands a little, and start talking confidently about some features they can see from where they are then standing. That feature may be an amenity you can physically demonstrate by turning a dial, opening a panel, or throwing a lever, or it may be something that requires explanation before its full value can be understood. It will get easier to claim their attention each time you use this technique on a given couple—when you handle it right. If you're telling them things they want to hear, if you're not pounding their ears when they want to quietly absorb a house's ambience, they'll listen because they know you're about to say something interesting. But, if their attention is getting harder to seize each time, you're not being selective enough in choosing amenities for demonstration, or you're going into too much detail—for them—at that particular stage of their progress toward a house choice. Speak briefly and to the point. In cases of doubt, don't demonstrate a feature or explain an additional point. They'll ask about items that are important to them at their current level of interest in that house. Avoid mentioning the obvious, especially never chat about the obvious for the sole purpose of killing the quiet. If silence with a buyer troubles you, reread *Silence is never more golden* in the previous chapter.

Choosing a good position when you take your demonstration stance helps. Any break in the interior will do: a step between levels, a doorway, an open space between rooms. If they continue talking to each other (why should they instantly shut up?) wait, silently and without moving, until they conclude their exchange. Then say your piece, and move on. Your control will be intermittent, and will grow throughout the showing session—if you don't try to maintain it in rooms and houses that lack anything worth demonstrating. If you feel compelled to dominate the entire showing session, consider joining the Marines; they still need a few good people for drill sergeants.

There's one time when you'll want to demonstrate features even if you expect your buyers to have little interest in them. This is where you show your own listing and the sellers are at home. Prepare your buyers for this before they get out of your car.

"At this point, I know you're mainly interested in the overall picture, but the lady of this house will probably be home now, because she's expecting her small children home from school. If she's there, and I don't tell you about a few of the improvements they've made here themselves, she'll be quite upset. Please bear with me this one time."

How can they refuse?

10. Go Back to Year One

Buyers are interested in the area they're moving to, and giving them a little history subtly establishes you as an old-timer there, an expert. I ask my buyers, "Do you know that in 1900, the Iversons bought 50,000 acres right around here for a dollar an acre?"

There's history all over North America. I could go into any town, talk to some alert and knowledgeable agents about their area's early landowners, and then be able to tell an interesting tale in the car while I'm driving buyers from one house to another. And my buyers—anywhere—will be impressed. Mix a touch of history in with your discussion of recreational facilities, schools, shops, and churches. Knowledge of all these things is vital. Sell the area while you're touring it.

11. Don't Show Too Many Houses

If you show them more than five or six the first time out, you're going to confuse people. They're not going to remember. "Now was that the one with the blue carpet? or the red?" It all gets muddled in their minds.

12. Give the House a Chance to Speak

Don't be afraid of silence. If your buyers aren't talking, that's good. It means they're reacting on an emotional level with the house, and they have to do that to fall in love with the place. So be sure that your mouth isn't in motion purely to eliminate a silence that frightens you. Don't be a talk-pest when people are making that intimate selection of their new home. This doesn't mean that you don't say anything; it means that you don't talk unless what you say will advance the sale of that home.

13. Sell Possibilities

It was a plain little house. A box. No style. But it was as high as the neat young couple I was showing it to could go. They wanted more but couldn't stretch their dollars. The place had no dining room. The dining area looked out on a grubby but fully fenced side yard where dogs had been kept. The house was vacant and the side yard was filled with junk. I told my buyers how easy it would be to replace the window with French doors, pave that sideyard, and create a romantic outdoor dining court.

"You've even got room for a fountain," I said.

They loved it. When we got back to the office, they immediately spoke of the house "where we could have a dining court with a fountain." They bought that house. A few months later, that young couple called up to rave about their dining court and invite me over to see it. They bought an idea—something that wasn't there—and then proceeded to install and enjoy it.

Train yourself to spot salable possibilities. You'll miss many opportunities if you only talk about what's there now. Possibilities that no one else has seen are free. Sell them. It's a beautiful way to create genuine value that will bridge the gap between what the sellers will take and what the buyers will give.

> Next time, next time, I'll surely know
> All For Sales, and in the warm glow
> Of great knowledge, hard won, will earn
> So much silver I'll have to learn
> New ways to spend, new sights to see
> New joys to sing of with such deserv'd fee.

14. Play the Ace Last???

There's some practical psychology here that often seems to work. Many agents swear by this system, but I don't use it anymore.

Play the ace last calls for you to route customers through the houses you think they'll like *least* to begin with. Then, after they've rejected a few properties, you take them to the house you've decided will catch their fancy. The theory behind this is twofold: that people feel better about making a *yes* decision after they've demonstrated control by saying *no* a time or two; and that your ace, the house you've picked to sell them, will look better by contrast to the others than it would had you shown it to them first.

In the beginning, I always placed the ace last—sometimes by accident because I had to show people several houses to find out what they wanted. Then, when the right house for them popped into my head, I'd get excited and say, "Wait'll you see the next house I'm going to show you. I promise you it'll be the very best you'll see all day. It really fits your needs." This approach always worked fine because I built up enough rapport to carry it off before using it. When you have that rapport, people react with delight to your spontaneity, enthusiasm, and involvement, to your injection of excitement and fun into the making of their big decision. If they're positive people, they'll react that way; if they're negative, go slow with the high excitement until you're sure it won't just make them more negative. Even now, I would show markedly negative people the homes I thought they'd find least attractive first, and save the best till last, so they could run their grouch-string out before getting down to business.

But, with normally pleasant to highly positive people, when you've reached the stage of knowledge, credibility, and confidence where you immediately know the house they'll buy, why waste time? Show them the house they'll love first—and tell them that's what you're doing. Then everything else they see just can't compare and, when they get tired of looking at can't-compares, you close them. But that stage takes a while to reach.

Later on, when you've perfected deep-dish qualifying, you can find out what they want in a hurry. When you have the Quick-Speak Inventory that'll enable you to match them one-to-one with the right house, lead with your ace—if you have rapport and they're warm-thinkers. But always game-plan your people based on their personalities. You can also show the ace in the middle of two or more can't-compares.

Play your hunches. That's how you develop reliable intuition about people. And in the beginning, unless you have a hunch to the contrary, show your buyers at least two other houses before you play your ace.

15. Steer clear of Razzle Dazzle

It's always safer to give people information at a deliberate, friendly pace than to rattle off intricate details too fast for them to understand. Let them hurry you along—and feel superior and smart, rather than make them slow you down—and feel inferior and stupid. When you squirt out information faster than they can comprehend it, people think about—and resent—you instead of thinking about what you're telling them. They know you've drilled yourself on the data, and that now you're showing off. Your methods are showing. You don't sound like someone who really cares about them. Slow down. Smile. Make sure your listeners are listening; make sure your words are turning prospects into customers, not turning customers into walk-aways.

16. Read Their Signals

Buyers send messages to you constantly with body language even when they're not talking. You can't necessarily understand, or rely on, the words more than the unspoken signals. Both often conflict with other parts of their total message. Don't try to read their minds; don't evaluate them; ask courteous questions to clarify how they feel. And, when your questions reveal important contradictions, ask further questions to clarify their meaning, purpose, or preference. Be careful not to sound argumentative or superior. Soften your questions with phrases such as: "So I'll understand exactly what you mean, could you—"

With some people, hearing the meanings between their words, and reading their body language signals, will tell you more than they will deliberately say to you at that stage of your relationship with them. Foster the feeling in their minds that you are a professional devoted to putting the customers' welfare first as you watch their body language and listen to their words.

Folded arms indicate tension, or that the person is feeling chilly. You may have moved too fast too soon, or invaded their comfort zone. The distance people want you to stay away varies. Be sensitive to that bubble of private space most people need. Don't bear-hug everyone; don't keep a ten-foot-pole distance from everyone either. Take your cue from their feelings. Time your approach to what their comfort zone is, rather than rigidly apply your own get-close, or stand-off, feelings to everyone.

When you detect signs that their emotions are churning, proceed with caution to find out what's happening inside their heads. You may need to close them, or pull back, or make some other move.

Smile a lot when you're with buyers. Cultivate a relaxed manner. Otherwise your tension infects them. After they've opened up, a little pat on the shoulder, and saying, "I'm going to take care of you," can work wonders at reassuring them.

Watching their facial expressions is vital. When you see a lot of confusion on the buyer's face, or a frown, gently find out why. Watch for restlessness or you'll lose them. Restimulate them if possible. Be alert for boredom. Move along. When the customer interrupts, or comes on with hostility, in many cases they're feeling the onset of buying fear.

Yawning is often a sign of fear too. Some people will yawn when they see the house they know they should buy, because now they're hard against the big decision—and the pressure scares them.

Others will smile to conceal irritation. Excessive throat-clearing or coughing can indicate fear, annoyance with not seeing what the person wants to see, hunger, boredom, or any number of things. And, of course, the yawners can be tired, the smilers happy, and the coughers sick. The signals of body language, like words, are often spoken with forked tongue.

Be alert for signs of fatigue. Some buyers tire quickly from the emotional strain. Fatigue stops all positive thought. Be careful not to exhaust your buyers with an overload of information and hustle before you show them the house you think they'll love. Don't take them there so tired they can't react to it.

17. Create Involvement

The wife mentions a favorite grandfather clock, or the husband tells you his hobby is woodworking. Be alert for opportunities to ask the wife how her grandfather clock would look in this hall, or the husband how well that garage would serve his hobby needs.

18. Build from Their Emotional Tone

As you proceed with your showing presentation, they will either get excited about what you are showing them, or discouraged. If you suspect discouragement, draw them out; don't allow them to suffer in silence. In my area, out-of-staters often say something like: "We didn't realize prices were so high out here. For this much money you get a mansion where we come from."

Turn their discouragement into enthusiasm by talking about lifestyle. Winning Scripts (under *Lifestyle*) gives you the words.

19. Show Bright

Show buyers five properties initially. Be prepared to show more. Especially with the ready-to-buy-today prospects, mix other brokers' listings in with your showing of in-house listings. Unless you do, the buyers will realize you're only showing them one company's share of the market. Such actions tell them, loud and clear, that they'd better find themselves another agent or they'll probably miss their best buy. Don't be disloyal to your buyers' interests.

Take the most attractive routes to the various properties with your prospects. Relax with them, and enjoy their company. Talk about the community and the reason why it's a nice place to live. This is a tension-filled task at best (for your buyers too), so be as relaxed as you can.

If you're showing many properties, take mini-breaks. If your buyers see more than five, all those properties start swimming together. Then it's time to suggest that they, or you all, have lunch or coffee.

Don't show more than five properties to buyers getting a "feel" for the area who are not in a financial position to buy today. Say this: "I would like to familiarize you with the area. I have selected a cross section of properties that best suit your range and needs. This will give you an opportunity to evaluate what you see today, and to go home and make some decisions."

20. Be Excited

About your showing presentation. Say things like, "If you enjoyed the last property, I know I'm on the right track. So I'm really excited for you to see this next one." Be sincerely involved in the drama of fitting the clues together (as in a mystery story) between the proper home and your buyer.

Developing the ability to pick out three to five homes during the qualifying interview that zero in on your buyers' needs should be your initial goal. You can soon reach this point by putting forth the necessary effort. Then your goal should be to raise your professional skills to the level where you can pick out and show *the* house, their future home, to buyers first. You'll never be able to do it every time, of course, but doing it at all takes a high degree of sensitivity and expertise. To be able to hit it once in a while is an admirable, and profitable, talent—and the source of much satisfaction.

21. In the Car

Before your buyers arrive, get your car washed or clean it out. Also clean all your other problems out of your head. Nothing will help you more than having a fresh mind and a large Quick-Speak Inventory of houses, winning scripts, and streets.

Be prepared for people. Give each person one of your imprinted scratch pads, and suggest that they keep notes for later evaluation. Have an extra amortization book in the car. CPAs, bankers, and engineers especially like to poke around among the tables of figures while you're driving around. Keep a few inexpensive games and toys in the trunk in case your people bring along children; keeping them happy and occupied will enhance your chances of selling their parents.

22. Never Get Caught

Between a husband and wife having a disagreement. That's easier said than done when they're disagreeing about what house to buy. Hearing from a third party often helps resolve the problem. To help, the agent takes the disagreement and rephrases it in a more positive light.

Let's treat an argument that flares between Joe and Clare after you've shown them some houses:

Clare: "I like the two-story, three-bedroom that needs work. The location is better, and you could easily repaper and paint some rooms."

Joe: "I hate that pit. Not only that, I'm sick and tired of following you around taking orders, spending my weekends painting, when I could be watching football. I like that little one-story four-bedroom with everything done. Not only that—it's cheaper than the pit you like."

Clare: "You're plain crazy if you think I'll move into that phone booth."

At this point you must become creative and, in an unbiased way, start getting through the problem. The way to solve any problem is through it. So we must start sorting. Check out the way we get through this murk:

Agent: "Now, as I understand this, Clare, you like to go in and put your own stamp on a home. You and Joe usually work together to renovate a property, is that correct? Good. Well, you must both have talent for that sort of thing. I'm all thumbs when it comes to taking something apart and putting it back together again."

Clare: "Oh, we've done some marvelous work on the properties we've lived in, haven't we Joe?"

Joe: "Yeah."

Agent: "Sounds like you're really talented, Joe."

Joe: "Well, I'm probably the best darn wallpaper hanger in town—and the least willing."

Clare: "Joe's really done some very nice work."

Notice that we are trying to restore some affinity and admiration between them. That's step one. Here's step two, finding the path to the solution:

Agent: Now, you have two choices here. First of all, you could renovate this place, something you're both good at, or you could move into something that doesn't need quite as much work. Is there some special reason, Joe, why you don't want to tackle another project right now?"

Joe: "Yeah, there sure is. I'm sick of fix-up work. I'm good at it—but it just takes too much time, and I want to start playing a little golf and enjoying life. Heck, I'm forty-five."

Agent: "Have you ever considered doing this for people who aren't as talented? You and Clare could start a business."

Clare: "Well, that's a thought. But Joe, are you really getting tired of it?"

Joe: "Yeah, Clare, I am. Maybe you'd like to start playing golf with me."

Clare: "I hate golf."

Joe: "Well, I know you like to play tennis, and so do I. With the money we'd save on that smaller home, we could travel more. Remember, you said you wanted to go to Tahiti."

Clare: "Oh, Joe, could we?"

Now the solution is in sight. By remaining neutral, by maintaining a professional attitude, the agent changed an argument into a discussion. Then the agent could act as the discussion's moderator. By staying cool, by looking for ways to renew their good feelings about each other, the agent toned their anger down and got them back to the business at hand. If you can't do this, you're almost certain to lose them as prospects. Stepping in, firmly and calmly, at least gives you a chance to save the situation and your opportunity for a fee.

Whenever I'm working with a couple who aren't getting along, I always try to get them talking about something good that exists between them. Even if there's no argument, two good openers are: "Tell me how you met" and "How long have you been married?" Once they're talking about the good old days you can cut right through the core of their problem and drum up a solution that pleases everyone.

23. When They're Too Agreeable

They love everything. It's driving you frantic. How can you deal with it?

First, recognize that their excess of good feeling probably stems from (a) they can't afford what you're showing them; or (b) they desperately want everyone, including their agent, to love them. So they just can't bring themselves to tell you what they dislike about the properties you're showing them.

It's almost always one or the other. If love-need seems unlikely, probe deeper into their finances. If you continue to work with them, they're going to be taking up lots of time—so find out if you're drilling a dry hole. You of course found out what they claim their financial situation is during the qualifying interview. Take a hard look at your notes. Call people where they come from. Run a credit check on them. It's cheaper, and less frustrating, than continuing to work under a cloud. Set up a confidential lender interview.

With people who seem to need everyone's love, you'll need to show a touch of displeasure that they aren't making any decisions.

If that doesn't work, have increasingly blunt discussions with them—over a period of a few days—and either bring them to a decision or send them on their way.

POTPOURRI

Choose:

Competent agents to associate with, and exchange information about houses of special interest. Working with buyers will cause you to miss caravan days occasionally, so develop contacts who can quickly fill you in on the newly listed houses that you should check out on your own.

When your buyers live nearby:

If they're comfortable with the idea, see their present home. While there, ask them what they like and dislike about that dwelling. Notice their favorite colors and the furniture they'll take with them to the home they're going to buy through you. Sometimes you'll want to measure some of their furniture. Take notes on your clipboard.

Possessing this information about their lifestyle (provided that they welcome your interest) will give you a strong hold on their loyalty, and enable you to quickly steer them to the best house available for their needs. Be very professional as you gather this information so that you'll never seem nosy.

L.A. TO SEATTLE, AND THE LOYALTY OF BUYERS

Whenever I think about the loyalty, or lack of same, that buyers display toward us worthy, hard-working agents, I'm reminded of the time I caught a plane for Seattle at Los Angeles International Airport right after Thanksgiving. I was flying north to present a training seminar.

In the LAX terminal that afternoon were a lot of college kids going back to school. I noticed one young couple embracing and carrying on with all young parting's sorrow. He was going to Seattle; she was staying in Los Angeles. I felt sad for them. It reminded me of my college days, and of all the tears when I used to say goodbye to my sweetheart as he went one way and I went another. I felt like walking up to them and saying, "Aw, don't worry. Before you know it, all the pain will be over: You'll be married, you'll have kids and house payments—and everything will be peachy."

I got on the plane and watched this fellow because I felt sorry for him. When we landed at Seattle, he walked ahead of me toward the terminal. I figured he'd crawl out, weighted down with sadness that his girlfriend was still in Los Angeles. All of a sudden, I noticed he had this little snap in his step. I thought, "I'm going to follow this guy for a minute." I walked behind him into the Seattle terminal. There, waiting for Mr. Sad-Down-South, stood a beautiful blonde. They hugged, and they kissed, and they were so happy to see each other. I wanted to yell, "Hey, wait a minute, his girlfriend's back in Los Angeles!"

Buyers are like that too. But they can't help it either. So just take it as a fact of life when they're motivated and it's hurting, you better be working, because if you don't handle their needs somebody else will.

SELLING THE WILLIAMSES: A ROLE PLAY IN ONE ACT

Cast: Manager
        Danny, the agent
        Mary Williams
        Jack Williams

This role play is to be read by four people at an office meeting to train themselves and the other agents present. If all four members of the cast have copies of this book, no rehearsal is required. The manager or broker conducting the meeting obtains volunteers to play the other three parts, and reads the manager's role himself or herself. The agent may be a man or a woman.

Props required: three chairs, arranged to represent the front and back seats of an agent's car. Comments to be made directly to the audience are enclosed in parentheses (like this). Stage directions [enclosed in brackets like this] are not to be spoken.

Manager: (The time is 11 A.M. Our agent, Danny, has just finished a fine qualifying interview with Jack and Mary Williams, played for us today by _____ and _____. As the action starts, Danny and the Williamses are ready to go out and see property. Five houses are on Danny's show list. Appointments have been made to show four of the houses. At the fifth house, no one answered.)

[Danny and the Williamses enter from the side and walk toward the three chairs set up to represent the car.]

Danny: Here are copies of the show list, and scratch pads. [Hands one of each to Mary, and then a set to Jack.] You can make notes on the houses if you care to.

I'm certainly happy that you've given me the opportunity to show you our town today and hopefully, to serve you in the manner that you're accustomed to. I'd like to ask both of you a favor before we begin. [Pauses.]

Jack: What is it, Danny?

Danny: Well, I'm a real estate agent, but I'm also a human being with the same needs you have. I own a home, and I had to look for property as a customer when I first moved to this area, just like you're doing. I wasn't in real estate then. Anyway, I can remember how disheartening it was to look at a group of homes that were too much money, or too far from my taste buds—and then going back to the motel discouraged. I sort of hated to say anything to the agent for fear I'd hurt his feelings because I knew that he was excited about the properties he was showing, and thought they were special. [Pauses.]

Jack: So what are you saying?

Danny: I just want you to know that, although I took a lot of information from you at the office, and sense what you need in a home, I'm never really sure until I get some "audience reaction," as I like to call it. It's sort of like the opening of a play—you never know how it will turn out until you read the reviews. So, if I am on the right track and you like what I am showing you, great. But, if I'm off track, please do me a favor and tell me—when the seller isn't present—or in the car. I can change my game plan fast. And I'm not the owner of any of these properties, so there's no way you can hurt my feelings. I'm interested in what you feel, think, and want. Please promise that you'll confide in me.

Mary: Of course we will, Danny. You seem anxious to please.

Danny: I am. [Makes car-starting motions and noises.]

Manager: (Danny, of course, has carefully thought out the best route to each property.)

Mary: How are the schools here, Danny?

Danny: We'll be looking at homes in two school districts. My children have been in one district for the last eight years, and I'm very pleased. The other district has also established an excellent reputation. I've visited both district offices, and they seem very similar. I have clients and close friends with children in the other district, and I get good reports about those schools. And we've followed the reports of the college board exams of kids out of both districts. They've scored high on college preparation.

Jack: Sounds like you keep informed.

Danny: I have to, or I wouldn't be doing my job. Real estate agents have a deeper responsibility to their people than just showing homes. I can tell you about good doctors, lawyers, gardeners—almost any service you might need later. Just ask, or call me—anytime.

Mary: Oh, I'm glad to hear that. I hate like heck to give up my pediatrician. I just love him—and my two-year-old does too.

Danny: Well, our kids love Dr. Zwillig. I'll give you his number when we get back to the office.

Manager: (Danny parks across the street from the property to be shown because it has curb appeal.)

Danny: [Raises arm as though to open car door and pauses, staring across the street. Jack and Mary follow their agent's gaze.] Well, this is our first showing. I pick out homes that have pride of ownership whenever possible. This one is clean and neat and a delight to show. It may not be right for you though, so please let me know. Don't forget our agreement. [Gets up, making motions of opening car door. Mary and Jack follow, as Danny walks ahead of couple to the front door.]

Manager: (Have your lock-box key handy, and a card ready to leave at the property. Keep cards in a side pocket of your blazer or suit, or in an easy access area of your purse, ladies.)

Danny: The owner said she was leaving. [Makes knocking motions.] We'll just give it a moment to make sure we're not disturbing her.

[Danny turns toward lawn area and looks through Jack and Mary. That causes them to turn around also.]

Danny: Lovely front yard, isn't it?

Jack: Someone here has a green thumb.

Danny: Everyone has a green thumb in this country. Nothing to it. Automatic sprinklers. The sun's free. Just throw ten bucks' worth of fertilizer on the lawn now and then. Well, I guess she's not here. [Uses lock-box key to open door.]

[The Williamses walk slowly into the house as Danny holds the door open, closes it, and then walks quickly—but smoothly, around them to get in front. Danny pauses, and looks in all four directions. The Williamses stop and imitate her four-corner looking.]

Jack: [Tentatively.] Nice place.

Mary: It's not bad.

Danny: Follow me. I'll take you through the living areas first.

Manager: (Danny leads the buyers through the house, walking with a confident stride that's not too fast, not too slow. The stage has been beautifully set at this house. The lights are on, and music is playing softly.)

Danny: As we go through, I'll point out a few things that perhaps you wouldn't otherwise notice. The owner tells us this carpeting was installed just six months ago, over $9/16$-inch rubber padding. It's in perfect condition, don't you think?

Mary: It's beautiful.

Manager: (Now our agent takes the buyers down the hall and steps aside to let the Williamses go into the bedrooms. So no one feels crowded, our agent remains in the hall.)

[Danny stands back as though holding a door knob; Jack and Mary take a few steps and then stand, looking about.]

Danny: Though you'd never know it, due to the excellent craftsmanship that was used, this master suite has a new bathroom. The large jacuzzi tub is an addition, and so is the matched pair of basins. Isn't that a neat feature?

Mary: Yes, it is.

Jack: It drives me up the wall to share a single basin with Mary. Double basins are an absolute must for us.

Danny: Okay, I'll make a mental note of that—and I'm going to scratch the next house on the list because it has a very small bath in the master suite—no chance to add the second basin as these people've done.

Jack: Yeah, scratch it—let's not waste time.

Danny: Did you notice the large walk-in closet?

Mary: [She looks.] Yes, it is big.

Manager: (Throughout the showing our agent has been alert for any sign of impatience, and for any sign of desire to linger. The pace of the showing has been matched to the couple's natural rhythm of absorbing and reacting. Our agent has maintained a good balance of silence between brief comments on the less-obvious amenities that particular house contains. Then, after they've seen the whole interior, our agent pops the question.)

Danny: I'm eager to hear your feelings about the basic floor plan and the color scheme here.

Jack: It's a very nice home, Danny, but it's too small for us. I can't stand a family room off the kitchen, because that means I have to listen to my wife's dishwasher every time I catch a game on TV.

Mary: Yeah, but Jack, I like having the family room right off the kitchen because I can watch Tim and Cindy play in there while I'm getting dinner.

Jack: But I hate the noise.

Danny: How about taking a quick peek at the yard now? Then I have some thoughts about family rooms that we can discuss in the car.

Manager: (Why take them back to see the yard now? Because Mary likes the house, and Jack may decide later that Mary should have her way on the family room since she's there all week, but he's only home on the weekends during the day. Then our agent can say, "Remember? It had a very nice yard, too.")

[Danny drops a card, and they quickly go through the motions of leaving the house. At the door, they pause while Danny makes exaggerated—but fast—lock-box-using gestures. Then the three of them get back in the car.]

Danny: [Making car-starting motions.] Now, let's think about this. Mary, you like the family room off the kitchen, and Jack likes some privacy. How about using a fourth bedroom for a combination den and guest room? Jack could put a TV there and have a place to call his own. And Mary, we'll find you a floor plan that still gives you a small family area off the kitchen.

Mary: Great. But is there such a beast in our price range?

Danny: There sure is. I was going to show you one just before lunch, but now I'm excited about that house because I see you have a specific need for it. What do you say we go over there right now? Jack—is that okay?

Jack: Sure. But, listen—I like the idea of the den, but I'm less than happy about the idea of also using it as a guest room.

Mary: Jack, how often do we have anyone stay over? About twice a year.

Jack: But the double bed in our fourth bedroom takes up all the space—that monster and your sewing machine and stuff.

Danny: Instead of having a double bed taking up space all year, how about selling it and using the money to buy a convertible sofa? They have reasonably priced ones now that fold down fast to very comfortable beds.

Mary: I'd put my sewing stuff in the family room so you could have a nice, private den, Jack.

Danny: It's astonishing how cheap portable TV sets are these days.

Jack: I'm not too big on small screens.

Mary: At least you could always see what you want. Old softie here always lets the kids watch their programs—except for football.

Jack: We ll, getting a little T.V. is a thought. How much would you guess a fairly good convertible sofa would cost, Danny?

Danny: I don't have to guess. They start at [ad-libs a current sofa price]. I have a couple of brochures in the car about the convertible sofas our local furniture shops carry.

Jack: You're a traveling encyclopedia, Danny.

Danny: Just part of my complete service. [Danny makes parking motions, then looks intently to the left.] There it is, folks. Take a careful look, because I really feel that's your next home.

[All three stare to the left with great interest.]

Manager: (Our agent has made this house-hunting expedition exciting by reacting quickly to clues about what will make these buyers buy. The vital element is to know the inventory well enough to be able to do that.)

Jack: [Doubtfully.] Does it have double wash basins?

Danny: Sure does.

Jack: How much are they asking for it?

Danny: [Ad-libs a current price for a four-bedroom-with-family-room home in your locality.]

Jack: Will they take less?

Danny: I know they'll take the price I mentioned. Anything other than that I'm perfectly willing to present to the sellers, and work with them to negotiate an agreement that's good for both parties.

Jack: But what's your feel for it? Do you think they're soft?

Danny: I wouldn't think so. This house just came on the market, and it's priced right—

Jack: [Interrupts] Its price is right, huh?

Danny: Definitely. So we really shouldn't look at it with the idea that we'll be able to buy it for less. It's a very sound value as priced.

Jack: Can you back that statement up?

Danny: Absolutely.

Mary: Guys, I'm dying to see the inside. Let's not sit here all day.
[Mary gets out of the car. Danny and Jack follow her, still talking.]

Jack: I don't mean back the price up with a list of numbers on a printout. I want to see some of the houses that justify that price.

Danny: No problem. I can drive you right to several that will.

Jack: Yes, I'll bet you can. I get the impression you know what you're doing.

Danny: Jack, I have to—for my own self-respect. Real estate is heavy stuff. The decisions are very important to the people who make them. I treat this business as a very serious matter.

Jack: It shows.
[They arrive at the front door.]

Danny: I didn't get an answer when I called here, but the lady is very neat, so I'm sure she left it nice. Do you mind waiting here at the door just for a minute while I run in and turn on some lights and open the drapes? I'd love for you to get a good first impression.
[Danny hustles around, making light-switching and drape-opening motions.]

Mary: Okay—but hurry. Danny can't hear us right now. Jack, what do you think? Could this be it?

Jack: Could be. This neighborhood gives me a good feeling.

Mary: Can we swing it?

Jack: Listen, we wouldn't be here if we couldn't. We're with an agent who's loaded for bear.

Mary: I'm so excited.

Danny: Come in—come in.

  [Spreads hands wide as Jack and Mary walk forward, and gestures in time to] Ta ta ta *ta*—BOOM.

  [Mary and Jack take a few steps forward, stop, and look around.]

Mary: I love it. I **love** it.

Jack: Not bad. Not bad at all. Where's my den?

WINNING SCRIPTS

Lifestyle

Here's how to turn house hunters' discouragement into enthusiasm:

New-to-the-sunbelt-buyer: "We never dreamed we'd have to pay so much for such a little house in this area."

Agent: "I understand how you feel. I'm from a colder climate too, and I thought the same thing when I first came here. Then I discovered that it doesn't matter, that you don't want so much space inside, because the accent here is on the outside.

  "No one else has a huge house either. Our warm sun just pulls you outdoors constantly. Before you know it, you'll find yourself sailing on the lake in January wearing a swimsuit, or playing tennis in shorts in February—without giving it a second thought. And your kids won't spend as much time indoors anymore, so you don't need large bedrooms."

  Natives should say, "I understand how you feel because so many people tell me that when they first come out. Then, before you know it, they're in the swing of things here and saying it doesn't matter anymore because—"

Reverse the reasoning if your buyers are coming the other way.

New-to-cold-climate buyer: "I'm not used to these huge rooms. I don't know if I want the hassle of keeping this much space clean."

Agent: "On our cold winter days, you'll be glad to have the extra room so the children can get out from under your feet and play games indoors to keep from getting bored. And, of course, they can always learn to keep their own space tidy. It's easier for them to do that when they aren't crowded."

Park Across the Street

"Doesn't this home make a fine impression from the street?"

"Wouldn't it be fun to have your guests see that impressive front when they drive up?"

"Doesn't this home give you a good feeling of strength and stability, just looking at it from across the street?"

"Here's a home that seems to say to the world, 'Important and cultured people live here.' Do you get that feeling too?"

"They've taken great pride of ownership in this particular home, haven't they?"

"You have to get inside to appreciate the real charm (the secret, the fine quality, the emotional appeal, the many features, the outstanding value) of this one."

Crossed Arms as a Buying Sign

Go gently. Pretend you are mentally removing one arm, and then the other, from the crossed position. Try a smile. "I see a little glimmer of hope in your eyes. Could it be that I've struck oil?" Humor is the best tension-breaker.

When You Haven't Excited Your Buyers

People always respond to honesty, or to your admission of a mistake. When the houses you select don't excite the buyers, say, "I'd like another crack at this. My houses today weren't what you like, so please let me select a few more, now that I have a better view of your needs."

New Home Competition

"Before I make a decision, I want to look at the new homes."

This happens frequently in areas where there are new tract homes, or semi-custom building going on, and direct buying from builders.

Here's the medicine:

"I certainly understand your wanting to look at the new property. Please feel free to do so, because I want you to have total peace of mind when you make your purchase—especially if it's with me. However, keep in mind that the home you're considering with me has approximately $15,000 worth of landscaping improvements (the owner gave me these figures) and that work was done five years ago, so you can imagine what the cost to reproduce the outside of that home would be today. Also, be sure to price out what the carpeting and drapes and, of course, the extra mirrors, paneling, wallpaper, and so on that you'd be getting here. In the resale all that work is in. It's part of the purchase price, and included in the new loan you'd be getting. But on the new home, all those improvements will be additional cash out of your pocket. Also, be prepared to live with dirt and dust for a while. I know some folks who didn't have carpeting laid until the initial landscape was in because they hated to get their new carpets and drapes full of dust and dirt. I tell you these things not to discourage you, but to give you some reality on what a new home involves, as opposed to a resale. Look at that carefully. It's not only the cost of improvements that's involved, there's the time and trouble of putting them all in to contend with too.''

If you are a resale salesperson selling new tract homes for a builder, as well as resales, turn it around:

''I know you're considering a resale home, but keep in mind that this new home has never been lived in. It will truly be yours to decorate and landscape in the colors and ways that fit your family, rather than someone else's. Your new home will have the unique touch that only you two can create. It will be an original because you are the original owners. It may take a little longer, but don't you always have to wait for quality? Your new home is worth waiting for because you can be assured it's what you want.''

Splash These Questions and Declarations into Your Time Together When It's Opportune

''Are you presently working with another agent?''

''Is there anything I could do to better serve you, that perhaps isn't being handled right now with any other agent you are working with?''

''I want to serve you so well that you won't feel any need to go to another agent in this area. I can't help you in all areas of the county, but this area is my specialty. It really is easier if you have one person you can count on for everything in each area. Otherwise, you may feel confused and torn in your loyalties. All that takes energy away from house hunting. I really want to fill all your needs. Is that possible, do you think?''

''Tell me about yourself. Do you spend a lot of time in your home? Are you goers on the weekends? Do you prefer just being home and having projects and hobbies around the house? I want to know as much as I can, so I can better serve you.''

''Describe your color scheme inside your present home. Do you want to repeat those colors in your next home?''

''What's the outside of your present home like? Colonial? Contemporary? I don't know about you, but when people think of me they see country and oak and tiny windows. What do you think your friends see when they picture you and your home?''

''I wish I could see your home. It would help me get into your skin and be you for awhile. All of that increases my awareness of how I can serve your important housing needs.''

"How am I doing? Am I on the right track? Are you disappointed at what we have done together so far, or pretty happy?''

Always Confront the Buyers Along the Way so You Know Where You Stand. Don't Ever Be Afraid to Confront the Truth

"I'm really enjoying our time together. Please don't hesitate to point out anything you feel I've forgotten to inform you about.''

"Let me tell you about our wonderful school system here.'' (Use the sales speech you prepared for this purpose.)

"Let me tell you about the convenient shopping we have here.''

"Let me tell you about the terrific access to freeways (highways, the Interstate) this area has.''

"Do you like sports and athletics? Here's a schedule of what's going on at the local Y, or recreation center, public park—''

"We have some great night life just minutes (miles, hours) away. Here's a list of some of our best nearby restaurants.''

List all the amenities your area offers and write winning declarations similar to the ones just given, to be used when qualifying and working with buyers. This is all great glue to laminate them to you.

"I'm going to take real good care of you two.''

"I know everything that's on the market around here, so you can be absolutely sure I'll show you every house you'd be interested in owning.''

Overly Talkative and Reactive

They are nervous about their coming change. This occurs frequently with the first-time buyer. "Do you think we'll qualify? I've only been on this job a year, and my wife just got her degree.'' Try to make them feel safe about their decision. "Now listen here, guys, I wouldn't do a thing to harm you and every step of the way I'll make sure that this is right for you. Remember we've all ready figured what you can afford on the lender qualifyer. We have respected loan people to assist you, too.''

17

CLOSING THOSE GOLDEN NUGGETS BEFORE THEY TURN INTO LEAD

The Natural Close Is the Greatest Close • Closing Craft • There Are Limits to Closing • When to Shut Off Your Yak • What's the Seller's Motivation • When You Sell One Spouse First • Three New Things You Said • Add a New Facet to Your Powers of Persuasion • Do You Take This House in Rain and in Sleet? • Ten Tips on Obtaining Salable Offers that Stick • Closing Scripts that Win

Unless we can close—unless we can bring about a situation where the customer will make, and carry out, a decision, success in real estate will elude us. But effective closing isn't a clutch of verbal traps that force people into decisions they don't want to make. Salespeople create that unprofitable situation for themselves by failing to qualify thoroughly, and by failing to fully understand their customers' needs, desires, and capabilities.

I've already talked about closing in many chapters in this book, in FSBO, listing, and prospecting. Now, in this chapter, we're going to work on the classic closing situation: getting the buyers' name on the line, and separating them from their earnest money.

The agents I see creating the most trouble for themselves are the ones who regard buyers and sellers as adversaries to be defeated. Certainly, some customers are disloyal, eager to take unfair advantage, careless of our time, and unaware that we agents have rights. But we must remember that most people when they make real estate decisions, are dealing with sums that frighten them. Be charitable. Learn to be genuinely warm hearted and kindly toward your people. Cherish the idea that you are serving their needs first in order to serve yourself well, but second. Never think of sellers and buyers as enemies. Your life becomes a war if you decide to make one. You can also decide to make peace. You can determine that you will serve your buyers to the best of your abilities in spite of whatever quirks their natures have.

This attitude is never more helpful than in closing. Unless you are in tune with your buyers, and working for them, you won't be able to take advantage of this fact:

THE NATURAL CLOSE IS THE GREATEST CLOSE

What is a natural close? It's the close that's part of the big picture. First you build rapport, and then you talk money and qualify. Then you laugh and show, then you take the good points and the bad points and add them up, then you fill out a buyer's net sheet, call the other agent to get the feel, and then end with, "I don't know about you guys, but I think this must be the place."

That's the natural close, as natural as going to sleep when you're tired, eating when you're hungry, and buying a home when you need shelter. This close occurs by itself when you follow all the natural steps leading to it. You don't wait to build rapport until after you write up an offer; you don't write up a purchase agreement before you show property. The natural sequence here is the same as Tom Hopkins teaches and it's just common sense. The only reason people have trouble with the natural close is that they get impatient—they try to put the roof on before they're through pouring the foundation. The natural close is the greatest close when you take it step by step. You simply do all the things you're supposed to do, thoroughly, skillfully, and at the right moments. The natural close is you being you, loving what you do, and knowing what to do. It's combining your knowledge with the needs and wants of people who are just like you and me.

CLOSING CRAFT

I've found in my travels that the agents who can bring people to a decision about a home are the agents who believe in what they're doing. They have faith that their people will benefit, personally and financially, by taking their help and advice on real estate matters. These agents believe in their own worth, and in the fact that their job is important to the continuing prosperity and security of their country. If you don't believe, convince yourself. If you can't convince yourself, get into another line of work. Because your disbelief will come through to the buyers, multiply your problems twentyfold, and rob you of all pride and joy in your work.

When I first came into the business, I wasn't really proud that I sold real estate. It was the only way I could think of to make more money than I'd spend on babysitters, and still have time to mother my four small children and the fifth on the way. I didn't know that outstanding people had dedicated their lives to selling real estate, and to creating a better work environment in the industry. I wasn't aware such people existed, or that they were giving generously of their time in political action committees, and at state and local levels of real estate jurisdictions. I thought, quite frankly, that most agents were too pushy. I was simply doing it as a stepping stone to what I knew not. You have a conflict when you feel that way about a job, whether you're aware of it or not. You subconsciously feel guilty because you're doing something you don't believe in. Unconsciously, you rationalize ways to be less effective, to be less than totally committed. Perhaps you even question whether you're leading people astray by selling them property, instead of knowing that their purchase, if it's one you recommend, will ultimately increase their net worth and immediately increase their well-being.

The sharp edge of doubt cuts deepest on what should be the closing stroke. That's when all our guilt comes crashing down, blocking our path to a smooth close.

Agents who fall into this category frequently

- Fail to see opportunities to close. This means that they never *sell* anything, although they will allow people to *buy* from them if the buyers are sufficiently anxious to do so.

- Get this sort of reply from a feeble attempt to close:

      Buyer: "I'll have to think about this. And I want to talk to my sister—she knows quite a lot about real estate."

      Doubting Agent: (With relief, because now he can go home.) "Can't say I blame you. Go ahead. Think on it. I'll call you in the morning."

      At best, Doubting Agent is good for no more than: "Well, what is it you want to sleep on? Can't we bring your sister down here, and all discuss this together?"

- Can't close even though they have all the proper closing statements memorized. But, these fine words are delivered without heart, conviction, or drive. Doubting Agent won't close in a closing situation for the simple reason that he's saying one thing when he means another. Sometimes these buyers, if they like the house well enough, will go to another broker for "an opinion." All they want is to be told, with unfaked conviction, that they're doing a wise thing. The agent who convinces them that he believes they should buy will sell them.

Every active agent will frequently encounter situations where people want to buy houses they should not buy, where he or she must advise against the purchase in question, or even against any purchase at all. The point is to apply doubt selectively, and not project one's own internal uncertainties into other people's lives.

Belief in what you're doing must come from within yourself, but it is the product of what you choose to put into your mind. Retailing bad news is a giant industry. If you're hooked on it, if you insist on your daily fix of worldwide disaster, don't be surprised if your lack of optimism costs you a bundle. You can also choose to look for the brighter side of the news. It's a little harder to find, because it's not as popular as bad news, but it's there. Being an optimistic realist is as valid as being a pessimistic realist because prediction will always be very chancy.

The buyers' ability to carry the investment in question is established in the qualifying interview. That leaves only one doubt to be resolved: Have you shown them every valid solution to their housing problem? Any property that's a valid solution must be a reasonable compromise of their preferences and dislikes, and be available within their price range. Once you've convinced yourself that they've seen every valid solution to their housing problem, you'll feel good about heartily recommending that they buy their choice.

When buyers see in your eyes and actions

- well-meaning intentions, and the conviction that you have their best interests at heart,
- confidence in your own expertise,
- and confidence in your own worth as a person,

your closing scripts will carry tons of persuasion—and they'll win. The same words, spoken with no genuinely felt conviction, won't even carry ounces of persuasion—and they'll lose every time.

THERE ARE LIMITS TO CLOSING

There are limits to closing beyond which it's not wise to go. Here are some cases:

- When your buyers have listed their present home for sale and must sell it to buy, and you know that the house sales contingency isn't acceptable in your community on offers.
- When husband and wife are deeply upset with each other, and pitting one against the other is what you would have to do in order to close them. Wait. It's far better to remain friends with both, and let them straighten out their marital situation at home.
- Overly excited people who are easy to close. Everything is wonderful. Money is no problem. They're ready to sign after one session in the car with you. I always suspect the easy ones. One time I had a miracle occur, as they do now and then between the easy-come, easy-fallouts. On a Sunday morning, one of my sellers called. A couple driving by, completely new to our area, saw the sing in front, went up to the door, and were shown the house by the sellers. They loved it. "Call your agent, and tell her to bring a purchase agreement

over here; we want to buy it." I was deeply suspicious. Believe me, when you're one of the walking wounded, you're suspicious. So I went over there rather reluctantly, purchase agreement in hand. (I was a three-year salesperson when this happened. Had I been new, I would've expected this one to be easy. Then, when it went thunk, I would've been crushed. But, thank goodness, experience teaches us not to celebrate until the check is in hand, and the closing statement is delivered.) As I went through the qualifying interview in the presence of the sellers, alarm bells were going off in my head. After the buyers approved the purchase agreement and left, I told the sellers that it was highly unusual to sell so easily. "Don't pop the Cold Duck yet, because this is a VA transaction and our buyers have to meet strict qualifying rules." But, of course, they just felt that I was being overly cautious (like new salespeople do when their broker tries to convince them to use the buyer's analysis for better service form *before* they show property). In this case, the buyer's credit had at one time been very bad, and there were a lot of job change problems. I never worked so hard for a transaction, but we finally closed this one. But, more times than not, the overly excited couple who drop out of nowhere and never find a thing wrong with the place are the people who need to be checked out the closest. Of course, we can always run into a dream situation, but please regard them strictly as icing on the cake.

- When they need to borrow money from relatives—who aren't with them—in order to purchase the property. Such buyers always say, "No problem. Our relatives will love it."

Tell your buyers, "I'm positive that your Uncle Squinch and Aunt Squat will adore this place, and want you to have it, but let's get them in on this now, before we involve the sellers in our excitement." Keep the pressure on your buyers to do what they must do before they can buy.

- When only one partner is present. This often happens when the husband comes out to start a new job, and the wife remains behind in their old home. Put a contingency in the purchase agreement that the offer is subject to her approval within a stated period, five or ten days. Make the sellers and their agent aware that they have nothing firm until Big Mama sees the house and says *yes*. It doesn't matter how often Pop tells you she'll be crazy about it.

- When they have an appointment with another broker or two after you. They love one of the houses you've shown them, but they have a hangup. In the past, they've always bought a house in each new area they've been transferred to from the first agent they've worked with. Then they never stopped worrying that they might've missed a better buy. This time they've vowed to each other that they'll keep their other appointments. "But we're really excited about this house, and we don't want to run the risk of losing it while we're looking around." Tell them to submit an offer through you that calls for their final decision within 48 hours. That will put them under some obligation to you, and allow them to ease their curiosity about other properties.

In this situation, many agents try to talk the buyers out of keeping their other appointments by saying something like, "Do you really feel it's necessary to see the other agents? I'm a Multiple Listing broker. I can show you any property they can show you. May I ask if you feel that I'm doing a good job for you?"

If you know the inventory well, and did a professional job of matching their needs to it, how much chance is there that another agent can show them a better house? You destroy your credibility by applying too much pressure now, especially if they say they won't buy any house that you showed them through anyone else. Insistence that they don't need another agent will convince many people that they'd better check out what another agent can offer them.

And some people can't handle much pressure in a straightforward way. Push them hard and they'll sign an offer—they'll give you an earnest money check. Then they'll hustle out to look at houses with other agents. If they find something they like better, you'll get a message canceling the offer they placed through you that's been accepted by the sellers in the meantime. The only certainty in the resulting havoc is that you'll have a lot of trouble coping with it. Closing is much more than merely getting an offer and earnest money. Closing is building enough conviction in your buyers' minds to carry them through to the settlement of the transaction.

I believe that the limits we must consider when we close are the following:

- Is the situation financially sound?
- Will your close merely create a temporary sale that will fall out? Show me a salesperson who pushes too hard, and I'll show you a salesperson whose cancellation rate is phenomenal.
- Do they really like the home, or are they the type of people who'll say anything to get out from under the pressure of decision making?
- Do they like you?
- Do you like them?
- Have you done a thorough job, or are you simply hungry for a sale?
- Are you handling too many customers at once, and trying, so that you can move on to your next appointment, to force speed on people who think slower than you do?
- Do they really want it, but you know it will be detrimental to them at this time? Several years ago, I was able, with hard work and creative financing, to get Max and Tina into their first home. During the following year, the appreciation rate was sensational, and they got the move-up itch. Max and Tina called me over to tell them what their net would be if they decided to sell. We were all impressed with the figure but they were a one-income family, and his take-home hadn't increased enough to carry the larger house they liked. They were eager to move up in the community although Max was getting bored with his job, and a promotion to another area was a possibility. I knew I could list their home, and also sell them the move-up, but I also knew that

Max and Tina would be stretched too tight for safety in the larger house. So I felt that this situation was outside the limits, and refused to close them. I said what had to be said as nicely as I could, and left them feeling not too happy. Six months later I did list and sell their house when Max got a healthy raise and a transfer to an area with less-expensive housing. I missed one transaction with Max and Tina, but I gained many more elsewhere because of the faith I gained in myself by doing what I knew was right for them. There's no better investment than in your own integrity.

WHEN TO SHUT OFF YOUR YAK

Knowing when to stop talking is one of the most valuable qualities an agent can have. I know agents who are blabber-junkies with a twenty-thousand-a-year habit. They're terrific closers. The problem is, they're also terrific reopeners. A cure for their loose lip would make more money for these agents than anything else could. Excessive blab can be caused by anything from simple high spirits to deep-seated anxieties. Cures range from validations (see Chapter 27) and in-depth review of one's goals and capabilities, to professional counseling and therapy.

Most of us don't have such a deep-seated chatter problem. We just talk too much part of the time. *Shut off your yak* means not saying anything that doesn't have to be said. Watch and listen, analyze what you already know about the situation, and keep silent until you think of something to say that has a good chance of advancing the cause.

Here are some good times to shut your yak:

- When showing property. That, of course, is when you set up the close. You can't set yourself up for a smooth close by talking when there's no need for your input. Too many tie-downs expressed too cutely, "Ooo, I just love this darling little kitchen, don't you?" and the recital of obvious facts, "This room has a huge window," don't advance your cause. If you irritate your buyers by talking too much, they'll think you'll probably irritate the sellers when you present an offer. Guard your words well when you're with buyers.

- When the husband and wife are fighting. Even if you know who's right, and a clarification of some point has to be made, wait until the charge is off, and their batteries are in normal operating condition, before speaking.

- When a third party, a friend or relative of the buyers, drops in on the scene and disagrees with everything you've told your prospects. Keep your cool until the steam blows off these people. You can only throw coal on the fire by talking. Sit there quietly, and let them battle. "You guys work it out, and then I'll follow your lead. As my Dad used to say, I'm a lover, not a fighter."

- When buyers and sellers talk at the property. Otherwise, you plant the seeds of suspicion in your buyers' minds that you're trying to conceal things about the area. Let the seller be the expert on the community at this moment. You can talk about other advantages of living there when you're alone with the buyers again.

    But if the conversation gets lopsided, rescue your buyers by saying, "I hate to break in, but we should be going now because the sellers are waiting to leave at the next house, and there's no lock-box key."

- When you return to the property with excited buyers who need to be by themselves and absorb the loveliness of the moment.

WHAT'S THE SELLER'S MOTIVATION?

Keep your antennas extended to catch any hints of seller motivation as you keyview houses and talk with other agents. Understanding why sellers are selling sharpens your eye for the perfect fit of buyer and seller.

Here's how it works. Agent Footmouth has a very strong buyer who needs a house fast, and can make a clean offer. It's the slow season, there's an oversupply of properties on the market, and the house that sounds ideal for Footmouth's people is listed at $159,900. His buyers' top limit is $145,000. They are reluctant to look at the $159,900 house because they don't want to get excited about something they can't afford, but Footmouth assures them that, because of the season and the oversupply, he'll be able to talk the sellers into accepting their offer. They view the house, love it, say go. Footmouth presents their $145,000 offer on the $159,900 property—and the sellers reject it contemptuously. Only then does Footmouth discover that the sellers' new home won't be ready for six to eight months. They don't want a quick closing, like most sellers do, because they want to stay where they are until they can move directly into their new home. So Footmouth's most important selling point for his low offer—a quick close—counts as a negative with them. They are not willing present-time sellers.

Had Footmouth known that before exciting his buyers about the property, he would have avoided showing it and avoided losing them. Because now, after reminding Footmouth that they only looked at the property because he said it could be had for their price, they find themselves another agent.

Here are some clues to seller reactions:

SELLERS' MOTIVATION	WILLINGNESS TO COMPROMISE
Quick transfer	Often willing to negotiate, especially if the employer will pay the brokerage.
Waiting for new home to be built ...	Depends on time span. Usually easier to negotiate with as completion date of new home approaches.

Purchased next home with swing loan and is now making, or soon will be making, payments on two houses unless this listing sells	Often willing to negotiate.
Purchased next home with savings . . .	Usually less willing to negotiate than swing-loaner.
Listed, but has nowhere to go yet . . .	Difficult to negotiate with unless they have their eye on something special, or unusual circumstances exist.

Chapter 18 has winning scripts for these seller motivations.

WHEN YOU SELL ONE SPOUSE FIRST

When either the husband or wife finds a house that they want before their spouse comes looking, don't try to sell the second half of the couple. Let the one you've already worked with do that for you. Stay in the background, ready to answer questions, but far enough away so that they can talk privately. If one spouse can't sell the house to the other, you can't either.

THREE NEW THINGS YOU SAID

Be aware of what you're saying, and ever on the lookout for sayings that go well. After each meeting with a buyer, take a few moments to think about the conversation. Write down the three new things you said that went over best on 3 × 5 cards, and review these cards frequently. This habit of writing down your best words will remarkably increase your memory for what you've said. And it will provide your own rapidly growing arsenal of Winning Scripts that are especially effective for you because they are original with you.

ADD A NEW FACET TO YOUR POWERS OF PERSUASION

''At this point in time, I'm not sure what you're thinking or feeling.''
    You could say that sentence more concisely: 'I don't know your mind now,'' but that's much too abrupt for many people when they're skipping about on the hot skillet of decision.
    Buyers have a lot to think about in the closing room, and abrupt speech can crowd them. Unless they're snapping back their replies quickly, use the comfortably slow, roundabout phrases that stretch out your meaning, and allow their preoccupied minds time to cope. School yourself in this technique, and its opposite, staccato speech that's stripped down to bare essentials. When you need to keep the

ball in their court, you can do it with a quick zip of short words. And their effect is heightened if you've been speaking in long-winded phrases before. Compare:

FORCEFUL	LONG WINDED
now	at the present time
today	during the current year
think about	give careful consideration to

There are hundreds of these odd pairs. Look for them, and practice switching back and forth from the quick and forceful to the slow and roundabout. Learn to alter your speaking style at will, and add a new dimension to your powers of persuasion.

DO YOU TAKE THIS HOUSE IN RAIN AND IN SLEET?

Do you take this house in rain and in sleet, to have and to hold, in dark of night and shine of day, when payments fall due, and when flowers bloom at your door? Do you take this place to be exclusively yours, to be your refuge from the world's cares, to be the shelter where your children grow and your friends gather?

Say yes.

I'm searching for the right words, the right timing, and the right price to draw four people's okay to an agreement that will benefit all of them. I'm just the go-between; only they can perform the act of buying and selling, of replacing the tired old wishes under that roof with fresh new dreams. I can't push too much, and I won't lie, but somehow I must provide the reassuring phrases and setting that's required if I'm to be the conductor of this transfer-of-hopes symphony, the minister for this union, the successful bearer of commodity expertise.

TEN TIPS ON OBTAINING SALABLE OFFERS THAT STICK

1. If your buyers insist on making a low offer, push hard for
   * no contingencies,
   * timing the close to suit the sellers' convenience,
   * terms that cash the sellers out (if that's what the sellers want),
   * no unusual or nit-picking clauses,
   * no grabs for the seller's furnishings,
   * and an extra large deposit.

   A low-price offer that meets all six of these requirements stands the best chance of being accepted. As a rough guide—and that's the best possible because every case is so different—each complication introduced into a low-price offer cuts in half its chances of being accepted.

   If your buyers are willing to offer only the earnest money that's customary, instead of an extra-large deposit, your chances of getting the offer accepted are reduced to 50 percent. If they offer a smaller-than-usual deposit, their chances are cut in half again, to 25 percent.

But your buyers aren't done yet. They specify: that the seller's patio furniture be included in the purchase price, and chop their odds to 12½ percent; that the dead tree in the front yard be replaced, and reduce their chances to 6¼ percent; that the sellers take back a small second mortgage for part of their equity, and thereby drop their odds to 3⅛ percent; that the settlement date be 90 days, although the sellers want to close in 30, and knock their odds to 1½ percent; and finally, they make the offer contingent on their present home selling within 30 days, and drive their odds below 1 in 100.

(Note that the final odds would be the same if we started with the house-sale contingency and ended with the patio furniture.)

And, if the buyers' credit is less than solid, cut their offer's chances in half again.

If you're questioning whether a low-price offer is damaged as much by a trifling provision (like the request for the patio furniture) as it is by a major item (like the settlement period), you've never seen, as I have, a seller grow pale when the price is stated, and then flush with rage when the trifle is mentioned. Never forget the part emotion plays in all aspects of real estate.

So, if you have to go with a low price, fight hard to eliminate every other negative that can be eliminated.

2. Do your homework during the qualifying interview and don't show people homes they can't afford. All you'll do is whet their appetite for what they can't have. That's cruel to both their feelings and your pocketbook.

3. Don't try to close too soon. Your buyers must really want the house. They will be eager to hear your full explanation of the buyer's net sheet. They will listen intently as you describe how an offer works. When they've reached that point, you've reached the time to say, "Are you ready to proceed? I'd like to make this home part of your future."

4. If possible, type the offer. If that isn't practical, take time to print carefully. (If both your writing and printing look like the work of a not-too-bright six-year-old, it can start hurting you in the wallet now. Libraries and bookstores have books on printing legibly. Get one, practice ten minutes a day for three weeks, and you'll be able to print beautifully for the rest of your life.)

Difficult-to-read offers, or those that have clumsily worded clauses that are difficult to understand, turn sellers off. Already it sounds like a troublesome transaction, and they haven't even deciphered the whole thing yet. You may not be able to type it, but you can always print it, and you must insist, for their benefit, that your customers give you time enough to word their offer clearly and concisely.

5. Explain this to the buyers at the time you write and they approve the offer: "I'll be presenting this offer to the seller in good faith. In other words, I'm

going in there with the understanding that if your offer is accepted, you are committed to the purchase of this property. You do understand that, don't you?''

6. Get a sufficient deposit.

7. Don't socialize after you write up the offer. Get down to business and present it. Suggest that the buyers go for a cup of coffee, or whatever, until you can get back to them.

8. Be sure the buyers are given a signed copy of the offer before you leave them.

9. Always call the listing agent and get a feel for the sellers' motivation. Then tell the buyer what the story is before you write up the purchase agreement.

10. Be sure you close your meeting with your buyers on an up tone! ''I will do everything in my power to secure this property for you. If I get a counteroffer, it won't be because I didn't give all I've got—and that's plenty. But wish me luck.

CLOSING SCRIPTS THAT WIN

Closing scripts, to be effective, must be spoken with sincere empathy. Your buyers must know that you're interested in them, are concerned about their welfare, and want them to have a trouble-free transaction. To instill confidence that they are safe in your hands, emphasize those points repeatedly.

Closing Scripts to Be Used in the Car on Your Way Out to See Property

''Let me tell you some things about this great community. The school system here is the finest. I happen to live just two blocks from this home, and I can tell you of my own personal knowledge that this grade school has as dedicated a staff as you'll find anywhere. And my friends tell me that applies to our entire school system. And our recreation and parks system is —. The public library is within walking distance and it's—. The stores here are—.''

''One of the things I like best about living here is _____.'' (Paint a picture of the change they're making that appeals to their interests.)

Closing Scripts to Be Used at the Property

Find an area with the features, such as proximity to work or highways, that seem to be important to them, and emphasize those features. ''I know how important freeway proximity is to you, Jim. Guess what, this house is only two blocks from the main artery to the freeway. Also, the hospital is only four miles away, Isabella. So perhaps we can go by there right now and see if there are any nursing positions open at this time.''

''Can you picture your furniture in this room?—How's it fit?''

When You First Get the Objection

Ignore it.

There are a lot of things they like about this house, but they say, "The color of the carpeting is *bad*. No way." Ignore that statement. Pretend you didn't hear it. And then say something like, "Oh, I forgot to tell you! This house has air conditioning."

Ignore the objection and bring out something you know they want. The second time the objection comes up, *go for it.* "But I told you, Danny, this carpeting—the color's atrocious. There's a lot of good things here, but I don't want to put new carpeting in. If I'm spending $95,000 for a house, I want the carpet to be good, and the color I want."

"Okay."

Be happy that they're telling you what the objection is. Because that means they feel safe with you now. The first thing about handling objections is, be happy. *Rephrase the objection* when they say to you, "I don't want to spend $95,000 and have to replace this carpeting."

Pause. Think a moment. Then say something like this (and make it sound the worst possible when you rephrase it): "Oh, this carpeting clashes with your furniture, does it? Then we've eliminated this house from consideration."

Now you've given them perspective, and brought what they're doing into focus. If there's any possibility that they'll buy that house, they'll say something like, "Oh, it's not *that* bad, but—"

After You've Rephrased the Objection, Get All the Problems Out in the Open

"Is there anything else, besides the carpeting, about this house that bothers you?" All this happens after you know they like the home. They're serious about it. Your cancellation rate will be much lower if you'll take time to explore all your customers' objections this early in the game. Some people are reluctant to reveal objections. Gently urge them to do so. Show empathy. Give your buyers time to find words for their feelings.

Here's how to overcome objections after they've given you all of them. It depends on what they don't like. If it's the carpet, say this: "You know, you can't change the location of a house. We can't physically move the acreage; we can't change the floor plan. But the carpeting we can always change. And, quite frankly, this is one of the finest locations in the area. So let's think in terms of a carpet allowance, maybe the seller would accept that. I'm not sure [because you're not], but it could be an option."

As salespeople, we provide *options* by opening the principal's eyes to them, by negotiating them, but primarily, by seeing them. That's part of our job: to be alert for options that the principals aren't aware of. Very often, what buyers object to is something they can live with temporarily. In the case just mentioned, they can manage with the carpet's unwanted color—if they choose to—until they can afford to recarpet.

"In view of all the other advantages this home has, is the carpet color something you can live with for a while?"

"Tell me what you're thinking about the possibility of purchasing this property. It's really important that you and I keep in good communication so I'll know if I'm truly serving your needs. Am I on the right track?"

I often interject something like this into conversations with my buyers: "If you decide to make a proposal to the owner, do you feel you'd want to include the refrigerator in your offer? You mentioned that was important to you."

"I think this place pleases you both. You're indicating to me that you'd possibly like to make an offer on it. Let's talk about that now."

Closing Scripts to Be Used in the Car on the Way Back to the Office

If they've found the house they like, and you're on your way back to the office, take the pressure off in the car.

The husband is thinking, "Uh-huh, she's going to want to buy it."

You just know. There's that buildup of tension in the car. Now is the time that you must relieve the pressure a bit, because it hurts. Say, "Now, Mr. and Mrs. Johnson, I don't want you to do anything that you're going to regret later. I want all the facts out in the open. So, as soon as we get back to the office, I'm going to prepare a buyer's net sheet for you, and tell you exactly what it's going to cost you to purchase this property, what the monthly investment will be, the loan origination fee, everything. Then we'll look at that and see whether you feel comfortable with it."

They think, "Oh, boy. That means she's not going to write up a purchase agreement. She's not going to try and close us."

Now they're sitting back like the rosebud was when we first met them, all tight and tucked in again. You can relieve some more pressure by saying now, "I want you to see the facts and figures before you make a decision. It's gotta be right, guys. If it's not right, I'm not going to live with it either." They feel safe again. You've created a safe environment. They're going to love you for doing that.

"Won't it be nice to have this decision out of the way?"

"It'll be great when you're all settled in and living in our community. I know you'll love it. I sure do."

Closing Scripts to Be Used at the Office When You've Returned with Interested Buyers

"I Want to Think It Over"

This is the house for them; they really love it; they want to move in. But the husband says, ''I want to think it over.''

Is their present home sold? It's the contingency problem again. Swing financing. Think about all these things again. If their present house is sold and all systems are go, but they're saying they want to think it over, try two things:

1. ''It's funny how many people have said, 'I want to think it over,' and I can understand that—I don't like to be pressured either—but then, when I call to be sure the property is still available the next day, a lot of times it's gone. The market is excellent in March, April, and May. So I feel an obligation to tell you this, Mr. Buyer, the property might not be here tomorrow. Are you willing to risk that?''

2. Suggest a 24-hour first right of refusal. If they've pretty much settled into the house you've shown them, but they've got an appointment with another broker, and there's no way they're going to make a decision tonight, try to get an offer with a 24-hour contingency requiring their final approval tomorrow evening at 5 o'clock. The listing agent and the seller have to go along with it, of course. I've used this device and saved sales I would otherwise have lost.

"The Interest Rate Is Too High"

She wants the house; he's hesitating. The interest rate is the peg he's hanging his fears on. He expresses concern about having their fun money consumed by high interest.

''As far as not being able to do things with your family— [What these buyers really need now is outflow. If they can talk out their anxieties and frustrations, these things will reduce themselves.] —what type of activities do you engage in with your family?''

''Well, we like to ski.''

''Oh, so do I. But, you know, you can't ski all year round. Perhaps you could have everyone save money throughout the year for the ski fun at winter time. But your property and your real estate investment isn't a seasonal, sometime item. That's a permanent security-building thing for you and your family over the years. When you consider the tax advantages, and the ongoing effect of inflation, it's really vital that you get started on owning your own home.

''I know the interest rates are higher than you expected, but that's not the whole picture. Consider what this home will cost in another year. Our rate of appreciation last year was _____ percent. Over the last three years it's averaged _____ percent. Okay, let's take the lower figure of 10 percent. You're considering a $110,000 home, a property that'll be worth $121,000 in 12 months' time—if inflation and our price trends continue, and I don't see any indications that they won't.

"I think that interest rates are going to hold steady, or go up, but what do you think is the most they can go down in the next year? A point? Two? Okay, let's figure what you'd save if they dropped *three* full percentage points, because I just happen to know that's a savings to you of about $2.20 per thousand of the loan, per month, on the term we'd be using, 30 years. Okay, on the $88,000 loan you'd need to buy now, that would work out to a $2,323 interest savings. That's a lot of money, but to get it, you'd have to pass up $11,000 in appreciation. You'd be out $8,677 by waiting.

When It's a Seller's Market

"Property in this area is on the market for an average of only _____ days now. That's the *average*. Homes that are priced right for today's market, as this one is, are being snapped up even faster. Based on this reality, it's simply not to your advantage to delay executing a decision that I think you've made. There just isn't that much property available here now, and the property you like on _____ won't wait long for a buyer. If you want to live in that home, the time to act is now. Right now."

"I just talked with the listing agent on this property, and there is presently another offer pending. So, I suggest that we write up a full price offer if we expect to acquire it." Of course, you never say this unless it's true.

Your Own Stamp of Approval Is Required

"This is absolutely and positively the best way for you to go." You can never use this strong a statement successfully unless you've worked closely enough with the buyers to have strong rapport as a person, and strong credibility as a real estate expert. However, if you've achieved this great rapport and credibility, but fail to use it at the right moment by decisively placing your own stamp of approval on the purchase they're considering, your strength will throw you for a loss. Credibility and rapport are self-defeating unless employed positively. Your buyers' faith in your integrity and knowledge demands that you believe they are doing the right thing—and that you also tell them so with no ifs, ands, or buts about it. If you don't, they'll believe you—and not buy. If you force them to pull reluctant approval from you, their faith in you will crack—and they won't buy.

When It's a Buyer's Market

The someday-you're-going-to-thank-me close. "I live and work in this town, so it behooves me to not just make a sale but to make a friend for life. I'm going to run into you at the grocery store, the bank, almost anywhere. Lots of people in town will ask you about your house and how you found it. My reputation is at stake here. Someday you'll thank me for bringing you to see this house—I have to be sure of that.''

Buy low in a high-interest-rate market.   In a high-interest-rate market, tell your buyers, ''Now is the time to buy in order to ensure that you'll have the best selection and the best terms.

''People think that buying property when interest rates are high is a poor decision. Most people don't understand what's going through the sellers' minds today. When someone puts a house up for sale in this market, they're motivated. They need to sell. So they'll carry paper, and they'll take a lower price than they would in a more favorable market. What a great way to buy on the lower end of the appreciation scale—before the next upward cycle of prices.

''Buy low—when interest rates are high!''

Here's another version of that effective sales dialogue for a hard market with high interest rates:

''Most people follow the crowd, but the crowd is almost always a step behind. When purchasing real estate, don't follow the crowd—lead them. The best buys in anything are made according to the contrarian theory of going against what everyone else is doing.

''When percentage rates are high, people don't buy. This is foolish because there are far more houses to choose from now, and the percentage of highly motivated sellers is also high. As a matter of fact, the effective rate of interest you'll be paying, in many cases, won't be all that bad.''

Then go back to discussing with your buyers how their negotiating power is far greater today than it would be in a lower-interest-rate market where the selection of available housing is poor, the prices are escalating, and the sellers are greedy.

Approaching the Offer Write-up

''I'll do everything in my power to make this transaction run smoothly. This is what is necessary if you decide to make a proposal to the seller: First, we fill out this purchase agreement. [Bring it out of the drawer, and have them touch and read it.] Then I'll need a check from you for an earnest money deposit of about $_____. Your check will be deposited upon the acceptance of this offer, or returned to you if the offer is declined. Then I will proceed to do all these things. [Present them with a checklist of the steps involved in the processing of their transaction from beginning to closing.]

''Then I present the offer. Here's what happens when I do.'' Start telling this to every buyer. If they say, ''Oh, we've been through this many times,'' I reply: ''Oh, you know how this works? Good. I won't go through that, then.''

But, most of the time, they listen while I explain how offers work: that I have to make the appointment with the listing agent. ''I'll go over there and present this offer. If the offer isn't accepted, you get your check back. It's invalidated. If the sellers change anything on this agreement, you have another chance to make another decision.'' Explain the whole thing.

''If you decide on this property, I intend to make it as easy for you to buy it as possible. I'd like to introduce you at the bank carrying the present loan. We can all go to the bank together and fill out the necessary paperwork, and perhaps get a new account started for you in this state. It'll be my pleasure to help you through this busy period.

''If you both decide you want to buy this property—I should say, 'If you both want to *try* to buy it by making an offer to the owners—then what happens next is that I'll call the listing agent and get some facts regarding possession and general motivation from him about his seller. Would you like me to call the listing agent and see what the scoop is?'' This only calls for a minor *Yes*, and many people can handle that who would freeze up and say *No* to ''Shall we proceed?'' because they haven't reached that point yet. Then, while you talk to the listing agent, they have time to get used to the idea. And, by allowing you to call the listing agent, they've put their foot in the air to take the next natural step—approval of your suggestion to write an offer.

For the Still Not Sure

''Let's go back there again and look at that property as if it's already your own home. Let's just go in there and relax—and enjoy the place. I'll sit on the living room couch, and let you people walk through and look, and measure, and picture your own furniture in there. Really get in there and pick it apart in your minds.'' Say that, then get up, and start moving for the door. Keep in control.

18

NEGOTIATING

Negotiating the Sale • Prepare for the Offer Presentation • Don't Talk Outside • Warm Up the Buyers' Image • Accent Minor Positives Before Price • Don't Wait Too Long to Mention the Price • Presenting a Realistic Offer to an Unrealistic Seller • Your Obligation to the Seller • Selling the Counteroffer • The Eight-Dollar Persuader • The Penny Persuader • Take the House Away From Them • If the Buyer Says "Yes" • The Three-Day Option When All Else Fails • Winning Scripts

In the last chapter we discussed methods of obtaining the most salable offer possible. Let's assume you've done that, and now you're ready for the next step—

NEGOTIATING THE SALE

Make the appointment to present the offer to the sellers through the listing agent. If the listing agent isn't available promptly, ask for his manager or broker, explain your problem cordially, and request that someone make the arrangements with the seller and be there when you present the offer. If you can't reach anyone in that office within a reasonable time, call the homes of everyone in that office. Burn up the wires to everyone *except the sellers*. Never go direct to the sellers to criticize their agent for not being on hand; not only is such conduct unethical, it damages your offer's chances of being accepted. Unprofessional conduct on the part of agents frightens sellers, and there's no worse time to frighten sellers than when they're about to hear an offer.

If diligent effort fails to locate someone in the listing office to represent the sellers, call an officer of your Realty Board for help. Your board has very specific rules on this point: follow them.

Seal Your Lips

News travels fast. Don't discuss the offer with the listing agent, the sellers, or with anyone else before you present it to the sellers and their agent in person.

And don't telephone the sellers during the time you have an unpresented offer. If it's absolutely necessary for you to communicate with them, have a third party (their listing agent, if possible) relay the message. Don't give the sellers an opportunity to question you about the offer before you're eyeball to eyeball with them.

If you know the sellers personally, they may call you and try to discuss the offer over the phone. It's quite easy to avoid doing so. Just say, "Oh, Mary, I understand how eager you are to know what's happening, but you see, you have an agreement with your listing agent that I'm required to honor. I know you wouldn't want to put me in a difficult position. I'll see you at seven. Thanks, Mary." Click.

When you have an offer on your own listing, it's just as vital not to discuss the offer with your sellers on the phone. If you allow phone negotiations to start, your seller is very likely to say, "Call them back and tell them to bump their offer up $2,000. And don't come over until you've got their okay on that." Why should your seller take the offer seriously if you don't?

With some sellers you can simply say, "I don't want to get into the terms until I see you. Is seven o'clock okay?"

With others, you may have to go further: "If this was an offer on someone else's listing, I'd never discuss it on the phone. I'm representing you in this transaction, and this particular set of buyers too, and I don't think it's fair to you or to them to make a phone offer. Will seven o'clock be a good time for you, or should I come right over?"

When another broker has an offer on one of my listings, I don't want to know what the offer is; I tell the buyers' agent *not* to tell me what the terms and the price are if he sounds like he's going to. That way I can truthfully say to the seller, "I'm sorry, but I don't know what the offer is."

They'll often reply, "Oh, come on—you must know."

"No, I don't. When I'm working an offer, I never tell the listing agent what it is. After we all get together and hear the offer, I'll help you analyze it and decide what to do."

"You really don't know what the offer is?"

"Absolutely not. And I think it's better this way. I'm your representative, not the buyers'. It's my job to get you the best price and terms that can be had to fit your time schedule. There's no advantage to my knowing what the offer is before you do because I can't accept or reject it. But there are several reasons for me not to. For one, some sellers would think I've teamed up with the buyers' agent to try and get his offer accepted. One of the ways to avoid suspicion is to avoid acting suspiciously—and that's one reason why I don't want to hear the offer before you do."

Sellers feel exposed when an offer is coming. Keep everything open and above board. All of the foregoing assumes that in your area, both agents are present when the offer is presented to the sellers. If the custom where you work is that only one agent is present, of course be guided by that. Your broker will explain precisely how this crucial step is to be handled in this case.

PREPARE FOR THE OFFER PRESENTATION

I don't care if it's not your listing; if it's your sale, do a Guidelines to Market Value and a seller's net sheet. Maybe the listing agent will have the guidelines form, maybe not. Have two rather than lose the transaction because you have none. And you're the only one who can have a net sheet filled out because you haven't told the listing agent what the offer is in advance.

As the buyers' agent, you should have all this vital data in hand. Go prepared. Psych yourself up and have the tools with you to give the offer its best possible launch.

DON'T TALK OUTSIDE

This is one of my pet peeves because buyers' agents chattering on sellers' doorsteps have strained many a fragile client relationship for me, and I believe several transactions were blown apart by that bit of carelessness. Here's how it should work:

An agent calls from another office and tells me, "I've got an offer on one of your listings."

"Hey, that's terrific. Thanks for showing it. Thanks for taking the time. I really appreciate it."

"When can we present, Danny?"

"Let me call the sellers. I'll get right back to you." I call the sellers, make the appointment, then call the offering agent back. "We're all set. I'll meet you at the property at 7 o'clock." End of conversation.

Notice that I didn't stay on the phone chit chatting with the buyers' agent, nor did I ask any questions about the offer; had I done so, I could very quickly find myself knowing more about that offer than I'd want to admit to my client.

And notice that I said, "I will meet you *at* the property." Not in front of it, or around the corner. Here's a recipe for disaster:

Two cars pull up in front of the seller's house. The seller is watching from the window and sees one of the agents climb in the car with the other agent. While the two agents chat, the seller is thinking, "What are they cooking up out there? They're trying to figure out how to beat down my price, that's what they're doing. Those turkeys! I'll show them. I'm not budging a dime off my price."

Don't kibitz with anyone. Just get out of your car, walk right up to the seller's door, and ring the bell. If the other agent is standing there, don't talk to him. Get inside the house with the sellers and then talk.

WARM UP THE BUYERS' IMAGE

When the sellers open the door, I introduce myself to them and the listing agent. Then we sit down and have a very brief bit of small talk before I get at it. But I don't present my offer just yet. First I say something like, "Let me tell you a little about Frank and Betty Lowe. They love your house. Oooh, do they love your house. You know, they have a three-year-old boy just about the size of your Mary over there, and your kitchen facing the back yard fits their needs perfectly. The swimming pool is great—they're a very sports-minded family. She's expecting, so it'll be just great that she won't have to drag all the stuff into the car to go down to the rec center— she can stay home in the afternoon and sun herself by the pool." I tell the sellers this kind of thing. Now let me tell you something: Many a house has been sold because the sellers liked the buyers better than the price. People often have a lot of themselves built into the house they can't live in anymore, and they want it to go to someone they feel good about. So talk up your buyers early in the game; it's usually the only chance you'll get because after the price hits, that aspect tends to carry less impact.

ACCENT MINOR POSITIVES BEFORE PRICE

I talk about the buyers first and then get into the purchase agreement. Before reaching the meeting, I've worked out my game plan. Every game plan is different, to fit the particular offer. Let's follow one through.

Before writing the offer, I found out (from the listing agent) when the sellers want to finalize the sale. Since my buyers' offer meets this important seller requirement, the favorable settlement date is the second item I talk about.

The sellers want to carry back a second mortgage and earn some interest income. Since a second mortgage is part of my offer, this is the third item I tell them about.

The sellers asked for a large deposit. Any money item gives them a good opening to say, "Okay, now that we're talking dollars, what's the price they're offering?" For this reason, I discuss the deposit as the final item before stating the price offered.

By speaking firmly and to the point, I have no trouble remaining in control. I'm able to guide the conversation the way I want it to go, without being loud or pushy, because I keep it moving.

DON'T WAIT TOO LONG TO MENTION THE PRICE

What you say about the buyers should be well thought out and right to the point. Don't drone on and on; the sellers have a lot hanging on what the offer is. Especially if you have a low offer, don't play all 18 holes first. I've seen agents lay on a fabulous presentation and build up to a dramatic crescendo: ''—and they're offering $120,000!'' The seller almost throws a punch across the table at the buyers' agent because he's been listening to this buildup for fifty-nine minutes and his asking price is $155,000. Sellers aren't stupid. They'll react well to a little concise drama, but not to a ramble down Yak-too-much Lane. Talk briskly, clearly, intently, and don't waste words before the price comes out.

You should also come on early with the price when the offer is weak in other ways, such as: the possession date specified isn't convenient for the sellers, the buyers may not qualify, contingencies, the terms offered do not meet those set forth in the listing, and so on.

PRESENTING A REALISTIC OFFER
TO AN UNREALISTIC SELLER

We discussed working with your own overpriced listing in Chapters 11 and 12; here we're concerned with negotiating the sale of someone else's overpriced listing.

How you should proceed depends on how long the property has been for sale, and on how active the market is. There's no point in pressing owners to sell a *new* listing at a figure well below their asking price in a market that's moving upward. At the opposite extreme is the listing that's been on a falling market for a long time. Here your realistic price is probably a genuine shocker to the sellers, and whether they will accept it will often depend on whether they can handle it emotionally, rather than financially. Come on softly in this situation even though you're the driver and they're the driven.

Tell them that you're there to help all parties reach a fair solution that's helpful to everyone concerned. Emphasize your buyers' concern about coming into an inactive market at any price and justify their need to make an intelligent decision for themselves. Defuse the situation with sympathy and understanding.

Most transactions take place between these extremes, on listings that have been available a few weeks in a moderately active market. If you're at the beginning of the normal selling season, emphasize the uncertainty of it all, the number of houses on the market, and the possibility that interest rates will rise. If the selling season is over, work that fact hard. Ask the sellers to give careful consideration to the likelihood that they'll have to carry the house through to the next selling season.

You're playing match point. So fight for it. Remember that you'll fight best if you remain courteous, calm, and considerate, but you can do that and speak forcefully too.

YOUR OBLIGATION TO THE SELLER

If your offer is not accepted, and the sellers and their agent start talking about a counteroffer, you should say, "There's something I'm obligated to tell you. If anything is changed on my offer, it's invalidated, and I no longer have an offer. I have the responsibility to tell you that."

If there's not a large spread between the offer and the asking price and terms, go a step further. Tell the sellers, "My offer is firm, and you can sell your house right now by accepting it. You can put all this uncertainty behind you so you can devote all your energies to moving forward. But a counteroffer puts us back to square one. I don't know what my people will do with it. Is it worth taking the risk that you'll have to wait for the next buyer? Who knows what the market's going to do in the coming weeks and months. But here we have this fine couple ready to go on your property now. Before you get committed to making a counteroffer, Mr. and Mrs. Sellhigh, wouldn't it be wise for you to talk about this privately? Maybe we [indicate the other agent] should leave you alone for 15 minutes. Don't you think that would be worthwhile? This is an important decision, and I feel you're rushing into a bad one."

Get up and start moving toward the door. Unless they stop you, you've probably made the move that will save the transaction.

SELLING THE COUNTEROFFER

Prepare the buyers for a counteroffer when you write their original offer. There's no guarantee that any offer will go. To improve my chances, I talk to the listing agent and learn everything I can from that person before I write up the offer. Then, after finishing the offer, I tell my buyers: "I'm going to try just as hard as I can to get this offer accepted. I'm really going to work for you. But there's always the chance it won't go. You know, they have five months to sell this house, so they don't want to move out soon. We're asking for possession at settlement in 30 days. That's tough, especially since we're not meeting their price." At that time, very nicely review the weak points of their offer. "So be prepared. Maybe this won't fly."

Many buyers will then say something like this: "I don't care. That's all I'll go. If you come back with anything changed on that offer, I'm not going for it."

Tell them, "That's understandable. But let's play one domino at a time. I'll sure do everything I can to put this through for you. By golly, I'll go in there and give 'em both barrels."

Your Negotiating Posture

Your negotiating posture should be calm, pleasant, and patient. Whenever another party speaks, listen attentively and hear them out fully. But don't expect the same courtesy in return from the principals in the negotiation; make allowances for their emotional strain and retain your professional cool. Direct the conversation toward making decisions that will solve problems and yield benefits, and away from personalities. If emotional demands or arguments are made, restate them in concrete and impersonal terms and ask the person who spoke emotionally if your restatement is correct. Stress benefits and work on problems; avoid attacking persons.

Never try to make anyone admit they've been unethical, unreasonable, un-smart, unkind, or un-anything.

Don't get sidetracked from real issues that involve money. Not only is it difficult to get people to admit they're un-whatever, you can't put such admissions in the bank—unless you're the one who makes them:

"I agree with you: On this point my sellers are being unreasonable. Unfortunately, they feel very strongly about it. You're absolutely right, but is it worth passing up this terrific buy because of a trifle?"

Sympathetic gestures and facial expressions, and empathic phrases, work wonders at smoothing the way over the rough spots. There are 12 empathic phrases in Winning Scripts at the end of this chapter that you should use often.

Influence the Counteroffer

Get the lowest price the sellers will accept at this stage nailed down first. Then go for the other items that are important to your buyers. You know what they are. Make sure the sellers understand the value to them of giving you selling points that can get the counteroffer through your buyers.

Take It to the Buyers in Person

Take it to the buyers in person when you get a counteroffer. Unless it's a long-distance transaction, don't call them on the phone if at all possible. And don't overlook this: The dramatic impact of a long trip by car or air can often swing the decision your way.

If you phone, tell them, "I need to talk to you and I'm on the way. I'll be there in _____ mintues."

Start with the Positive When You Present the Counteroffer

Continuing the example, they've told you that they must be settled in about 35 days. That's got to go. So you lead off with, "Hey, you know what? They didn't fight the 30 days. They said okay on that. Even though they don't have a place to go, they said they'll find a place and pay rent—so that's good news."

Start out something like this: "I want to give you the good news first. And the bad news I'm hopeful we can work out."

How to Sell the Difference

Do just that. Sell the difference, not the price.

Some agents sound like they're announcing the world's heavyweight championship fight when they tell their buyers, "The sellers countered for ONE HUNDRED AND FIFTY-EIGHT THOUSAND DOLLARS." They leave no doubt in the buyer's minds: We're talking about a very impressive and frightening amount of money now. No wonder so few of their counteroffers are accepted.

It's just as accurate to calmly say, "They countered for $3,000 more." Your buyers know what they offered: They can add 3 to 155 and come up with 158 every time. Never mention $158,000 until you have the counter signed. Here's how it goes:

"The sellers countered for $158,000," agent Bangwords says.

"Wow," says the buyer. "That's a lot of money. That's almost 16 percent of a million dollars. Unreal. I can't believe I offered $155, 000 and got turned down. They're nuts. You could buy a great house for $55,000 not so long ago—never mind about the extra hundred grand. They can keep their stupid house—let's forget the whole thing."

"The counter is for $3,000 more," you say.

"They want $158,000, huh?"

"Yes, $3,000 more." Repeat the difference, not the price. Then get right on with:

THE EIGHT-DOLLAR PERSUADER

If you're working with 30-year loans, each additional thousand-dollar loan amount will increase your customers' monthly investment by:

INTEREST RATE	MONTHLY COST PER THOUSAND DOLLARS
9%	$ 8.05
10%	$ 8.78
11%	$ 9.53
12%	$10.29
13%	$11.06
14%	$11.85
15%	$12.64
16%	$13.45
17%	$14.26
18%	$15.07
19%	$15.89
20%	$16.71

Tell them this (assuming a 9 percent interest rate and a counteroffer difference of $3,000): "You're already going in with enough of an initial investment, so we can put all the difference on the loan. The spread amounts to $24.15 more a month. As you consider this counteroffer, that's the effective figure to keep in mind, of course. $24.15."

Why talk about $158,000 when you can realistically talk about $24? I had a lot more success selling people on $24 than I do on $158,000. I'll bet you will too.

The $8.00-a-month persuader is not a gimmick; it really is the effective, important figure to people buying their own homes. It's vital that you keep putting things back into proper perspective for your buyers. In the counteroffer situation, both buyers and sellers tend to lose perspective. If you and the other agent aren't careful, your negotiations will degenerate into a power struggle: The principals will take and hold to positions regardless of what's best for them. Don't let them lose sight of the benefits that will flow from agreement. Get away from the power play thing. Get your buyers back to why you're doing the job for them, to what the real problem is, to how you and they are going to solve it.

Sometimes they'll say, "I'm just not going to pay that price." They can afford the house. They want it. But some ego item is interfering with their thinking. Buyers and sellers can irritate and frustrate each other without ever meeting. Be the peacemaker. Keep thinking of nonaggressive words to express what has to be said. You're there to soothe everybody down and clear the rabbits off the runway. So always—

Sell Amenities

Never argue money. Sell the amenities.

"Don't forget, this house is close to the schools. The kids can walk. And that beautiful park is just down the street. From the other house the kids would have to take the bus to school. And you'd have to take them to the park, Mary."

"Yeah, but it's $3,000 more."

Now you have to hit them with—

THE PENNY PERSUADER

With 30-year loans, each extra thousand dollars added to the loan will increase the buyers' daily investment by:

INTEREST RATE	DAILY COST PER THOUSAND DOLLARS
7%	.22
8%	.25
9%	.27
10%	.29
11%	.32

INTEREST RATE	DAILY COST PER THOUSAND DOLLARS
12%	.34
13%	.37
14%	.40
15%	.42
16%	.45
17%	.48
18%	.50
19%	.53
20%	.56

Pick out an amenity and sell the savings value of that amenity against the difference. We're still working on that $3,000 difference with Frank and Betty Lowe. The interest rate will be 9 percent, so the $3,000 will cost them 81 cents a day. You look at Betty and say, "We've covered the whole area and we know what's available. We know we can buy the house you like best for a price you're happy with, plus 81 cents a day. That's really what we're talking about—81 cents. I know it all adds up, but so do the other costs, like driving the kids around. I don't think gas will get cheaper, and I know you'd rather have your kids walk to school than go on the bus three miles each way. But it's hard to reduce a benefit like that to dollars and cents, isn't it?"

"I have a feeling you're about to," Frank says.

"I wouldn't try. Quality-of-life values just don't translate into dollars. Anyway, the money has to work out for you, or it's not a good situation—and I wouldn't want you to go on it. I really mean that. Okay, zero for the kids walking to school, but how often would you say you'll drive to school yourself, Betty? Once a month? Or once a week, counting all the different activities for all three kids."

"At least once a week," Betty says.

"Okay, six miles round trip at 10 cents a mile—60 cents. That only pays for about one day a week. I don't know how often the kids will want to go to the park—"

"Frank," Betty Lowe says at this point, "I can't believe we're sitting here talking about 80 lousy cents. I want that house."

Give the counteroffer to Frank and say, "I know you folks are going to love that place. I'm really happy for you." Put your finger where Frank is to sign and say, "That's were you approve it, Frank."

And away you go.

It isn't always that easy, of course. But, if they can qualify for the loan and want the house, you're dealing with personality hang-ups that will yield to the right approach. Here's one that often works:

TAKE THE HOUSE AWAY FROM THEM

Run through their other house choices again and then say, "Frank and Betty, I think we should forget this house we've made an offer on."

Decide whether the husband or the wife wants the house the most, and address that person: "Betty, what do you think? Shouldn't we take another look at your second and third choices? Maybe, in view of this counteroffer, you'll see them in a different and better light now. We could see them both in 30 minutes. What do you both say? Shall we take off right now and go look at them?"

You've just taken the house she wants away from Betty. Close your mouth now and wait. Find a very interesting knot in the knotty pine to stare at. By your silence, force one of them to say something. Betty is working on Frank with her eyes, so don't watch. If you'll just sit there counting the nails in the paneling, the chances are the buyer will say "Yes."

If the Buyer Says "Yes" Notify the Seller Immediately

Notify the seller immediately if the buyer says "Yes." Right away, because another offer may be in the wind, and somebody may have an attack of remorse.

Give Everyone a Copy

Many a transaction has been lost because everybody didn't have a copy. The listing agent, the sellers, the buyers, and the buyers' agent must all have a signed copy of the offer and counteroffer, if any. Do it. Get those copies signed and delivered before you go to bed that night so you don't have to worry.

Now Pat Yourself on the Back

Go back to the office, jump up and down, and hug everybody. Then go home, tell everybody there that you're great, pat yourself on the back again, and *take time to celebrate*. Really do this. Take the time to feel good. What you just did was no easy job. Some days it goes on and on for hours and far into the night.

There are solid reasons why you should make a big thing of patting yourself on the back immediately following a success. Unless you do, you'll cheat yourself out of a vital, sustaining part of the reward, and weaken your future drive.

THE THREE-DAY OPTION WHEN ALL ELSE FAILS

Wait three days and resell the original offer. Waiting is dangerous. But let's assume you haven't been waiting: You've kept on working with Frank and Betty Lowe, and after three days they're still in the market. They still want the Sellhigh's house but they won't—or can't—pay $158,000 for it.

When you go back to the sellers with the same offer, don't schedule the full offer presentation meeting. That will be an irritating formality at this point. Anyway, you tried it face-to-face, it didn't work, and now the only thing you can change is the presentation method.

Call the listing agent at home about eight or nine on the third night. Say that you want him to participate in a conference call about the original offer right then with the seller. You'll pay for the call.

Never go around the listing agent and call the sellers direct. They'll turn you down cold and complain to their agent, who'll then file a complaint against you at your board. Stay clean with the listing agent, and get his permission to make the conference call, or don't do it. The listing agent will tell you whether other sales activity on the Sellhigh's house makes your rehash of the old offer pointless.

The third night after the original offer was turned down seems to be the right moment for this option. Maybe your buyers will sweeten their offer, moneywise or otherwise. But, sweetened or not, make that call.

After three days, the sellers are very likely having third thoughts: "My house hasn't been shown since the Lowes were here; the selling season is almost over for this year; how much longer can I dance on my toes?"

This option can work in any market when you're only 2 percent apart, as we are in this example, and it can work in quiet markets when you're much further apart.

Few agents come back after three days and present the same offer. It takes very little time or trouble—you've already done all the work. You only need to get one success from a hundred tries to justify the effort, and your success ratio with this move will be far higher than that.

WINNING SCRIPTS

Use a Dozen Forms of Empathy

Trade rhetorical concessions for substantive concessions, verbiage for concrete, points of discussion for points of value. It costs nothing to say—

"I know you're right about that. If this was a just world, that's the way it would work. Unfortunately, there isn't much justice, so we won't be able to do that."

But it can cost you a great deal *not* to say those blow-softening words when the occasion arises for them. If you can't give them the value, at least give them, whenever possible, the satisfaction of hearing you justify their position. Only the score goes in the record book. When the game is over, the grandstand yells count for nothing. Here are some soft phrases you should be quick to drop into negotiations to smooth their way:

- "I understand." Very simple, very powerful. Practice saying it with varying tones and emphasis.

- "I know what you mean."
- "I've been there."
- "I know what you're saying."
- "I sympathize with that."
- "I know the problem well."
- "You're right."
- "I agree."
- "I see your point."
- "That's only right and reasonable."
- "I'm with you 100 percent."

Scripts that Help Close These Seller Motivations

Quick Transfer

"I would've been delighted to bring you a full price offer, but this is the very best I could do, based on my buyer's thinking, and the other properties that are available.

"May I emphasize again that my buyers are financially sound, and they can complete this purchase very quickly. This means that, within _____ days, you'll be cashed out of this house, free of the monthly payments here, and you'll be off and running in your new life. Won't it be great when this problem is solved?—I'm happy to say, I've got the solution. All you have to do is approve it right here."

Waiting for New Home

"Because you have time, you have a cushioned price on this property that reflects a future evaluation, rather than today's price. My buyers obviously prefer your home to all others, or I wouldn't be here with an offer from them. But they've become experts on today's values in our area in the last few days.

"They want your home, but they want to buy it at today's prices. This is a very cyclical business, and there's no guarantee that prices will actually rise [continue to rise, turn around] over the next six months.

"In half a year, the scene might look very different, so I believe we're justified in asking that our offer be considered in the light of today's market conditions only."

"Is it possible for you to consider interim housing? Perhaps my people may be interested in a rent-back situation for you. Would you consider that?"

Purchased Another Home

"Obviously, it's no fun paying out all that interest. I offer you a well-qualified buyer who can eliminate this problem for you within _____ days from today. We'll make this as free of worry as possible for you."

Nowhere to Go Yet

"I appreciate the fact that you wanted to wait for a well-qualified buyer before you went ahead with purchasing another property. My people are willing to give you 60 days to close this one out, and to find your next home."

Distress Sale

In cases of pending foreclosure, divorce, bankruptcy, or financial disaster brought on by the loss of a breadwinner's income, it's important to help people save face. Even if they're hurting and you know it, play that aspect down. Introduce your offer like this:

"Again, I wish I could have brought you a full price offer, but this is my buyer's best shot. Due to the number of homes available now, he's taking a rather hard line. If you have the holding power, then this offer may not be for you. Holding power is mostly an emotional thing rather than a financial question. Most folks would rather have it sold and go on to something new."

19

FALLOUT AVOIDANCE

Do it Now • Look Ahead with a Piece of Paper • Sleeping Dogs Wake Up and Bite • Meatball Mortgage Company • Only Half the Battle • Get It Moving • Keep Your Clients and Customers Informed • Work with the Appraiser • Choose Hard-and-Now over Later-and-Easier • Go to the Source • Assume Nothing • How to Push Details with Minimum Effort • Be There at the Settlement

We won't waste time on transactions that can't be saved because they collide with immovable obstacles. Grieve not for what might have been. Think about the lost transaction only long enough to understand what really happened. You've paid a price for knowledge, so get it. Instead of blinding yourself to truth by seeking someone to blame, look at the circumstances with cold eyes—and learn. Don't try to convince others that your performance was faultless. If it was, they'll know it. If it wasn't, your protestations merely prove that you don't use your energy wisely. Don't talk on and on about the dead transaction. Bury it. Go on to newer and neater things.

Sales that shouldn't have been made because the buyers can't qualify are covered in Chapter 15, not here. Fallouts are failures to close due to circumstances that arise or change after the purchase agreement is signed. And circumstances can change radically at any time. This brings us to the first principle of fallout avoidance:

DO IT NOW

Leaving details undone kills transactions; letting precious time slip away kills transactions. Unsigned documents. Loan applications not pursued with vigor. Inspections not made. The list is long; it includes every detail necessary for the close. Today's easily handled detail becomes day-of-closing's unmanageable monster.

Why do transactions fall out?

For reasons as countless as snowflakes in a blizzard. People stumble into new reasons every day. Fortunately, the best method of saving your transactions and collecting the fees you've earned is to rely primarily on simple common sense. Basic to this is checking frequently with the lender and the escrow officer (or whoever is processing the paperwork) to make sure everything that's required is started, and then is completed, in good time.

After a disaster, surprisingly enough, many agents will say, "Nobody ever told *me* the durn thing had to be done." These agents don't understand that when they hang their license on the wall, and tell the world they're in the real estate business, it's *their responsibility to know* what's required. Nobody is fanning their face anymore. Nothing but inertia stops them from studying their office's file of closed transactions, from asking their escrow officer, lender's representative, or manager what's required, and then bulldogging those requirements through.

LOOK AHEAD WITH A PIECE OF PAPER

Another surprising thing is how often agents will fail to sit down and make a list of all the things that must happen if that particular transaction is to settle. The night the sale is made, it's easy to get carried away in the excitement, and to be certain that no item will be forgotten. The sellers are enthusiastic and happy, and you know how badly they need to get their money out of the house. So you believe their assurances that they'll get right on with replacing the water heater and finding the permit for the greenhouse, as agreed. It never occurs to you that they simply won't get around to it, or that you could forget about these items. But each of the following 60 days of the settlement period generates its own pressures. You're working on new sales and listing opportunities with the intensity that real estate demands. These pressures blow those water heater and permit problems right out of your mind—until you get a phone call, a few hours before the scheduled close of this transaction, telling you that there'll be no close at all unless the permit is on file and the water heater is replaced *today*. Now it's tear-hair-and-tires-time. You have an appointment to show property, and no time to handle these details. But handle them you must, and postpone your appointment to show property you must, whether you lose the buyers or not.

So, sit yourself down, the morning after each sale, and think through everything that must be done to get that transaction closed, and your share of the fee safely tamped down in your bank account. Go over the purchase agreement's special provisions word-by-word; review the negotiations step-by-step; then think about each room in the house, the appliances, and the grounds. Don't overlook the counteroffer. Compile a special checklist for that closing as you do that. Then check your list regularly. Keep everything moving. You're the one who gets paid—or doesn't get paid—for doing all this.

SLEEPING DOGS WAKE UP AND BITE

If you're working on a government-financed transaction and there's a patio cover outside, don't assume there's also a building permit for a patio cover. Any additions or remodeling work done since the original construction are a time bomb ticking away unless you have copies of the building permits for the work in your files, especially if you're working on a VA-financed transaction.

Instead of worrying abut it, find out. Call or visit your city or county building and safety department, and make sure building permits have been issued, and that the work is properly signed off.

But sometimes you'll find yourself working with buyers who are ready to make an offer on the weekend. If so, protect your buyers by inserting this clause into their offer:

"Sellers to furnish copy of building permit for patio cover within five days of acceptance of this offer."

Then make sure you get that copy.

If you've ever made a last-minute, tire-screeching run to the building department with a transaction hanging in the balance, you'll swear there's nothing worse than not avoiding this avoidable problem.

MEATBALL MORTGAGE COMPANY

Above all, select with great care the lender you recommend to your buyers. Then closely follow the path through approval to funding that their loan application must take. Here's something that cost me $3,000 to learn: When approval of a customer's loan application takes longer than promised, you better worry even though the loan representative says, "Don't worry." In fact, you'd better cancel that application and take the loan to a reliable lender. There may still be time to save the transaction. Losing one at the last minute because Meatball Mortgage Company ran out of money, and couldn't fund the loan, ranks very high on real estate's list of greatest frustrations.

ONLY HALF THE BATTLE

Foresight and prompt action can save most of the transactions that fall out between offer acceptance and the settlement and collect-your-fee time. I say *"most"* with confidence, because most of my transactions have squeezed through tight places. Many experienced agents swear that *every* transaction hangs by a thread at some point during its perilous flight from acceptance to settlement. Only half the battle is getting an offer accepted and the transaction opened. The second—and often the toughest—half of the battle is getting that open transaction closed. Heed this warning: Your work is only half done when an offer is accepted.

GET IT MOVING!

Start processing your transaction the first available business hour. Make up a schedule that shows when each item required for the close must be completed. If the transaction hangs on a contingency, consider whether you should incur any processing cost until that contingency is removed. Unless you plan to pay for those costs yourself if the transaction falls out, have it clearly understood who will pay for the processing charges (for example, an appraisal fee to a lender) if the transaction doesn't go through.

KEEP YOUR CLIENTS AND CUSTOMERS INFORMED

''I've got the termite report in my hand. No problems.''

''The appraisal came through okay. Isn't that great?''

''Good news: We have loan approval.''

Whether your clients or customers are the buyers or the sellers, they've made a big decision, and they'll have moments of doubt about the wisdom of that decision. Perhaps they'll have moments of panic. You are the flight steward or stewardess during that transaction's bumpy flight from opening to settlement, and part of your job is to reassure the anxious passengers—your people. You are also the navigator and pilot, so use all the outside help you can. Your problems will multiply if you try to do everything yourself.

What if the news is bad?

Tell your people. Keeping them informed means just that, Everything concrete that affects their interests—except those items that are obviously too trivial to mention—must be promptly divulged to all interested parties. Make a distinction between the bad news (something actually happened) that must be immediately passed on to your customers, and the bad mouthings (nothing actually happened) that will merely plague your customers' sleep in the wee hours of morn. And bear this in mind: When something necessary to the settlement of the transaction does not happen on time, that nonhappening is bad news. Both buyer and seller must be promptly informed. Use a communication log for all good and bad news connected with the transaction. Record all conversations you have with your people on this log. Record every conversation with all parties involved during the open transaction period. See Chapter 24.

WORK WITH THE APPRAISER

Meet the appraiser at the property, and give that person a list of comparable sales. A copy of the Guidelines to Market Value that you used to make the sale will do just fine. Never make appraisers dig up the list of comparables for themselves.

Why bother?

Because appraisers don't have much time. Compare their fee to yours and you'll see why they don't. They can't dig and dig; they have to furnish your appraisal fast and get on to their next assignment. So they're very likely to miss the best comparable sales that you used to justify the sales price to the buyer, and turn in an appraisal that's too low to carry the loan. By the time you go through the whole process with another lender, something else can change that will kill the transaction. It happens all the time.

CHOOSE HARD-AND-NOW OVER LATER-AND-EASIER

Make that drive to get the documents signed. Go see for yourself that the missing screens were replaced, as agreed. Between the time that the *Sold* sign goes up and the close of escrow or settlement, you must supervise the details. When things don't happen on schedule—

GO TO THE SOURCE

For example, you represent the buyer. Your accepted offer called for a preliminary title report within ten days, but on the eleventh day you still don't have it. Call the title company first and ask them what's holding up the prelim. Then call the listing agent and ask that person why they aren't abiding by the contract.

ASSUME NOTHING

Make sure that everything happens that has to happen if your transaction is to finalize. And don't wait until the transaction is in serious trouble to start rescue operations. At the first hint of danger, move fast to cure the problem.

HOW TO PUSH DETAILS WITH MINIMUM EFFORT

Select dependable people and companies to perform the services called for on your checklist. Make inquiries before using anyone. Meet the people involved. Tell them you're going to do a lot of business, that you expect prompt and efficient service, and that you'll be loyal to them if they'll perform for you.

Be a good customer. Always order the work as soon as you can. Don't forget that the services you use have other real estate agents they must please if they're going to stay in business. Cooperate. Don't waste the time of your service people. Limit your demands for special attention to those occasions when you really need it, and you'll find they'll come through for you.

Be forceful, but always be courteous. As you're pushing the details along, remember that many of the people you're dealing with are on salary. They'll get paid whether your treasured transaction falls out or closes, so don't expect them to feel as intensely about it as you do.

Bug people briefly and frequently. Repetition is more effective than rage. Firm persistence pays. Make people want to help you, not determined to foil you.

BE THERE AT THE SETTLEMENT

In some states, this means sitting in on a settlement ceremony at which papers are signed and a deed is exchanged for a check. There's no such settlement meeting in California, but the principle remains the same: Both agents must be available to react to any sudden emergency. If you can't be in town the day your transaction closes, designate another competent agent in your office to cover for you, and make sure everyone concerned knows who that covering person is.

After hundreds of transactions, I still worked with checklists. Although I've developed a sixth sense for trouble that served me well, sometimes my sixth sense was out to lunch. A checklist never is.

Tailor the basic checklist given in Chapter 24 to your state laws, climate, local conditions, and customs.

20

A 100% REFERRAL BUSINESS

The Referral • But What Will They Take • Doing Volume Business • Put a Good Bit of Warmth in Your Fast Professional Job • Return Messages • When They Move In • How to Get Letters of Recommendation • Getting Referrals • "We've Moved" Cards • Stay in Touch • Remembrance Programs • Inhale New Information, Exhale New Business • Drop One, Pick Up Seven • Winning Scripts

You can't service 20 listings and farm too. You can make big money in real estate by farming—but not the top dollar. So why bother with a farm in the first place? Because farming is one of the fastest and surest ways to build referral business. First develop a farm that's producing a steady crop of fine listings. While you're doing that, the phone will start ringing with a very special kind of call:

"I hear you really know what you're doing, so I want you to come over and list my house."

Then it'll ring again. "I'm Joe Justgotin. I'd like to see some houses. Herbert Kelly said you were the best agent to call."

And all of a sudden you've got referral business. You can't slack off in your farm yet. You'll still promote. You'll still send thank-you notes, advertise, work open houses and floor time, and the business will keep on coming to you because you've earned it—by effective promotion and then by effective performance for your clients. At first, you'll spend all your nonlearning time searching for buyers and sellers. When you're working with some people, you'll perhaps cut your search-for-client time in half, but you'll still have to do it or you'll soon have no clients and no income. It will come home to you very forcefully how much more you could accomplish if you started each day with a client or customer who has a need, rather than with your need to find a client or customer.

This whole book is about how to maximize your time so that you can create a loyal clientele that will keep on feeding you the first shot at listings and sales. Then, by knowing how to hit the target with lots of those first shots, you earn a large income.

By stick and piece, as a house is built, you build your loyal clientele. First acquire the site: your real estate listing farm. Guided by plans as a contractor is, work effectively at preparing that site. Lay the strong, straight foundation for a loyal clientele by performing the basic services of real estate with the competence, friendliness, and integrity that makes people glad you were their agent. In house construction, as in clientele construction, a crooked or weak foundation makes for a ramshackle structure of little value. Erect the walls of your clientele structure by following through, by using your expertise to foresee problems, by doing the extra things we'll talk about in this chapter. Roof your clientele structure by asking for referrals; furnish it by keeping in touch so that former clients will remember to recommend you when real estate comes up in conversation. Your clientele structure, can be a shack or a mansion; it depends on how much effort and material you're willing to put into its construction.

One Christmas season I got a call from a family where the husband and wife had been married 60 years. They were the closest couple I ever knew. I'd sold the family several houses: to the grandparents, the parents, the newlywed children. Every time they had a real estate problem during the last five years, they'd call me up. "What should I do about a home improvement loan? Who should I call for a swimming pool bid?" I was the real estate member of that family.

Christmas Eve, the patriarch of the clan called me. "My wife died today. I wanted you to be the first to know." He was sobbing on the phone. Because his single son lived with them and there were three names in joint tenancy on the title, he was very concerned about what he had to do legally. He said, "I can't think of anyone I'd rather call, because you're part of our family."

When you're building a clientele, remember what a family intimate you want to become. Go out on every listing presentation, and work with every buyer, with that in mind.

Before I ever made a listing presentation, I instinctively looked on everyone in my farm as someone who could decide to move tomorrow. I did that because I didn't know how to tell the move-sooners from the stay-put-forevers then. I'll tell you something: I still don't know how. People have told me, "I'm never moving; my roots here are driven all the way to the center of the earth," and four months later they're calling the moving van. You never know. Everyone on your farm is a possible client, and a source of vital information and referrals.

The first place I went when I started in this business was out to greet people. All those housewives vacuuming on Saturday morning, and all husbands shining their cars in driveways, turned and looked when the big mama made her first appearance in the local neighborhood. I came equipped with giveaways: free litter bags for the husband's car, rain hats for the ladies. Information began leaping (along with baby in the tummy) my way.

"Hey, the guy next door is being transferred." It kept coming at me because I kept going back after it.

"My brother may want to move out here. Do you have any information about Mission Viejo you could mail him?"

I sure did.

"Brad Johnson just decided to take that job in Pennsylvania. Told us so last night."

And so it went. Looking back, I can remember dozens of leads like that. Not all of them worked out, but I followed up on every one. It's those early leads to a fee that still stand out in my memory—the hundreds of doors I knocked on, and the thousands of phone calls I made that led nowhere, have long been forgotten.

I did things differently later in my career. In the early days I was looking for a break, couldn't find one, and then I realized I had to make my own breaks. I worked a farm and the for-sale-by-owners, checked birth announcements for leads, held open houses, and so on. Later my major real estate sales work consisted of handling three areas: (1) come-list-me requests; (2) show-me-homes requests; and (3) servicing listings and open transactions.

THE REFERRAL

The phone rings. They want me. Me, lil ol' me. "We heard you're good." They are giving me their Academy Award. I love it. "We heard you really know the score." Hot diggety! A firecracker goes bang! I've arrived in someone's mind—isn't that the cat's pajamas? Whoop-dee-doo—Wow! Wham! It's the Fourth of July in my mind.

I keep a current Rolodex file of all my closed transactions since 1972, and work that file at least twice yearly. Sometimes I send out crazy notes, or drop over and say hi. Every Christmas I have special tree ornaments made up and delivered to my clients and customers. I send out a lot of flowers all through the year.

The 100 percent referral business doesn't mean you go up on a mountain, squat in front of a cave, and wait for people to climb to you. You're still working; you're still farming; only now it's exclusively the Everybody-I-know farm that you're watering and fertilizing and reseeding with the changing seasons. You may spend more money on giveaways now than you ever did on the ordinary 300-house farm, but the returns are far greater because you average more payoff work each day. Your gifts now go to people who've already worked with you, are likely to do so again when they have a need and, in many cases, those people have already given you fee-winning referrals. Instead of trudging door-to-door, much of your time is spent on the phone gathering information and pushing transactions toward their closings.

That Rolodex file is your stock in trade. It's your umbrella of protection against the rapid changes of climate that hit the real estate business. Start filling yours today.

BUT WHAT WILL THEY TAKE?

When the buyer says, "They're asking $169,000, but what will they take?" please don't answer, "Oh, I know that's just an asking price. They'll take less."

Today's buyer is tomorrow's seller.

When they ask that question (and every buyer does), look at them and say, "I know they'll take $169,000." Pause an instant, and then go on. "Anything other than that, I'm perfectly willing to present to the sellers, and work with them to negotiate something that's good for all parties."

A significant part of today's buyers will remember how you handled that question when tomorrow comes and they find themselves selling. Three years after buying a house from me, I've had people call up and say, "C'mon over; we're moving." I take the listing and, as we're talking afterwards, one of them says, "You know why we listed with you? Your Christmas tree ornament was nice, and we liked getting your notes, but here's the real reason: When you were showing us a million houses before we bought this one, we remember how you represented all those properties. You never said, 'I know they'll take less.' We thought, 'Someday, if we ever sell again, we don't want an agent who'll tell every buyer, 'I know I can chisel them down,' like the first guy we worked with did. On about half the houses we'd go in, he'd say, 'Here's what they're asking, but I can get it for you for a lot less.' "

Whether it's your own listing or not, don't knock the price. Some agents on an open house will announce to everyone who walks in, "They're asking $149,900, but this is my listing and I know that price is soft. Believe me, it's *soft.* They're really *mo*tivated." This agent believes he can tell a genuine buyer from a self-appointed spy—if he's ever thought about sellers' spies—so before long, he's telling the seller's uncle or bridge partner how soft the price is, and a short time later is groaning around the office: "I just can't believe this. I've always been solid as granite on my $149,000 listing, and they were all set to extend it for another 90 days. So just now I call up and he's an iceberg—says he's listing with Sell Fast Realty tomorrow. Wouldn't give me a reason; wouldn't hardly talk to me. And after all the open houses I've held for them! People sure are ungrateful."

DOING VOLUME BUSINESS

Doing volume business means working efficiently. You don't have time to patch avoidable mess ups because there are so many *un*avoidable mess ups coming at you:

Stay on top of phone numbers and names.   If you have only one transaction a month, you can spend 30 minutes looking for the phone number and name you wrote with eyeliner on the back of a candy wrapper. The top producer can't do this.

Caravan alone.   You don't have time for jolly chit chat in a car full of agents. And you can't afford their distraction while you're emotionalizing a home into your Quick-Speak Inventory.

Work to a plan.   Certain things have to be done each day or your problems multiply. List what you have to do and make people wait, if that's unavoidable, while you do them.

Schedule time off and take it.   Otherwise you burn out, mentally and physically. Sustained high production must be supported by quality recreation that meets your needs.

PUT A GOOD BIT OF WARMTH IN YOUR FAST PROFESSIONAL JOB

Many otherwise strong agents fail to build a large and loyal clientele because they are too coldly efficient, too much the big operator, too surface slick. Their clients know they were well served, but they feel vaguely taken advantage of, machine-processed instead of treated by a warm and caring person. Let a wart or two show, prove that you're down to earth, friendly, and real. Make them glad they've contributed to your success. It's better not to be absolutely perfect. You're in a highly emotional business and, while you can easily get too involved in your customers' problems, you can also easily be too aloof, too uncaring, too determined to preserve a strict professional relationship. Functioning on a large scale in residential resales requires more than efficiency; it requires an efficiency that's camouflaged by friendliness and warmth. Fly the happy medium between concerned, unforced friendliness and overinvolvement in your clients' problems. Sometimes only a fine line divides the two, a fine line that will run in different places for different people at different times. There's no simple rule, but you should be thinking about whether you're operating at the right distance from each set of clients each time you meet with them.

RETURN MESSAGES

Return messages from customers just as fast when they're in process as you did when you were showing them property. This can be difficult sometimes, but you've got to do it if you're going to build a loyal clientele. This is what people will think if you don't: "Now that she's sold us a house, now that she's got what she wanted from us, we're suddenly nobody. When she was showing us property, she always got back to us the same day. Three days ago I called her, and she still hasn't called back. All she cares about is quick money." So when these people decide to move again, in two months or two years, they'll remember how you slighted them after they bought, not how you catered to them before. Agents who unconsciously—or deliberately—slow down services after the sale are sometimes heard to say, "I'm the unluckiest guy in the world when it comes to finding loyal clients."

WHEN THEY MOVE IN

Help Them Move In

Hand them a flyer you've prepared that gives information on utilities, cleaning services, schools, and so on. Arrange to have any utilities connected that you can (some require the owner to sign) as of whatever date your buyers specify. Suggest that they consider your office their message center while they're en route.

Dinner on You the Night They Move In

This is remembered with special gratitude by wives too tired from unpacking to shop and cook, and by husbands who're a bit edgy about unexpected moving expenses. You'll save time and money—and make a better impression—by not inviting yourself to that dinner. Let them go by themselves and relax.

The free dinner is easily arranged by talking to the manager of a good restaurant, and perhaps making a cash deposit. One highly successful agent runs a tab for this purpose at a country club, and needs only to call and say, "Mr. and Mrs. Ed Tracy and their two children will be in for dinner tonight. Put the charges on my bill." Don't worry if your clients have the extra thick filet mignon just because you're paying; they will feed you referrals—a far richer diet for you than any restaurant will serve them.

Bring a House-warming Gift

A home-furnishings gift certificate, a class card to a local health exercise class if they are fitness people. How about a lush green house plant? Or maybe a pen-and-ink sketch of the home framed? Brainstorm gift ideas with fellow salespeople.

HOW TO GET LETTERS OF RECOMMENDATION

Ask. Do it softly. Wait until they're settled. And ask enthusiastic people, not those who see everything in two shades of gray. When you make your second follow-up call to see how they're getting along three weeks after they're in, if they say something along these lines: "I knew I liked this home before, but now I love it. My kids are on the swim team, and everything is really clicking."

That's the time for: "Can I ask you a favor? Would you mind writing a letter of recommendation, stating that I did a good job for you? Because I want to put it in my Listing Presentation Manual. And I'll keep a copy in my desk, so when I have a down day, I can read it, know that I helped somebody, somewhere, and feel good about myself again."

Ask for letters of recommendation; you'll get a hundred times as many as you would if you didn't ask.

GETTING REFERRALS

You have to ask for them too.

You have to tell people you're eager and able to handle more business. You might think that's always obvious to everyone, but you can so easily slip into appearing hassled, overworked, in desperate need of time off—just when you're in desperate need of a hot buyer more than anything else. Never let a client think for an instant that you're anything but thrilled with the real estate business. For clients and customers you are always up.

Referred customers are quicker to refer their friends to you than picked-up customers are, partly because referred clients often are the sort of people who habitually seek recommendations when faced with an important decision. Refer to the Winning Scripts at the end of this chapter for referral-breeding phrases to use with them.

With pickup clients and customers, there's even less reason to leave the referral idea to chance. Do it delicately, but plant the thought firmly in their brains that recommending you to their friends is something you need and want. Unless you take the initiative, it may never occur to them.

They may even like you so well that they won't refer you. Here's how that happens: Art and Cheryl are a charming young couple you pulled in from an ad call. They buy their first house from you, and they love it and you too. A few weeks later, they invite two friends of theirs, Joe and Scrappy Loudslap, over to see their new house. After a few more visits, the Loudslaps are very enthusiastic about your area, but when Art and Cheryl talk it over, they decide not to mention you to Joe and Scrappy. They feel that their friends are too crude for you, that they probably won't buy a house anyway, and that you're so busy you'll be annoyed with them for bothering you with Joe and Scrappy Loudslap. Fortunately, you run into Art and Cheryl and, as you're talking to them, you sense that something is on their minds. You draw them out and then give strong assurances that you'll be happy to take your chances with the Loudslaps. So Art and Cheryl put their friends in touch with you.

An experience like this convinced me that I had to be more direct about asking for referrals. (I sold a house to the couple I've called the Loudslaps in three days.

They were fun to work with.) It dawned on me that I'd been Shy Shelia when it came to telling people that I was working for, and dreaming about, referral business. So I started making a bigger thing of asking for referrals in a nice way, and I began getting a lot more of them.

"WE'VE MOVED" CARDS

My friend Marleen has ten of these notices typed up for each of her buyers after they've moved in. She drops them off a day or two after they arrive, before the newcomers have time to send their new address to their friends. These cards are complete, with the customers' name and new return address typed on the envelope. They're so convenient, they get used, and Marleen's personally endorsed advertisement goes out all over the country. Marleen tells me it's a real business-builder for her.

We are proud to announce we have recently moved to Huntington Beach. Our new address is:

98281 WORTHPORT DRIVE
HUNTINGTON BEACH, CA 92646

We would also like to mention our Realtor, Marleen Litzel, who helped make our move a pleasant one. If you're looking for a home in this area or think of selling your present home, give Marleen a call at _____. We're enclosing her card for your convenience, so be sure to mention us!

Our schedule is a little hectic right now as we're in the midst of boxes, but we're looking forward to seeing you soon,

STAY IN TOUCH

Stay in touch with your sellers who move away. They might move back. And, wherever they go, people around them will know where they came from, will tell them when someone is moving to their old home town, and in this way give them a chance to send you a referral.

With your buyers who stay, keep in touch. You can't go off into space (bury yourself in your office and your daily routine of working with new clients) and expect your old clients to remember you when they move three years later. If your old clients haven't heard from you, you won't even be fourth on their list.

Stay in touch means an annual gift plus a phone call, a visit, or a note every six months. Magnify your impact by varying your touch: sometimes phone, some-times visit, sometimes send a note.

And don't direct all your keep-in-touch toward just the wife or the husband. You can learn that the hard way, or you can take this tip from me, and save the fees you'll otherwise lose. I kept in touch with only the wife in several couples who'd bought from me because that was easier—and first learned they were moving when their houses appeared on the hot sheet as new listings.

I had slipped up on keeping in touch with the husbands because I thought I was solid with the wives; when it got down to the ''Honey, I'm sorry but'' stage, the locker-room referral won out. Never put all your eggs in one basket. A couple is two people (count 'em) and they both are important in the listing decision.

Remembrance Programs

Schedule time during each of two off seasons during the year to remember your entire clientele. And stick to your schedule, or your referral business will dwindle, not grow. Decide what your annual gift system will be: birthday, anniversary, Christmas, Mother's and Father's Day; or you can create your own gift day: Jive up January Day, September Surprise, whatever.

A note that says you're striking a blow against dull February, when enclosed with a gift, will have more impact than the same amount of money spent two months earlier at Christmas time. Do what turns you on, suits your personality, and fits your schedule. Stay within your budget—but think big. Careful planning will speed the day when you can maximize your impact, and doing that will maximize your income.

Don't overlook stopping by, and leaving the good old scratch pad that's extolled in Chapters 6 and 7. If no one answers your knock, write a note like this: ''Sure hope you like your home now as well as you did the day you moved in. Just thinking about you, Maria Hall.''

The important thing is to make those twice-yearly contacts every spring and fall, and deliver a unique special remembrance sometime during this year. Instead of the gift, some people follow a birthday and anniversary card program. I've never done that. But other agents have, with good results in building up the clientele. If you feel comfortable with that approach, do it.

Keep Clients and Customers Informed of Your Success

They love to hear about it! They really do. If you have done all the things we've talked about, all this detail work, all this follow-up, you're not an agent to your clients, you're a friend! They love you. You're part of the team they're rooting for. When your picture is in the paper, or they hear you're doing this or that, write them and say, ''Thanks. I couldn't have done this without you. I get by with a little help from my friends.''

INHALE NEW INFORMATION, EXHALE NEW BUSINESS

It pays well to keep current with local happenings by reading the local papers, but it pays off fabulously well to stay ahead of what's printed as news. The right proportion is: 2 percent read the local papers, 98 percent get out and see the people and the places, and do something about what you learn.

For example: Going to your office from an early morning meeting with a seller, you follow your usual practice of keeping your eyes open while you take a route that will lead you through areas you haven't been in for a few days. In a shopping center you see a merchant putting a "Going Out of Business Sale" banner in the window of his paint store. You have no intention of diluting your concentration on the home resale market, so you call a business opportunities broker you know, and tell him about the banner. Your biz op friend says "So Charlie Pealing has finally had enough. That guy just isn't the type to be in retail sales. I'll hustle right over and see him. He should sell the business, not close it. The right owner could make a bundle. Do you have an in with Charlie?"

"No. See if you can find out whether they're planning to sell their home and move out of town, will you?"

"Two days later, Biz Op calls you back. "I listed the paint store. And the Pealings are leaving town. The wife's name is Mabel. I'd go over and see her this afternoon, if I were you."

DROP ONE, PICK UP SEVEN

When I met Steve and Tina for our second appointment to look at property, Steve said, "I guess we wasted yesterday morning for you, Danny. We've decided that a view isn't so important after all. Everything else is still the same. Sorry to spring this on you without warning."

"That's no problem at all, Steve. Okay, I can think of—"

"You'll need some time to research a new bunch of houses, won't you?"

I shook my head. "Just give me a few minutes to phone our new group of sellers. And yesterday wasn't wasted, because now I know exactly the house for you."

Steve and Tina looked at each other a little oddly, so I went on quickly, "But there are three other really sharp homes I want you to look at also. While you finish your coffee, I'll let the owners know we're coming."

A few minutes later, we were on our way. "Want to see the house I think you'll like first, or shall I save that to the last?"

"Save the best for last," Tina said.

They went through my three comparison houses carefully. Today the emphasis was on finding reasons to eliminate each house; yesterday they had talked about how they could repaint the wall and change the carpet everywhere they went, I realized that they'd found something they really liked. Ideally, I would've worked with them all day, but I'd had to work Steve and Tina around another out-of-state couple who were in town, house hunting at the same time.

Driving toward the house I thought they'd really like, the tension felt like it would pop the doors of my car. At last we turned into a small cul-de-sac where only one house was for sale. "I knew it," Steve said. "Did I tell you, or didn't I, Tina?" Both of them jumped out of the car and hurried up the sidewalk toward the house I'd brought them to see. But not for the first time, obviously. Here I'd thought I was smart to hit on just what they wanted in two days—somebody else had done it in one afternoon! I forced a smile, let them inside, and watched while they dashed off in different directions. I stood there, knowing there wasn't anything I could do to sell them; somebody already had. I qualify all my customers before showing houses, so of course I knew they could afford the place or I wouldn't have brought them there; I also knew the house was priced right.

Steve and Tina finally put their heads together for a moment of quiet talk. Then they walked up to me, eyes shining. "This is it, Danny. Let's go back to the office and write it up."

The listing agent on that property was a well-known agent who closed a lot of buyers she picked up on open houses. She hadn't been able to close Steve and Tina though. Neither had I; they'd closed themselves—but, I thought, we all need some gravy now and then.

Driving back to the office, I named the listing agent. "I'm surprised she held that house open—it's tough to find. She likes to work the ones that are right off busy streets."

"It wasn't open yesterday," Steve said. "We floundered in there with a brand new agent. Look."

I glanced at the card he held out, and saw a woman's name written neatly on one of the local realty firm's cards. "She was working her very first open house somewhere around here."

"She might be brand new, but she was really sharp to take you to that house right off," I said.

"Pure dumb luck," Steve said. "She thought it had a view until we got there. We only went in to be nice, and then—whammo. Who wants an agent like that to represent them? Okay, if I lived out here and could stay on top of it—maybe."

"Except for her being new, did you like her okay?"

"Sure," Tina said. "But we've got to fly back home as soon as possible, and Steve doesn't think she can look out for our interests the way you will. After all, we'll be 2,000 miles away."

"Let her get some seasoning first," Steve said. "She doesn't even know her way around town."

"Oh, you just rattled the poor girl," Tina said. "When we walked into her open house, it was really sweet how excited she got. Hadn't seen anyone for three hours, and she was just closing up. So we just had to let her show us some other houses."

I remembered the feeling. You're so new it hurts, and you know it shows. You're scared of all the things you don't understand about the business, and you wait, and wait, and wait on those endless Open Houses before you learn how to use your time. You're praying that people will come because you need a transaction bad—and at the same time you're afraid to have anyone come because there's so much you don't know. I remembered—in an eye-moistening flash.

Tina had kept on talking, "We stayed at our house—Steve, I'm already calling it our house—until it got dark on us. So it took her a few minutes to find her way back to where we'd left our car, and old grump here—"

"I just told her she needed to learn the streets," Steve said.

"But by that time, she was quivering from head to toe," Tina said. "She figured she had made her first sale."

"Because she'd had some dumb luck," Steve said, "I don't see that we owe her anything. In fact, we gave her some badly needed experience—free."

We were back at my office by that time. Thinking about that new agent, I led the way inside. It's no fun to be quivering hungry for a sale. I've been there and I know. But that was past for me; by that time I had three very good years behind me.

"Steve, Tina—it'll break that gal's heart if you buy through me the house she found for you. We can work this out so you're protected. I know her broker and he's good. I'll call him right now and get his word that he'll stay on top of this transaction all the way through, so there's no way you'll have problems with her inexperience."

"Danny, you took us there today anyway. What did she really do for us?"

"Steve, she took you there first. Now she's pacing the floor, wondering what happened, sweating out the phone, jumping every time it rings thinking it's you or Tina wanting to make an offer. Please go through her. Let's all feel good about that great house you've found."

That's the one I dropped. I'm no Pollyanna: had I been struggling, I never would've done it. But I had money in the bank and a success pattern established; I didn't need to step on heads. So I called her broker, explained the situation, and of course he agreed to watch the transaction. The customers were pleased with how it went.

The seven I picked up came about because that office sold nine of my listings the following year, compared with only two the year before.

WINNING SCRIPTS

When you've wrapped up a sale for referred customers, it's quite easy and natural for you to say, "Martin and Georgia, can I tell Jack and Helen that you're satisfied with my service?"

"You certainly can," Martin says. "In fact, I'll call Jack myself and tell him what a great job you did for us."

(If Martin calls Jack, so much the better, but don't depend on it. Call Jack and

Helen later and thank them yourself.) Now you tell Martin, "I'd appreciate it so much if you would call Jack. You know, people feel responsible when they recommend someone, and that's just one reason why I go all out to justify the confidence they had in me. I depend completely on referrals from satisfied clients—from *very pleased* clients, I hope—and I really like it this way because it's so much nicer to work with people who've been referred. I can do so much better of a job for people when there's that feeling of mutual confidence from the start. Martin and Georgia, don't you think we had mutual confidence right from the beginning?"

"We did. We certainly did," Martin says. "We saw everything we needed to see, didn't waste time,and we bought right—I feel good about the whole thing."

"Wonderful. I can't tell you how pleased I am to hear you say that. Would it be asking too much if I'd say I hope you'll recommend me to your family and friends if the opportunity arises?"

"Oh, we certainly will," Georgia says.

"You wouldn't happen to know of anyone who's thinking of a real estate move now, would you?"

Martin shakes his head. "No, 'fraid not. You know, we hate to rush off, but—"

"Martin," Georgia says, "What about the Hensons?"

"Oh, that's right," Martin says. "Funny I'd forgotten about them—must be all the excitement. Now that we're moving down here, I think the Hensons might too. They've talked about it for a couple of years, but they didn't want to go where they didn't know anybody. I'll give you his phone number—you should call him."

Even if you don't sell them, ask for referrals. Sometimes you'll show property to people for three or four days, and they think you're great, but they buy in an area outside your working range. When they call to drop the bad news, why not say, "I'm really glad you found what you wanted. I really am."

"Well, we just wish we could've bought it through you."

"Do you feel I did a good job showing you this area?"

"I sure do."

"Can I drop you a couple of my business cards in the mail? Would you mind referring people to me who might be moving down to this area?"

If you're this tight with them, they'll always tell you they'll be happy to. And this works—I've sold several people who were referred to me by people who had bought elsewhere.

TIME PLANNING

• How to Plan Your Day • Setting Priorities • Use A Pencil • Use Checklists • How to Close Rings • Controlling the Phone Monster • Interruptions • Time Log Yourself • Schedule Your Days, Weeks, and Seasons • Jugging Personal and Professional Time • Communicating Right the First Time • Watch for Danger Signs in Communicating • The $8 Million Listener • Set Aside Some Alone Time • When Depression Starts Eating Up the Clock

Time—Have You Got Enough?

When it comes right down to it, there are only two things life can offer us: time and each other. The 86,400 seconds in each day are all we'll ever have. Time is like no other concept—it is life itself. Because its importance to us all cannot be exaggerated, I want to devote a chapter to the effective use of time, both personal and professional.

Systems that help you "Do the most productive thing possible at every given moment" are great. As a matter of fact, I will suggest a few effective systems here. But the biggest problem people face with time isn't *time* management—it's *self-*management. You and I can control everything that happens in our immediate universe, but we can't be effective if we're nonselective. Getting control of your life means letting go in the areas where you are ineffective, and taking control in the areas where your time is well spent. It means that you make, and carry out, basic decisions about how you'll invest your most precious, irreplaceable, and nonrenewable asset: time.

We lose control (lose the ability to exercise our authority and manipulate our talents to further our growth) in areas in our life that we have closed to positive change. All too often, we close off areas of our life from positive change because we allow the small emergencies of the moment, instead of our own carefully thought-out plan, to control our lives.

Closing off areas of our life from positive change means that we have ceased to grow in those areas. Since we cannot remain constant, when we stop growing in an area, we start decaying there. Life is a series of growth or decay rings, built one on the other. We open a new growing ring by choice, compulsion, or chance. Then we nurture it with care, action, and energy—or we allow it to wither. And finally, either soon or late, we close the ring. Call it change, call it growth, call it getting older, life is a series of rings. Each ring has an opening, an effective period, and a close. Each ring of your life is either a growing ring—or a decay ring.

Learn to think in terms of change. Be aware that everything is growing or decaying: our love, our skills, our friendships, our spirit, our fortune, our health, and our surroundings. But don't hate or fear decay; it's the natural process that provides us with nutrients for future growth rings.

What you think in terms of change, you can see more clearly how you are making choices—or are letting circumstances make them for you. Make choices after weighing your conflicting opportunities instead of letting things happen to you. Before we can be effective, we must plug our minds into now; this day, this hour, this minute, this second. Plug into now. Some people should carry a tape player around that endlessly repeats "Plug into now, plug into now, plug into now." Living in yesterday or yesteryear, regretting what was, or wasn't, said or done five minutes or years ago, is living a decay ring. Living in the now, while preparing wisely for the future, is a growth ring; living in the future is a decay ring because, for the people who live in it, the future can never arrive—except as a shattering blow.

How can you plan your time in a business that demands that you be at the beck and call of buyers and sellers?

Recognize that it isn't easy. Then go on from there. Of course any time plan you set up will be interrupted—frequently, you hope—by the urgent demands of your clients and customers. That means business and business means fees. If people interrupt your schedule, make them pay for the privilege—don't begrudge them.

Recognize that you'll frequently have to decide whether to abandon a planned day because of something that just came up, or refuse to change your game plan. Rehearse how to say no politely. Always be ready to say, "I can't make it today, but do you have any free time tomorrow?" And, as often as possible, make your nonbusiness appointments tentative so that you can jump on a fast-breaking opportunity.

"I'll do it later when I have the time," is an illusion you can't afford. You'll never have more time. Unless you retire to Mars, you're never going to have more than 24 hours between now and this same minute tomorrow. The largest step you can take toward packing your hours with action, success, and fun is to recognize that using time productively is the most valuable skill you can have. With it, anything physically possible can be achieved. Without it, very little of your potential will be used, and you'll achieve only a fraction of the success you're capable of.

HOW TO PLAN YOUR DAY

Do it the night before. Always. Every night.

To begin with, allow 15 minutes each night for this vital element of your personal growth, income, and time control system. You'll soon learn to do a thorough job of planning each of your tomorrows in 5 minutes or less.

Three Actual Time Plans

Here are daily time plans prepared by three successful real estaters. Note how much easier the veteran's time plan is. He's paid the price for a 100 percent referral business, so now he's enjoying a high degree of control over his time along with a high income.

FEBRUARY						
S	M	T	W	T	F	S
				1	2	3	4
5	6	7	8	9	10	11
12	13	14	15	16	17	18
19	20	21	22	23	24	25
26	27	28				

MARCH						
S	M	T	W	T	F	S
				1	2	3	4
5	6	7	8	9	10	11
12	13	14	15	16	17	18
19	20	21	22	23	24	25
26	27	28	29	30	31	

APRIL						
S	M	T	W	T	F	S
						1
2	3	4	5	6	7	8
9	10	11	12	13	14	15
16	17	18	19	20	21	22
23	24	25	26	27	28	29
30						

Monday March 13

8	Pick up kids at Jr. High **3**
Floor time	Basketball game (Jeff,
9 Return messages	Sue, Jamie) **4**
Organize what to show, check if available, set **10** appointments to preview.	Prepare dinner **5**
11 Organize newsletter, ad or flyer	**6**
12 Preview properties	Go over listing presentation, **7**
Printer--newspaper appt.	comps, etc.
1 Calls to customers, escrow prospects.	Listing presentation **8**
2 Children home--call	**9**

NOTES:

Married woman   3 million volume
4 children
2 years in real estate

FEBRUARY	MARCH	APRIL
S M T W T F S	S M T W T F S	S M T W T F S
1 2 3 4	1 2 3 4	1
5 6 7 8 9 10 11	5 6 7 8 9 10 11	2 3 4 5 6 7 8
12 13 14 15 16 17 18	12 13 14 15 16 17 18	9 10 11 12 13 14 15
19 20 21 22 23 24 25	19 20 21 22 23 24 25	16 17 18 19 20 21 22
26 27 28	26 27 28 29 30 31	23 24 25 26 27 28 29
		30

Thursday March 16

8		Door knocking (15)	**3**
	Check Multiple Listing book,	FSBO appt.	
9	hot sheets, expired in office		**4**
		Expired appt.	
10	Printing pick up		**5**
11		Cold calls	**6**
	Floor duty		
12	No lunch today--Do mail--outs		**7**
		Appt. expired listing	
1	Preview property		**8**
2	Post office run		**9**

NOTES:

Single guy   2 million volume
31 years old
3 weeks--no days off
3 days--goes & hides
2nd year in real estate

Make planning tomorrow an integral part of your getting-ready-for-bed routine. Follow the same steps each night and you'll find your planning going faster, and nothing will slip past you. Here's my step-by-step system for tomorrow-planning:

- First, I review my monthly and weekly pages for all the items I've accumulated there over the past weeks that must be done tomorrow.

- Then I list them on the daily work plan, along with the new things that pop into my mind at this time.

- Next, I give my short and long-term goals a fast mental run-through, and then set activity targets (how many doors to knock on, or how many fizzbos to see, for example) that'll enable me to reach my goals.

FEBRUARY						
S	**M**	**T**	**W**	**T**	**F**	**S**
			1	2	3	4
5	6	7	8	9	10	11
12	13	14	15	16	17	18
19	20	21	22	23	24	25
26	27	28				

MARCH						
S	**M**	**T**	**W**	**T**	**F**	**S**
			1	2	3	4
5	6	7	8	9	10	11
12	13	14	15	16	17	18
19	20	21	22	23	24	25
26	27	28	29	30	31	

APRIL						
S	**M**	**T**	**W**	**T**	**F**	**S**
						1
2	3	4	5	6	7	8
9	10	11	12	13	14	15
16	17	18	19	20	21	22
23	24	25	26	27	28	29
30						

Monday March 20

8		Constant follow-up on	**3**
	Exercise program & tennis	leads	
9			**4**
10	Office to service transactions		**5**
11		Dinner	**6**
12	Lunch with old client	Phone canvassing	**7**
1	Showings	Listing presentation	**8**
2			**9**

NOTES:

Single guy
4 million dollar volume last
3 years
6 years in business

- Finally, I highlight the must-be-done details that have a way of turning into monsters if not handled when they should be handled.

That's all there is to it. When I first stated doing this, it was a hard quarter-hour's work, but the results on those first tomorrows were so great that I've never stopped planning my days this way. After a week or two, I was getting my planning done in two or three minutes a night, and I often felt I'd saved two or three hours a day because I was organized. That adds up fast—as extra listings taken, and more houses sold.

Planning tomorrow every night lets you sleep better. When I first got into real estate, I didn't do this for months. I'd toss and turn in the middle of the night, wondering what time I had to be where the next day, and how I'd get the loan documents delivered before ten o'clock so the loan would fund that day. I was doing my planning the hard way—with my conscious mind in gear instead of asleep. Then I discovered that the subconscious mind works on your problems in the middle of the night if you'll commit them to writing. Then your conscious mind rests, and the subconscious takes over and does its job. You wake up and the solution to many of your problems is as plain as the new day's sun.

But, this is important, the next morning when you wake up, do present-time exercises—DON'T READ THE TIME PLAN. Wait until your morning routine is out of the way and you've reached your work area. Then open the planner. By doing that, you open the first of the day's growth rings. Check off each item you complete; each one is a win you should feel good about. It's so nice to see lots of boxes checked off at the end of the day, knowing full well that you've done all you could.

How to Make Things to Do Pop into Your Mind at Planning-Tomorrow Time

As you run across things through the day that will go on tomorrow's time plan, jot them down. Or record them verbally on a cassette recorder that you carry with you (the slim pocket kind is great). That night, when planning tomorrow, play it back.

Fill out your tomorrow's plan in a quiet place where you can do it alone—go in the bathroom and lock the door if necessary. Take a moment to relax, and free your mind of hassle. Then jot down your things to do as fast as your memory pours them to you. Don't slow down the process by assigning priorities. Do that tomorrow morning.

What a thrill it is—what a tremendous feeling of power it gives you—when this system is working reliably for you.

The New Day's Growth Rings

Every night before planning a new day, check your today's plan for growth rings you haven't closed that day. Make a decision on each one. Carry the project forward to tomorrow, plug it into a later date, or abandon it.

I always plan both my personal and professional time together. Keeping your promise to a child that you will attend a 3:00 basketball game is just as important as keeping a 6:30 listing appointment. Any type of agreement should be honored, both at home and in business. Of course, if this is to work, you can't make more agreements than you have time to honor. The solution is simple: Set priorities, and learn how to say no.

Present Time

Get into present time when you wake up in the morning. Maybe we had a bad dream. Maybe our fears about a sale falling out made us sleep fitfully. Maybe we just have a lonely feeling in the pit of our stomach. So, first, we must concentrate on the now, the present. Work out your own routine for getting into present time and putting dead yesterday away. Here are the exercises that put me into present time in the morning:

Sitting on the edge of the bed, let your feet rub the rug. Feel its texture. Look out the window at something outside you like. Look at something in your room you like. Turn on music. Stretch. Reach for the ceiling. Touch your body, your shoulders, your nose. Touch three walls in your room fast. Pick up a perfume bottle or vase. Feel the shape.

Do sit ups to music. Touch your toes repeatedly. Make up a creative dance. Sing in the shower. Buy a water massage. Enjoy it in your early morning shower. Go out and jog. (If you're not in shape, start walking.)

Pick up a book and read a familiar happy passage. Do all this fast. The goal is to get into present time quickly, to feel good about yourself, to feel aware of now.

Now commit your day to a greater force than yourself, to the Supreme Being if you believe. Say something like this: "Please help me be all that I can be today. Help me play my part in the creation of a better world. Help me concentrate on just today, so that at the end of this day, I'll know that I did all I could do, as fairly, wisely, and effectively as I could."

SETTING PRIORITIES

List everything to be accomplished the following day, both personal and professional, but don't put a priority on them until the next morning. Then, when you arrive in the work area the following morning, use A B Cs to set priorities.

A showing appointment and a child's dental appointment are both *A* priorities. So the following morning write *A* beside all these appointments on the time plan. A *B* priority might be something like making a bank deposit, and grocery shopping. A *C* priority in the middle of October might be "start your Christmas list" today. You could do it a week or two later, but if time permits, today is the day!

Apply priority setting to clients and open houses also. For example, you've listed a vacant house. It's Tuesday. You get a note from a couple in New Jersey you've been corresponding with. They are arriving in California this weekend, but they don't say when you'll hear from them. Plan an open house at your vacant listing as a *B* priority, and make showing property to the people from New Jersey an *A* priority if they show up. That's what's nice about priorities. It gives you options. And in our business the more options we have, the better our careers will go.

You also need to set priorities at home. If you plan on setting your farm on fire this month to build up a big listing bank, then everything on your time plan for this month should reflect that goal. Don't create conflict by telling the family that you intend to see a lot of them this month when the farm and listing bank is foremost on your mind. If you set career priorities this month, set some personal priorities with the spouse and the kids for next month. Balance is the key to an effective juggling act between personal and business demands.

USE A PENCIL

Use a pencil when time planning. Let's face it, we must be flexible in real estate. The best laid plans of mice and men are flushed down the drain in real estate. You start on expired listings, intending to work on them all day, but a hot buyer pops in off the street. Naturally, you go for the buyer. With no trouble, you erase your original time plan, and plug the expired listing routine into another day. If your schedule is in ink, you feel guilty.

USE CHECKLISTS

The greatest way to keep control of the changing patterns of our business is to use checklists. People ask me how I kept on top of 20 to 30 transactions a month as a salesperson. I had checklists inside every folder, and I used a communication log for each transaction to record every conversation, phone or in person, relating to that transaction. When you call the lender, and they tell you that the loan on one of your transactions has been approved, record that information in writing, along with the day, time, and name of whoever gave it to you. You also write down when you called the customers to inform them of the good news. Also, when you and another agent are arguing about who is supposed to order the termite reports two minutes before the closing, you can refer to the entry in your communication log dated two weeks ago that stated he promised to order it that day. These communications logs are powerful allies in court, should that ever be necessary.

Since the form has the names at the top, you will need at least one form for each transaction you're working on. In order to keep the forms organized, you might want to keep them in a loose leaf binder, alphabetized by client name, then keep the binder handy to the phone. When the sheet is filled, it can go into the client folder and a blank one with the client's name can be added to the binder.

Checklists that make for smoother cruising when you're servicing listings, holding houses open, and pulling up-time are all gathered together in Chapter 24. You'll find step-by-step checklists there to help you keep on top of things in a variety of real estate situations. A sample of the communication log also appears in this chapter.

Imagine yourself with a listing that just sold, a sale that was made two weeks ago on which the VA appraiser is due out any day, another transaction about to close that needs loan documents signed and a cashier's check. How do you manage all these things without feeling overwhelmed? It's easy—if you've been working systematically. You simply pick up each folder and, by reviewing the checklists, you know exactly what the status is of each. But, don't forget, all this servicing must not take up the major portion of your time. To maintain volume, your main effort must still be directed at contacting new business. You have open houses to set up, and fizzbos to call on. How do you know what invitations you have sent out, what owners you are working with that need to be followed up, and so on? Right. You have checklists on each of these programs, and cards filled on each of these people. By pulling the card from your file, you can tell the status and progress of each situation.

HOW TO CLOSE RINGS

One of the biggest problems real estate people have is not being able to finish phone conversations, meetings, and projects. Many things started, nothing finished. So what happens? Confusion and guilt runs wild, as it always does when people fail to complete what they've started. They get nervous and ineffective. Notice how it works in a real estate office. The salesperson comes in, first thing in the morning, with the best of intentions. Perhaps he's started his growth rings for the day properly: The night before he wrote his plan, and he walked into the office ready to go—20 open house invitations he's going to write the first thing this A.M. After his floor time, he's going to brown bag it for lunch, and then rap knuckles on three blocks' worth of doors. But what happens? He never closes any of these rings. He starts. But visitors, phones, and donuts get in the way. Paperwork that should've been done three weeks ago now is urgent, and must be done *A* priority, and suddenly the day is done but the work is not.

Here's how to handle paper and people interruptions in your day:

CONTROLLING THE PHONE MONSTER

The phone is strictly a message machine. It's not a living, breathing organism that attacks our day and make us its slave. There was a time when the phone controlled me. I would be eating dinner, talking to my family, and giving them some badly needed time, when the phone would ring. My goodness, it might be the big deal of the year. It might be Ford. It might be Chevrolet. It might be Rockefeller. So, like Pavlov's dog salivating on signal, when the phone rang I'd pick up the receiver ready to do anything it told me to do. Now, granted, this instrument is a big item in the life of a real estate agent, especially the real estate agent who needs to connect with any possible house buying or selling creature, but there are times when this instrument must be excluded from your life. You just have to ignore it. Let it ring or buy an answering machine to record messages.

Do You Prolong Conversations?

Someone says, "I'll see you Saturday night," and you immediately introduce a new matter into the conversation. "Oh, did I tell you, my brother bought a new house?" We do this subconsciously. Studies prove that we do it because we hate endings— even phone conversation endings—it's the old fear of finality. Train yourself not to introduce new topics into old phone conversations. If the other party tries it on you, say something like "Oh, tell me all about when I see you on Saturday, I've just *got* to run now."

Do You Always Have to End Up on Top?

Some agents are so competitive that they fight to win even when nothing worth winning is involved. It happens like this: You call in to report a sale, just as excited as can be. You've been with these customers for two days straight, so you haven't had a lot of time to service your transactions. Last night you were at it almost until midnight calling back on messages. After all, these out-of-staters have to be given first priority. So you call in to ask the up-person to write your sale on the board. Whoopee.

    Instead of congratulations, the up-person lectures you for not returning Mrs. Brown's calls about a termite inspection that isn't needed for 30 days. "She called back twice, and boy, is she mad." You spend the next 10 minutes trying to come out on top by making the up-person admit you're right about your priorities. But the up-person wants to come out on top too and won't admit anything. It's all so useless. Be alert for no-win conversations, and chop them off with quick "Sorry about that, bye." Quit playing games with the precious minutes of your life. Hang up, not on.

Open Your Phone Conversations Closer to Their End

You'll save chunks of time by getting right to it. Let's take this situation: You need some information about a listing from an agent you know.

    Here's how the slow-and-open phone start goes:

    "Hi, Ed. This is Danny. How's it going?" Wasn't that friendly and polite? Unfortunately, Ed doesn't know it's not nice to tell people you're anything but "fine." So he says, "Not too good, Danny. I was talking to a fellow in the parking lot yesterday and a beer truck swung wide and ran over my big toe."

    "Ed, that's terrible." The appraiser, who is standing at your elbow waiting for Ed's information, shifts his weight impatiently. "Listen, Ed, I'm terribly sorry but—"

    "Thanks, I appreciate your sympathy. I really do. You know what else happened to me this week? You won't believe this, but—"

    Let's try the quick and closed phone start on Ed's big toe (all in one breath): "Hi Ed I was wondering if the sale of your listing at 2436 Poplar has settled yet?"

"Settled yesterday, Danny. Say, did you hear what happened to me?"

"Ed, the appraiser is standing here waiting—I'll talk to you at the board breakfast—Thanks, bye."

When you have calls by the score to make, as every agent handling several transactions at a time does, you have to press to keep those calls from eating up your get-new business time. Better start practicing that art now.

Some Other Ways to End a Phone Conversation

"I sure look forward to seeing you on Tuesday." (That was the purpose of the call) "Bye."

"I sure appreciate all your information. That's all I want today, but I'll call you again when I need further help."

"My doorbell's ringing."

"I have a commitment—sorry, but I must run."

(You do have a commitment—with yourself. Be careful. Don't allow yourself to be the most neglected friend you have.) Commitment covers a multitude of sins. Use it freely.

Use a Time-efficient Call-back System

Return messages right before quitting time or lunch. People who're thinking about going to lunch don't want to keep on jabbering.

INTERRUPTIONS

Controlling Drop-ins

See your friends on a regular basis, and really work on the friendship. Then no one will drop in on you quite as easily and say, "Where have you been?"

If you're in the back office doing something important, set up a fellow salesperson to help you out when a drop-in visitor stops in to eat up your time. Prime them to say to the visitor (usually the other salespeople know who the pest is), "Would you like me to interrupt him?" That usually wakes them up to the reality that yes, you are busy right now. If you are interrupted, stay on your feet—and fidget. Keep looking back at your desk. Or else put limit on it by saying "I am right in the middle of preparing a Guidelines to Market Value for a seller, so I only have about 10 minutes right now" or "I have a commitment." (It could be with yourself.)

Coffee

Many agents have a $50-a-day coffee habit. "Gosh, I need a cup of java. Gosh, it's too hot. Gosh, it's too cold. I better fix another cup. I just can't get started without a cup of coffee."

If they worked the time they spend drinking coffee, they'd close another transaction a month. Then, of course, we must have the donuts with the coffee. How about rewarding yourself with one coffee break a day—if you're on target with your goals. But put a time limit on it. Remember that every time you break your concentration to drink coffee when you're in the middle of a project, you stop that growth ring. Even if nothing prevents your reopening that ring again after your coffee break, it still takes a certain amount of energy to regain the momentum you've lost.

Lovely Long Lunches

Lovely long lunches slay time. Oh, what fun. What violence to your production and energy level for the entire afternoon. What you'd spend on daily long lunches will finance a terrific referral-business builder of the sort staged each month by a broker friend of mine in El Paso, Texas. She hosts lunch and welcome get-togethers for her recent buyers and past clients. Everyone meets one another, and this gives her a priceless opportunity to follow up with clients and customers in a social situation. It's a profitable idea that's lots of fun.

Paper Interruptions

What does your desk look like? A time trap? Do you regularly spend a few calm seconds filing papers where you can go right to them, or do you regularly spend frantic minutes searching through the rubble for papers you must have? If you're a paper junkie, take the clutter cures in the next chapter.

TIME-LOG YOURSELF

Unrealistic time plans are worse than useless. Instead of efficiency, they deliver frustration. The way to connect yourself with reality on time planning is to log a 48-hour stretch of your activities. Record the hours and minutes you spend sleeping, eating, dressing, lunching, shopping; taking care of the car, yard, home; commuting and recreation; paying attention to details, and talking on the phone.

But first, time-plan the 48 hours you're going to log. Then, after you've logged the real time spent on your cycles of action for two days, compare how much time you estimated for each activity and how much time you actually spent doing it.

The data you gather this way will guide you to creating realistic time plans that will expand your efficiency.

SCHEDULE YOUR DAYS, WEEKS, AND SEASONS

There's a best time to do everything. When your timing's right, your efforts go further. Good timing multiplies your effectiveness by a factor of ten.

Here are the best times of the day, week, and year for working:

For Sale by Owners

5:30 Sunday night.

September through December the market slows up for everyone. Fizzbos need extra help. Take an especially long listing—through March, if possible.

Send fizzbos a note of encouragement timed to arrive on Saturday: "Hope the weekend is going well for you. I might stop by Sunday after my last showing to give you an update on general market activity in the area for the weekend."

Your Farm

3:00 to 6:00 on Friday afternoons.

10:00 A.M. and 12:00 noon Saturday mornings.

Double your prospecting schedule between September and December. You'll get few signatures on listings. Instead, you'll create opportunities for follow-up that you'll convert into listing agreements from January through March.

Cold Calls

Any day between 7 and 8:30 P.M. (Don't worry about calling on Saturdays or Sundays. Most people will think you're hard working.

September to December: Do lots of phoning and prospecting so you'll have many things to solidify after the first of the year.

Listing Presentations

Intensify your efforts in this area September through December. Many of these presentations will be for later follow-up. "We want to wait until after the holidays," is a common refrain. Be sure to send these new prospects Christmas cards, and January letters with predictions about next year's market. A good time for appointments with both spouses is 7 to 8:30 P.M., nightly or weekends. January through June are big months for new listings. Make sure of your share of those listings by laying heavy groundwork to get them during the final third of the year.

Showings

Intense activity from March through August. It starts building, depending on climate conditions, between January and March. Plan to keep days free to show quite a bit. Many companies transfer right after the first of the year. Do errands and follow-up listings at night and early mornings; leave 10 A.M. to 6 P.M. free to show property.

Expired Listings

Work them the day of the week that your Multiple Listing book is published. Early A.M. phone calls. Your comment might be something like this: "I noticed that your home was removed from the multiple. Are congratulations in order?" (no pause) "Has it sold?" *Wait* for their reply.

"Oh, that's a shame—I remember thinking how lovely your paneled den is with the Norman Rockwell paintings on it." They're delighted when you remember things like that. It certainly helps you get your foot in he door. But you'll need to have your Quick-Speak down pat.

To Heal Wounds

You'll have disappointments. Unless you're physically exhausted, schedule the next day for office catch-up. Make sure you don't spend the time dumping on your associates. Time-plan a heavy day of specific goals. Then hit the office door early and tear into those projects. Double check your transaction files. Catch up on all reports. Organize some new sales and listing aids. Clean out your desk. Answer correspondence. Send notes to people you think about on a hunch. Sit at that desk for the time-planned number of hours and pound out all the dirty work. All day long, cross off like crazy on the detailed list of Things to Do you prepared the night before. At the end of that day, you'll have a great sense of accomplishment because you've done a lot of thinks you dislike. That relieves guilt and releases energy. The following day, you'll want to get out amongst them again.

Schedule One Service Day a Week
to Tie Strings Together

Spend a full morning each week (preferably Monday or Friday) working on transactions already opened. Call lenders and check on status of all loans and funding. Make sure the client and customer has delivered or sent everything necessary. Prepare comparables for appraisers. Check on inspection reports, patio permits, and the like. If the buyer needs to secure a projection of future earnings from his company in order to qualify, is it now ready to be picked up? Check present listings still unsold. Call owners and give them a pep talk. Call agents who have shown your listings and communicate the feedback to the seller.

JUGGLING PERSONAL AND PROFESSIONAL TIME

Get Help if You Need It

This item is written especially to my ladies (but show it to your husbands).

How can you possibly clean house, wash clothes, cook, care for children (a full-time job in itself) and knock on doors, show property, have listing appointments and still sleep nights? You are not Houdini. For a long time, I thought I was, and tried to prove it to my family and neighbors. "I'll show them. I can do it all without help. If anyone sees a cleaning crew coming to my house, they'll think I can't handle the pressure. And, God knows, I don't want them to think I'm neglecting my children." After three years of doing laundry at 2 A.M., and generally not enjoying life or the money I'd had the good fortune to make, I decided to employ a full-time helper.

At first the family didn't think they would like having someone "hang around." But, after much discussion, we all decided that having clean socks in the morning and a Mom who could sit down five minutes out of the day would far surpass any loss of privacy we might experience.

Finding the right person took some doing. We ran through a few until the right lady came along. I don't need help now. I just have a once-a-week cleaning service. But things change as kids grow up. It takes time, patience, good recommendations, and perseverance, but good help is out there if you need it.

Here are some tips. If you live near a retirement community, there are a lot of able-bodied and capable people over there who are lovely, and need people to care about. Run an ad in their local paper and say something like, "We have an active, happy home with two children and two working parents who need domestic assistance. We like people, and will enjoy the company and aid of another member of our team." Run an ad in the local junior college or university's paper. Get to know some of the counselors (try the high schools, too) and tell them about yourself. Maybe they can match you up with a kid who will blend well with you and your family's personality. Try the employment agencies, or run an ad in several newspapers. A dear friend of mine, who is raising his children on his own, did that. He got the cream of the crop!—a couple in their fifties who love kids and do cleaning, cooking, grocery shopping—the works.

But never forget that you are the parent. Help should provide you with more quality time with your family. In the summer, go to the office at the crack of dawn, after telling the children that at 1 P.M. you'll toot the horn out front and everyone can jump in the car for the beach. Then you have the rest of the day to enjoy your family, without having to worry about dishes, clothes, and food because you have capable people doing it. Having reliable help should be one of your first goals as you progress up the real estate ladder.

Establish Family Goals

Goals are great. Cut out a picture of a Cadillac, put it on your desk, and tell yourself: "If I make x amount of dollars next month, I'll buy this one for me." That's neat. But after that, how about asking a travel agent for a ski poster from Aspen or Snowbird? Tack it up on your 9-year-old's bedroom wall and say, "If I achieve this number of listings, we're all going skiing next month." Watch how those kids will keep you posted on happenings that can help your career. Including them in the family's goals makes the youngsters accept your being away much better.

Spouses

You must make it up to her or him frequently by saying, "Okay, tonight is our night," and you don't let the phone, clients, or kids interrupt. Wives or husbands who've constantly put up with no time or attention from a spouse, due to that person's compulsive work habits, won't be around when the spouse finally makes it and has time. Sometimes that takes 20 years. Even though the couple may not be physically separated, emotionally they have abandoned one another long before.

Sometimes the Family Has to Wait

Keep that in mind. If you have out-of-state customers and they need to find a house in three days, you and I know that you'll be with them early, and until well into the night. This is when I say to the gang, "Okay, this next couple of days, make your lunches the night before, get up in time for school, and generally help keep the place straightened up, because Mom is helping some people find a home in our area."

Sometimes the Business Has to Wait

Of course, that's for a school play, Little League game, a parent-teacher conference, or maybe just a lost child who needs your attention. Often a misbehaving child is a discouraged child who simply needs some good communication with Mom or Dad.

Do the Things You Hate Most
Earliest in the Morning

That might be making a casserole for dinner, answering phone messages, writing follow-up notes, picking up keys and lock boxes—or dropping bad news on someone. Do the things you hate first. Then you have a free mind for the rest of the day. Then you can concentrate on really important things like facing clients and giving them 100 percent of your attention.

COMMUNICATING RIGHT THE FIRST TIME

Communicating right the first time saves a wonderful amount of time. Good communication means taking an idea and putting it into clear and concise words, delivering it to a receiving point (hopefully, a listening ear) and then receiving acknowledgement from the mouth of the receiver that he got it okay. Breakdowns in communication occur when people don't listen properly, and can't duplicate exactly what the message was. Then the misinformation spreads.

Here's a case: The listing agent is telling people, when there's trouble in Unsettled City, that Mary, who represents the buyer, said the escrow officer would order the termite report. Mary didn't write down in a communication log form (stapled to the inside of the transaction folder) what she told the other agent, so no one believes that she ever said that. What she actually said was, "You're the listing agent, so please order the bug report, and tell the escrow officer that you've done so." But the message didn't get through because (1) Mary yelled at another agent to take a message from the guy holding on the other line for her; (2) Mary had a donut in her mouth; (3) the listing agent wasn't listening at first because he was watching a pretty redhead walk by his real estate office. Then, when hearing Mary bite into the donut made him hungry, he put down the phone while she was talking, and walked over to the candy box for a chocolate drop. This is communication? Yes, it goes on every day in real estate offices across the country. And the funds of our buyers and sellers are at stake. Please follow these simple rules during communication, and no one will be able to believe the way you handle 20 transactions at once without getting rattled.

Use a Communication Log

There's a sample form in Chapter 24. Record all phone conversations pertaining to a transaction on this log. Make a new entry in the communication log for every phone conversation with the client, lender, escrow officer, attorney, mother-in-law, or whoever. You don't have to quote verbatim, but give the sense of the conversation. Write something like, "12-12: Talked to Sunny Westbrook of American Savings. Appraisal ordered, bank verifications returned, buyer loan application filled out and back, expect to go to loan committee on the 6th of next month." Record the length of conversation.

Be Single Minded

Concentrate on the person you're with, the project you're doing, the day and hour you're living. Push everything else out of your mind. Tell yourself, and other people, "I'll handle that later."

Do this especially when you're with clients or customers. Make them feel that there isn't another living soul on earth, and that you have nothing but time for them. I used to say to my hot prospects, "You are my most important concern right now, so don't worry about me being busy with anyone else." How they love that. It sure beats the salesperson who thinks he can catch every fish in the sea. "Well, I have until three o'clock and then I have to pick someone up at the Holiday Inn." How would you feel?

Acknowledge the Message

When someone calls you, sends you something, writes you a note, or just says hello, please acknowledge that message. Say thank you, say yes, say anything, but let that person know you received. Everyone wants to know where they stand, whether the beautiful pass they threw 30 yards downfield was received and carried for a touchdown—or fumbled. And, when you send or speak important messages, follow up until you get acknowledgement, and know you've completed your communication.

With Loved Ones

Communication is also important to your loved ones at home. Have you ever heard this said? "Home is where you go when you're tired of being nice to people." Now that is a sad thought that can come true for any of us. Oftentimes the phone's ringing when we walk in. The house is a mess. "Get this place cleaned up," we scream and yell as we walk to the phone. Then we pick up the phone and say in our *wonderful-me* voice, "Hello there, can I help you?" And when we hang up, it's scream time again.

WATCH FOR DANGER SIGNS IN COMMUNICATING

Blame Sentences

Do you use them?
> "They are to blame."
> "She made me feel bad."
> "He made me late for the appointment."
> "She didn't do what she was supposed to do."

Do You Ask Intimidating Questions?

Spouses despise this. "What did you do all day? God, how I hate that one.

> "Oh, nothing. I just sold six houses, washed four floors, changed 26 diapers, swore 16 times, stubbed my toe 13 times, and had one affair with Carlo Ponti during the TV program, *As the Bubble Bursts*."

Do you answer direct questions by making excuses? Questions from broker, "Did you go farming today?"

> "Oh, boy, have I been busy. My kid forgot his lunch so I had to deliver it, and—"

Fatigue Stops Positive Communication

If you're tired, shut up and go to bed before you make a fool out of yourself. Who cares about anything when they're tired? You'll definitely get messages mixed up, so put a blanket over the phone and let it sleep too.

THE $8 MILLION LISTENER

Listen, listen, listen. Do that more than you speak, and you'll save lots of time. Listen especially with clients and customers on listing appointments and property showings. A friend of mine did almost $8 million in volume in 1 year. Barbara is basically a quiet, reserved human being. But does she listen! Her follow-through is legendary. From her files, Barbara can duplicate every significant conversation she was party to concerning each and every one of her transactions.

SET ASIDE SOME ALONE TIME

Everybody needs time for themselves occasionally. You just can't keep pouring from the pitcher forever stopping to fill it up. I escape for a few minutes almost every day to be by myself. Maybe to walk along the beach. How I love the sea. Or throw myself into music. I have found a new alone-time favorite. Skiing down a mountain with ear phones on, listening to music. After I've had a lot of transactions to keep up with, or a week away from home giving seminars, I really need to heal myself. Sinking into relaxation for a couple of days and just regaining emotional energy is important to me.

WHEN DEPRESSION STARTS EATING UP THE CLOCK

I find one of my close friends to be with. Then we stay clear of the serious things, and how heavy life can be. Just laughing, dancing, and enjoying their company snaps me back fast. Everyone needs three or four people they can be perfectly themselves with, and know that their genuine self is accepted and appreciated. We have to learn how to protect our spirit above everything else. Life is for growth, not decay. If you identify with certain people or events that have a destructive effect on you, you must either change your thoughts, or disconnect from the influence. Be around people who make you feel good about being you. Remember, all we have is time—and each other.

22

SELF-ORGANIZATION

Winning the Paper War • Clutter Cures • Your Real Estate Car •
Profit Stations • Work Methods • Think Kits

Use your low-pressure time to organize, so you'll be cool and competent when the pressure shoots up, and be able to use that high pressure to drive your career forward instead of being blown apart. The money is where the high pressure is. Organize to handle it. Organize for specific purposes:

- To take a listing without prior notice,
- To show property without prior notice,
- To qualify new customers anytime,
- To close old customers anytime,
- To use large blocks of time effectively,
- To use odd moments effectively,
- To prospect efficiently,
- To learn efficiently,
- To succeed with open house and up-time,
- To follow through successfully,
- To have time for your loved ones,
- To enjoy life.

Self-organization has a specific objective: to free you from as much frustration as possible so that you can concentrate your time and energy on doing those things that earn fees.

Organize.

Organize to stay organized.

Organize yourself, because no one else can.

Do it fast.

That's the secret. Speed. Plan. Make the minutes count as you organize yourself. Act boldly. Act with speed. Then you'll have the time to do it, and the benefits received will encourage you to keep on spending a few minutes a day organizing and keeping organized.

The beauty of getting organized is, once accomplished, very little time is required to maintain a high level of organization. Not that you can ever neglect it entirely, but most of the necessary action becomes automatic. It's merely a matter of forming the right habits.

WINNING THE PAPER WAR

As long as you're in real estate, that blizzard of paper will keep beating down on you. Have you ever noticed the way many agents go through the pile of paper that's in their office slot? First, they look through it quickly for something important, such as a check made out to them. Not finding one, they leaf through the material dispiritedly, reading nothing, throwing nothing away, and then they set it all aside in one pile to be gone over later. That stack of papers is all important stuff—too important to be thrown away, not important enough to be acted on now. Action waits until later, "Until I have more time."

Don't fool yourself.

The first step toward uncluttering your desk is to unclutter your mind of the idea that there'll ever be more time later. There never will. You're working hard to increase your clientele—to increase the demands on your time. You'll have less time to waste tomorrow, less time every tomorrow. The real estate business, our legal system, technology, and life in general are all complicating themselves more every day. Convince yourself that, "I won't have time tomorrow to catch up with what I should've done today; I do today's work today. And I organize today for my busier tomorrows."

CLUTTER CURES

Here's how to go through that pile of paper in your office slot and be done with it when you reach the last item:

Grasp the pile by a corner, shake out all the same items—phone messages and letters—and act on them first. But, instead of skipping about like a child under a Christmas tree, dispose of each item as you touch it.

- Throw it in the wastepaper basket,
- File in it an easy-clean file (see next section), or
- Act on it. Pick up the phone and call someone; write a letter; note what has to be done at a future time in your tomorrow's action list or appointment book;

refer it to somebody else for handling; file it in a specific file—do *now* whatever is required. The secret is to *touch paper once*, and only once, whenever possible. Easy-clean files let you do that without losing control of anything you need. If you're suffering the pangs of paper-choke because you can't separate what you may need later from what you'll never need, here are three specific remedies that will heal the most virulent case of keep-it-all-itis:

Easy-Clean Files

1. This/Last Files

So that you can find any item you might need quickly, set up a this/last file for each type of document you receive 20 or more of each month. If you get a daily hot sheet from your Board of Realtors®, and have been letting them pile up on your desk and in your attaché case because you hate to throw them away, label a file folder, HOT SHEETS/THIS MONTH. Keep that folder in the ready position and you'll never have to worry about whether you'll want to look at last week's hot sheet again or not. Look at each hot sheet when you first see it. Concentrate an instant to remember any detail you might need, jot down in your appointment book any action you'll take that hot sheet in the future, and then pop it in HOT SHEETS/THIS MONTH.

You need one more file folder: label it HOT SHEETS/LAST MONTH. On the first day of each month, dump the content of the HOT SHEETS/LAST MONTH in the wastepaper basket, transfer the content of HOT SHEETS/THIS MONTH to the last-month folder, and you've easy-cleaned your hot sheet file. It's a matter of moments, once a month, to clear several this/last files. Here are some other this/lasts you might want to set up:

- Caravan sheets
- Other broker's flyers on their listings
- Loan company flyers
- Other service flyers

You might ask, "Why not just have a this-month file and dump it once a month?"

Then you'll be dumping out yesterday's material, along with 30-day-old items. This/last folders guarantee you'll keep every item at least 30 days, so there's no worry that you'll throw away items you'll need. It's a system you can set up quickly, put on habit control, and forget about.

2. Throwaway Files

You need only four folders for this complete, quarterly throwaway system. Label them:

- Throw away March 31
- Throw away June 30
- Throw away September 30
- Throw away December 31

These folder are great places to drop various bits of paper you might—but probably won't—need again: raffle tickets, claim checks, coupons for a free lunch, miscellaneous notes. The first time you think of it after the date on a folder passes, dump the entire folder without looking at any of the material in it. That must be the basis on which you put items into the throwaway folders: unless you rescue them before the date shown, out they go. If you find that your four throwaway folders are overcrowded, use:

3. Rotating Monthly Files

Label a dozen folders, one for each month. Suppose you start the system in March. The first folder in the group is March, then April, May and so on through December, followed by January and ending with February. During March, drop everything into that March folder you might want to keep for an extended period of time. At the end of March, place March's folder behind February's, and start dropping incoming items into April's folder. Repeat that process through the 12 folders. On the first of March of the following year, dump the one-year-old material in March's folder in the wastebasket and start the process all over again. If you haven't crowded these folders with material that should go into this/last folders, there won't be too much filed in each of the monthly rotating folders. Finding a needed item there will be easy: Think about when it came in, and then skim through the items in one or two of the monthly folders until you see it. The rotating monthly file allows you to keep items readily accessible for a full year, and to clean that file in less than one minute per year.

There you have it: Three systems that'll prevent the paper blizzard from stalling your movement forward. You can set the three up in only 10 minutes with two dozen folders, then you can start efficiently disposing of all the papers you're not sure you'll need again, and still be able to find them if you do. That takes care of the most numerous and least important papers. With them out of the way, we can concentrate on handling vital papers effectively. To do that, set up fast-working tickler files.

Monthly Tickler File

Label 12 folders, ACTION January 1, ACTION February 1, and so on through December. These are great for reminders to pay bills, order farming tools, send anniversary cards to clients, and a thousand other things. Put everything you need to handle each item in these files so that you can work through them quickly. On the first of each month, pull the folder, do the work, and put your repeating reminders back in the folder. (The Smith's anniversary will be in April next year too, so it should stay in ACTION April 1.) Then put that folder at the back of your ACTION folders and let it start working its way to the front again.

Tickler 1/31

Any office supply store will have Oxford Stock No. 152–31 on hand, a set of 30 folders numbered 1 through 29, and 30–31. To set up a tickler 1/31, all you need do is put these folders in your desk and start using them. Here's how:

Suppose today is the 20th of the month. Take the folders numbered 1 through 20 and put them behind 30–31. You'll then have a set of folders arranged as the dates will come up for the next 30 days. File all your action notes in the folder for the day you should take action, and tickler 1/31 will automatically place that file in your hands at the right time. All you need do is clear the file once a day. Three obvious uses are:

- To trigger follow-up on your transactions. ("Loan documents due back from Smith.")
- To remind you of events. File the complete invitation or announcement. When the date comes, just pull the papers and go—no hunting around for the ticket.
- To kick off follow-up on your leads. Choose the date you want to call that party back, and drop the paper with the information in that day's folder. The fast fact grabber form in Chapter 24 is set up for this kind of operation.

Less obvious, but more powerful in effect on your income, is the heightened sense of timing you'll develop with this system. Use tickler 1/31 to spread your workload to the lighter days, to trigger phone calls at the best moments, to put yourself in the right place at the right time. The advantage of tickler 1/31 over the calendar pad is that you can drop original documents or complete files into it—no copying is necessary.

Every night, as you're working up your tomorrow's action list, go through the next day's tickler 1/31 folder. If it's the night of the 19th, pull the folder marked "20," take all the papers out of it, and file that folder behind "19." Don't carry the tickler folders around with you or, when you need them to file new tickler material, they'll be who-knows-where.

Put tomorrow's material in a folder marked ACTION NOW, a folder you carry with you as a ready-made plan of action for the day. Tickler 1/31 works best when filed at the profit station you visit and work at every day, the profit station from which you make most of your fee-winning calls.

Daily Action Folders

This set of seven folders is easy to carry in your attaché case. It lets you constantly rearrange your schedule for the next few days, as developments demand. Label them ACTION MONDAY, ACTION TUESDAY, and so on through the week.

These three tickler systems bring the ore from which you refine your tomorrow's action list gold.

TAL Yourself to Big Money Fast

Success is certain if you do these two things: (1) Each night, prepare a list of the things you must do tomorrow to achieve your goals and; (2) do those things tomorrow.

On your TAL, your tomorrow's action list, rank the opportunties you've set out for yourself in their order of importance. Jump on those items you like least the very first thing in the morning and get them out of the way. Don't keep them hanging over you all day. This habit, of making sure that you *clear all disagreeable tasks first every day*, will do wonders for your morale and double your efficiency. No longer will you carry guilt around all day, and go in fear of the unpleasant duty. By doing what you don't want to do early, you save hours of excuse-making and exhausting internal debate. And while you're procrastinating, that nasty problem is getting worse, and your fear of dealing with it is getting stronger.

After the disagreeable is out of the way, tackle the tasks on your TAL in order of their importance. Push item 1 as far forward as you can before moving on to item 2. The TAL form is shown in Chapter 24.

The Control Book

You're an outside person. The money is out in the field. You do your business where it can be done, in your clients' homes, in vacant houses and coffee shops, on the hood of your car. So make it a firm habit to keep whatever book you use to control your activities with you at all times.

Name and Phone Naildown

Every real estate office periodically sees one of its agents tearing his desk apart searching for a client's phone number while bemoaning the fact that, unless the number is found, all chance of a transaction with that party is gone. A common surname, when the city they live in isn't known, or an unlisted number, can cut off all chance of getting back to a prospect.

Curiously, even after hearing about a few of these fiascos, agents will continue to jot phone numbers on any scrap of paper and let it go at that—until they need the number.

Always write the number in a second place. At once. An excellent second place is your control book. The quick scribble, "Jones, 234-0987," can save you a frantic hour—or a large fee. The important thing is to do it as soon as the prospects give you their number. Write it in a second place while you're talking to them. They won't mind your taking them seriously.

But the phone number you have at the office doesn't help when you're at home, on open house, or pulled over at a roadside phone to call and postpone an appointment. Regularly, every day, enter all the important new phone numbers you've acquired that day, along with the date, names, addresses, and any other pertinent details, in a triplicate dispatch book (available in office supply stores). If you keep your dispatch book at your office, that nails the phone numbers down at the office.

Tear one copy out, take it home, and nail the number down there. Put the third copy in your car trunk, and nail it down wherever you drive. The number already in the address book or control book you usually carry nails it down wherever you walk—if you have that book with you. If not, that phone number is safely in your car, home and office. This thorough approach might seem like overkill—until you drop a fee by losing a phone number. Organize to do this as a routine and the time saved by not having to hunt for numbers will more than offset the moments it takes to nail them down in the dispatch book.

YOUR REAL ESTATE CAR

Although they're great for casting an aura of excitement and glamor over the proceedings, you don't have to drive a luxurious four-door sedan to sell real estate. I won top volume awards in our board showing property in a little red squareback VW. Keep the car you're using clean. Don't let trash accumulate in it. Store all that stuff in your garage that's bouncing around in the car's trunk now, and use the space to carry:

- *Kid Controller Kit.* Gather some games, puzzles, and books (they don't have to be new or expensive) for those occasions when your customers bring their children. Avoid gooey eatables that'll be used for polish on your car seats.

- *Last week's Multiple Listing Book.* Carry this week's MLS book with you, but if you mislay it, that trusty copy in the truck will see you through.

- *"Just Sold" doorhangers* that you can spread in the neighborhood the same day you close a sale. News is the most perishable commodity in the world. Get it out fast.

- *Giveaway Kit.* Always carry a supply of your personalized scratch pads. Give them, and other farming items, out at every opportunity. People remember gifts someone they know personally hands them far better than gimmicks hung on their doorknob by a phantom.

- *Keep a few of your customer-catcher maps* made up and ready to go in your trunk, too. Chapter 9 describes this useful sales tool in detail.
- *Forms Kit.* Keep a few extra copies of listing forms, purchase-agreement forms, counteroffer forms, buyers' net sheets, sellers' net sheets, and any other forms you might need handy in your car's trunk. You can't close without these vital forms, and by the time you get back, Cousin Charlie may have called and said he's getting into real estate.
- *Coping Kit.* A small pair of pliers, a screwdriver, a few extra ballpoint pens, a handful of bolts and nuts for your signs, a *Sold* sign, a *For Lease* sign, tape, boxes of raisins for when there's not time to eat a regular meal, paper clips, and spare batteries for your calculator, are all items that'll keep unexpected small problems small.

Protect all paper items carried in your trunk from dust and moisture or they'll probably be unusable when you need them. Plastic bags closed with rubber bands are great for this because you can see what's inside. Cardboard boxes with lids kept on by masking tape work well too. Label them so you won't be tearing everything apart when you need something in a hurry.

All these kits will easily go in one 11 x 14″ cardboard box with lid, such as R-Kive® No. 725, available at office supply stores.

PROFIT STATIONS

Doesn't that sound better than "work stations?"

Don't let it stop you if you can't immediately have a large, well-lighted desk in a separate room, with telephone and files handy. A work station can be effective if it's only a shelf in the pantry within reach of a wall phone. That's what my home profit station was. Don't knock the shelf in the pantry. With a 25-foot cord, you can range far and wide, stirring soup and quieting restless babies, while prospecting, following up, or negotiating on the phone.

Any shelf or nook can be an effective profit station if you have a phone, a place to write, and a shelf to keep the things you need. The less space you have, the more pressure there is to get down to essentials.

An open house is an effective profit station if you organize to work effectively while you're there, in addition to holding the house open. Chapter 9 discusses this in detail.

The Traveling Profit Station

Everything you need to prospect effectively; to follow up on expireds, fizzbos, your current clients, and your transactions can be chucked into your second attaché case. Your first attaché case contains your Listing Presentation Manual and all the forms and tools you need to list and sell. By grabbing these two cases, you're ready for anything.

Inexpensive attaché cases are available in variety and drug stores.

WORK METHODS

Mood Governed or Scheduled Batch

Be aware of how you work now. You may want to change your fundamental method to one that's more productive. One of the most popular methods of working is to allow your mood to govern your pace and direction. You work continuously at whatever seems like a good idea at the time until your mood changes. Then you do something else as dictated by your new mood.

Often that new mood is created by a phone call or some other stimulus from the outside. If this is your work method, your output is controlled by external forces, by stimulus from the world beyond your skin, not by your internal determination. People who swing rapidly from periods of enthusiastic action to glum apathy have not organized themselves well enough to take full control of their careers. A keen sense of your own worth; a warm regard for yourself as your own best friend; a set of goals you want to achieve, believe you can achieve, and are excited about achieving; the habit of encouraging (positively validating) yourself—these are the bedrock on which you build the discipline and sense of purpose that success demands. That's the essence of self-organization. Take control of your career. Instead of letting anyone and everyone you come in contact with govern your mood, and then letting your mood govern your output, take control of your life. Set goals, work to schedules, control your mood and yourself. A useful concept is:

Scheduled Batch

No matter how efficient you are, there will always be more work available in your real estate practice than you can perform. You can work until you're exhausted, and always feel defeated. Or you can schedule a batch of work, finish it, and feel good. By organizing a constant flow of wins in this way, you reinforce your good feelings about yourself and build your confidence. You begin a cycle of working happier, of having more success, of achieving goals. As your abilities grow, as the brake of negative thinking grab you less and less, you'll find yourself setting higher and higher goals—and continuing to achieve them.

Plan your work in batches. Schedule yourself to do preparatory work during the hours when you can't door-knock or phone. Set up batches of ten expireds or ten fizzbos that you'll visit or phone at the right time of day and week. Research these opportunities; drive past each of the houses, and have the files all set up so that you can start promptly when the good time rolls around. Plan ahead so that you can get through your batch with smooth self-confidence. Let your constant mood of confidence inspire people to place their trust in you. Govern them with your mood instead of allowing their fear, anger, guilt, and failure to govern you.

THINK KITS

You get a come-list-me call. "Joe just came in, and he got that terrific promotion."

"That's really neat, Lisa."

"Only thing is, they want him there in two weeks. We want our house on the market right away. Can you come over here now?"

"I can be there in ten minutes."

From your files, you pull the Guidelines to Market Value that you prepared when Lisa first told you they would probably be moving soon.

Grabbing your attaché case and your listing kit, you hustle out to your car. Everything needed to take a listing is in your two hands because you think in terms of kits, not long lists of miscellaneous items. And you won't forget anything in the hurry and excitement because you've carefully organized those kits during quiet time.

PREPARE AND PERFORM—OR PASS OUT

Preparation Is the Vital Concept • Preparation Prevents Poor Performance • Be Mentally Prepared • How to Create Sales Dialogues Fast • Make Money on Your Area's Yearly Buying Pattern • Your Important Information Notebook • Services • Put the Numbers Book Away • Fast Numbers Are Fee Earners • $44.25 Is a Figure to Remember

You're lying back in a dentist's chair, staring goggle-eyed at the ceiling, hoping it won't hurt. A man you don't know walks in. He's wearing a white coat. He leans over you with a drill, gives you a cherry smile, and says, "I hope you don't mind me practicing on you. This is my first day on the job, you see, and I'm not too sure of what I'm doing. But trust me—I'll take good care of you."

Have you ever sat nervously in a doctor's office, and suddenly noticed all the diplomas and certificates hanging in neat frames on the walls? Reassuring, aren't they? Since the competence of their real estate agent can have a heavy impact on their financial health, clients and customers expect you to be prepared. When you first contact them, they're looking for some reassuring signs that you know what you're doing. They're seriously thinking of relying to some degree on your competence in making a decision that, including interest, may involve nine times their annual income. That's important money to anyone.

PREPARATION IS THE VITAL CONCEPT

Preparation is the key to closing a sale. Preparation is the key to closing a listing.

Learn the inventory. Know your area intimately. Understand thoroughly all the different financing methods available, all the costs of borrowing, all the closing costs. Understand, and be able to explain concisely, the tax and investment advantages of owning your own home.

PREPARATION PREVENTS POOR PERFORMANCE

In real estate, the same situations are played over and over again in endless variations on a few basic themes. Prepare in depth to meet these situations with smooth confidence. Learn the closes, the qualifying methods, the techniques. Watch the hot sheets. See new listings constantly. I did it every single week, year in and year out.

When the ad or sign call comes in, you've got to know more about what's in that house than the ad tells, more than can be seen from the street. If you don't, why should the caller talk to you? And you've got to know more of what's on the Multiple Listing than just that one property. Prospective buyers immediately spot the salesperson who knows the inventory. It just stands out.

Know the area. Know about schools, parks, churches, doctors, baby sitters, bowling alleys, tennis, soccer—know it all. And, especially, know those things that are unique, outstanding, or unusual about your area. Know its history, special parades, customs. You're not just selling homes, you're selling a way of life.

Know the comparables. That means you've got a terrific comparable file that you're constantly updating. Someone should be able to come up to you and ask any questions about the area's housing when you're actively listing and selling, and that answer is there, on the top of your tongue.

Don't shoot yourself. When opportunity walks in, it takes preparation to be able to grab it before it walks right out again. The difference between an outstanding salesperson and an average salesperson is preparation. One is armed, the other isn't. One has the weapons to win; the other has only a silly grin and a naive trust in luck.

BE MENTALLY PREPARED

This means that when I close the door on my house and get in my car, no matter what's happening there, all my problems click off. Before I'm moving toward a meeting with clients, all of my attention is directed toward them.

Sometimes it's not easy to do. But often it's the best possible way to handle your personal problems—to put them out of your mind for a while and let one of the world's greatest healing systems—good honest hard work—do its magic. A move well worth developing is this one of clicking the inner conflicts off for a time. "I'll think about that later—right now the best thing I can possibly do is to concentrate on solving Mr. and Mrs. Hottewbye's housing problem." That's an excellent habit and skill. Find the tricks that work for you. Squeeze your toes. Whistle Dixie. Take three deep breaths. Something will work for you.

HOW TO CREATE SALES DIALOGUES FAST

You'll need a tape recorder.

Why do we call them dialogues when you're obviously going to do most of the talking—why not monologues?

Because these sales talks should be two-way communications between you and the client or customer. Don't set them up for you to go on and on. Constantly insert questions.

"That makes sense, doesn't it?"

"Do you agree?"

"Are you with me?"

"Look, this is my profession, and I work with these concepts every day, so it's easy for me to forget for a moment that my clients are experts in other areas that I know nothing about. So please interrupt if I get carried away. I haven't been throwing realty jargon at you, have I?"

Keep them involved. You're not selling them or listing them if they're staring at you, thinking abut their golf swing or wondering how they can get away from you.

Define exactly what each dialogue is to cover. Rumbling sales speeches result when your purposes are vague; effective sales speeches result when you have specific objectives. For example, Objective: To persuade someone to list with you.

Pick someone you've met (a client, a friend, anybody) to address your speech. Let's say you choose Jubal Late, a 40-year-old bachelor who's an engineer. Imagine that you're talking to him when you tape your sales dialogues. The second time you tape each sales speech, imagine that you're addressing someone other than Jubal, a young married couple, for example. The third time, address a retired couple.

But, before you start talking, outline your speech. Here's how to do this quickly: Take not more than five minutes to jot down two or three words to remind you of each of your main ideas, the six or seven reasons why Jubal Late should list with you. Take another minute to recopy your notes into logical order. Put your strongest point last, and your second-strongest point first.

Now tape your speech. Talk to that imaginary person or couple. If you can think of real people, so much the better. Don't talk for more than three minutes.

Listen to the recording once for content. Stop the tape to make notes on parts you want to add or cut.

Listen to the tape again. This time be alert for avoidable repetition of the same word, for ahs, ohs, and slurred words, and for talk that's too fast or too slow, too loud or too soft. Make sure your speaking style is easy and natural. You don't want to sound stiff, superior, or condescending on the one hand, nor do you want to come across as being a hard-selling phony. Make sure you're not throwing in real estater's jargon. Use plain English. Pare unnecessary words that obscure your meaning, but do repeat your basic ideas in other words. It's been said often: Tell them what you're going to tell them, tell them, and then tell them what you've told them. That applies only to your main ideas. Go over your prime points in plain but varied language when you express them the second and third times.

Listen, think, and immediately make a second tape of your speech. Repeat your double analysis. Then tape the day's final version. This third version will be your starting point when you review your short speech tomorrow.

Use this method to tape all nine sales dialogues called for in the Breakaway Schedule of special achievements given after Chapter 28. Here's the list of dialogues and the day they're scheduled:

DAY

12: "Why should you list with me."
13: "What's happening now in our local resale housing market?"
14: "The communities of Greenpretty (your area) Valley."
15: "Why Greenpretty Valley is a great place, Mr. and Mrs. Homebuyer, for you and your family to grow and prosper in."
16: "Here's what happens in today's market when you limit your offer with contingencies."
17: "The outlook is optimistic."
18: "The tax advantages of home ownership."
19: "Why you should buy a home now."
21: "The various ways you can finance a home purchase, and the advantages and costs of each method."

As you listen to these tapes, and learn your material thoroughly, you'll need to be on guard that you aren't repeating it like a mynah bird. Practice constantly at speaking with conviction and clarity. Pause occasionally for effect. Ask your imaginary listeners questions. Use a bright and pleasing tone. Vary the speed and force with which you speak. But be careful you aren't going for a Shakespearean performance; talk naturally or you'll sound insincere—and you'll talk yourself right out of business.

When you've made the best tape you can, put it away for a few days. Then listen to it again. Cut a new tape whenever you think you can improve on your old version. Keep your first tape or two. When you listen to them a month or two from now, you'll be impressed with how much you've improved.

Listening to your own tapes frequently will rise your critical abilities to new heights. You'll find yourself making minor but important improvements in facets of your speech you didn't even notice the first few times you listened to your voice. And you'll find that listening to those perfectly delivered lines of yours is a very effective learning device for the content of the sales dialogues.

When you're actually face-to-face with a buyer or seller, you'll want to break your speeches up into small segments. What the clients want to say is more important to you than what you want to say to them. Your chance will come. Be prepared to make it count with effective and expressive speech that compels attention because it's informative and direct.

Rehearse spontaneity, verve, and facts *in*; rehearse drone, hesitation, and ramble *out*. Tips on four of the dialogues follow. You'll find ideas for the others in the chapters on listing and selling. But the real power of planned and practiced sales speeches comes from the accurate and up-to-date information that's in them. Only you can supply that.

Day 14: "The Communities of Greenpretty Valley"

Tape your remarks and listen to them carefully to make sure you're not speaking condescendingly about any part of your sales area: The locality you knock will be the only one that some of your buyers will feel comfortable in. Make sure you don't talk yourself right out of any chance to sell in that area—unless that's what you want to do.

Day 16: Here's What Happens in Today's Market When You Limit Your Offer with Contingencies"

You'll need to tailor this one to your prospects' degree of sophistication in real estate. If you haven't had experience with this yet, talk to several other agents. Call someone in the Multiple Listing book who has several listings. Ask that agent, "If I had a customer interested in your listing at 12345 Fir Street, how would your sellers feel about an offer contingent on my people selling their home?"

Day 17: "The Outlook Is Optimistic"

You'll need this dialogue when buyers ask you things like, "Where do you think the general economy is going? Are we headed for another recession? Aren't we about due for another downturn? Aren't interest rates too high?" Here's what they're really saying: "I'm afraid. Tell me something that'll ease my worries about taking on the risk of buying a house. I need reassurance."

Give them reassurance.

Those buyers need a crutch. Unless you shove strong support under them fast, they'll fall victim to their fears and back off from investing in their future as they should. Prepare your optimistic outlook speech before need. Stiffen it with facts. Make it a tight strong argument that you've practiced until you can deliver it with convincing power.

Where are the facts? In news magazines, newspapers, bank newsletters. The Kiplinger letter is an excellent source. Be on the lookout for good news constantly. But don't wait. From what you know now, or can quickly find, perfect the first version of your "Optimistic Outlook" sales dialogue. Improve it in the future whenever you can.

Day 19: "Why You Should Buy a Home Now"

Talk with understanding about the real reasons why people buy homes instead of renting apartments: to satisfy their yearning to belong, their urge to call some territory their own, their aspirations for prestige, security, and comfort. Work in some words about the indestructible nature of a land investment, the accumulation of equity, the appreciation of value. Simply mention the tax advantages, which another dialogue covers in detail. Don't let dollars dominate this discussion, as so many agents do. Money reasons are rationalizations people use to justify their emotional decisions. If you outline the money advantages adequately, while treating the emotional factors with dignity and completeness, you will create a powerful selling tool in this sales dialogue.

When higher housing prices and interest costs seem imminent, these items should find a place in this sales talk, but your basic speech should be built around the factors that don't change. Don't be discouraged if your first attempts don't sound convincing or detailed enough. You're dealing with deep emotions here. It's worth working hard on this talk over a period of time. Do the best you can now. Continue to develop and refine this sales dialogue in the coming months until your clients and customers listen carefully, and nod their heads in agreement, as you talk.

MAKE MONEY ON YOUR AREA'S YEARLY BUYING PATTERN

The demand for housing in your marketing area may have a pronounced seasonal pattern, or one that is affected less by the weather and more by calendar events such as school summer vacation. This pattern of change in month-to-month demand repeats itself from year to year. Other factors influence the demand for housing in your area, of course. Changes in the economy will make it more difficult to see the yearly pattern—but it's there. Knowing that pattern intimately makes you a local real estate expert.

Being able to discuss that pattern in detail and with confidence not only will impress prospects, and help you convert them into clients and customers, it will frequently provide you with powerful arguments that will induce your clients to make realistic price decisions.

Suppose your sellers are considering an offer late in the year that's well below the price they want. You know they should take it because, for openers, they can't afford to carry the house through the winter. For closers, your chances of hanging in as their listing agent until spring are doubtful. So it's vital for them and important to you that they accept the offer. In this situation, most real estate agents can't fire any ammunition except vague but vehement assertions such as, "The market around here is really dead in the winter."

"How dead is it?" the seller says.

"Well, all I do in the winter is public relations. I might as well be fishing."

Doesn't sound very professional or convincing, does it? Even when delivered by the grayest of heads, such arguments don't bend bullheaded sellers intent on being their own worst enemies (such sellers are a breed you'll encounter often). How much better if you can marshal arguments that are based strictly on facts of record, arguments that run along these lines:

"Based on the record, only about 13 percent of our annual sales are made in the winter months. Of course, if house sales were evenly distributed throughout the whole year, 25 percent of the sales would be made in the winter fourth of the year. So winter sales are roughly half of the average for the entire year—okay? But that 12 percent not sold in the winter is added onto the rest of the year, so the difference between winter and summer is more like three to one. Are you with me? The actual average for the last three years is 13.2 percent in the winter and 38.4 percent in the summer, or just about exactly three to one."

Let that sink in for a moment. "I've got my charts right here. Would you like to look at them?"

You open the book. "Excuse me for throwing all these numbers at you so fast, but they're important for you to know. If you're to make the best decision on this offer, our seasonal buying pattern has to be a key element in that decision."

After you get that point across, follow up with this clincher that you've dredged up from your statistics: "There's another vital aspect to this seasonal pattern that should also be given careful consideration at this point: Winter prices are lower than summer prices by an average of 9 percent. My data cover that last three years, and they're adjusted to eliminate the effect of inflation. That is to say, I've isolated the price effect of the season.

"Now, what does that 9 percent price differential actually mean? Well, it tells us that, for the most part, only the most willing sellers sell their houses in the winter. Putting it another way, nobody sells in the winter unless they sell for less. Since you're working on the high side of the market price, what this boils down to, in all probability, is that you'll carry the house through the winter if you turn this offer down. Maybe all the way to summer—unless you decide to take considerably *less* than this offer in the meantime.

"Of course, what I'm attempting to do now is predict the future, and no one can be sure of what the future will bring, but the recent history of this area bears out what I'm saying. The choice is between taking a long gamble against the future's odds, or taking the sure thing now."

Let's tune in on a conversation with a FSBO who is fooling around with selling his house. It's January 14. Your FSBO wants to move out of state, so you tell him:

"In each of the last three years, resale home sales in this area have peaked in March. Before then, the best month was always August. But every year—the largest number of new listings—and the largest number of total listings—still hits in August.

"So what does this mean to you? If you want to delay listing your house until summer, like you're talking about doing, the odds are you'll have to accept less than you could get for your house in March, simply because they'll be so many more houses on the market.

"We're talking about a supply-and-demand situation here. You have a very unique house, one that people will fall in love with. But why put *them* in the strongest possible bargaining position, and *yourself* in the weakest possible bargaining position? If your house is in the market well before the peak—and not too many people know our market has been peaking in March—buyers are thinking, 'They've got the whole summer to sell; they won't go for a low offer now.' But if you're trying to sell in August, then the buyers are saying to themselves, 'If they don't sell in the next couple of weeks they're stuck with the place until spring.' That's an enormous difference in buyer attitude.

"My graphs detailing all this are in my car. I'd like you to think about the advantages of having the entire Multiple Listing Service on your team—all 1,300 of us—plus a strong, professional agent—me—directing the marketing effort. I gather that your plans hinge on selling this house. Wouldn't it be wiser to put this gigantic team to work for you at the *best* season rather than at the poorest season? Is it worth taking the chance?

"Would you think about that, please, for the moment it'll take me to run out to my car and get my graphs? I think you'll be impressed with their market information. You know, I've done many things like this. I'm a professional. I devote a lot of time to searching out ways that'll help my clients sell faster and for more money. There are so many aspects to marketing real estate that only a dedicated professional thinks about."

You must have your facts documented in case you're challenged. Here's how to come up with the data that will support your statements:

Your Board of Realtors® will have the following information summarized by month for several recent years:

- Total number of housing units sold, per month
- Average price

Let's say that for Greenpretty Valley in one year the sales were as follows:

	UNITS	PERCENT OF YEAR
January	195	3.9
February	250	4.7
March	320	6.2
April	410	8.0
May	520	10.1
June	601	11.7
July	690	13.4
August	640	12.4
September	599	11.6
October	415	8.1
November	395	7.7
December	110	2.2
Total	5,245	

Plot the data on graphs. Show each year in a different color. You need two graphs:

- PRICE CURVE. See the sample graph that follows.

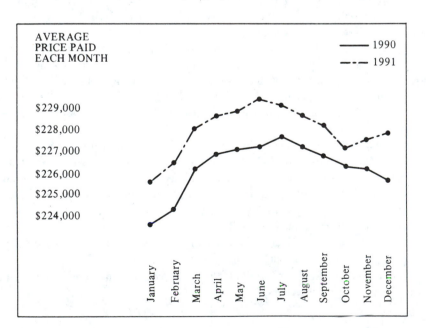

• MONTHLY SALES AS PERCENT OF THE YEAR. See the previous table.

Powerful stuff. It just takes a little preparation—perhaps four hours' worth. What is the average commission you expect to earn? Divide that by four to get your hourly rate for preparing that data if it only sells one transaction for you, or wins one listing that sells, during the several years you'll use it. You will, of course, need to spend an hour each year updating the data. If your average commission is $900, you'll have made $15 a *minute* for updating that data after it's saved one transaction for you.

YOUR I.I. (IMPORTANT INFORMATION) NOTEBOOK

Put a small notebook in your ataché case in which you keep, filed alphabetically, important information that you might need at any moment.

A	Advertising phone numbers, deadlines, rates
D	Deadlines for reciprocal listings, caravans, ads, Multiple Listing
S	School District boundaries, phone numbers
T	Tax rates, local
U	Utility office locations, hook-up information

Do more than work on this notebook in spare moments on floor time or at open houses. Make up flash cards and memorize everything in it.

SERVICES

You should be ready to recommend someone to perform every conceivable household repair and type of construction work. Suppose a client calls and you don't know about the trade he needs. You've got electricians, plumbers, roofers, and tree-sprayers on tap, but Gus Smith, who bought a house from you, needs a tile-setter.

You can say, "Sorry, Smitty, I've never had a call for a tile-setter. Can't help you on that one."

Translation: "I'm not as much of an expert as you think I am."

Here's how to handle this one: "Tile-setter, yeah—who was that fellow?—Smitty, you'll have to give me a minute on this one—I just can't think of the man's name. I'll have to check my file at home [at the office if you're at home] and call you back."

Then get on the phone, locate a tile-setter, and get back to Smith that same day. Be sure everyone you recommend has a proven track record with someone you know. Preferably you! A bad recommendation can hurt you more than none at all!

PUT THE NUMBERS BOOK AWAY

You look like a beginner when you pull out the little book of numbers and drop your nose in it. Usually, all you need is one number, and that you can memorize (or write it down on a strip of tape you stick to the back of your calculator). When interest rates are moving, perhaps you'll need to have three numbers at your finger tips, ready to punch into your pocket calculator. Here are some of the numbers, all for 30 year loans:

INTEREST RATE	FACTOR PER THOUSAND
9-1/2	8.4086
9-3/4	8.5916
10	8.7758
10-1/4	8.9611
10-1/2	9.1474
13	11.0621
14	11.8488
15	12.6445
16	13.4476
17	14.2568
18	15.0709
19	15.8889
20	16.7102

Suppose you're figuring a buyer's net sheet for a $67,310 loan amount, a 30-year loan at 10-1/2 percent.

A glance at the information you've written on the back of your calculator tells you that $9.1474 is the payment for each thousand dollars of such a loan. Enter 9.1474 in your calculator and hit the multiply button.

Now enter the loan amount: 67.31. (Since "thousand dollars" is your unit, the comma after the thousands in your loan amount becomes your decimal point: $67,310 = 67.31. The final zero in the loan amount means nothing in this calculation.)

9.1474 × 67.31 = $615.71 monthly investment for 30 years to pay off a loan of $67,310 at 10-1/2 percent.

This answer is accurate to the penny.

Where do you find the $9.1474* in your real estate numbers book?

In the monthly payment schedules, on the 10-1/2 percent page for 30 years, find $100,000 at the bottom of the page. That figure, the monthly investment to retire a $100,000 loan, is $914,74. Moving the decimal point two places to the left divides by 100, giving the answer carried out to 4 decimal places for a $1,000 loan.

---

*Some amortization books give this value as $9.1475.

Note that the figure given in the table for a loan amount of $1,000 is $9.15. Applied to the loan in this example, the rounded figure of $9.15 gives an answer that's about 18 cents off per month from the actual payment.

Why fool with $.18 per month? Because some people, when they come right down to making a commitment, are put off by rounded figures about their monthly investment. They prefer round figures on house values, closing costs, and the like, but that monthly outgo figure, if given approximately and without conviction as to its accuracy, is a wonderful excuse to put off making a decision. Close that loophole by giving them the exact figure. It's easy when you know how.

FAST NUMBERS ARE FEE EARNERS

Whipping out the numbers fast allows you to concentrate on your clients and customers. Learning the shortcuts frees you of fluster and distraction at the crucial moments when people make their big decisions. Why inflict the serious handicap on yourself of being slow at, and afraid of, the arithmetic you know is required to earn a fee? While you're fumbling, buyer's remorse is whispering in your customer's ear: "Wait. Don't commit yourself. Think it over."

$44.25 IS A FIGURE TO REMEMBER

That's how much a $100,000 loan is reduced in principal by the first monthly investment of $877.58, when the rate is 10 percent and the term is 30 years. The other $833.33 is the first month's interest cost.

No wonder sellers so often overestimate how much they've reduced the balance of new loans. Many of them reason somewhat like this: "Okay, my payment is $877.58, so figure three hundred bucks for interest. Let's say $377.58 for quick figures, and to be on the safe side. So I must be paying the loan off at about five hundred a month. Let's see. I took the loan out last December, so I've made six payments. We can't owe more than $97,000 now." The man thinks he's paid off more than three thousand dollars; actually, he's paid off *less* than three *hundred*.

By remembering $44.25, you can quickly estimate rough payoff figures for any size loan that's new, carries an interest rate in the 10 percent range, and has a term of 30 years or more.

This rough estimate will warn you when your prospects are indulging in wildly wishful thinking. Here's an example of how this can help you:

You're talking to George and Mary Cosby, who want a larger home. Even though George has received a promotion, you suspect it's going to be a tight squeeze to qualify them for the loan they'll need. One of the things you need to know is how much equity the Cosbys have in their present home. But they're hazy about their loan's exact terms. Most people are. They're certain that when they bought two years ago, they took out an $85,000 loan. They guess their interest rate at 9 or 9-1/4, and the loan's term at 35 years. George says, "We must've paid it down to about eighty-one thousand after all this time, wouldn't you think?"

"Instead of taking a wild stab at it," you say, "let me make a quick calculation." It's obvious to you, of course, that in only two years the Cosbys paid off much less than $4,000 on a long-term 9 percent loan. But rather than slap George down by instantly saying no, you dignify his wishful statement by calculating an answer.

You know that $44.25 is the first month's payoff on $100,000 at 10 percent for 30 years, and that 35-year loans pay off even more slowly. But you don't think they've got a 35-year loan, though you don't say so yet.

- Put $44.25 in your calculator.

- Multiply it by 85 percent (Use .85 if your calculator doesn't have the % button; $85,000, of course, is 85 percent of $100,000.)

- The result, $37.61, is the first month's payoff for an $85,000 loan for 30 years at 10 percent simple interest. Multiplying that by 24, the approximate number of monthly investments the Cosbys have made to date, gives $902.64 as the answer. The caution flags are flying; the Cosbys have paid off about one thousand dollars, not the four they think they have. Now you need to let them down easy, and without making them feel stupid or poor.

"Well, you know, George and Mary, these long terms pay off very slowly at first. I work with them every day, and I'm still surprised every time I figure one. If you happen to remember the exact amount of your payment, I could figure the whole thing for you in a minute."

"That's easy," George says. "I write the check every month. It's $699.28."

"Does that include property tax and fire insurance?"

"No. I pay that separately."

"Okay, this is great, George. You've given me everything I need."

Divide $699.28 by 85 on your calculator. The answer you get is $8.2268. A flick of your wrist allows you to consult the numbers you've written on a piece of tape stuck to your calculator's back. You see that $8.2268 is the payment per thousand dollars of original loan amount for a 30-year loan at 9-1/4 percent.

"You've got a 30-year loan at 9-1/4 percent interest," you announce.

"That's right," George says. "I remember now. You really came up with those numbers fast." They're impressed. They don't have any doubt anymore that you're competent to handle their real estate needs. Now that you've qualified yourself in their minds, you can get on with solving their housing problems and earning a fee.

"Knowing the numbers is just part of my service, George. My clients and customers have more important things to think about than the details when they're making a big decision like buying or selling a house. Okay, if I can just have another second."

You pull out the little book of real estate numbers and flip to the loan progress chart. (It sometimes has a different name.)

- Find the page for 9-1/4 percent loans. You know that's the Cosbys' interest rate.

- The heading reads "Original term in years." Their loan term is 30 years, so you look at that column.

- Their loan is two years old. In the "Age of Loan" column you find 2. On the 2 line in the 30 column is "986." This number means that, for every thousand dollars the Cosbys borrowed originally, they now owe $986.

- The original amount of their loan was $85,000. Multiply $986 by 85 to get the current amount they owe: $83,810.

"Well, your loan has a balance of $83,810. But, of course, you've gained two full year's appreciation on your house. You put down 20 percent when you bought?"

"Yeah," George says. He's blinking from the shock of being told that he owes $2,810 more than he thought he did.

You then multiply $85,000 by 125 percent (1.25) and get $106,250. The Cosbys took out an 80 percent loan on their present house when they bought it; 80 percent of $106,250 is $85,000.

"I take it you paid about $106,250 for your house?"

George gives you a surprised look. "That's exactly what we paid for it, not counting fees."

You know that the appreciation rate was 8 percent two years ago and 12 percent last year. You multiply $106,250 by 1.08, leave the result in the machine, and multiply that number by 1.12. Your answer is $128,520.

"George and Mary, let me ask you something, and let's agree that we're just talking. What do you think your house will sell for on today's market?"

"I wouldn't take a dime less than $120,000." George says. "I've really put a lot of work and money into that place. Sprinklers, a concrete patio, lots of things. And I just painted the place."

They were able to get a full 80-percent loan going in, so there's a good chance they bought at a fair market price. If so, their home has probably appreciated at about the average rate, and should now be worth about what you figured: $128,500.

Multiply $128,500 by 92 percent or .92 to get $118,220. They will gross about $118,220 if their house sells for $128,500. Subtract what they owe, $83,810, to get their net walkaway of $34,410. However, you don't drop that figure on the Cosbys yet because they would lock onto it. Then, if it turns out that they have strange ideas about decorating or housekeeping, or have otherwise downgraded their home's salability, you're in trouble. Their house won't bring an average price, and you've needlessly thrown away a pad that could put you into two transactions.

"Let me work out a sellers' net sheet for you based on one hundred twenty-THREE thousand," you say.

"Will our home sell for *that* much?" Mary asks.

"Well, Mary, we've been talking for a few minutes, and you know by now that I'm a conscientious professional, so it goes without saying that I'd want to do my usual thorough market study of your house before giving you a definite answer to that question, but—" pause just an instant "—I'd never mention a figure like that if I didn't think it was a distinct possibility, based on what you've told me. If your house could be sold for $123,000, would you folks be definitely interested in the home we've been talking about?"

Now zip your lip and let the big question hang in the air. Enjoy the silence, as only a pro can. The most important part of salesmanship is knowing when to keep silent—and having the strength to do just that for as long as it's necessary. While communicating nonverbally, wait. Don't straighten things up, fidget, make notes, or run figures on your calculator. Sit still and count spots on the opposite wall. Let the pressure build.

Your fast methods have kept you right up with them anyway. Their net walkaway figure is $29,350 from a sales price of $123,000. (.92 times $123,000, less $83,810, equals $29,350.) Call it $30,000 for round numbers. That's about what they'll have for a down payment without drawing on their savings. Since 5 times 20 is 100, 4 times the down payment available gives you the 80 percent loan that's necessary. The Cosbys can pay about $150,000 for a house, if they can qualify for a $120,000 loan—you figure this in your head in a flash.

The interest rate is 10 percent, and 30-year 80 percent loans are available. That works out to $8.7758 per thousand dollars borrowed, a figure you have memorized because it's the going rate on the most common type of loan at the moment.

No calculation is necessary to get a tight figure on an easy number like $120,000. Jot down rounded figures from $8.7758

$878	for the hundred thousand
88	for ten thousand, and
88	for another ten thousand
$1,054	payment

Multiplying $8.7758 by 120 with the calculator gives the payment as $1,053.10. The jot and add figure of $1,054 is close enough at this stage.

Don't wait until you're with people to learn the real estate numbers. Professionals practice prior to performing. Amateurs don't. Anyone can tell the difference—professionals earn fees; amateurs work for nothing.

24

MONEY-MAKING FORMS AND CHECKLISTS

MONEY-MAKING FORMS: QSI Slot Sheet • Fizzbo Cross-File Cards • Communications Log • Buyer's Progress Chart • Fast Fact Grabber • Results Record • Show List • Tomorrow's Action List • Farm File • Lender Qualifyer Form • **MONEY-MAKING CHECKLISTS:** Prospecting • Farming • Listing Appointments • Listing Presentation Manual • After-Listing Checklist • Open House Checklist • Checklist for Property-Showing Appointment with Buyer • Real Estate Car • Coping Kit • Fallout Avoidance Checklist—After-Sale Checklist • Marketing Plan of Action

MONEY-MAKING FORMS

There are two kinds of forms: those you *have* to fill out for someone else's convenience, and those you *can choose* to fill out for your own benefit. Don't confuse the two. For many of us, the mere sight of the word *forms* brings up sour memories of drudgery, taking tests, and taxes due. But forms have another part to play, the organizing, time-saving, money-making role they'll perform if you'll let them. The trick is to choose, and use in a systematic way, forms that are designed to help you achieve your goals. Such forms allow you to get more work done in less time. They free your mind of detail, and allow you to concentrate on the clients and customers, and on the points that earn fees. Used wisely, effective forms will put the right facts in front of you when you need them, facts that will often make the difference between capturing or losing a client, between closing people or opening them up for another agent.

Forms and checklists: Good ones are priceless. They'll prevent errors that at best are time consuming to correct, and at worst destroy opportunities. If you think of forms as barriers to progress, and checklists as crutches for the incompetent, you're cutting yourself off from tools of great value. The forms and checklists that follow may or may not fit your area and work methods. If they don't, adapt them. Or design and compile your own. The important thing is go get rid of the helter-skelter, and organize your work for maximum efficiency. Using effective forms and checklists will make an enormous difference in your production.

Quick-Speak Inventory Slot Sheet

The walk-in looking for an elegant view home in Exclusive Heights won't be impressed by your knowledge of the fixer-uppers in the valley. Nor will someone interested in smoked glass and wood be charmed if you show them nothing but brick. There's a wide variety of property available in your sales area, and most of it falls into broad categories—slots for short—that people ask for. Your inventory knowledge will be bunched into a few of these categories—leaving you unprepared to cope with buyers for other categories—unless you work effectively to prevent that bunching. The slot sheet provides you with a fast and dependable way to do that. It allows you to design your Quick-Speak Inventory to meet the widest possible range of needs. It guides your keyviewing and QSI flashdecking along the lines you've selected as being the most efficient for you. As your Quick-Speak Inventory grows, you may want to use additional slot sheets to cover more localities. Here's how to put this idea to work.

Select your first zone of specialization for your first slot sheet. This should be an area of at least a thousand houses or condominiums. Then take out a blank sheet form and insert the name of the zone or area you chose. At the top of the columns write five headings. Do it in pencil to begin with. These headings should classify the housing in your zone in ways beyond the number of bedrooms each unit has. Classify them by price, number of stories, style, lot size, specific amenities. Use what works in your area; choose headings that reflect what buyers want and how they think in the here and now. Price, of course, is where the heaviest cut almost always comes, so you'll probably want to head some of the vertical columns. *Under* $250,000 (250K), or whatever figure now marks the top of an active demand slot in your area.

Once you've decided on how you'll organize your inventory, fill in the headings you've chosen for your slot sheet in ink. Then get busy finding houses to fill those slots. Now you know exactly what sort of houses your Quick-Speak Inventory needs to give you a complete sample of what's available. Now you know exactly what to look for so you'll be prepared to work with any and every serious buyer that your area can provide housing for.

The slot sheet aims at developing an inventory you can show on the shortest

UNDER 200K	UNDER 150K		CONDOS	ELM DIST.	CLUB ESTATES
140 W. "E" ST.		V	66 S. NET	5502 W. ACE	
1020 BLUFF		O	2131 4th E.	4901 DIANTE	65 PRESS WAY
		V			
2 BEDROOMS	2 BEDROOMS		2 BEDROOMS	2 BEDROOMS	2 BEDROOMS
		O			
		V			
3 BEDROOMS	3 BEDROOMS		3 BEDROOMS	3 BEDROOMS	3 BEDROOMS
		O			
		V			49 S. 60th
4 BEDROOMS	4 BEDROOMS		4 BEDROOMS	4 BEDROOMS	4 BEDROOMS
		O			
		V			
5 BEDROOMS	5 BEDROOMS		5 BEDROOMS	5 BEDROOMS	5 BEDROOMS
		O			

QSISS   QUICK-SPEAK INVENTORY SLOT SHEET

*V   Vacant   O   Occupied

FIXER-UPPERS	GREAT TERMS	VIEW	POOLS

possible notice—preferably with no notice at all. For this reason, the form gives special attention to vacant houses. In each row of slots, the top line is marked *V*. To qualify for these lines, a property must be vacant, available for showing without your having to notify anyone, and its house key should be in a lockbox on the premises, or kept in your office.

The lower lines are marked *O* for occupied homes that require a phone call before you take buyers to see them. For each slot, select the property that represents the best value you know of that is available now. As your inventory knowledge increases, and as new properties come on the market, update your QSISS so that it lists the best buys you know of every slot on it.

For example, you might decide to call your first area of specialization *Greenpretty West*. Use the first two headings to focus attention on hot price categories. Three areas of special interest to you, a condominium development, an average neighborhood, and a prestige section, should have their own columns. Since houses with a fine view, a pool, or solar-assisted heating are in special demand in Greenpretty Valley, use the spaces for special categories at the bottom of the form to spotlight properties with those amenities that are best buys.

To speed the updating of the slot sheet, prices are not given because they should be flashdecked and memorized.

Additional tips for fast building of your Quick-Speak Inventory are given in Chapters 2 and 3.

Fizzbo Cross-File Cards

When filed by phone number (which can be written in large numbers in the corner) the FSBO X-File gives you a quick and effective way to work for-sale-by-owners. Chapter 5 shows a partly filled-in form, and tells you how to pack loads of money-making follow-up information onto this 3 × 5 card.

Communications Log

In the sample communications log that partly filled out here, the transaction is Stuart to Meigs, and the client is Stuart, so you are the listing agent. It's important to show who your client is on this particular document because you might be representing Meigs in a few weeks. The first conversation started at 11:10 A.M. on June 9, and lasted two minutes. This data about time, date, and length of call makes all the difference if your word is questioned later. You'll find it's a real cruncher to say, "According to my communications log, I gave you that information on September 12 at 2:05 in the afternoon. I'm sure you remember now. My log shows that we talked for six minutes." Should gripe come to growl, your communications logs will carry great weight in court—if you've made a consistent practice of keeping them.

The first call noted on the sample log was made by you, as indicated by the code "OC" (as explained on the form). The subject of the call is given next. You'll often use several lines for a single communication. Don't clutter up the page with pointless detail, but do take sufficient space to record the bones of the conversation. In the last column, show who the other party to the communication was. With a little practice, you'll find yourself entering this information without difficulty or delay as you talk.

Buyer's Progress Chart

Whether you represent the sellers or the buyers, you'll want to keep close tabs on what isn't happening. Staple a buyer's progress chart to the inside of your transaction folder, review it at least once a week, and keep the fees flying to you. Chapter 19 talks about fallout avoidance in detail, but the heart of the matter is right here on this form. You'll have far fewer fallouts if you'll diligently do the detail work on time.

Fast Fact Grabber

Here's a form that'll not only let you catch information quickly while you're prospecting, but, by using it, you'll also be able to find that information rapidly when you follow up. On the back of this form are spaces for scheduling and

COMMUNICATIONS LOG

CLIENT/SUBJECT				TRANSACTION				
Stuart				Stuart		TO	Meigs	

COMMUNICATIONS LOG

					YEAR	PAGE

START TIME	DATE	STOP TIME	CODE	CODE: OC/outgoing phone call V/visit L/letter IC/incoming phone call
				GIST OF EACH COMMUNICATION AND NAME OF PERSON CALLED
11:10 AM	6/9	11:12	OC	

BUYER'S PROGRESS CHART

BUYER'S PROGRESS CHART			DATE OF SALE	NAME	
			TARGET CLOSING DATE		
			FINAL ITEM COMPLETION CHECK		
STEPS REQUIRED TO CLOSE	PHONE	DATE ORDERED OR SENT	DATE COMPLETION EXPECTED	DATE ACTUALLY COMPLETED	DATE CLIENT INFORMED
APPLICATION FOR LOAN					
APPRAISAL					
BANK VERIFICATIONS					
CREDIT REPORT					
EMPLOYMENT VERIFICATIONS					
INSURANCE, FIRE OR HOMEOWNERS					
LENDER FUNDS AVAILABLE					
PRELIMINARY TITLE REPORT					
REPAIRS					
TERMITE INSPECTION					
INITIAL INVESTMENT DEPOSITED					

©1989, Danielle Kennedy Productions, 219 S. El Camino Real, San Clemente, CA 92672

FAST FACT GRABBER

DATE OF FIRST CONTACT		PRIORITY	BEST TIMES TO CALL	
LAST NAME		_____		
FIRST NAME	H U S B A N D	SEE OVER ☐	DON'T CALL TIMES	
WORKS AT				
JOB OR TITLE				
FIRST NAME	W I F E			A C T I O N
WORKS AT				
JOB OR TITLE				

NOW	☐ OWNS	☐ LEASES	☐ RENTS	BEDROOMS	BATHS	STORIES
	ADDRESS					
STYLE						
CONDITION						
AMENITIES						

WANTS	☐ TO SELL ▲	☐ TO LEASE-OPTION	BEDROOMS	BATHS	STORIES
	☐ TO RENT ☐ TO BUY	FINANCING DESIRED (CIRCLE ONE)	VA FHA CONVENTIONAL CASH OTHER		

STYLE & LOCATION WANTED

SPECIAL REQUIREMENTS

HIS $	HERS $	OTHER $	TOTAL INCOME $

PRICE RANGE OF HOUSE THEY WANT TO BUY $		TO SELL $	per MO YR
CASH AVAILABLE FOR INITIAL INVESTMENT $		FROM SAVINGS	FROM SALE OF PRESENT HOME	FROM OTHER SOURCE

WHAT'S ON THEIR MINDS NOW

SPORTS, HOBBIES, SPECIAL INTERESTS

PETS	RELATIVES LIVING WITH THEM	CHILDREN	
CATS			
DOGS		LIVING WITH THEM	
	FAST FACT GRABBER		

BACK—FAST FACT GRABBER

NAME						PHONE NUMBER				
FOLLOWUP CALL NUMBER	1	2	3	4	5	6	7	8	9	10	
PLANNED DATE TO CALL											
ACTUAL DATE CALLED											

RESULTS OF CALL NUMBER

1

2

3

4

5

6

7

8

9

10

FAVORABLE ASPECTS

UNFAVORABLE ASPECTS

HERE'S HOW I'LL CONVERT THIS CONTACT INTO A TRANSACTION:

recording ten calls. Just as important are the three boxes at the bottom that are designed to direct your attention toward figuring out how to turn each contact into a transaction.

Results Record

Most of us tend to remember the negatives, and dwell on our hurts more than is good for us. It's easy to do that and overlook the steady progress we're making. Results records keep the good stuff up front. Make one of these forms out for all your prospecting sessions—even if you make only one call.

Study the results records you've completed from time to time. You'll discover that the more you have, the more you'll learn from them. Unless you keep track of your course, you can't correct it.

Show List

This is a form that always impresses customers. After I've made it out, I often run it through the office copier and make one for each of my buyers.

On the form "*page* number" is the page number of the current Multiple Listing book where the listing appears. This is handy when a customer starts shooting questions under several houses at you that you're not prepared to answer.

Under "*status*," o/o and t/o mean owner-occupied and tenant-occupied. The distinction is important when you're showing property. Tenants have been known to be less cooperative and less careful than owners about setting the stage. The "OK" means that you've reached whoever lives there and received their permission to show the property.

Tomorrow's Action List

Every night use an appointment book planner, a TAL, or any piece of paper, but plan your tomorrows. Unless you do, every breeze that blows will push you hither and yon. You won't get where you want to go until you take charge of your life. Be sure to check out my Time Planner that includes this form.

Farm File

Here's a form that has the space you need to record all the good things you'll learn about the people in your farm. Knowing these details helps you talk to them and earn their friendship and trust.

For your convenience, space is given in the farm file for entering information

RESULTS RECORD

	DATE CALLS MADE
RESULTS RECORD	TYPE OF CALLS

START TIME(S)	STOP TIME(S)	TOTAL TIME SPENT

TALLY OF CALLS MADE	TOTAL NUMBER OF CALLS COMPLETED	AVERAGE TIME PER CALL
	☐	☐

SOURCE OF PHONE NUMBERS   OTHER SOURCE

FSBO ADS   MY FARM   CRISS CROSS   OTHER DIRECTORY

THE THREE BEST THINGS I SAID DURING THIS PROSPECTING SESSION ARE:

1 _____

2 _____

3 _____

NEXT TIME, WHAT I'LL DO BETTER IS: _____

REMARKS

I MADE ☐ CONTACTS DURING THIS PROSPECTING SESSION THAT I WILL FOLLOW-UP IN THE FUTURE

DURING THIS PROSPECTIVE SESSION
I MADE ☐ APPOINTMENTS

FORM KJ-6   PRINTED IN U.S.A.

SHOW LIST

SHOW LIST			B E D R O O M S	B A T H S	S T O R A G E	A G E O F H O U S E	S T Y L E					
PREPARED ESPECIALLY FOR												
DATE	**SALES COUNSELOR**	**PAGE NUMBER**										
▲ **PROPERTY** PERSONS TO CONTACT ▼	▲ **PRICE** PHONE ▼	▼ **STATUS** ▼ OK ▼										
1 ADDRESS	$											
CALL BEFORE SHOWING	PHONE											
2 ADDRESS	$											
CALL BEFORE SHOWING	PHONE											
3 ADDRESS	$											
CALL BEFORE SHOWING	PHONE											
4 ADDRESS	$											
CALL BEFORE SHOWING	PHONE											
5 ADDRESS	$											
CALL BEFORE SHOWING	PHONE											
6 ADDRESS	$											
CALL BEFORE SHOWING	PHONE											
7 ADDRESS	$											
CALL BEFORE SHOWING	PHONE											
8 ADDRESS	$											
CALL BEFORE SHOWING	PHONE											

about the house they live in. Transfer the permanent part of this data to your property catalog.

Each time you work your way through your farm, try to record at least one additional fact about every family you visit with. Do that immediately after you talk with them or you'll lose a lot of the small details that are vital to winning control of your farm. There's a fine line you must walk here. On one hand, you must show a pleasant interest in your people. On the other hand, you must not come on as a nosy busybody. Back off if you encounter someone who is secretive and suspicious; you can gain nothing by pressing such people.

Before you hit any house again, take a moment to quickly review the details you've already learned through your past casual conversations with the people who live there. This will allow you to start off the new conversation about where the last one ended. People are flattered by what you remember about them if you're not too obvious about it.

A word of caution. You can lose your farm file, so don't write anything in it that would offend the people involved if it turned up in the wrong place.

TOMORROW'S ACTION LIST

T.A.L.   ►DO DATE _____
TOMORROW'S ACTION LIST

MUST DO   DONE

☐

☐

☐

PRIORITY

☐ _____ ☐

☐ _____ ☐

☐ _____ ☐

☐ _____ ☐

☐ _____ ☐

☐ _____ ☐

☐ _____ ☐

☐ _____ ☐

☐ _____ ☐

☐ _____ ☐

FARM FILE

ADDRESS			LAST NAME		
	◀ HIS	FIRST NAMES	HER ▶		

CHILDREN		

HOUSE INFORMATION		BEDROOMS	BATHS

CAREER INFORMATION ◀ HIS HER ▶

LEISURE INTERESTS ◀ HIS HER ▶

FARM FILE

BACK—FARM FILE

VISITS	LAST NAME		DATE MOVED HERE
DATES	FACTS LEARNED		
FRIENDS AND RELATIVES			
REFERRAL POSSIBILITIES			

FARM FILE

LENDER QUALIFYER - A FORM BUYER FILLS OUT AT FIRST INTERVIEW

EXAMPLE:

For a family with gross annual income of $42,000 and monthly long-term obligations of $400 (installment debt, auto loans, credit cards, child support, etc.)

A. Gross Annual Income   **$42,000**
(Before Taxes)

B. Gross Monthly Income   **$3,500**
$42,000 divided by 12

C. Monthly Allowable Housing   **$1,260**
Expense and Long-Term
Obligations
$3,500 multiplied by .36 (36% of gross monthly income is usually allocated for principal, interest, taxes, insurance *and* monthly long-term obligations.)

D. Monthly Allowable Housing Expense   **$860**
$1,260 minus $400 (Subtract monthly long-term obligations from line C. Remainder is allowable principal, interest, taxes and insurance payment.)

> NOTE: Monthly Allowable Housing Expense on line D should not exceed 28% of Gross Monthly Income on line B. If it does, enter the lesser amount on line D and continue.

E. Monthly Principal   **$774**
and Interest Payment
$860 multiplied by .90 (90% is the amount of the monthly allowable housing expense usually allocated to principal and interest payment only, *excluding* taxes and insurance.)

F. Estimated Mortgage Amount*   **$96,100**
$774 divided by 8.05 multiplied by $1,000 (8.05 is the factor for a 9% loan amortized over a 30-year term. Factors for other interest rates and terms - consult a lender.)

G. Estimated Affordable Price Range   **$120,125**
$96,100 divided by .80 (80% is the mortgage loan amount, assuming a 20% down payment. Use .90 for a 10% down payment.)

ACTUAL:

A. Gross Annual Income $ _____
(Before Taxes)

B. Gross Monthly Income $ _____
Line A divided by 12

C. Monthly Allowable Housing $ _____
Expense and Long-Term
Obligations
Line B multiplied by 36

D. Monthly Allowable Housing $ _____
Expense
Line C minus long-term obligations or line B multiplied by .28, whichever is less

E. Monthly Principal $ _____
and Interest
Line D multiplied by .90

F. Estimated Mortgage Amount* $ _____
Line E divided by the appropriate factor from the interest rate chart and multiplied by 1,000

G. Estimated Affordable Price Range $ _____
Line F divided by .80 or .90 depending on down payment

Should you select an adjustable rate loan, your Sales Associate can also show you how to use this Worksheet and Interest Rate Factor Chart to determine your affordable price range and monthly payments.

This material is intended for example purposes only and is not a commitment for financing.

This work sheet is intended for use on primary residences. Your mortgage amount and price range will vary depending on the size of your down payment, the specific terms of your loan, other monthly obligations and the amount of association fees, if applicable.

*Rounded to the nearest $100.

An estimated and itemized list of closing costs seller should expect to pay when their home sells.

SELLER'S NET SHEET

SELLER'S NET SHEET

PREPARED FOR _____

REGARDING _____

SALES COUNSELOR _____

MANAGER'S APPROVAL	_Date_
	SELLING PRICE .... $ _____

ESTIMATED SELLING COSTS

TITLE INSURANCE	$ _____
TAX STAMPS	$ _____
ESCROW FEES	$ _____
TERMITE INSPECTION AND REPORT	$ _____
OTHER INSPECTIONS	$ _____
PREPAYMENT PRIVILEGE, IF ANY	$ _____
RECONVEYANCE FEE	$ _____
BENEFICIARY STATEMENT	$ _____
PRORATION OF INTEREST	$ _____
FHA OR VA LOAN DISCOUNT FEE	$ _____
DISCOUNT TO CASH OUT BUYER'S SECOND TRUST DEED	$ _____
_____	$ _____
_____	$ _____
_____	$ _____
_____	$ _____
_____	$ _____
APPROXIMATE* TOTAL OF SELLING COSTS . . . . $ _____ $ _____

LOANS

(Indicate where the information was obtained by circling one of the sources for each loan.)

FIRST TRUST DEED	Seller	Lender	Document . . $ _____	
SECOND TRUST DEED	Seller	Lender	Document . . $ _____	
OTHER ENCUMBRANCES	Seller	Lender	Document . . $ _____	
TOTAL ENCUMBRANCES . . . . $ _____ $ _____				
TOTAL OF ESTIMATED SELLING COSTS AND ENCUMBRANCES . . . . $ _____ $ _____				

APPROXIMATE* NET CASH TO SELLERS . . . . $ _____

*This estimate has been prepared to assist you in computing your costs and net walk-away cash. Whenever possible, we have used the MAXIMUM charges that are expected. However, unusual circumstances may arise, and lenders, inspectors, and others may vary their charges. Therefore, these figures cannot be guaranteed.

POSSIBLE CREDITS OR DEBITS NOT INCLUDED ABOVE:
Return of balance in impound account.
Proration or cancellation of fire insurance.
Proration of property taxes.
Proration of association dues.

An estimated list of costs buyer can expect to pay when they purchase a home.

BUYER'S NET SHEET

BUYER'S NET SHEET

PREPARED FOR _____

PROPERTY ADDRESS _____ SELLING PRICE _____

SALES COUNSELOR _____ DATE _____

⬤ FINANCING METHOD

_____ LOAN FEE . . . . _____ _____ _____

INTEREST ON NEW LOAN . . . . _____ _____ _____

at interest rate of . . . . ____ % ____ % ____ %

SETTLEMENT (ESCROW) FEE . . . . _____ _____ _____

DRAWING LOAN DOCUMENTS . . . . _____ _____ _____

ALTA TITLE POLICY . . . . _____ _____ _____

TAX SERVICE . . . . _____ _____ _____

RECORDING FEES . . . . _____ _____ _____

FIRE INSURANCE . . . . Premium _____
(or Homeowners')   or   _____ _____ _____
                                       Impound _____

PROPERTY TAXES . . . . Proration _____
                                          or   _____ _____ _____
                                       Impound _____

CREDIT REPORT . . . . _____ _____ _____

APPRAISAL . . . . _____ _____ _____

INSPECTIONS . . . . _____ _____ _____

ASSOCIATION DUES AND TRANSFER FEE, IF ANY . . . . . . _____ _____ _____

_____ _____ _____ _____

_____ _____ _____ _____

MISCELLANEOUS . . . . _____ _____ _____

TOTAL CLOSING COSTS . . . . _____ _____ _____

INITIAL INVESTMENT . . . . _____ _____ _____

TOTAL CASH REQUIRED TO CLOSE . . . . _____ _____ _____

MONTHLY INVESTMENT . . . . _____
(see other side for the breakdown)

MANAGER'S APPROVAL

This form breaks down the buyer's monthly payment.

BACK—BUYER'S NET SHEET

BREAKDOWN OF MONTHLY INVESTMENT

Principal and Interest

    on First Mortage ----------------------

    on Second Mortgage -----------------

Association Dues, if any -------------------

Monthly Cost of Fire or

    Homeowners' Insurance --------------

Monthly Cost of Property

    Taxes ----------------------------

TOTAL MONTHLY INVESTMENT -------

AMOUNT DEDUCTIBLE* on

your Federal Income Tax

Return -----------------------------------

*NOTE: YOU MUST VERIFY THIS AMOUNT WITH YOUR TAX ADVISER BEFORE RELYING ON IT TO MAKE A DECISION ABOUT REAL ESTATE. THESE DEDUCTIONS MAY NOT BE AVAILABLE TO YOU.

All figures given on both sides of this form are based on present information. Actual figures at the settlement may vary.

A form realtors use when they interview a buyer prior to previewing homes.

BUYER'S ANALYSIS FOR BETTER SERVICE

Date _____

BUYER'S ANALYSIS FOR BETTER SERVICE

Names of clients _____

Is this your first visit to our community? _____

Where are you folks from? _____

How long have you been looking for a home? _____

How many are in your family? _____

Then you have _____ children? _____

May I ask their names and ages? _____

Where do you live now? _____

How long have you lived there? _____

Are you investing in your home, or do you rent? _____

How is the resale market in your area? _____

May I ask, Mr. _____ where are you employed? _____

_____

How long have you been there? _____

Have you seen any homes you really like? _____

What prevented you from owning that home? _____

_____

_____

_____

How soon had you thought of making a move after you've found the right home? _____

How much time will you have to see homes today? _____

How many bedrooms would suit you best? _____

If they own now:
How much do you feel you will realize from the sale of your home? _____

Will it be necessary to sell your present home to purchase the new one? _____

_____

BACK—BUYER'S ANALYSIS FOR BETTER SERVICE

Will you be converting any of your other investments to cash in order to complete the purchase of your next home?_____ ____

_____

If we are fortunate enough to find the right home today, will you be in a position to make a decision to proceed? _____

_____

Not to be personal, but to do a better job for you, may I ask, how much of your savings do you wish to invest in your home? ____

_____

What price range have you been considering? Better yet, since most people are concerned with their monthly outgo, how much do you feel you could comfortably invest each month in your new home, including everything?_____

_____

Use on lower price range properties:
A rule of thumb most lenders use is that the monthly investment should be approximately one-fourth of a person's gross monthly

income, after payments on long term bills are deducted. Are we in line here? _____

_____

Please take a moment, Mrs. _____ , to describe your present home to me, including all your likes and dislikes.

_____

_____

_____

_____

_____

What are your special requirements for your next home? _____

_____

_____

_____

_____

Are there any other special requirements that I haven't noted yet, such as (Suggest some of the popular amenities available in your

inventory) that you'd like to see in your next home?_____

_____

_____

_____

_____

_____

A comparable form to use with the homeowner during the listing presentation.

GUIDELINES TO MARKET VALUE

GUIDELINES TO MARKET VALUE

PREPARED FOR _____

REGARDING _____

PREPARED BY _____   *Range $_____ to $_____*

DATE _____

RECENT SALES	SALES PRICE	DATE LISTED	DATE SOLD	LIST PRICE	AMENITIES	FINANCING	LOCATION		

HOMES AVAILABLE NOW	LIST PRICE	DATE LISTED	DAYS ON MARKET	AMENITIES		FINANCING	LOCATION		

EXPIRED LISTINGS	LIST PRICE	DATE LISTED	DAYS ON MARKET	AMENITIES		FINANCING	LOCATION		

©1989, Danielle Kennedy Productions, 219 S. El Camino Real, San Clemente, CA 92672

Note: All forms can be purchased "camera ready" for realtors at Danielle Kennedy Productions.

MONEY-MAKING CHECKLISTS

Prospecting

Before the best time to prospect that you've chosen for this particular session, gather the phone numbers you'll call. Have these items at your elbow when you begin calling:

- *A pad of fast fact grabber forms*, or plain paper.
- *Results record form.* Fill in the date, time you'll start calling, type call, and source of the phone numbers before you start. Keep track of what you're doing so that you can evaluate what you've accomplished, and improve results for future prospecting sessions.
- *Mirror.* Keep it in front of you as you call so that you can constantly check your expression. Strain that shows in your face will travel over the wire to the other person.
- *Pen.* And pencils. Have plenty.
- *Timer.* A stopwatch works best. Any clock will do.

- *A cassette recorder* if you want to tape yourself.
- *The Danielle Kennedy Planner* to record a possible appointment you might acquire during this session. Be ready to set up meetings that don't conflict with your present commitments.
- *Your office's current sheet of listings and the Multiple Listing book* in case the conversation turns into property inquiries.
- *Your comparables file.* But be careful not to give them too much information over the phone. Do that in person with a Guidelines to Market Value form.
- *Winning scripts.* Have handy a list of statements to make and questions to ask.
- *Goal.* Always set a goal for each prospecting session that's completely within your control. Build on wins.

Checklist for Farming

- In your car:
  Bottle of ice water.
  Multiple Listing book.
  Farm file.
  Property catalog.
  Backup supply of giveaways.
- In your purse or pocket:
  Supply of business cards.
- In your hand:
  A few of your current giveaways.
  A few of your imprinted scratch pads.
- In your heart:
  Firm resolve to meet your goal for farming that day.
  Firm belief that a single soft yes is worth 100 hard no's.
- In your brain:
  Your goal for how many contacts you want to make today.
  A number of opening remarks.
  Alertness.
- On your face:
  A confident smile.

Up-Time

The tea cart checklist is given in Chapter 10.

Checklist for Listing Appointments

- Clipboard for taking notes during the tour.
- Calculator.
- Multiple Listing book.

- Title insurance rate card.
- Amortization book.
- Your Listing Presentation Manual.
- Listing folder that contains:
  Guidelines to Market Value filled out for the property you're there to list.
  A seller's net sheet form to be filled out during the appointment.
  A blank listing form.
  Your marketing plan of action flyer.
  One of your imprinted scratch pads.
  Copy of your latest newsletter.
  Flyer-packet of your other listings, or of a sample of your office's listings.
    Place them on top of a copy of your profile of a pro (you).
  A copy of your personalized flyer, ''A Dozen Tips that'll Bring My Sellers
    More Money.'' (See Chapter 12.)

Listing Presentation Manual (LPM)

The most convenient page size is 8½ × 11. You need the stand-up kind that's easy for your prospects to see, and that leaves both of your hands free. You have two choices of format in this size sheet:

- *Flip Chart.* The horizontal page size is 11 inches, like a school notebook turned on its side. K & M's model E3V-11 has one-inch rings. Sheet protectors are available.

- *Easel Binder.* The horizontal page size is 8½ inches. K & M's model ES311-1½ has 1½-inch rings. 20th Century Plastics of Los Angeles offers a top-loading sheet protector (their model RB-3) that makes updating your LPM fast and easy. If your local office supply doesn't have these items in stock, they can order them for you.

I prefer the flip chart to the easel binder because most of the certificates and 8 x 10 photos that I used in my LPM were right side up in that format. And the flip chart looks less like a high-school notebook and more like a professional's working equipment.

Select the format you prefer. Then create pages with scissors and paper cement that usually present your LPM's points. Office supply stores carry rub-on letters (transfer lettering) in various sizes that look terrific. Use lots of color. Highlight important items with a felt marker. Strive for a smooth presentation, but keep it very personal to yourself, and avoid making it too slick, because the most important element in your presentation is selling yourself.

Although your LPM will have three sections, flow smoothly from one section to the next as you use it.

Section One: Sell the Real Estate Industry

Explain the Multiple Listing Service.

- Sample page from the MLS book.
- Highlight number of agents.
- Emphasize the referrals from other areas that all these agents get.
- Give the volume done by the entire board last year in graph form. As you talk, tell them what the volume was last month and last week.
- Printed copy of the code of ethics, published by the National Association of Realtors® (if you are a member).

Diagram of buyers:

Show this diagram visually, and explain when you give the presentation that first-time buyers are afraid of fizzbos, and people coming in from distant points don't have time to work with them. Both kinds of buyers want a professional they trust to represent them. So, without professional help, sellers are left with the local bargain hunters and lookielews. (Don't bring all this up if it's obvious that the sellers have no intention of trying to sell themselves. Don't plant the idea in their minds.)

Section Two: Sell Your Company

Have 8 × 10 color pictures of your entire staff, the interior of your office, and the exterior of your office. (If you have a good location, talk about it at this time.)

If your company rates favorably in your community on sales volume, have a page that shows how strongly they rate, and then tell them.

Samples of your company's advertising.

Explain how advertising works in the local real estate resale market. A diagram showing how much business comes from signs, from classified ads, and from other sources will be helpful to back up your position on advertising.

The special awards your company has won or a shot of your staff holding trophies is most effective. Show your pride in your office and tell how your staff works together.

Deadlines for getting the listing into the board office, for advertising, for having their house caravanned. If your office has its own preview of new listings, tell them about it now.

Show your company's relocation affiliation, and talk about it.

Section Three: Sell Yourself

- Training certificates. Show the sellers that you keep up with new trends in marketing homes.
- Samples of flyers you've had printed on some of your listings.
- Your profile of a pro flyer.
- Your "Dozen Tips to Bring My Sellers More Money" flyer.
- Your track record, if you've been in the business long enough to have an impressive one.
- Photos of your office awards. Newspaper clippings.
- Copies of ads you've placed yourself.
- Letters of recommendation from satisfied clients and customers are powerful convincers.
- Your marketing plan for selling their home, should you be selected to represent them. A sample marketing plan is given at the end of this chapter.
- Photos of you and happy clients putting up *Sold* signs. These have great emotional impact. Use several.
- A blank Guidelines to Market Value form, and a blank seller's net sheet, makes for a smooth transition to the money phase of your presentation.

At this point set the LPM aside, put your listing folder on the table, take out the guidelines form, and go for it.

After-listing Checklist

- Stick your temporary *For Sale* sign in the front lawn.
- Have your broker approve the Listing Form.
- Submit copy of listing to Multiple Listing Service.
- Obtain key from sellers and place in lock box.
- Order permanent *For Sale* sign installed.
- Distribute *Just Listed* doorhangers in the neighborhood.
- Check with the present lender about the existing loan or loans. Can they be assumed? Is there a prepayment privilege? What costs are involved? Explore what other lenders will do for a buyer now, so you'll be able to answer when one asks.
- Have an extra key made if the sellers will allow you to.
- Put your marketing plan into high gear.

Open House Checklist

- Open house signs, arrow signs, and flags.
- Refreshments, if desired. (Bring paper cups, napkins, sugar and creamer, if needed, paper plates, trash bag.)
- Your plan for making effective use of your time on open house.
- Display on the most visible table, or on an easel:
    Purchase agreement.
    Guest log.
    Information flyer about the property.
    Stack of customer-catcher maps.
    Stack of flyer-packets.
    Giveaway package promoting your area.
    Stack of your imprinted scratch pads.
    Business cards.
    Net sheet made out for asking price of that property.
- Have available, but not necessarily in sight:
    Listing forms.
    Amortization book.
    Title insurance rate card.
    Calculator.
    Multiple Listing book.
    Your appointment book.
    Pad of fast fact grabbers, or plain paper.
    Something to eat.
- Display in the front room:
    Easels with storyboards about your area and you.

Add if the House You're Holding Is Vacant

- Card table and three folding chairs.
- Roll of hand towels, box of tissues, soap.
- Drinking cup.
- High-intensity lamp with extension cord.

Checklist for Property-showing Appointment with Buyer

- Show list prepared for this buyer.
- Deposit receipts (purchase agreements).
- Title insurance rate card.
- Calculator.
- Amortization book.

- Multiple Listing book.
- Counteroffer forms.
- Buyer's net sheets.
- List of schools and churches in the area.

Real Estate Car

- Open house signs, arrow signs, and flags.
- Temporary *For Sale* sign.
- *For Lease* rider.
- *Sold* rider for your office's sign.
- Kid kit with games to occupy the small people some buyers bring along.
- Coping kit (see next section).
- Backup kit containing a supply of your
    Business cards
    Personalized scratch pads
    Latest farming giveaway
    Latest newsletter
    Buyer and seller net sheets
    Listing forms
    Purchase agreements
    Counteroffers
    Lock boxes
    Extra batteries for your calculator
    Supply of pens and pencils
    Extra amortization book and title rate card
    Stationery
    Letterheads, notes, and envelopes
    Stamps
    Customer-catcher maps
    Flyer-packets

Coping Kit

- Small rolls of masking and transparent tape.
- A few push pins, paper clips, and rubber bands.
- Small stapler, scissors, screwdriver, pliers.
- Handful of bolts, nuts, and washers for your signs.
- Work gloves.
- Box of tissues. Bandaids.
- Large flashlight.
- Measuring tape (cloth, not metal, so as not to scratch furniture.

Put these items in a small cardboard box and keep them in your real estate car's trunk. You'll be pleased at how often they'll ease your way, and keep you looking cool and competent.

Fallout Avoidance Checklist—The After-Sale Checklist for Both Buyers' and Sellers' Agents

- Be alert for developments that might blow *this* transaction apart. Every real estate transaction is unique, special and different. The most important item on your fallout avoidance checklist is alertness and quick reaction—in cool, professional manner that employs plenty of sound common sense—to whatever occurs. Chapter 19 has more details.

- All copies of the accepted offer (and counteroffers, if any) signed by all parties. Copies of each of these documents delivered to all parties.

- Buyer's loan application delivered to lender.

- Complete legal description of property to lender and to the person processing the paperwork.

- Inspections ordered promptly. Termite, roof, mechanical—whatever is required in your area and by the special provisions of this purchase agreement.

- All other special provisions of this agreement cleared.

- All contingencies, if any, cleared.

- All repairs required by agreement ordered in good time, and then completed. Who has responsibility for each item? Are they doing what has to be done? Are the sellers making timely arrangements to move out?

- Loan approval.

- Keep a communications log on all conversations touching on this transaction. Use a buyer's progress chart to keep track of the vital steps necessary to close.

- Will the lender have the money to fund the loan?

- New fire insurance obtained by buyer.

- Preliminary report of title, if required by this purchase agreement. Ordered? Received? Any problems?

- Have escrow instructions (or whatever document is used in your state to tell the person handling the paperwork exactly what to do) been signed and returned?

- Have the buyers done whatever must be done before they can get the necessary initial investment money?

- Have they deposited that money in escrow or the proper account?

- If the buyers are to move in before settlement or close of escrow, has a rental agreement been signed and a substantial amount of money released to the sellers before they take possession? (Allowing the buyers to move in before the property is legally theirs should be avoided whenever possible. Some people see this as removing all incentive to complete the purchase. Others find little things around the house to bicker about. But sometimes it's the only way to save the transaction when things that the buyer can't control delay the close.)

It's your responsibility to protect your clients' interests, and also to help them give friendly and honorable cooperation to the other party. Transactions have been lost because one of the agents felt that loyalty to his or her client or customer required rude conduct or unreasonable actions. Never forget that your job is to solve problems, not create them.

Add to the After-Sale Checklist if You're the Buyers' Agent

- Introduce your buyers, by telephone or in person, to the processor (or whoever will be handling the paperwork involved).
- Think through the paperwork problems involved in this particular transaction, and work out a schedule to get everything done on time. Whenever possible, allow yourself a pad of time to cover slip-ups in the paper flow. If necessary, hand-carry documents. Fly there and get them signed. Ship them out by air freight parcel service. Use the post office's latest priority and express services.
- Review with your buyers all the details that have to be cleared before they can get title to their new house. Do this as soon as possible after their offer is accepted.
- Fire insurance ordered.
- Copy of fire insurance policy delivered to processor or lender.
- Work through the listing agent to make sure that the sellers have arranged to move out on time.
- Make sure your buyers understand what type of check is required. If they show up on the closing date with a personal check drawn an out-of-state bank for the amount for the initial investment, your transaction won't close— unless they can have the funds wired from their bank to a nearby correspondent bank *that day*.
- Keys to the house (and garage door openers). When, where, and from whom will you get them? Don't wait until the last minute. The listing agent may be out of town when the sellers move out with the keys in their pockets.
- Housewarming gift to buyers. (Dinner on you the day they move in?) Cement your relationship with them and ensure future referral business.
- Ask for referrals.
- Call two weeks after they move in.
- Add these customers to your twice-yearly contact file.

Add to the After-Sale Checklist if You're the Listing Agent

- Notify your office, and your association, of the sale.
- Obtain your broker's approval of the purchase agreement.
- Copies of any permits for alterations and additions in the file if required.
- Put a *Sold* rider on your *For Sale* sign.
- Remove the lock box. Tell the sellers, "With your permission I'll keep the key in the safety of our office so I can let the appraiser and the inspectors in and not have to bother you. Will that be okay?"
- Distribute *Just Sold* doorhangers in your area.
- Prepare list of comparables for appraiser.
- Meet appraiser at the property with list of comparables, and key.

Marketing Plan of Action

This plan was written by one of my students. Adapt it to your area and methods, quick-print your revised version, and add one to your Listing Presentation Manual. Put a copy in the listing folder that you make up for each listing appointment.

I SALES PROMOTION AND ADVERTISING
   A   List property. Place lock box, if agreeable.
   B   Distribute listing to all members of the staff.
   C   Submit listing to Multiple Listing Service, and check book weekly to make sure listing is accurately recorded.
   D   Caravan for our staff on Tuesdays, and acquaint them with the amenities and strong sales features prior to entering client's home.
   E   Caravan for Saddleback Valley Board members on Thursdays, with refreshments served to encourage their lingering to enjoy the home. Phone offices for a personal invitation prior to caravan.
   F   Write no less than three ads about property for advertising in some or all of the following media: *The Register, The Pennysaver, The Saddleback News*, and the *Los Angeles Times*.
   G   Printing and distributing of a marketing sheet. Sheets are given to offices of the Saddleback Valley Board of Realtors, passed out at board breakfasts, and also left in client's home for those viewing it.
   H   Open house, when convenient for client.

II MONITORING
   A   Request that sellers save all business cards of agents for follow-up by you.
   B   Follow up with people met during open house.
   C   Personal notes notifying neighbors and others of listing, and open houses.
   D   Telephoning top salespeople in board.

E A continual effort to keep client's property in front of board members, and to sell to each agency that calls in about client's home.

GOAL— To continually, and always in good taste, keep client's home in front of MOTIVATED salespeople and MOTIVATED BUYERS until SOLD!!!!!!!

III FINANCING THE SALE OF THE HOME

A Contact the current lender, inquiring about their lending policies.

B Conduct a lender survey of interest rates, loan fees, and other data to compare with current lender.

C Report and discuss findings with client.

IV CONTACT WITH OWNERS

A Present samples of all sales promotions and advertising.

B Call and visit with client frequently as to the progress of the sale of the home, response of showings, and general market activity.

C Re-evaluate marketing program often as to possible changes.

V THE PROCESSING PERIOD

A Suggest and implement, if possible, hand-carrying of documents.

B Suggest that all documents be signed, and returned to the respective parties, as soon as possible.

C Keep in constant contact with processor, lender, title company, and buyer's agent during the entire processing period.

25

Dead Cats, Weeds, and Holes in the Walls

About noon on a hot September day, I took a call from an agent who said she would show one of my listings in an hour to a very ready buyer if I would get rid of the dead cat in the backyard. It was pretty bad, she said. When she previewed the house, one of the neighbors had complained to her about the cat. As I walked out of the office, I told Melinda on the up-desk, "I'll be back in 20 minutes. Got to run over and bury a dead cat." I picked up a shovel at my house and drove over to the listing. It was a vacant house that the owners had left in immaculate condition, but as soon as I stepped out of my car, I realized that the neighbor had good reason to complain.

I dug a deep hole in the backyard with the shovel, placed the poor little creature in his grave, and refilled the hole. Then I drove back to the office and called the showing agent.

"You're all set."

"When's it going to be taken care of? I can't show that property to my people unless I know for sure—"

"It's done. I took care of it myself. And I turned the sprinklers on for a bit. It's April in Paris around there now."

I went over to the up desk to check with Melinda for Messages. She said, "Danny, did you really go out just now and bury a dead cat?"

"I took care of it, Melinda. I'm sure it had been somebody's darling pet, but I couldn't leave it in the back yard. What a total turn off for buyers."

"Of course. Only—why you?"

"Because I'm the *listing* agent, Melinda, The owners are a thousand miles away."

"But couldn't you have called someone?"

"Like who? I figured I could take care of it myself quicker than I could locate someone to do it for me. How would you have handled it?"

Melinda shook her head. "I don't know—except that I wouldn't do it myself. I'm a real estate agent, not a yukky-thing-doer."

I thought about that incident again two months later when Melinda dropped out of real estate. She just couldn't bury the dead cats.

THE DIAMOND

The hardest and, at the same time, the most beautiful fact about this fascinating business of ours is this simple truth: You get paid exactly what you're worth. This will seem very hard when you've just had two transactions fall out, four offers turned down, and eight bills you owe go delinquent. It will seem beautiful when you bank in one month more than the average wage earner takes home in a year. "There's a lot of pure, dumb luck in this business and all of mine is bad," too many of us say, and believe, when things go wrong. Whenever you're tempted to lay your problems on some nebulous force outside yourself, it's time for you to act as your own best friend, and have a little talk with yourself. "Friend, I tell this to you for your own good: You make your own luck 99.99 percent of the time. In listing you make your own luck. In selling you make your own luck. In every aspect of life you make your own luck. So get out there and make yourself some good luck. Sitting around complaining pays just what it's worth: nothing. The longer you talk negative, the longer you'll earn nothing—and fella, you can't afford it."

Are you throwing yourself into real estate with all your energy? Or are you just testing the water, dipping a toe in to see if it's too cold?

IT'S COLD, ALL RIGHT

Pull on a wet suit and dive in—or get in your car, drive away, and forget about it. There are determined, knowledgeable agents already in the water—and they think it's just fine. One thing you haven't done is join a monopoly; there won't be a protective tariff holding off the competition.

But there's space for everyone who's willing to work effectively. This will always be true: The world in general, and the real estate business in your area in particular, will always have room for another effective worker. So learn to be effective.

That means, quite simply, that you do what has to be done to open and close transactions. We are not talking about trickery, misrepresentation, and unethical conduct: All unfair tactics are degrading and self-destroying. Learn how to win people's trust and confidence. There's no better way to begin than by convincing yourself of your own trustworthiness and competence.

Many people unconsciously hold back from all-out effort in real estate because, if their all-out effort fails to bring them success, they'll have no excuse. They can't face the risk of defeat without a prepared excuse. These people do not see that:

ALL-OUT EFFORT MAKES SUCCESS CERTAIN

If you've chosen goals that are achievable, all-out effort makes success certain. Success in real estate is an achievable goal for anyone capable of obtaining a real estate license, if they'll make a full commitment of their energy and resources—if they don't hold back. They must make that decision and only one other: "I must change and adapt and grow; the world won't change and adapt to me."

Do what has to be done to merit your clients' and customers' faith in you. Tell them the truth, the whole truth, and nothing but the truth. So far as you know the facts, tell them everything that legitimately affects their interests, everything that's important to the decisions they must make. Do this even when you talk yourself directly out of a fee. It will come back. Believe in your own integrity, and others will believe in you too. Nothing can happen in real estate until people like and trust you.

Do what has to be done to prepare a property for sale. Tell the sellers the doggie do-do in the backyard must be shoveled up, that the bathroom fixtures must be cleaned and shined. Do it diplomatically—but do it.

Sometimes there are serious problems with the property that have to be corrected before it will sell. If the sellers are merely slow to accept reality, work with them. But you have to make a decision here. Will they accept reality and fix the problems before they decide it's your fault the property hasn't sold? Look ahead and make that decision early. The most effective use of your time may be to work on listing other properties to replace the problem house. A large part of being effective is successfully avoiding unpromising situations.

Agents who have only one listing or one buyer to work with will put up with much flakiness in that client or customer as you pick up a good workload of people to service, make sure that you also pick up:

A LOAD OF INDEPENDENCE

Keep your balance, but remember that people can keep you working so furiously that you never realize how much money they're preventing you from making.

A few sellers and some buyers are too demanding, too unreasonable, too destructive of your time and energy and positive feelings. You can't make money even if you succeed in closing a transaction with them. By the time you've collected your fee, you've spent more time working with them, and more time healing yourself afterwards, than you would've spent earning two or three fees with normal people.

If you're starting to wince every time the phone rings, if you're beginning to suspect that you secretly hate people, stop and take stock. Are you selecting the worst people to work with by allowing such people to monopolize your action? If so, they're blocking you from having sufficient time and energy to find prospects who are more of a pleasure, and less of a pain, to cope with. Lots of nice people are out there, mixed in with lots of un-nice. Never lose sight of that fact. For the sake of your health—and for the benefit of your fortune too—start sloughing off the worst of the grumps and growlers as soon as you can. Start jumping for the prospects who say please. Remember that they are the kind who'll go away quietly if they're neglected. Let the howlers howl when you give priority on your time to the say-pleasers. That's the way you select a reasonable clientele instead of allowing an unreasonable clientele to select you. Relax. Keep your mind refreshed. Put yourself in the way of pleasant people to work with. You'll make more money and like your days better if you do.

FALLBEHIND, MOVINGUP, AND HYFLIER

You'll encounter more properties with minor problems than with major problems: landscaping that needs attention, squeaking doors, a broken window that lets in rain.

Agent Hyflier calls a dependable handyman. "Fix it. I'll pay you." Hyflier may or may not get repaid by the seller at the close. "My time is valuable," Hyflier says, having done the things necessary to make it so. "No handyman can do what I get paid the most for, but he can take what I'd get paid the least for off my back."

Agent Movingup feels the same, can't afford the handyman yet, makes the repairs personally—and gets the house sold.

Agent Fallbehind is too busy squeaking his office chair to do what must be done. Things slide until, three days before the listing expires, Fallbehind has a sudden burst of energy. Lots of phone calls. Intense pressure on people to move fast. Money is spent. Things get done.

Too late. The sellers list with someone else.

Fallbehind sinks back into a dazed funk, rousing occasionally to refill a coffee cup and say that Hyflier isn't really good. "He just knows an awful lot of people."

Something underhanded is going on there somewhere, Fallbehind intimates darkly, pounding back to his desk. ''And this new kid, Movingup—let me tell you, nobody goes that fast in this business without cutting too many corners. Just a flash in the pan. No real depth there. Wait'll things get really tough. Wait'll the chips are down. Then we'll see if these prima donnas can sing.''

When the market turns and the chips *are* down, Hyflier is flying too high to notice, Movingup is solidly entrenched with a 100 percent referral business, and ex-agent Fallbehind takes a job outside real estate ''until the market straightens itself out.''

Here are a dozen ideas that, if followed, will turn Fallbehind into Movingup, and Movingup into Hyflier:

DANNY'S DOZEN FOR SUCCESS AT LISTING AND SELLING

1 Honor your time and your integrity.

2 Keep specific, written, achievable and exciting dreams always fresh and alive in your thoughts.

3 Validate yourself positively every morning and night.

4 Build your pride on achievements won fairly; never forget or apologize for a humble beginning.

5 Know the inventory.

6 Know your area.

7 Make promises you can keep and then keep them.

8 Learn the golden phrases people need to make decisions that are favorable to them and to you.

9 Find your winning shots and have a game plan that you play hard.

10 See the world through your clients' eyes; feel their hopes and fears; be part of their ups and downs. Develop referral business by putting your peoples' needs ahead of your own.

11 No matter how busy you become, take time to be kind to your body, and to learn and live and love.

12 Be responsible to and for yourself, to and for your family, to and for your company, your community, and your country.

WATCH YOUR JARGON

Caller: ''I've decided to sell, Tillie. Come over and list my house.''
Tillie: ''I can't. I'm on the floor.''

A GOOD-STUFF NOTEBOOK (INNER TRAINER JOURNAL)

Good-strokes go in the front section. These are all the clever dialogues, zingers, and convincing arguments you thought of after the people walked out the door and it was too late to use them. And you also record here the effective lines you did think of in time to use.

Briefly jot down the circumstances that set the stage for your good stroke after you record the good stroke itself. Make a habit of capturing your effective words on paper as soon as you're alone. Read them over and role play them occasionally so they'll be on the tip of your tongue the next chance you get to use them. You'll get many chances; the situations of real estate constantly repeat themselves.

Feel-goods go in the back section. These are your victories. Read them to pep yourself up when things go wrong; read them when things go right to accelerate your enthusiasm. We tend to remember and dwell on our defeats and rejections, large and small, and to forget our good shots. Turn that around: Reject your rejections and dwell on your sharp shots. The quick oneliner that got a good laugh and saved a shaky negotiation. The time you listened right to a grumpy garbage-can kicker and came away with his listing. The fee-winning hunch you acted on. Jot down your smaller victories too. If you're held back by fear that someone will read your feel-goods, abbreviate them into code. Keep a list of the scores you've made. Read and relive them when you're tempted to dwell on defeat. If you prefer hashing over faults and failures to remembering strengths and successes, that's not just a clue you're self-destructing your enthusiasm, forcing a defeatist attitude on yourself, and driving fees from your pocket: It's proof.

Take delight in your victories. Remember what you did right. Record your right moves, your strengths, your effective phrases. Review them constantly. Build confidence to match your rapidly growing competence. Low achievers have neither; mediocre performers have one without the other; high achievers have both. Success flies on two wings.

STAY AWAY FROM JOLLEY J. FLOPPE

Every office has one or a few jolly flops, people who have loads of failure fables on Quick-Speak.

"That's me, the fall-out king of the South."

"I've screwed up so many deals, I've learned to look good doing it."

"When it's your turn to get a good break, it'll find you wherever you are. No sense knocking yourself out looking for it."

"Take it easy. Rome wasn't built in a day."

"You don't have to do that."

"Nobody does *that* anymore." (J. J. Floppe will tell you this about any effective technique, such as door-to-door farming, that the Floppe is too negative minded, fearful, or lazy to do.)

These are the people who think they know exactly how much business they have to do to hold their desks. Occasionally they have to find a new wall to hang their license on. By doing well, you become an emotional threat to them: You can do it, so why can't they? Although they may not admit it even to themselves, they aren't really for you if you're a comer. Don't let them pull you down to their level.

WEEDS

Weeds are easy. There's a kid in the neighborhood who'll do them for you. And I've pulled a few thousand weeds myself at my listings. Now that's past. The hardware stores have these terrific Weed-Eater gadgets for the price of a good dinner for two. Get one if you have a weed problem on vacant houses. It might be worthwhile having a Weed-Eater to lend your sellers who still occupy their houses. Get that landscaping shaped up somehow and sell that house.

EVEN OUT THE PEAKS AND VALLEYS

Even out the peaks and valleys with investment income. Buy a fixer-upper at the year's low point, fix it up during the slow season, and put it back on the market when demand quickens. Build up a rental portfolio. Invest in the field you know. You'll gain insights and make contacts that will boost your career.

MAKE HABIT WORK FOR YOU, DON'T FIGHT IT

"I'm set in my ways. They're winning ways. I change my ways whenever I learn something better. Habits are my friends, not my masters, not my enemies. They help me do more, and get it done better and faster. My habits don't control me; I control them."

If you don't believe all of this you've located a serious barrier to your success and happiness. Beat this barrier down. You put it up; you can knock it down.

If you find the idea of changing your personality unsettling, explore your fears. Why don't you want to change? When you can answer that question, you'll be ready and able to take charge of yourself.

CHECK YOUR MOP EVERY MONTH

The real estate market is changing constantly. The *methods of operation* that worked well last month may not work as well next month. Long distance races aren't won on dying horses, and your real estate career is definitely a long distance race.

Consider every month whether you should adopt new methods to deal with changes in

- The resale market as it is *today*, as it is likely to be in the immediate future.
- Your growing referral business.
- Your increasing professional stature.

And, every month, consider these questions:

- Should you work with creative financing methods to maintain volume in the face of a tightening money market?
- Should you concentrate on finding buyers, or on acquiring new listings?
- Should you farm more—or less?
- Should you start looking for an assistant?
- Should you advertise more? In newspapers? By mail?
- Should you spend more time with clients, and less time however else you're spending it?
- Should you review fundamentals?
- Should you take some time off and heal yourself so that you'll be more effective?

THE PIGEON-TOED UNDERSOLD REAL ESTATE PERSON

It's 6:00 P.M. He's been pounding the pavement all afternoon. "Hi, I'm Paul Roberts, your local real estate expert. Can I be of service?" This morning he sat on floor duty at the office. Not one decent prospect. "Sell Fast Realty, this is Paul, I'm sorry; Mr Jones isn't in right now. Can I take a message?" Four hours of taking messages, an afternoon on the street and now he's home. "Hi, Paul. How's my honey? How'd you do today? Any listings? Did you show anyone property, or sell a house?" Sounds easy. But it ain't. I make a motion that the whole world swap skin for a week with the real estate man—no salary, no steady flow of income—only himself to turn to. Let them experience the days of desperation and loneliness. Let them earn our days of self-fulfillment, cocksure power, and creative drive.

THE RULES

Play it strictly by the rules. Take this from me as the absolute truth, and save yourself a lot of hard knocks: The rules give you your best chance. Ethics aren't entanglements that hinder you; they are defenses that protect you. Use them.

During my 10 year career as a salesperson I was never called to court even one time. I'm very proud of that; more so than a track record.

EXCUSES ACCUSE

Whenever you're tempted to marshall lengthy arguments rather than admit an obvious failure on your part, remember that the more you excuse yourself, the more you accuse yourself. Confess the mistake. Don't ramble. Accept full responsibility and move on fast. Blame hanging in the air clouds the client's view of you.

"It's all my fault. I was very busy that day, but that's no excuse. I should've handled it but I didn't. That won't happen again, I guarantee you. What's done is done; now let's focus on the future—"

DEVELOP YOUR POWERS OF DECISION

Quick decision making is a skill that becomes habit. It can be developed. Indecision is a habit that can be overlayed with your new habit of decisive action. Here's how to do it:

- Make important decisions when you're fresh. A tired mind makes weak decisions, if it makes any at all.

- Don't postpone decisions and do nothing. If you need more information, decide how much new information you need and how you'll get it. Then make a decision about when you'll make that important decision.

- Always make small decisions fast. Always make big decisions deliberately. Always make the distinction. The common practice is to make large decisions fast, perhaps because analyzing their pros and cons seems overwhelming, and to reserve the longest periods of indecision for the smallest matters. Turn that around: Make the right decisions about decisions. Quickly snap off the little decisions, where mistakes hurt little, or not at all. Put your long thoughts and detailed reasoning into the large decisions.

When you've paid your dues in this business, and the volume you're doing starts attracting attention, eager beginners will ask for more help with their problems than you have time to give. Tell them to read:

OLD HAND TO NEWCOMER

How's it going?— See you later;
We'll talk when you're much greater.
Don't bother me kid, go do as I did.

Though it wouldn't be a strain to,
I hardly get paid to train you.

I have eager people to see
Who are busy waiting for me;
I have lots of doorbells to ring
And some very hot deals to swing.
Don't bother me kid. Go do as I did.

Let me make you this blunt declaration:
I'm no part of your indoctrination.
Why, all this time of mine you'd like for free,
Is time that will earn me a great big fee.
Don't bother me kid. Go do as I did.

You see, my time is all I've got,
And if it seems I'm such a sot,
As not to give a jig or jot,
Not a worry about your lot,
Say, guy, don't be so very dense
I mean no great big old offense.

Sure. I was a slow starter once,
Now I'm busy 'cause I'm no dunce.
Let me wish you the best of luck
And hope you make the great big buck.
But bother me not, just do as I did.

Learn wide, learn deep, and on your own,
Knowledge learned is never on loan.
I wouldn't say, this you should do,
Unless I knew that it's true,
Because, deep in this cold shell that you see,
Lives warm mem'ry of how it was for me.

HOLES IN THE WALL

There are so many when some people move out, their house looks like the O.K. Corral after that bad day. Those holes in the wall are the main topic of conversation whenever that house is shown. It's pure disaster.

Root around in the garage for the rusty, skinned-over cans of wall-matching enamel such people always leave. But a small can of spackle from a hardware store, and enough children's water color brushes from a variety store to give you one for each color. Press dabs of spackle into the picture holes with your thumb or a putty knife and then touch up that spackle with the paint. Anyone who'll take the time to work carefully can do a beautiful job of hole repair their first time out. Even tired old paint dries out to match.

Adjust to reality. There's no justice. Bury the cat, pull the weeds, touch up the holes. Sometimes, the way this unjust world operates, you'll make a thousand dollars an hour doing just that.

GOALS

Recall the Picture of Yourself as a Child • Pick Four Targets • Imagine Your Targets. Do They Balance? • Hazy Targets Are the Hardest to Hit • Ask Yourself These Questions • Give Yourself Wins • Review Your Targets Periodically • Break Up Your Work Cycles • Life Doesn't Have to Be

People who have purpose find goal setting easy. Their purpose is more important to them than the difficulties they face carrying it out. Their minds are too filled with purpose to allow space for difficulties to expand there. They are impatient with barriers, and think constantly of how to avoid or get through them, not on how formidable and distasteful those barriers are. Because such people have no interest in difficulties except to solve them, they find themselves constantly achieving goals, and then setting new and higher ones for themselves.

The future looks far different to people without purpose. Forced to function without a driving purpose to crowd their minds, they find their problems expanding like hot air in a balloon. Purposeless people devote most of their time and energy to trivialities, and see their lives enclosed by walls. Their chances are small of ever finding a purpose outside their self-imposed walls because they think those walls can't be scaled. With purpose, one sees the handholds, scampers over, and is away to the greater world outside.

It all comes down to purpose. Is your mind filled with expanded purpose?—or expanded problems? Your mind must be dominated by one or the other; it cannot be dominated by both. Pump up your purpose, expand the positive side, and the negative side must diminish.

You're here. Why not make an impression? Why not be an influence? Why not have a special effect on one person? Why plod when you can fly? The limitations you place on yourself are enormously greater than any that can be imposed from the outside.

It all comes down to purpose. To me, purpose derives from having other human beings in your life who care, who love you—yes, who are dependent on you. Nothing nourishes purpose from seed to great oak like being special to your own special people.

Find your purpose. Find big and small reasons to want more from life. Then fulfill your potential. You may think we're all worms—then be a glowworm. Glow as you worm your way along. I remember the glowworm stage. At first I was delighted to glow a little, and then I wanted to be a butterfly. Then a meadowlark. And after that, an eagle.

It all starts with purpose, purpose that's more important to us than the barriers we must go around or through to achieve our finest destiny.

Everyone must develop on their own, and at their own particular rate of growth. But growth would be dull without people who care about us, who provide the spark, who encourage our development. At every step of the way, from birth to the present time, I've had people—adults or children—around me. These people have given me more purpose. I've felt loved. I've been loved, and the more I'm loved by my children, and by the adults in my life whom I care about, the better I get. I could never have opened a real estate company with partners I didn't love. I could never work for anyone unless there was some emotional feeling there. I've been accused of mixing my head and my heart on decisions. If God permits, I'll stay that way the rest of my life because working strictly for my own satisfaction is not my ambition.

RECALL THE PICTURE OF YOURSELF AS A CHILD

Before thinking about the targets or goals you wish to achieve, let's go back to a point in your life when you were quite free—about age five. What did you like to play? What did you pretend? It's important that you think about this, because often we had purpose as a child. We were born with some innate talents, needs, and wants that so often lie latent in adulthood. If we can recall a time when pretend and mental imagery were part of our everyday life, we can regain some failed purposes in our life. Let me talk about myself for a minute. As a child, I did a lot of pretending and talking to myself because I was without brothers and sisters. I can recall wanting to be grown up and have lots of children around me. I wanted to be a mother very badly, but I never saw this as a restrictive thing. I wanted to be a dancer, a singer, and a doer at the same time as being a mother. My parents never gave me the impression that if you were a mother, you couldn't do anything else. As a teenager, I loved President Kennedy and Bobby and Ethel and their eleven children. I used to cut all their photographs out of *Life* magazine. I loved the action going on in that group. People running for office and playing touch football—it was fascinating. My mental imagery always painted me in the middle of a picture like that. So, when I began my family, and had one baby after another, I was delighted—and I always had something else happening. I'd take courses at the local university, read textbooks, burp babies, and practice a new dance step at the same time. People who didn't like surface confusion would come into my house and wonder how I could stand all these growth rings I had going on at the same time. Then, when the expansion of the family brought out the need for money, I entered real estate. I wanted things for my family that my imagination told me we could have. I was inspired to work because my purpose was great. I tell you these things so you will examine your own life. Remember our motivation is rooted in our reality.

Because, if you don't have the excitement in your soul that creates purpose, the simple suggestions I'm about to give you on goal setting will be futile. Many writers and speakers can turn people on for an hour or a day, but that turn-on is an external thing and it's only temporary. Only you can motivate you!

Purpose that remains powerful for long periods of time must be internally generated. All I can hope to do is picture the growth ring. You must open that ring, and all the growth rings that lie beyond, for yourself.

Purpose comes from self-knowledge, and from your love of the people who kindle that purpose. Make a list right now of your purposes in life, and of the people who will bring those purposes out loud and strong. Keep in mind that these faces must undergo changes from stage to stage of our lives. Life is change, but as long as you have significant persons in your life—in present time, in memory, or in imagination—you can be strong in purpose, happy and effective, and you can grow.

PICK FOUR TARGETS

Take a notebook to a quiet place. Go there alone and get comfortable so that you can think in clear and large terms about the four vital areas of your life. Consider each in turn. Begin by writing these two words across the top of a page in your notebook:

Financial Targets

Below that heading, write a short paragraph to describe what you want to attain financially. Don't begin with specific sums of money. Focus on the *purposes* that you want the money for initially.

Your first paragraph might read something like this:

"My purpose is to be independent of outside financial aid for the rest of my life, and to support myself and my family. I wish to provide my children with college educations, and ourselves with two wonderful trips together each year."

Think about what that will cost, and then write a second paragraph:

"My purpose is to have a steady income of _____ for the rest of my lifetime. I can realistically achieve this in the field of real estate by attaining a volume of _____, and by investing in _____ on this program: _____."

On this first page, keep your thoughts on the overall picture. Then write out your financial purposes in great detail on succeeding pages as you refine your thinking.

Work at recording your purposes with all the freedom that intensity can give you. Remember as you write that you can always revise your purposes whenever you close one series of growth rings and open another. Set your purposes on what is excitingly alive for you now. The next target area to cover, with a fresh page in your notebook, is:

Social Target

Here is the format: Write your own purpose that reflects your emotional needs.

"My purpose is to have three significant people in my life who are outside my family. These three will be people I love, people I can count on in times of joy and sorrow. I would like to share common interests with them. I am not a club joiner, and prefer a small, select group of intimate friends. I recognize that this will take time and patience to develop."

You may be a club joiner. Beautiful. You may prefer having a wider circle of friends. Perhaps traveling abroad, and developing friendships with people of other cultures, intrigues you. There's an enormous variety of social purposes. Having ones that strengthen your will is what's important, not who they are. Now head another page of your notebook:

Spiritual/Mental Target

"I wish to read at least two books a month, and attend at least one new seminar quarterly. I want to go back to college and _____ . I wish to develop my spiritual awareness, and increase my understanding of the supreme forces in life by _____."

Now explore the last of the four target areas:

Physical Targets

"My body is healthy and I intend to keep it that way through good diet and adequate exercise. To this end, I will _____ [jog, lose weight, play tennis, whatever]. I intend to reach these measurements, _____ , and remain there. I also realize that if I follow this good physical program all my life, I will be more desirable and the statement that you get better, not older, will be very true of me."

The most common barrier to strong purpose is the failure to throw off negative childhood training. Many of us are blinded to what *we* want by our compulsion to do what we think *others* value. We're so busy worrying what other people think that we don't tune in to what we feel. We must hear our own inner voices to have strong purpose.

You may have to think about these four target areas over a long period of time before you can truly get in touch with yourself on all four of them. But, unless you write them out, your purposes will tend to remain as flimsy as clouds. Write them out now. Your initial targets may stand for the rest of your life, or you may intensify them tomorrow. What's vital is to start the process of building powerful purpose through knowing exactly what you want from life.

IMAGINE YOUR TARGETS. DO THEY BALANCE?

As soon as you finish writing your four targets, take a critical look at their balance. Some people are too work-oriented. Others are too play-oriented. It isn't too much work, or too much play, that sends workaholics and high-life addicts to the mortuary too soon, it's lack of balance. I know about the destructive force of an out-of-balance lifestyle—I've been there. In my case, it was addiction to work that threw my life into turmoil. I'm not sure that problem is more easily cured than an overfondness for the bottle, but at least it gives you the energy to attack it.

Balance your income and outgo, not only of money, but also in the social, spiritual, mental, and physical target areas as well.

For a while, I was clicking out the listings, and clicking out the sales, night and day. Holding open houses by day, and washing clothes by midnight. Burping babies, healing wounds—all but my own. Was I tired! I wanted to go dancing, and didn't. I wanted to go golfing, and didn't. I wanted to fly, skate, ski, laugh, and click my heels—but I didn't. Maybe after this next closing. Just one more check. Just one more customer. Just one more referral. Tomorrow, tomorrow, I will do it. But by the time tomorrow came I was exhausted. I wasn't exercising. I wasn't eating. I was stuffing food down my throat at very odd hours of the day and night. Socially I was down to maybe two friends—everyone else had tired of being put on hold. Mentally I was a little nuts.

Now I'm practicing what I preach. You can sell as much real estate when you work smarter, not harder. That's on the short run. Over a period of years, you'll make more money by keeping your balance, enjoying life, acquiring new skills in other areas, and keeping your purposes strong.

HAZY TARGETS ARE THE HARDEST TO HIT

Now let's get down to specific goal setting. How many doors will you knock on today to pay for your trip to Europe—or the rental property you want to buy?

In the other areas of your life, set goals just as specific. If your target is to be a better parent, how much time each day are you going to spend with your child?

ASK YOURSELF THESE QUESTIONS

Are my targets real or pretend? Determine this by asking yourself:

- How realistic are my goals considering my time schedule?

    If you have floor time today and a dance to chaperone tonight, plus seven kids to drive places in between, your commitment to knock on 50 doors each day for the next two weeks is in trouble. At least it is today. Cut down the overall goal a bit, or modify it when your personal schedule is heavy. That decreases frustration and increases your energy for the hours when you can throw yourself fully into your work.

- How realistic are my goals, considering my natural talents?

    This is a tricky area, because your natural talents are so much greater than you think they are. But if your ankles are weak, don't try out for roller derby.

- How realistic are my goals considering the people close to me who frown on my every move?

    Don't draw back just because everyone doesn't agree with what you're doing. But, if you have a spouse or loved one who gives you a lot of trouble, you'd better recommunicate. When loved ones feel compelled to hold you back, there are deep-seated problems that should be pulled into the light and looked at. Such problems don't get better without loving attention bestowed in time.

- How realistic are my goals considering my pocketbook?

    Suppose your target is a super-promotion in your farm every single month this year, but you haven't had a transaction close in six weeks—and you're about to miss your second house payment. I suggest you cut the supers, order a good supply of scratch pads, and go from there.

GIVE YOURSELF WINS

Some people never pat themself on the back. I have a tendency this way. I'll give a speech to a group, and before I even say "Hey, I did good," I'll go after the critique cards. Sometimes, I catch myself hurrying through the wins looking for the guy who hates me and the fact that I'm on this earth. Then I have to get hold of myself, and take time to bask in the wins so when I hit the losses, I can keep my perspective.

When you make a goal and achieve it, stop and smell the roses. I don't care if your goal was only to close one transaction this month, even though you sit next to Mr. Realestate who's presently handling 30 transactions. You made your goal, so take your body to the best dress shop, men's shop, hobby shop or whatever's your turn-on—and go for it. Then grab your loved one and jump for joy. Record your wins on the calendar. Write the goals you've achieved in tall letters and add some whoopee stuff. Learn how to let yourself feel really good about winning—you'll win more often if you do.

REVIEW YOUR TARGETS PERIODICALLY

Decide if what you're doing is still what you want to do. Some people keep knitting sweaters when they're ready to open up a stitch-and-sew shop. You're changing into a bigger and better person, so keep your targets current. Goals age much faster than we do. Pearl Bailey, at age 60, went back to school at Georgetown University. She certainly is studying and growing.

BREAK UP YOUR WORK CYCLES

Here you are with lots of purpose. You're attacking your goals with vigor, and knocking them down left and right. But don't overkill. You can burn yourself out. Learn to take mini-breaks: five minutes, an hour here or there, an occasional afternoon, a long weekend. On those mini-breaks use another capacity, preferably physical. Exercise is the best healer for the pressures of real estate. If you don't allow yourself to get physically exhausted, an hour's exercise (especially if it's doing something you enjoy) can repair a hard day's damage—and leave you fresh for an evening's work or frolic.

Break your big goals down into simple, small tasks. If your goal is to become the listing king or queen, and that means you have to double your production, break your ambition down into small daily wins. Contact so many FSBOs, call so many expireds, write so many notes a day.

LIFE DOESN'T HAVE TO BE

Life doesn't have to be a series of failures looked at over your shoulder, and more failures seen ahead. Here are some phrases that have no place in your vocabulary:

- If only
- How I wish I
- If I had it to do over
- I could have
- It's too late

Life is for the living. You and I are alive now, and can do anything we want to do. It's just a matter of knowing what that *anything* is. Once we discover that new purpose, or rekindle an old purpose, we can be on fire carrying our message through our space of time. It's exciting stuff, flying our craft through skies that are sometimes stormy, sometimes calm, but never dull. Discover your goals, and let them guide you to any port you want. Viva La Dolce Vita.

27

VALIDATIONS

Tasting Blood • The Formula • Precisely What Is the Technique? • Getting Started with Positive Validation • Intensify Your Positive Input by Creating Your Own Validations • The Honest Validation • Put It Behind You Fast • Choking Off Negative Input • Negative Validations • Flip the Disk • 35 of the Winningest Scripts of All

Please don't think I'm trying to be a psychologist, or an expert on mind control. I'm a woman second, a human being first, and a wife, mom, author, and lecturer. I can write a book and expect it to be read for one reason only—I did what I said I did in sales. This is my credibility. My only intention in this chapter is to make you aware of a way I think that's been enormously helpful to me. Maybe you can try thinking the same way, and have a little luck with it too. This doesn't mean I never get down, make mistakes, or react as any human being sometime does. Please understand that I am just another person, and don't put me on a pedestal. Sometimes we glorify people and then, as soon as they go the least bit haywire, everyone is on their case. My main purpose in this chapter is to tell you that, number one, your self-esteem is going to have a whole lot to do with your success in real estate. You know that already—just look around. Success keeps on breeding success. And, number two, here's a way you can feed decent stuff into your head that will help your self-esteem. If you feel you are too down and out for this simple method to work, by all means get help. This chapter is really for us everyday Joes who have our share of ups and downs, and just want to take life a little less seriously. Some of us get deeply burdened at times. That's when we must make a reach for help. Just make sure that you reach to the right thing for answers. But this chapter is not meant for that deeply burdened type of situation, where a person needs counseling.

One other thing goes hand-in-hand with this chapter. It's called faith. It isn't any of my business what people's religious beliefs are. And I am never one to impose mine. But I must tell you that people who believe in a Supreme Being usually believe in themselves too. A long time ago I learned an expression that I always keep handy when I get down and out: "God doesn't make junk." So if you believe in God, and I do, then you should go along with this chapter. I happen to believe very strongly in a personal God, and I talk to Him and myself in the form of positive validations every day. Now, if you aren't interested in this side of Danielle Kennedy, fine. Skip this chapter. "Stick with real estate, Kennedy," may be your philosophy. No problem. I can understand that. But for those of you who wonder how I think, here it is. If it helps, if it brings more power to you as it has to me, I'll be thrilled.

TASTING BLOOD

A new agent goes out into the field, quivering with fear, and somehow makes a good contact. Hopefully, because that agent's entire future in real estate may hang in the balance, he or she will repeat over and over to himself or herself a positive validation like, "I'm a natural at this. I've got the touch. Nothing can stop me now."

But if he or she thinks, "That was a pure fluke. I'll never be able to do that again in a million years," then very likely it won't happen again in a million years. That's a bit long to try any broker's patience.

THE FORMULA

You have to want the validation to work. You. Not your mother-in-law. Not your mate. Not your broker. Not your godfather. You. And the intensity of your desire to make the validation part of your personality has everything to do with your successful accomplishment of that aim. The formula for calculating the effectiveness of validations is

$$S = ED^2$$

The probability of *Success* equals the *Emotion* you pack into your validation multiplied by the square of your *Desire*.

PRECISELY WHAT IS THE TECHNIQUE?

Write your validations on 3 × 5 or smaller cards. Put the cards beside your bed and review them the last thing before going to bed, and the first thing in the morning. For quicker results, also review them during the day. Every time you review them, take a moment to visualize yourself having successfully accomplished the validation. It's important not to float above your mental image and watch yourself smoothly closing a client, or whatever the validation is. Imagine yourself looking out through your own eyes at that client as you close. Positive validation is a participation activity, not a spectator sport. Feel yourself standing there, talking confidently and effectively.

GETTING STARTED WITH POSITIVE VALIDATION

Your effective new self will begin to emerge the day you stop negatively validating yourself. That effective new self will rapidly become stronger, more confident, and more successful when reinforced constantly by positive validation. Your morale, when freed of negative input, will soar. You will welcome new directions, learn new skills, plunge into new situations, make new contacts, close new business— and enjoy it all. You will brush aside obstacles and ignore rejections that formerly would have shattered your drive. You will know the joy of catching the tide of success.

The sharpest saw, if left in the toolbox, won't cut wood. Although goals and validations can work wonders for you, they'll do nothing unless they're used. Don't put them away for later. Later has a way of becoming forever. But goals and validations aren't hand tools. They are power machinery capable of high-speed, high-quality production, or steady output at a lower and more comfortable pace if that's your preference. They're fully controllable, and all the levers are in your brain.

Maximum results require carefully thought-out validations that are coordinated with your goals. It takes a little time to put this program into full operation, but you can begin today with the positive validations given at the end of this chapter.

Choose not more than 20 that are aimed in directions you wish to go, and start visualizing them twice daily. It's best to do this lying in bed or sitting down. Get physically comfortable. Relax. Close your eyes and project the image of self you want. Feel it. Solidly and deeply experience what you wish to be. Then go on to your next validation. With practice, you'll be able to project a validation, and fully experience its impact, within a span of only two or three seconds.

Practice will enable you to carry well over 20 validations, if you so desire, and still get through them in two minutes or less. Limit your validation sessions to 120 seconds each morning and evening. You'll always be able to spare four minutes a day to operate this machinery of vast potential. Longer sessions self-destruct from interruptions, loss of concentration, and other pressures. Bear in mind that occasional lengthy sessions have little effect. Only the constant repetition of images briefly seen but intensely felt can do the subtle work of changing the inner self-image that controls your outer action. This regular repetition of vivid emotional experience is most effective when your subconscious mind is most receptive: immediately before and after your night's rest.

INTENSIFY YOUR POSITIVE INPUT
BY CREATING YOUR OWN VALIDATIONS

You can train yourself to conjure up a mental vision of the performance you desire to achieve through validations. It usually helps to hang a name on these visions, and often words are useful as triggers or intensifiers, but the most powerful effects of the validation technique are achieved by vivid visualizations that go far beyond a mere silent recital of words. Emotional intensity is what you are seeking. It may come to you the first time you try, or it may require practice, but it is attainable with slight effort compared to the benefits that it will return to you.

Let's set out some rules for making positive validation effective.

- *Don't talk* to anyone about your personal validations. They are your most personal property. If you make them public, you will destroy their effectiveness.

- *Achieve* substantial gains with the validation technique before you admit to anyone that you are using it. Some of those around you will ridicule the idea and try to discourage you because, if you succeed, it will unsettle them. They may have to think. They might need to change. They might even have to face the choice between following your lead or falling behind.

- *Express* your validations in phrases that are vivid and emotion-packed for you.

- *Be direct.* Passive validations produce passive results. Choose the active construction over the passive one. Use "I understand people," not "I am an understanding sort of person about people."

- *Be concise.* State your basic validation in the shortest form that retains force. Then add as lengthy a reinforcing description as will add to the intensity of your review experience with that validation.

- *Be accurate.* Select precise terms. If your goal is 20 prospecting calls a day, validate: "I make 20 prospecting calls a day every working day. I look forward to it; I'm making money at it; I'm good at it." But don't validate 20 calls a day when your goal is only 10, to give yourself a margin. You'll have to make 20 calls a day, or piggyback negative input on that validation. Either way, you weaken the entire program's thrust.

THE HONEST VALIDATION

Validations deal with emotions, not facts. They are declarations of what and who you intend to become. They are private. You make them silently. No one else relies on them when making a decision. Keep in mind that if you think something is true, for you it is.

PUT IT BEHIND YOU FAST

Winning at real estate involves taking many hard-to-take defeats. Big ones and small ones. Sudden and unexpected. Like the fallout on closing day of a large transaction carrying a much-needed fee. *Un*sudden and expected, like the loss of a fine listing that just won't sell. Snubs from frightened sellers. Slights from harassed buyers. There are enough negatives for the gloomiest to dwell on.

Take the long view. These events and people are of minor importance to your life. Don't let them determine whether you enjoy life—not for a week, not for a day, not even for an hour.

CHOKING OFF NEGATIVE INPUT

If you're aware of what negative input does to you, you can shut it off. Negative self-validation destroys your confidence, kills your competence, and throws you into dangerous tailspins. First, realize when you're doing it. Then you can stop chopping yourself down.

Is this what you're telling yourself after you discover an error?—"What a jerk you are! Screwed up again. Really blew it this time. Dummy. Every time you get rolling, you do something stupid like this." That's the loser living in us all talking, trying to take over. Throw loser back in the cooler with this positive validation: "I'm surprised I let that one go by. That's not like me, because I'm always on top of things like that. Okay, I slipped this once. But I won't again."

Admit the mistake to yourself with dignity. Tell yourself you won't repeat it—and get on with your action. You'll always make a few mistakes; your performance will never be perfect. Neither will anyone else's. You strive for perfection—but settle for a realistic level of performance. Be aware that as you improve the quality of your performance, you will automatically raise the standards by which you judge yourself. Keep that fact in mind, and praise yourself for progress made. Never chastise yourself for falling short of unattainable perfection. Don't organize a system that excludes the possibility of enjoying success, a situation in which you cannot win, cannot be satisfied, cannot rest easy after fruitful labors. Instead, enter positive input into your system and produce satisfaction, peace of mind, and a personal climate where success flourishes, by focusing on improvements and done-wells and beauties and feel-goods, not on a wart or two.

NEGATIVE VALIDATIONS

Nobody escapes them entirely. But you can hold their damage down to minor levels. Here's a sampling of negvals, a dismal dozen. Some of them will be familiar.

1 "I never could remember names."

2 "That's just the way I am."

3 "I'm not quick with numbers."

4 "I won't kill myself for anybody."

5 "I just can't get started in the morning."

6 "I can't win for losing."

7 "Nobody ever gives me any breaks."

8 "The market is lousy."

9 "Buyers don't want to buy anymore, they want to steal."

10 "I just can't figure people out."

11 "I could never swing a deal like that."

12 "My sellers are the most unreasonable people!"

Many people have made negative validations a necessary part of their coping system, and regularly use them to announce failure in advance. It's a neat trick: It turns a defeat into a win. "I told you I couldn't do it. Wasn't I right?"

You sure were, buddy. That's quite a smooth game you're playing there. Keep it up a while longer and the guy with the loud voice and the rude manner will repossess your car.

FLIP THE DISK

Every negative validation can be reversed into a positive validation. Turn those drive-killing, enthusiasm-slaying, defeat-breeding monsters into drive-developing, enthusiasm-energizing, win makers with the validations in the next section.

35 OF THE WINNINGEST SCRIPTS OF ALL

Here are twelve positive validations you can use to overwhelm the dozen negvals just given.

1 I've got a quick keen memory for names because I like remembering people's names. I make the effort, and I make money doing it.

2 I'm continually learning and growing and changing. When I realize I've been on the wrong flight, I find the right flight and get on it.

3 I'm fast and accurate with numbers. I wasn't previously, but now I am because I made the effort. It pays. Wow, does it pay!

4 I'm a hard worker. I put out lots of extra effort. Sure, I've got a lot, but I've worked hard for it. One of my greatest satisfactions is coming home after I've hit it hard all day, knowing I've done a good job. Going all out makes you feel great about yourself. You don't have to make excuses or brag. You know you've got it.

5 I'm an early riser and a fast starter. Early morning is the best part of the day, the time when I get my best thinking and work done.

6 I can't seem to find time for losing because I like winning so much. Good things just keep coming my way. Why no? I deserve them.

7 I make my own breaks. I like it my way—I'm making it, not taking it.

8 The market may be bad, the market may be good, but I'm serving my clients, not the market. In other words, the market is what I make it, and I make mine good.

9 Sure, people are looking for bargains. They always are. I'm careful with my money too. But I convince most people that the value is here, that it's worth paying the going price. And they do.

10 I have a lot of success understanding people because I make a real effort to put on their shoes and feel how they feel.

11 I'm a professional. I can handle any transaction. Anything I don't know, I'll sure find out in a hurry.

12 I don't have problems with my sellers that I can't work out. I'm empathetic. I'm a hard and effective worker for my clients. For most people, selling or buying a home is an intense emotional experience. That's why they need me: to help them make the right decisions during a difficult time.

Here are 20 more positive validations to fuel your upward flight:

13 I like myself.

14 I am responsible.

15 I do what I tell myself I'll do.

16 I do what I tell others I'll do.

17 I'm proud to be a real estate professional.

18 Real estate is exciting, fast moving, and fun. Not only that, I make great money at it. What could be better?

19 I do the most productive thing possible every minute.

20 I never dwell on negative thoughts.

21 I am getting nearer my goals every day.

22 I expect problems and disappointments. Without them, how can I be sure I'm doing everything I can to reach my goals.

23 I'm going far, fast, and high.

24 I am changing and growing and adapting myself to the world. I don't expect the world—my fellow workers, my manager, my clients, the competition, the lenders, the law—to adapt to me.

25 If it can be done, I can do it. The only question is whether I want to or not.

26 I'm alert and I'm no fool, but that doesn't keep me from liking and trusting people. And they like and trust me.

27 I spend quite a bit less than I make, so I own impressive real estate investments.

28 I'm a hard worker, but taking care of my health and spending time with my family have high priority. I eat wisely, exercise sensibly, and get adequate rest. And I take quality time off.

29 I'm mellow and vigilant, and every day I close up more on my goals.

30 My clients expect and get a lot of service from me; that's why I'm so successful.

31 I'm knowledgeable, thorough, and effective.

32 If it's not right, I just don't do it. It's that simple. And that simple idea called integrity has saved me much trouble, many clients, and lots of money. I'm practical. I don't shine my halo every morning. But I do know the clear line between right and wrong. I don't cross that line because I don't want to. And I never need to, because real estate is a people business that's built on trust. Nothing builds trust better or faster than valuing and practicing integrity.

Here are three final positive validations to shield you from the slings and arrows of outrageous fortune.

33 I put trouble behind me fast, and get on to something promising. I know I can't change yesterday—I can't even change five minutes ago. But I can influence the future to go my way, so I work on the future—in the present—during this minute.

34 My self-respect is not dependent on fate or the approval of other people. I make my destiny with my own effort and courage.

35 My happiness is not hostage to the whim of the public. Clients and customers come and go; my composure and confidence remain.

28

BREAK LOOSE

Well, dear ones, we did it. We read all the instructions on how to start the engine.

Now let's take off. I did. So can you. But one final reminder as we conclude this book. Start today to concentrate on just the next customer. Don't try to do everything we have mapped out for you in one week. Sometimes we take a look at the long haul, and it scares us half to death. I don't want you to do that. Think, *"Just one more person,"* and follow these suggestions to help you:

- *Break loose* from people and places and things that take you down. Life is for the living, so seek out the situations that cause growth, not decay. Keep your responsibilities, but shuck your hungover habits.

- *Break loose* from negative thoughts and feel-sorrys. As soon as you start feeling down, take a walk around the block. Robert Frost always took his dog. Frost said he didn't know if it did the dog much good, but it sure helped him.

- *Break loose* from fear and panic. When you try something for the first time (like knocking on a door, or qualifying a buyer) pretend you've done it dozens of times before. You'll find that comes easy when you've solo-role-worked the task dozens of times before.

Chew a blade of grass first. Grin. Hum a happy tune. Not taking yourself too seriously really helps. "Always think that you *want* to do what you're doing, not that you *have* to do it. Have-to hurts; want-to has wings.

Don't let the grumps of this world control how you feel. Across everyone's path a few grumps stray—but you don't have to join them. In fact, you can't join the grumps unless you want to. You can just as well choose to enjoy each day, and to profit in some way from every minute of every hour. Make believe that you only care a little bit and the trick will keep you opening up, finding new friends, and making more joy and more money.

- Break loose from bad patterns like taking no exercise and living on junk food. A sound body and mind go hand-in-hand. Pay some attention to what you eat, and put yourself on an exercise program. What are your strengths in sports? Golf? Handball? Lifting weights? Playing hockey? Tennis? Figure that out, make time, and do it. However, don't go out there and try to beat the pants off some pro. This is supposed to relieve anxiety and frustration, not cause it. Some people do everything with the "kill" instinct. Relearn how to play if you've forgotten.

- Break loose from jealousy. That causes more physical and mental mix-ups than any other disastrous emotion. Become your own best friend, and don't worry abut who's better off than you. Keep in mind that you're an original. No one can replace you. If a customer goes elsewhere, he won't be getting you. If a loved one gives up on you, that doesn't make you unlovable. Jealousy is sick, both in and out of real estate. We all get the pangs. When they come on, do something exactly opposite of the feeling. If someone else in the office makes a sale, force yourself to congratulate him. Put a note on his desk with a pleasant thought. Pretty soon, jealousy will figure it can't win.

- Break loose from being on the defensive. Ask yourself: Would I rather be right or happy? Accept the possibility that you may not always have all the answers.

- Break loose from complaining about personal problems and health. There's only one time to talk about health, and that's when it's good.

- Break loose from gloomy facial expressions. Exercise your cheek muscles and start the smile broadening. Grandpa Barrett always recited,

> *Smile and the world smiles with you*
> *Weep and you weep alone,*
> *For the cheerful grin will get you in,*
> *Where the kicker is never known.*

- Break loose and laugh, laugh, laugh. There's a song in Mary Poppins called "I Love to Laugh." In most of the song there's a man laughing his head off. You just listen to it and roar. Just take a look around at the whole bunch of us, and think about some of the ridiculous jams we get in—it's hysterical. My whole family tries to make me laugh when I get real serious or mad. I'm so happy they're around. They are the funniest, kindest, happiest people I have ever met. For the rest of my life everything will continue to make more sense because of them. How lucky can one woman and one man (my wonderful husband Mike) be?

- *Break loose* and find the kid in you again. Remember what it's like at 6 or 16, when you wake up on a summer morning, when the air smells clean, and the breezes are warm? You can't decide who to play with today, if you should ride your bike, skip rope, or hug and kiss your boyfriend behind the garage. Wasn't it terrific? I can still be that way. Real estate is great—but living is even greater. Life is so fragile. Cherish every second. Begin now and

Break loose—

BREAK LOOSE—

BREAK LOOSE AND LIVE!

THE BREAKAWAY SCHEDULE—A SELF-TRAINING COURSE THAT WILL GIVE YOU HIGH EARNING CAPABILITY IN 21 DAYS

The Index gives the page numbers where explanations will be found for each of the special terms that we've coined for Breakaway.

NOTE. You can complete all *Special* Achievements in the 21-day schedule before you receive your license. Many of the *Repeating* Achievements require a license.

SPECIAL Achievements of Day 1

1 Take aim at what you want. Reread Chapter 26, then make a written list of six initial goals as suggested in that chapter. They may be major or minor goals, but one goal should be the exact sum of money you want to make in the next 12 months. Another should be an exciting thing you'll spend part of that money on.

Here are two secrets that will ensure your success with the dynamic goal-setting technique:

- Set your initial goals fast, review them frequently, and revise them whenever they stop pulling you forward.
- Validate your ability to achieve the goals you've just set for yourself. Chapter 27 gives the method in detail. Select at least ten of the positive validations given there (or write your own) and triple your goalreaching capability.

2 Reread Chapter 5.

3 Select your winning move from the variety of For Sale by Owner techniques given in Chapter 5. Your selection won't be chiseled in granite. Make it fast. You can always change it later. Then prepare a flashdeck of the winning scripts for the FSBO technique you've chosen. Chapter 3 details the flashdeck method of high-speed learning.

4 Use your new flashdeck to create a blank-interval cassette. Chapter 3 shows you how easily blank-interval (BI) cassettes are made on a portable recorder-player, and how you can use this system to rapidly develop a convincing delivery of the many fee-grabbing lines in this book.

5 Select your specialization zone. This can be a neighborhood, a community, a certain type of house, everything east of the tracks—any definable area or class of housing units will do. Don't spend much time picking your first zone: You're merely selecting an area you'll give special attention to until another area looks better. You won't farm there. But plan to drive your zone frequently, and give special attention to its houses on caravan.

6 Prepare your Quick-Speak Inventory slot sheet. Chapter 24 shows you how; Chapter 2 tells you why this is the golden key to success.

7 On a printed map of your sales area, define 30 neighborhoods of about 20 streets each. This is the first step in gaining complete street knowledge of your area with the fast and effective named-neighborhoods method. Getting lost with a customer destroys your image of competence. Knowing your streets so well that you can't get lost impresses customers and saves crucial time during property showings, when delay is dangerous. Chapter 3 gives full details.

8 Read about rapid image building in Chapter 13. Then make an appointment with a professional photographer to have your portrait taken. Use this portrait on your letterhead, newsletters, business cards, and display advertising. You also need this same photo of yourself for the single most important farming tool I know of: imprinted scratch pads. Chapter 13 gives tips on designing effective ones. Complete your scratch pad design now, and order 1,000 of them as soon as you have your photo.

REPEATING Achievements of Day 1

Note A. Repeat each achievement every day until you've wrung the fullest possible benefit from it.

Note B. Achieve the *specials* for each day first; they provide the tools you'll need for the *repeaters*.

Note C. You must have a valid real estate license before performing many of the *repeating* achievements.

A Keyview properties until you've filled five slots on your Quick-Speak Inventory form. Review Chapter 3. It tells you how to use the keyview concept for total house recall. (See today's special achievement 6.)

B Using the high-speed learning method given in Chapter 3, put the first two named neighborhoods in your memory.

C Make three runs through your flashdeck this evening.

D Follow immediately with three runs through your blank-interval cassette. Use the flashdeck to coach yourself when necessary. Don't stop. Keep the tape moving and concentrate on speaking the lines with sparkle and clarity.

E Make up your tomorrow's action list. Chapter 22 has tips on this simple technique that, if you make it a firm habit, will earn more money for you in fewer minutes than anything I know of.

F Just before retiring for the night, review the validations and goals you selected today. Give each one a few seconds of deep concentration. Experience yourself doing, having, and being what you want to achieve.

SPECIAL Achievements of Day 2

1 Reread Chapter 11, How Listings Are Won.

2 Flashdeck that chapter's winning scripts.

3 Use your new flashdeck to create a blank-interval cassette.

4 Hyperlearn your listing form. As you recall, Chapter 3 has the techniques that will enable you to conquer this form quickly.

5 If you don't have a farm yet, consult your manager and determine what areas are open. Then reread the sections in Chapter 6 on selecting a farm. Take your time making this important decision. On each of the next three days, an achievement is scheduled to help you select, on Day 6, the best farm available.

6 Reread Chapter 21, Time Planning. Write a daily schedule for yourself. Then choose three time-saving systems from that chapter and put them into action.

7 Conquer the seller's net sheet form (often called ''seller's net proceeds'').

Give this form one hour of concentrated attention. Study the closing statements in your office's file of completed transactions so that you'll understand the end result of the seller's net sheet form. If you discover anything on the form you wouldn't be able to explain to a client, find the answer. Direct your questions outside your office—to processor, title, and lender's loan production people. If you don't know the answer, you can be sure a prospective client or customer will ask the question.

REPEATING Achievements of Day 2

G Review your validations and goals as soon as you wake up. Take a moment to visualize each validation and each goal: Emotionalize them—make them live in your mind.

H Make three fast runs through your flashdeck in the morning.

I Follow immediately with three runs through your BI cassette.

J Check the daily hot sheet, if one is issued by your Board of Realtors®. Have any changes occurred in the five houses you put into your Quick-Speak Inventory? If so, update your QSI flashdeck, your slot sheet, and your memory.

K Keyview enough properties to fill five more slots on your QSI slot sheet and to replace any already on it that have expired or were sold (Chapter 3).

L This evening make three runs through your new and old flashdecks.

M Make three runs through each of your BI cassettes.

SPECIAL Achievements of Day 3

1 Reread Chapter 8, Prospecting.

2 Flashdeck that chapter's winning scripts.

3 You guessed it: Make a BI cassette for solo role working these winning scripts. Chapter 3 tells you the difference between role playing and role working.

4 Write your "I'm in the real estate business" letter for your everybody-I-know farm. Chapter 6 has sample letters, and Chapter 13 gives writing tips. Estimate how many copies you'll need (certainly at lest 300) and order that many from a printer.

5 Start your everybody-I-know farm. On file cards, list the names of 25 individuals or couples you know well. Chapter 6 tells you how to work the people-I-know farm.

6 Define on a map the various farms that are available to you. Then drive all the streets of each one. You may immediately eliminate some from further consideration. When you return to the office, determine the turnover rate of each farm you're still considering with the method given in Chapter 6. Read the discussion there on applying past turnover rate to your decision about the future.

7 Reread Chapter 22, Self-Organization. Then organize your automobile for maximum real estate efficiency.

I didn't say this would be easy.
Becoming a professional never is.

REPEATING Achievements of Day 3

Some fizzbo material may have passed the overlearned stage. If so, drop those cards to weekly review, as suggested in Chapter 3, and limit the FSBO cassette to one or two runs of solo role playing every other evening. This overlearned stage is ideal for developing the relaxed, confident delivery that's most likely to convert prospects into clients.

Here's a new achievement to be repeated daily until thoroughly learned:

N Flip open your MLS book or your office's inventory of listings, and prepare seller's net sheets for the first three houses you listed. Push yourself. Work hard and fast. Check your results. Then ask your broker to check and correct them. Never give a sheet to a client until you have your broker's permission to do so. Your company is liable for your errors and, through them, you are too. Whenever you figure a net sheet, remember that some of the dollars you're writing down on it could come out of your pocket if you make a mistake. You can't get a professional's rewards without accepting a professional's responsibilities.

SPECIAL Achievements of Day 4

1 Reread Chapter 15, Qualifying.

2 Flashdeck the winning scripts for the buyer qualifying session and make a BI cassette.

3 Spend two or three hours with a processor, attorney, title company officer, or whoever settles (closes) transactions in your state. Watch and learn. Make an appointment and they'll give you a pleasant reception. Later on, when you're working with lots of people, you'll find that you're making money from what you've learned watching these people.

4 Decide on the format for your farm file (see Chapter 6, and the form in

Chapter 24). Obtain the materials you'll need for it now so you can start developing this basic file as soon as you pick your farm on Day 6.

5 Start your important information notebook (see Chapter 23) by copying into it all the frequently-used listing form remarks and special provisions that you find by studying your office's file of closed transactions and current listings. Work with only two or three files at a time, and be careful to return them promptly to their proper file positions.

Orphan Clients. But, before you do that, ask your broker if you can have some of the orphans you find. Clients of agents who've left your company are orphans—unless they've already been given to someone currently active in your office. The orphans who bought a house three or four years ago are about due to move up, and some people expect to be transferred to another area even sooner than that.

6 Visit the farms you're considering. Walk around each one and get a feel for the different localities. Look at the way the people take care of their properties. Notice the cars they drive. Just by casually glancing from the sidewalk, you'll form an idea of the attitudes held, the lifestyles lived, and the recreational activities engaged in. Which farm do you feel most comfortable in?

The better you relate to the people in your farm, the more affinity you have for them, the better you'll do there. Talk to anyone you happen to meet who seems to live in the area. Tell them that you're selecting a farm and ask for their advice. People love to give advice, so listen carefully to what they have to say. (If you haven't received your real estate license yet, be careful not to offer your services as an agent. Don't talk about the values of specific properties, or do anything else that requires a real estate license.) Don't be swayed by a single grouch or booster; talk to several people in each farm. Ask them how they like their particular street. Is it convenient to shopping and highways? Are there any special problems in the area? If several of them tell you a certain agent has that neighborhood all tied up, you might want to look elsewhere. Investigate before you commit yourself to an area. You'll be making heavy and continuing investments of time and money in your farm for a long time, so pick it carefully.

7 Reread Chapter 23, Prepare and Perform—Or Pass Out. Review your schedule, goals, and validations; consider whether you're preparing yourself adequately to achieve those goals. Add these achievements to your daily schedule:

REPEATING Achievements of Day 4

O Add 25 more names to your everybody-I-know file. Continue to add 25 people a day to this card file until you get through all your old and new school, club and church rosters. Then work through your Christmas card list, shower party lists, and any other list you have of people you know.

When you've worked through all your rosters, add the people you trade with, friends, relatives and acquaintances—anyone you know—at the rate of ten name cards per day.

When you have everyone you now know in your file, don't stop. Every day you meet new people. Add at least one new name to your list every day.

P Send handwritten notes announcing that you're in real estate to three people in your everybody-I-know farm file. Handwritten notes are a must for people you know quite well.

SPECIAL Achievements of Day 5

1 Reread Chapter 10, Up-Time.

2 Flashdeck that chapter's winning scripts.

3 Use your new flashdeck to create a blank-interval cassette for solo role working the ad call and sign call situations and responses in those winning scripts.

4 Develop your knowledge of all forms of conventional financing currently being offered by banks, savings and loans associations, and other private mortgage loan sources in your area. Enter the details in your important information notebook.

5 Consider the farm areas open to you from the standpoint of providing yourself with a wide price range and selection of housing types. It may be necessary to select three mini-farms in three different locations to achieve this purpose. Can you do that? Do you want to? Explore these questions today. More details are given in Chapter 6.

6 Flashdeck the deadlines you'll be working with:
  • Your company's deadlines for cooperative advertising.
  • Local newspaper advertising deadlines. Call the newspapers for this information; don't ask around the office.
  • Your Board of Realtors® deadline for getting new listings in the next issue of the Multiple Listing book. There may be different deadlines for extensions and other changes in existing listings. Know them all. What's the deadline for adding a house to the next caravan? If this information isn't printed in each issue of the book, call the board office.

7 Conquer the buyer's net sheet form (It's sometimes called the "buyer's closing costs.") Learn how to quickly figure what the buyers' initial investment in their new home will be, and how much they'll be investing in it every month. Chapter 23 has helpful tips.

REPEATING Achievements of Day 5

Add this to your schedule and keep at it every day until you've acquired professional competence:

Q Open your Multiple Listing book or office's listing inventory at random and prepare buyer's net sheets on three houses. Work as fast as you can; then carefully check your work. Research any areas of uncertainty in your office's file of completed transactions, with lenders' agents and title people, or with the person who processes open transactions for your firm. Leave the agents around you out of this; they have their own problems.

Add to your schedule, and keep at it until you're operating smoothly at the level of success you've chosen for yourself:

R Put your winning FSBO system to work by contacting five for-sale-by-owners a day.

SPECIAL Achievements of Day 6

1 Reread Chapter 6, Sow That Farm and Reap and Reap and Reap.

2 Flashdeck that chapter's winning scripts.

3 Create a BI cassette of the verbal opportunities and barriers in those winning scripts and of the responses to them that enable you to take advantage of the opportunities and get around the barriers.

4 Weigh all the information you've gathered about the different farms that are available to you, and select your farm. Choose the one that scores highest on diversity, promise, and affinity. Inform your broker of your decision.

5 Decide how you'll compile your deed details folder on your new farm. Chapter 6 tells all about it. Work out a plan to get this information as soon as possible, and put your plan in motion now.

6 Start a property catalog of your farm by registering a tenth of your farm's properties today. Note that you record facts about properties, not people, in your inventory catalog. Chapter 6 tells you how this listing and sales aid will make you money, and how to create it. On each of the next nine days, a repeating achievement will be to record another tenth of your farm in your property catalog so that, by Day 15, you'll have every property in your farm recorded.

7 Organize your home work station for maximum real estate efficiency.

REPEATING Achievements of Day 6

Continue your daily schedule Repeating Achievements from Day 1 through Day 5. You now have six BI (blank-interval) cassettes:

FSBO   Qualifying Buyers
Listing   Up-Time
Prospecting   Farming

All the cards for your flashdecks of this material, plus the deadlines flashdeck you compiled yesterday, should now be in three groups:

- In your twice daily drill deck: material not overlearned.
- In your once or twice weekly review decks: learned material.
- In your monthly review deck: overlearned material.

Remember that your learning goal for all these phrases, facts, and skills is complete mastery. When you're able—instantly, accurately, and sincerely—to respond to the situations these tools are designed for, you'll usually be able to turn them to your advantage. Half learning won't get it. Continue your daily drills until using each item becomes second nature. Some of these situations don't happen often. If you depend on prospect contact to keep these words and skills fresh in your mind, you'll be unprepared for the less frequent situations when they suddenly occur. Schedule regular review of the overlearned material.

Add this new achievement to your schedule:

S Study the filled-out listing forms in your office's file for 30 minutes a day. Continue this daily study for as long as it helps you.

SPECIAL Achievements of Day 7

1 Reread Chapter 7, Danny Kennedy's Full-Year Farming Almanac.

2 Make a tentative schedule for your next 12 months of farming activity.

3 Select this month's giveaway (one you can get quick delivery on), and order enough of them for your entire farm. (If you're on a tight budget as a new salesperson, order scratch pads only until you can afford the monthly giveaway suggestions.) But don't order anything until you've checked with your broker, and made sure that it's okay to use them in your area.

4 Order next month's giveaway for your farm.

5 Order your farm giveaway for the month after next.

6 Pick your monthly farm decision day. Chapter 6 tells you why this is vital to an efficient farming program, and what to do. If you select the tenth day of each month, write "Farm Decision Day" in your yearly appointment book on the tenth of every month remaining in the year.

7 High-volume phoning plays tricks on you unless it's kept in control. Fast fact grabber and results record (in Chapter 24) are two forms that'll help you make phone prospecting pay off big. Order these forms today, or design your own and have a local print shop run off 100 copies of each.

But before you start on a phone-prospecting campaign, check with your broker and make sure that you won't be violating any local ordinances or rules.

REPEATING Achievements of Day 7

Add this item to your daily schedule:

T List another tenth of your farm's property catalog. (See special achievement 6, Day 6.) Let's review some of the items on your daily schedule.
  * As soon as you wake up, review your validations and goals. Take a moment to see yourself—in full color—enjoying each goal or living each validation. Emotion is what works the changes. Practice ''seeing'' your success clearly for a second or two on each goal and validation. Don't linger: The twice daily repetition of these mental images will start working their wonders as soon as you learn how to make them vivid.
  * Make three fast runs through your new and old flashdecks each morning and night. Concentrate—and never hesitate. Unless you know the response or answer instantly, turn over the card, read it intently, and pass on to the next card.
  * Make three runs through all your BI cassettes every evening and morning. Coach yourself with the flashdecks if necessary. Say your lines with confidence and sincerity.
  * Check today's hot sheet for changes in your QSI. Make any necessary corrections in your slot sheet, QSI flashdeck, and memory.

SPECIAL Achievements of Day 8

1 Reread Chapter 14 on capturing customers.

2 Flashdeck the winning scripts in that chapter.

3 Use your new flashdeck to create a blank-interval cassette for solo role working those customer-capture situations.

4 You'll soon be working with buyers—and writing offers and counteroffers. Before you do that on your own, get your broker's approval. There are a lot of pitfalls in offers that could be costly to both of you, so don't rush in before you're ready. Prepare. Don't terrorize your buyers into backing out by groping for words, and floundering through the form. Buyers making offers

need reassurance, not reasons to run—they scare themselves enough without our help. Know the forms thoroughly; memorize the phrases that cover common purchase situations; get ready for fast work at decision-making time. Do your job before their desire to buy cools. Chapter 3 gives you a rapid learning technique and tells you how to learn—before need—all the purchase offer situations that are frequently encountered in your locality, and what phrases best cope with those situations. Use them to make up a purchase offer flashdeck.

5 Spend one hour reviewing your income, personal, and family goals. Revise your written list of goals to include at least three achievable goals that inspire you in each of these three categories.

You're now able to drive without hesitation to about 160 streets in your sales area through your work with the named-neighborhoods program (special 7, Day 1). In the coming months and years, this knowledge will win many extra fees for you.

REPEATING Achievements of Day 8

U Add to your daily schedule: Use the purchase offer flashdeck (today's special 4) to drill yourself on making out this form fast. Take 30 minutes of drill, then spend another 30 minutes researching your office's files. Add any new offer problems you find—and the clauses that control them—to your purchase offer flashdeck.

V Reread the tips in Chapter 6 on farming. Then knock on 15 doors in your farm. Learn at least one fact about each family or house.

SPECIAL Achievements of Day 9

1 Reread Chapter 9 on how to make money holding open house.

2 Flashdeck that chapter's winning scripts for open houses.

3 Prepare a blank-interval cassette for solo role working the open house situations in those winning scripts.

4 Add to your important information notebook by copying into it the frequently-used purchase agreement (deposit receipt) clauses you find in your office's file of closed transactions.

REPEATING Achievements of Day 9

Schedule yourself to hold open houses both days of the coming weekend (if Sunday open houses are accepted in your area). The big listers in your office will welcome your offer to give their listings this exposure to the public because you're demonstrating a high level of drive, enthusiasm, and competence.

SPECIAL Achievements of Day 10

1 Reread Chapter 17, Closing Those Golden Nuggets.

2 Flashdeck that chapter's winning scripts.

3 Use your new flashdeck to prepare a BI cassette for solo role working the closing situations in those winning scripts.

4 From memory, sketch your sales area's highways, major roads, and most important streets. Use as many sheets of paper as you need to show all major traffic arteries in your area, and how they connect. Take not more than one minute per sheet. When you're through, compare your work with the printed map. If your sketches are wrong or incomplete, you've discovered a weakness you can correct before you get lost with a customer. Chapter 3 tells you how to do so quickly.

REPEATING Achievements of Day 10

Add to your daily schedule:

W Prospect for people interested in buying or selling real estate by making ten cold canvass calls in your sales area. Chapter 8 provides you with techniques for successful cold calling. Keep your results count for cold canvass calls separate from the other two types of calls you'll be making soon.

You are, of course, trying for an appointment to view a house, with the intention of expanding that appointment into a listing presentation. Don't be discouraged if you don't get an appointment; your goal is to complete those ten calls in a courteous and professional manner. If you do succeed in making an appointment, build on that success: Go for more appointments by finishing your ten calls. And then concentrate on preparing the strongest listing effort you can make today. Review Chapter 11; you'll find much there worth brief and intense study right now.

- You have now filled all 50 slots in your basic Quick-Speak Inventory. You started this project on Day 1 with special achievement 6 and repeating achievement A. Will these 50 slots adequately cover your sales activity? If not, design another slot sheet and start filling it in at five houses per day, and continue replacing sold and expired houses on your original slot sheet.

SPECIAL Achievements of Day 11

1 Reread Chapter 18, Negotiating.

2 Flashdeck that chapter's winning scripts.

3 Use your new flashdeck to create a BI cassette for solo role working the negotiating situations in those winning scripts.

REPEATING Achievements of Day 11

Continue your daily sessions with each of the incomplete achievements. Add this to your daily schedule:

X Make ten image-building calls into your farm. Keep track of who you're calling in your farm. If you don't have a farm, make ten additional cold canvass calls into your sales area.

SPECIAL Achievements of Day 12

1 Effective farming will make you a lot of money. A 100 percent referral business will make you a lot more, because all your time will then be spent working with clients who've called you. That happy situation is reached by doing a superlative job of farming, by working effectively with buyers, and by developing those and other contacts into a reliable referral network. Chapter 20, A 100% Referral Business, told you how it's done. Reread that chapter now. Let it inspire you to do the superlative job of farming that'll have you cashing in on referrals soon. Make referral business your goal. Start training yourself now to explore the referral possibilities of every person-to-person contact you make.

2 Assemble the best Listing Presentation Manual (LPM) you can from what's immediately available to you. Then write down everything that can strengthen your LPM. Plan how you'll obtain each item. Tips on preparing your LPM are given in Chapter 11 and 24.

3 A method for creating effective sales dialogues fast is given in Chapter 23. Use that method to develop a "Why you should list with me" speech for use with your Listing Presentation Manual.

4 Start your farm people flashdeck by listing a family name on one side of 3 × 5 card, and their address on the card's reverse. Take this information from any directory you can. The crisscross is the most convenient. Do 30 cards today, or a tenth of the households in your farm. This is the start of a project to be completed over the next nine days as a repeating achievement. Chapter 6 tells you some of the ways a farm people flashdeck will help you gain control of your farm quickly.

REPEATING Achievements of Day 12

Add this to your daily schedule:

Y Call the owners of ten expired listings. Chapter 8 has helpful tips. Keep a results record (See Chapter 24) on each call and hold it for future analysis.

SPECIAL Achievements of Day 13

1 Reread Chapter 13, Promotion, so you can sell your listings faster and sell yourself better.

2 Develop this sales dialogue: "What's happening now in our local resale housing market."

3 Develop your knowledge of government home purchase financing used in your area. Include any veteran or other financing your state may have along with the federal FHA, VA programs. Call the loan production departments of mortgage companies for this information, or the lender's agents who leave their cards in your office. Enter the details in your important information notebook.

4 Make up a master for your buyer show list form. Run off a hundred copies at the local quick-print shop—you're going to need them. Chapter 24 has a sample that works great—saves time and impresses customers. Use it as is, or modify it to suit the housing in your area.

REPEATING Achievements of Day 13

You should now be:

• Talking with 15 people on your farm each day. This will take you around your farm once a month.

• Talking with at least five fizzbos a day.

• Making ten cold canvass calls.

• Making ten image-building calls a day into your farm.

• Calling ten expired listings a day.

SPECIAL Achievements of Day 14

1 Make up the best "Our Beautiful Area" sales book that you can from what's immediately available. Include common floor plans; lists of churches, clubs,

schools, cultural, and recreational facilities; maps showing locations of malls, shopping centers, and scenic areas; driving distances to regional attractions and nearby cities; local tax information and utility rates—include all the things people moving in want to know.

2 List what you need to improve your sales book and plan how to acquire each item.

3 Develop this sales dialogue. "The communities of Green pretty (your sales area) Valley." Describe them as you would to a prospective buyer making his or her first visit to your area. State the types of housing available in each community and give price ranges.

4 Flashdeck all the churches in your sales area. On one side of each 3 × 5 card write the denomination; on the other side write the name of the church and its location or cross streets. Not knowing where the churches of their faith are in your area will hurt you badly with some people. I hope you won't have to lose a thousand-dollar fee before you'll act on this advice. Make a map if it'll help, but learn where the places of worship are.

REPEATING Achievements of Day 14

Your printed "I'm in real estate" letter will be ready by now. Add this to your daily schedule:

Z Hand address envelopes and mail this printed letter to 20 people in your everybody-I-know farm. Continue your mailing at 20 letters a day until you've mailed to everyone you know.

SPECIAL Achievements of Day 15

1 Know you area's yearly buying pattern. Chapter 23 told you why knowing it will make you money, and gave you a powerful self-selling speech. Review that section and acquire this knowledge.

2 Review the tentative goals you set for yourself on Day 1 and Day 8. Do they still excite you? Did you aim too low at first? Or do they now seem too high to reach? Take time today to reset your income goals for the immediate future at achievable levels that will inspire you to greater, but not impossible efforts. Write down income goals (revised if you so decide) for each of the next 12 months. As you set these monthly income goals, bear in mind the 60-day sale-to-payoff delay that's built into the average transaction. Always set believable, achievable goals. But first reread Chapter 26. You'll now see the discussion of goals there in a new light.

3 Develop this sales dialogue: "Why Greenpretty Valley is a great place, Mr. and Mrs. Homebuyer, for you and your family to grow and prosper in."

REPEATING Achievements of Day 15

- Complete your farm property file. This project began as special achievement 6 on Day 6, and repeating achievement T on Day 7.
- Add the final pair of named neighborhoods and bring your stock-in-trade of well-known streets to the top professional level of 600. This project started on Day 1 as special achievement 7.

SPECIAL Achievements of Day 16

1 Develop your knowledge of the seller-financed sales methods that are available in your state such as land contracts, second trust deeds, and all-inclusive trust deeds (wraparounds). Enter the details you learn in your important information notebook.

2 Develop this sales dialogue: "Here's what happens in today's market when you limit your offer with contingencies."

REPEATING Achievements of Day 16

AA Schedule yourself for two open houses this weekend. Make a reputation for doing a superlative job representing property on open house and you'll soon find that your office's top listers will be eager for you to hold their listings open whenever you have time. Being able to select the best open houses will give you the best possible shot at buyers. Start now to get everything together that you'll need to put on the kind of open house performance that builds your future.

SPECIAL Achievements of Day 17

1 Reread Chapter 19, Fallout Avoidance.

2 From that chapter and the checklist in Chapter 24, make up your own checklist of items to watch out for, and take action on, between sale and settlement.

3 Develop this sales dialogue: "The Outlook is optimistic." You'll need this speech when buyers ask you such questions as: ''Where's the country going? Are we headed for another recession? Aren't we due for another turndown?'' Unless you're ready to deal with these fears, you'll lose some fees. Chapter 23 has more about this.

4 If you're part of the Multiple Listing system, flashdeck the coding and abbreviations used by your Multiple Listing Service. Include everything a buyer or seller looking over your shoulder at the Multiple Listing book might ask you about.

REPEATING Achievements of Day 17

BB Would a call-back to any of the people you've already contacted be worthwhile now? If so, do it. Are you entering your better-call-backs in your appointment book? Unless you do, you'll miss out on vital follow-up. Calling back *at the right time* where you sniff business is the difference between success and failure on the phone. Set up your call-back system (keep it simple) and call all prospects back precisely when they say is the best day and hour. The back sides of the fact grabber forms (Chapter 24) and tickler $\frac{1}{31}$ (Chapter 22) combine to make an effective call-back system.

SPECIAL Achievements of Day 18

1 Develop this sales dialogue: ''The tax advantages of home ownership.'' Every time you give this talk, be sure you first tell your clients and customers to get their tax advice from tax experts, not real estate experts, and that your remarks are intended only to alert them to possibilities.

2 Analyze all the results record forms you've compiled so far. If you have 1 appointment and 3 opportunities for later follow-up to show for each 100 calls, rejoice—you're doing great. Anything more than that is sensational. Study every little part of your prospecting procedure. Look for the winning things you're doing—and do them more often. Also be on the lookout for any nonproductive habits you might have slipped into. About now would be a good time to tape your side of a few prospecting calls if you haven't already been doing that regularly. Play the tapes back, try to put yourself in the other person's shoes, and keep thinking, ''What can I do better?'' On your results record forms, if you've filled one out (completely) every time you've prospected, you'll find clear statements as to what wins and what loses. You've been talking, now listen to yourself. Be sure to take your own advice.

3 Your experiences have given you a changed viewpoint on the value of self-organization in the past two weeks. Read Chapter 22 again: You'll find some valuable tips there that you missed before.

4 Read entirely through Chapter 3, Build Money-making Skills Fast with Hyperlearn. Then select three methods to continue the rapid learning that's fueling your breakaway from the pack, and decide how you'll use them in the future to maintain your rapid learning pace.

REPEATING Achievements of Day 18

Fit this into your daily schedule:

CC Add one new validation on a day to your validation deck, or revise one old one. See Chapter 27 for a full discussion of validations.

SPECIAL Achievements of Day 19

1 Develop this sales dialogue: "Why you should buy a home now."

2 Write reminders in your appointment book for monthly review and improvement of "Why you should buy a home now."

REPEATING Achievements of Day 19

DD You've been making ten image-building calls per day into your farm. Continue at this rate until you've called your entire farm once. Then drop back to five image-buildings calls a day, and set that up as a permanent part of your daily work schedule. Remember that you'll always need a reason to call them, so be continually on the alert for reasons to do so. Chapter 6 talks about this in more detail.

SPECIAL Achievements of Day 20

1 Reread Chapter 21, Time Planning. No subject is more vital to your success than this one. If you don't own a good time planner: call me at 714-498-8033 and check mine out.

2 It's now been one week since you developed your first version of "What's happening now in our local resale housing market." Update that sales dialogue with the latest weekly data issued by your Board of Realtors®. Add details. Smooth out its flow. By now, you've probably given this talk to prospects on the phone many times. Tape yourself doing that, and then critique your delivery.

REPEATING Achievements of Day 20

Since Day 10, you've made a total of 100 cold canvass calls and 80 calls to expired listings, plus many other calls.

Congratulations. You're now a telephone pro. You've talked to some great people and you have business in sight. Keep after it.

Now use your results record form to help you decide which of the two prospecting fields is most productive for you. Split your future 20 calls a day between cold canvass calls and expired listings so that most of your calls go where you see the greatest return. But continue to make at least ten calls a week to the least productive field. There may be a seasonal factor, competitive condition, or soft spot in your technique preventing you from striking pay dirt in the field that looks least promising now. By making calls to this area, you'll soon discover what the problem is and be able to correct it.

EE On your permanent daily work schedule, block out time to make 20 prospecting calls a day, divided between cold canvass calls and expired listings.

SPECIAL Achievements of Day 21

1 Write ''A Profile of a Pro'' about yourself. Chapter 13 tells you how to make money with this self-advertisement, gives writing tips, and has a sample profile to help you.

2 Develop this sales dialogue: ''The various ways you can finance a home purchase, and the advantages and costs of each method.''

3 You've worked hard during the past three weeks, and you've tentatively formed many effective new habits. Make those winning habits a permanent part of your personality: Read the rest of this section about consolidating your gains.

And now at last it's finally over,
Time's come to gather the sweet green clover.

Congratulations, Awaybreakers. You've learned a great deal very quickly.

Now you're at a crossroads. Will you use this new input, review it, expand on it, and continue to grow—or will you slowly slide back to your previous level of performance? Here are some specific suggestions on how you can continue your growth habit:

CONSOLIDATE YOUR GAINS AFTER BREAKAWAY— MAKE A SMOOTH, SWIFT TAKEOFF INTO RAPIDLY RISING INCOME

Reward yourself. *Now*.

You'll sustain your drive longer and make more money if you'll alternate hard-driving work with high-quality play. Select whatever reward you think you should have, not what someone else thinks you should have. When you've done the job, collect the reward from yourself. Then continue the good habits you've learned through Breakaway:

- Prepare a tomorrow's action list every night. (Do this even on vacation—it maintains the habit: "(1) Get up late. (2) Go to beach, (3) Have fun—")
- Add five houses to your Quick-Speak Inventory every day your time isn't fully occupied with clients.
- Continue Hyperlearning information about real estate in general and your area in particular until you have all the data on Quick-Speak that distinguishes the competent, highly paid pro from the unreliable and unpaid amateur.
- You've learned how to prospect fast, and you've had success at it. Its terrors are behind you. Any day you don't have an appointment with a client or customer, get out in the field and prospect for two hours in the morning, another two hours in the afternoon, and by phone for an hour in the evening.
- While others stand around and gab before the weekly office meeting starts, sit down in a corner and bang off a few prospecting calls, or keep on top of your transactions, appointments, and action list. Carry your prospecting kit in your attaché case. If a customer calls in to say, "Sorry—I'll be 45 minutes late," pull out your prospecting kit and rap out a few more calls. Squeeze fees from those vagrant minutes by making them work for you.
- Leaf through the Breakaway schedule, and privately score how thoroughly you've put the material there to use. If you aren't satisfied that you've squeezed all the benefits you can from Breakaway, then;
- Repeat the course. Pass over the items you've thoroughly learned or completed. Look again at the achievements you were reluctant to try three weeks ago. The achievements you don't want to think about are the precise ones that will make the most dramatic improvements in your career.
- Are you charging ahead now?

If your answer is no, do you lack drive? Have you chosen goals that really excite you? Do you really believe you can achieve them? You have? You do? Then are you using validations to power your drive?

Or are you afraid to change? Afraid to be a winner? No. You're probably not. But if not, why aren't you charging ahead? The odds are that your problem lies in noninspiring goals, or in nonuse of the validation system. If you're not thrilled with your performance, restudy Chapters 26, 27, and 28. Remember every second I'm rooting for you. Consider me your invisible partner. Between you, me and someone greater than both of us, we can make this career of yours spectacular.

GLOSSARY

Adjustable Rate Mortgage (ARM):   A mortgage with an interest rate that changes over time in line with movements in the index. ARMs are also referred to as AMLs (adjustable mortgage loans) or VRMs (variable rate mortgages).

Adjustment Period: The length of time between interest rate changes on an ARM. For example, a loan with an adjustment period of one year is called a one-year ARM, which means that the interest rate can change once a year.

Amortization: Repayment of a loan in equal installments of principal and interest, rather than interest-only payments.

Annual Percentage Rate (APR):   The total finance charge (interest, loan fees, points) expressed as a percentage of the loan amount.

Assumption of Mortgage: A buyer's agreement to assume the liability under an existing note that is secured by a mortgage or deed of trust. The lender must approve the buyer in order to release the original borrower (usually the seller) from liability.

Balloon Payment: A lump sum principal payment due at the end of some mortgages or other long-term loans.

Binder: Sometimes known as an offer to purchase or an earnest money receipt. A binder is the acknowledgement of a deposit along with a brief written agreement to enter into a contract for the sale of real property.

Cap: The limit on how much an interest rate or monthly payment can change, either at each adjustment or over the life of the mortgage.

CC&R's: Covenants, conditions and restrictions. A document that controls the use, requirements and restrictions of a property.

Certificate of Reasonable Value (CRV): A document that establishes the maximum value and loan amount for a VA guaranteed mortgage.

Closing Statement: The financial disclosure statement that accounts for all of the funds received and expected at the closing, including deposits for taxes, hazard insurance, and mortgage insurance.

Condominium: A form of real estate ownership where the owner receives title to a particular unit and has proportionate interest in certain common areas. The unit itself is generally a separately owned space whose interior surfaces (walls, floors and ceilings) serve as its boundaries.

Contingency: A condition that must be satisfied before a contract is binding. For instance, a sales agreement may be contingent upon the buyer obtaining financing.

Conversion Clause: A provision in some ARMs that enables you to change an ARM to a fixed-rate loan, usually after the first adjustment period. The new fixed rate is generally set at the prevailing interest rate for fixed rate mortgages. This conversion feature may cost extra.

Cooperative: A form of multiple ownership in which a corporation or business trust entity holds title to a property and grants occupancy rights to shareholders by means of proprietary leases or similar arrangements.

CRB: Certified Residential Broker. To be certified, a broker must be a member of the National Association of Realtors®, have five years experience as a licensed broker and have completed a certain number of required Residential Division courses.

Due-On-Sale Clause: An acceleration clause that requires full payment of a mortgage or deed of trust when the secured property changes ownership.

Earnest Money: The portion of the down payment delivered to seller or escrow agent by the purchaser with a written offer as evidence of good faith.

Escrow: A procedure in which a third party acts as a stakeholder for both the buyer and the seller, carrying out both parties' instructions and assumes responsibility for handling all of the paperwork and distribution of funds.

FHA Loan: A loan insured by the Insuring Office of the Department of Housing and Urban Development; the Federal Housing Administration.

Federal National Mortgage Association (FNMA):   Popularly known as Fannie Mae. A privately owned corporation created by Congress to support the secondary mortgage market. It purchases and sells residential mortgages insured by FHA or guaranteed by the VA, as well as conventional home mortgages.

Fee Simple: An estate in which the owner has unrestricted power to dispose of the property as he wishes, including leaving by will or inheritance. It is the greatest interest a person can have in real estate.

Finance Charge: The total cost a borrower must pay, directly or indirectly, to obtain credit according to Regulation Z.

Graduated Payment Mortgage: A residential mortgage with monthly payments that start at a low level and increase at a predetermined rate.

GRI: Graduate, Realtors Institute. A professional designation granted to a member of the National Association of Realtors® who has successfully completed courses covering Law, Finance and Principles of Real Estate.

Home Inspection Report: A qualified inspector's report on a property's overall condition. The report usually includes an evaluation of both the structure and mechanical systems.

Home Warranty Plan: Protection against failure of mechanical systems within the property. Usually includes plumbing, electrical, heating systems and installed appliances.

Index: A measure of interest rate changes used to determine changes in an ARM's interest rate over the term of the loan.

Joint Tenancy: An equal undivided ownership of property by two or more persons. Upon the death of any owner, the survivors take the decedent's interest in the property.

Lien: A legal hold or claim on property as security for a debt or charge.

Loan Commitment: A written promise to make a loan for a specified amount on specified terms.

Loan-To-Value Ratio: The relationship between the amount of the mortgage and the appraised value of the property, expressed as a percentage of the appraised value.

Margin: The number of percentage points the lender adds to the index rate to calculate the ARM interest rate at each adjustment.

Mortgage Life Insurance: A type of life insurance often bought by mortgagors. The coverage decreases as the mortgage balance declines. If the borrower dies while the policy is in force, the debt is automatically covered by insurance proceeds.

Negative Amortization: Negative amortization occurs when monthly payments fail to cover the interest cost. The interest that isn't covered is added to the unpaid principal balance, which means that even after several payments you could owe more than you did at the beginning of the loan. Negative amortization can occur when an ARM has a payment cap that results in monthly payments that aren't high enough to cover the interest.

Origination Fee: A fee or charge for work involved in evaluating, preparing, and submitting a proposed mortgage loan. The fee is limited to 1 percent for FHA and VA loans.

PITI: Principal, interest, taxes and insurance.

Planned Unit Development (PUD): A zoning designation for property developed at the same or slightly greater overall density than conventional development, sometimes with improvements clustered between open, common areas. Uses may be residential, commercial or industrial.

Point: An amount equal to 1 percent of the principal amount of the investment or note. The lender assesses loan discount points at closing to increase the yield on the mortgage to a position competitive with other types of investments.

Prepayment Penalty: A fee charged to a mortgagor who pays a loan before it is due. Not allowed for FHA or VA loans.

Private Mortgage Insurance (PMI): Insurance written by a private company protecting the lender against loss if the borrower defaults on the mortgage.

Purchase Agreement: A written document in which the purchaser agrees to buy certain real estate and the seller agrees to sell under stated terms and conditions. Also called a sales contract, earnest money contract, or agreement for sale.

Realtor®: A real estate broker or associate active in a local real estate board affiliated with the National Association of Realtors®.

Regulation Z: The set of rules governing consumer lending issued by the Federal Reserve Board of Governors in accordance with the Consumer Protection act.

Tenancy in Common: A type of joint ownership of property by two or more persons with no right of survivorship.

Title Insurance Policy: A policy that protects the purchaser, mortgagee or other party against losses.

VA Loan: A loan that is partially guaranteed by the Veterans Administration and made by a private lender.

INDEX

O

P

Ms. Kennedy conducts sales training seminars and motivational programs throughout the world.

A complete sixteen tape video sales training program entitled "List, Sell & Act Fast," plus audio cassette programs along with other educational materials are available.

For information, or brochures call (714) 498–8033

D A N I E L L E

K E N N E D Y

Danielle Kennedy International Productions
P.O. Box 4382
219 S. El Camino Real
San Clemente, CA. 92672–4382
(714) 498–8033